MODERN POLO

BY

CAPTAIN E. D. MILLER, D.S.O.

(Late 17th Lancers)

EDITED BY

M. H. HAYES, F.R.C.V.S.

(Late Captain " The Buffs")

Author of " Points of the Horse," " Illustrated Horse-breaking,"
" Veterinary Notes for Horse Owners," " Riding and Hunting,"
etc.

SECOND EDITION, REVISED AND ENLARGED.

POLO

WORDS of wrath at Polo spoken
  Should forgotten be next day;
They're a sure and certain token,
  Good the game and fast the play.
Least words said they're soonest mended,
  Never are they worth repeating;
Do not therefore be offended
  If defeated or defeating;
Keep your temper and your place,
  Gallop at your fastest pace.
If a man you chance to cross,
  You or he may take a "toss."
Learn the rules and play the game,
  Then you'll never be to blame;
If your pony stops to kick,
  Beat him with your Polo stick;
If he shuts up like a cur,
  Ride him with both whip and spur.
See your girths are new and strong,
  Stirrup leathers not too long,
Saddle-tree correctly fitting,
  Pay attention to your bitting.
If to win is your ambition,
  Keep yourself in good condition;
Choose a stick of proper length,
  Weight according to your strength;
Bearing this in mind you may
  P'r'aps in time improve your play.

Horses – Sports and Utility

The horse (*Equus ferus caballus*) is one of two extant subspecies of *Equus ferus*. It is an odd-toed ungulate mammal belonging to the taxonomic family 'Equidae'. The horse has evolved over the past 45 to 55 million years from a small multi-toed creature into the large, single-toed animal of today. Humans began to domesticate horses around 4000 BC, and their domestication is believed to have been widespread by 3000 BC. We, as humans have interacted with horses in a multitude of ways throughout history – from sport competitions and non-competitive recreational pursuits, to working activities such as police work, agriculture, entertainment and therapy. Horses have also been used in warfare, from which a wide variety of riding and driving techniques developed, using many different styles of equipment and methods of control. With this range of uses in mind, there is an equally extensive, specialized vocabulary used to describe equine-related concepts, covering everything from anatomy to life stages, size, colours, markings, breeds, locomotion, and behaviour.

Sporting events are some of the largest and best-known activities involving horses, and here – communication between human and horse is paramount. To aid this process, horses are usually ridden with a saddle on their backs to assist the rider with balance and positioning, and a bridle or related headgear to assist the rider in maintaining control. Historically, equestrians honed their craft through games and races;

providing skills needed for battle, as well as entertainment for home crowds. Today, these competitions have evolved into racing, dressage, eventing and show jumping – many of which have their origins in military training, focused on control and balance of both the horse and rider. Other sports, such as rodeo, developed from practical skills such as those needed on working ranches and stations. Horse racing of all types evolved from impromptu competitions between riders or drivers, and has since become a multi-million pound industry. It is watched in almost every nation of the world, in its three main forms: 'flat racing' (long, even stretches), 'steeplechasing' (racing over jumps) and 'harness racing' (where horses trot or pace whilst pulling a driver in a small, light cart). A major part of horse racing's economic importance lies in the gambling associated with it.

All forms of competition, requiring demanding and specialized skills from both horse and rider, resulted in the systematic development of specialized breeds and equipment for each sport. Horse shows, which have their origins in medieval European fairs, are held around the world. They host a huge range of classes, covering all of the mounted and harness disciplines, as well as 'In-hand' classes where the horses are led, rather than ridden, to be evaluated on their conformation. The method of judging varies with the discipline, but winning usually depends on style and ability of both horse and rider. Sports such as polo do not judge the horse itself, but rather use the horse as a partner for human competitors as a necessary part of the game. Although the horse requires specialized training to participate, the details of its performance are not judged, only the result of the rider's actions—be it getting a ball through a goal or some other task. A similar, historical example of sports partnerships between human and horse is 'jousting', in which the main goal is for one rider to unseat the other. This pastime is still practiced by some sportsmen today.

There are certain jobs that horses do very well, and no technology has yet developed to fully replace them. For example, mounted police horses are still effective for certain types of patrol duties and crowd control. Cattle ranches still require riders on horseback to round up cattle that are scattered across remote, rugged terrain. In more urban areas, horses used to be the main form of transport, in the form of pulling carriages, and are still extensively used (especially in the UK) for ceremonial functions, i.e. horse-drawn carriages transporting dignitaries, military personnel or even the royal family. Horses can also be used in areas where it is necessary to avoid vehicular disruption to delicate soil, such as nature reserves. They may also be the only form of transport allowed in wilderness areas, often because of the fact that horses are quieter than motorised vehicles, therefore impacting less on their surroundings. Although machinery has replaced horses in many parts of the world, an estimated 100 million horses, donkeys and mules are still used for agriculture and transportation in less developed areas. This number includes around 27 million working animals in Africa alone.

As well as these labour intensive uses, horses can also be incredibly valuable for therapy. People of all ages with physical and mental disabilities obtain beneficial results from association with horses. Therapeutic riding is used to mentally and physically stimulate disabled persons and help them improve their lives through improved balance and coordination, increased self-confidence, and a greater feeling of freedom and independence. Horses also provide psychological benefits to people whether they actually ride or not. 'Equine-assisted' or 'equine-facilitated' therapy is a form of experiential psychotherapy that uses horses as companion animals to assist people with mental illness, including anxiety disorders, psychotic disorders, mood disorders, behavioural difficulties, and those who are going through major life changes. There are also experimental programs using horses in prison settings. Exposure to horses appears to improve the behaviour of inmates and help reduce recidivism when they leave.

As a concluding note, one of the most important aspects of equine care is farriery; a specialist in equine hoof care. Horses aid humans in so many ways, it is important to ensure that they are properly equipped and cared for. Farriers have largely replaced blacksmiths (after this specialism mostly became redundant after the industrial revolution), and are highly skilled in both metalwork and horse anatomy. Historically, the jobs of farrier and blacksmith were practically synonymous, shown by the etymology of the word: farrier comes from Middle French *ferrier* (blacksmith), and from the Latin word *ferrum* (iron). Modern day farriers usually specialize in horseshoeing though, focusing their time and effort on the care of the horse's hoof, including trimming and balancing of the hoof, as well as the placing of the shoes. Additional tasks for the farrier include dealing with injured or diseased hooves and application of special shoes for racing, training or 'cosmetic' purposes. In countries such as the United Kingdom, it is illegal for people other than registered farriers to call themselves a farrier or to carry out any farriery work, the primary aim being 'to prevent and avoid suffering by and cruelty to horses arising from the shoeing of horses by unskilled persons.' This is not the case in all countries however, where horse protection is severely lacking.

We hope the reader enjoys this book.

Photo by]

[W. ROUCH.

(WALTER JONES.) (G. A. MILLER.) (CAPTAIN RENTON.) (W. J. DRYBROUGH.) (E. D. MILLER.)

Rugby winners of the Champion Cup, Hurlingham, 1897, 8, and 9.

PREFACE TO SECOND EDITION.

DURING the six years since the First Edition appeared, several hundreds of polo ponies have passed through my hands, and I have taken part in many good matches, with the result that I have been able, from practical experience, to bring out this book in a revised and considerably enlarged form.

E. D. MILLER.

Tournay Barracks,
Aldershot.

CONTENTS.

CHAPTER I.

FIRST STEPS AT POLO.

CHAPTER II.

THEORY AND PRACTICE OF POLO.

CHAPTER III.

POLO APPLIANCES.

CHAPTER IV.

CHAPTER V.

TRAINING THE POLO PONY.

CHAPTER VI.

POLO PONY GEAR.

CHAPTER VII.

POLO PONY MANAGEMENT.

CHAPTER VIII.

VARIOUS BREEDS OF POLO PONIES.

CONTENTS.

CHAPTER IX.

POLO IN INDIA.

Remarks on polo in India—Polo ponies—Stable
management—The bitting of polo ponies—Indian
Polo Rules—Necessity for the better training of
ponies in India . . . . 221 to 251

CHAPTER X.

A RETROSPECT . . . . 252 to 257

CHAPTER XI.

POLO PONY BREEDING.

General remarks—Polo Pony Society—Experiences of
breeders . . . . 258 to 272

CHAPTER XII.

POLO IN THE ARMY . . . . 273 to 296

CHAPTER XIII.

POLO ABROAD.

United States of America—California—Argentina—
The Colonies—France—Russia . . . . 297 to 313

APPENDIX.

CHRONOLOGY OF MODERN POLO.

APPENDIX.

ILLUSTRATIONS.

Rugby winners of the Champion Cup, Hurlingham, 1897, 8, and 9
Frontispiece

MODERN POLO.

CHAPTER I.

FIRST STEPS AT POLO.

Development of modern polo—How to become a polo player—How to hit the ball—Forward strokes—Back-handers—Riding at polo.

DEVELOPMENT OF MODERN POLO.

As my theme is Polo of to-day, I shall not discuss the ancient history of the game beyond saying that it appears to have been played in Persia 600 B.C., and that the 10th Hussars had the honour of introducing it into England at Aldershot in 1871. It has made enormous progress among us as a popular sport, and has undergone many changes for the better, I venture to think, since the first regular match was played in that year, on Hounslow Heath, between the 10th Hussars and the 9th Lancers. On that occasion there were on each side eight players, who rode very small ponies.

The *Morning Post* in July 1871 gave the following account of that match :—

"Nearly all fashionable London journeyed from town to Hounslow on Tuesday, to witness a new game called 'Hockey on Horseback' between the officers of the 9th Lancers and 10th Hussars. The 10th are quartered at Hounslow Barracks, and the 9th came on from Aldershot for the match.

"The game took place on Hounslow Heath, and the various equipages quite surrounded the space allotted to the players.

"Four upright posts some twenty feet apart, marked the goals through which the ball (a small sphere of white bone) had to be driven by the players before either side could claim any advantage. The sticks used were like those for hockey, of ash and crooked at the end, and with these the ball was often struck a considerable distance. The distance between the goals was a little under 200 yards, and the players having taken up their position in front of their respective goals, the ball was thrown into the centre of the ground by a Sergeant Major of the 10th Hussars, who then galloped off, when each side immediately galloped for the ball at the best pace of their ponies. The 10th appeared in blue and yellow jerseys and the 9th in parti-coloured shirts of blue and red, and both sides wore mob caps with different coloured tassels attached. The game, which has been imported from India, and which has for a long time been in vogue among the Munipoories, one of the Frontier tribes, was watched with the keenest interest by the numerous and aristocratic company present. The game lasted for an hour and a half with an interval of ten minutes, when half time had been played. The players numbered eight on each side, and were mounted on active, wiry, little ponies about 12½ hands high. The sides were as follows :—

9TH LANCERS.	10TH HUSSARS.
Capt. Clayton.	Capt. Balthorpe.
,, Grissell.	,, Bulkeley.
,, Palairet.	,, St. Quirtin.
Mr. P. Green.	,, Okeden.
,, R. Moore.	Viscount Valentia.
,, F. Herbert.	Mr. Smith Do rien.
Lord W. Beresford.	,, J. Woods.
Mr. W. F. Fife.	,, E. Hartopp.

" At the end of the prescribed time, the Hussars had gained three goals to two gained by the Lancers ; and although the general remarks made it evident that the new game is the most fitted for cavalry soldiers, it was admitted by all who were looking on, that it was more remarkable for the strength of the language used by the players, than for anything else. Mr. Hartopp on the side of the Hussars and Mr. Moore on that of the Lancers were much applauded throughout the game for their activity and the speed of their ponies."

The first improvement was to reduce the number of players to five a side. Soon, regular polo sticks replaced hockey sticks, which were first used ; the size of the ponies was increased ; and the old-time game gradually developed into the fast-galloping, hard-hitting, and scientifically-worked combinations which now constitute Modern Polo.

The following are some of the early matches played in England, which I think may be of interest to players of to-day.

1 *

On the 27th June, 1873, at Lillie Bridge, the following teams met, and Light Cavalry won 4 goals. to 2 :—

HOUSEHOLD CAVALRY.	LIGHT CAVALRY.
Marquis of Worcester, R.H.G.	R. St. L. Moore, 9th L.
Lord A. Somerset, R.H.G.	Hon. E. Willoughby, 9th L.
Lord Kilmarnock, R.H.G.	Capt. Middleton, 12th L.
Hon. H. Boscawen, 1st L.G.	Lord M. Beresford, 7th H.
Hon. F. Fitzwilliam, R.H.G.	E. Hartopp, 10th H.

The first match recorded as having been played by the 7th Hussars was in August, 1875, when they opposed Staffordshire in Manchester :—

7TH HUSSARS.	STAFFORDSHIRE.
Capt. Hunt.	Lord Castlereagh.
,, Roper.	,, Ingestre.
,, Shuttleworth.	Capt. Hyde Smith.
Mr. Graham Smith.	Sir C. Wolseley.
,, Atherley.	Mr. Barrett.

Won by the 7th Hussars.

On the 12th June, 1880, the following match was played at Hurlingham for a gold cup presented by the Prince of Wales, and was won by the Military by one goal :—

MILITARY.	CIVILIANS.
Capt. St. L. Moore.	E. Baldock.
Algernon Peyton.	J. McClintock-Bunbury.
Phipps Hornby.	A. Peat.
L. H. Jones.	J. Kennedy.
F. D. Blacker.	J. E. Peat.

The number of players was reduced to four aside in 1881 at Hurlingham, though the Scots Greys won the All Ireland Open Cup the previous year with four men.

The Champion Cup (p. 318) was started in 1877, and the Regimental Tournament in 1878 (p. 316).

We now play four a side, on ponies varying from 14 hands to 14.2, which is the standard limit of height. In India it has lately been raised from 13.3 to 14.1 ; and in America, from 14.0 to 14.2. Instead of the old dribbling and scrimmaging game, in which every man played more or less for himself with but little idea of combination, we have now a carefully arranged organisation, in which every player has his own particular duties clearly defined, so that the success of a side depends more on the ability to work as a whole, than on the individual good play of the different members. Formerly, the only player with a special office to fill was the goal-keeper, who stayed far out of the game, and whose sole duty was to defend his goal, while the remainder of the side played up in front together.

HOW TO BECOME A POLO PLAYER.

A good horseman, whose eye has been educated by such games as cricket and racquets, and who thoroughly understands football or hockey, the tactics and combinations of both of which greatly resemble those of polo, will not take long to master the peculiarities of polo, and ought to be a really good performer after three months of regular play. Here, as in all other games which demand quickness of eye and skill of hand, assiduous and long-continued practice is imperative. At first glance it may appear strange to say that many men play polo well in spite of being bad horsemen. Hence, the fact that a man knows little about riding should in no way deter him from giving the game a trial. Indeed, it should be an argument all the other way ; for nothing improves one's horsemanship so much as polo. A great advantage which polo has over all other outdoor games, is that one can begin it comparatively late in life, and that one will continue to improve with age and experience. The reason for this is that coolness, command of temper, horsemanship, knowledge of the game, and "head," all of which come with age, are far more important factors in making a first-class polo player than activity, which is an attribute of youth. At football a man is as a rule at his best from twenty to twenty-five ; and at cricket, from twenty to thirty years of age ; yet there are few really first-class polo players in England under thirty. Men of mature years are in no way barred from polo. Although I have never heard of a first-class cricketer who did not learn to play as a boy, many fine polo players have begun comparatively late in life. The late Mr. Kennedy, who was a remarkably fine player, commenced polo when he was thirty-eight years of age, and continued to be in the first flight for at least ten years later. Although it is well to commence early, it is not always feasible to do so ; for few boys have the desired opportunity.

The fact that the number of polo clubs has been more than doubled in England during the last few years, proves the advance which the game has made in popular favour. Many hunting men see the advantage of reducing the number of their horses, and filling up the vacancies with polo ponies, so that they can have their fun in the saddle all the year round, and not only for six months.

The first want of the novice who is fired with ambition to play polo is a suitable pony, to obtain which

he should seek the aid of an experienced friend, who
had best make the purchase soon after the polo season
is over ; for then the supply will exceed the demand,
and an animal quite good enough for all reasonable
requirements ought to be procurable for, say, £50.
The great point about such a pony is that he must
be a perfect player. If he fulfils this condition, no
objection should be taken to him if he be somewhat
slow. For choice, the pony should have played for
more than one season ; for the more experience he
has had, the less likely will he be to learn new tricks,
such as stopping and shying off the ball. The
beginner should avoid "green" or tricky ponies ;
for it is impossible for him to learn to hit the ball
and teach his pony to play at the same time. If
he cannot get a trained pony, he will no doubt learn
a good deal on a raw one ; but he must not imagine
that his teaching will do anything but spoil the
pony, unless it is a marvel of equine intelligence and
handiness.

Apart from the saving of money, it is well for the
novice to get a steady pony at the end of a polo
season, so that he may have several months during
which to practise hitting the ball in every direction
and at varying speed before he essays to play in
a game. Most men, even the busiest, can generally
manage, if they live in the country, to get an hour
two or three times a week for practice. It usually
happens that if a man begins playing polo by
starting straight off in a game, he is put to play
No. 1, and is told to ride the Back and not to mind
the ball, the consequence being that he does not
get as much practice in a whole season at hitting

the ball, as he would do by himself in a month. Even if he were not put to play No. 1, he would become so hurried and would get so bustled, that most likely he would not hit the ball half-a-dozen times in a game. If a beginner cannot get, as would be advisable, a whole winter's practice, he should have at least a month at it by himself before engaging in a regular game. Although a good level field is an advantage to begin on, it is not absolutely necessary ; for any fairly even piece of grass, if large enough, will serve the purpose. Besides, the practice gained by hitting the ball on rough ground will be found invaluable when galloping over a smooth surface in a game. The novice will receive great assistance by getting a capable friend to teach him (as I shall endeavour to do further on) how to hold his stick, and how and where to hit the ball. From the very commencement, he should always try to hit the ball in a certain direction, as for instance at a particular tussock of grass, tree, mark on the ground, or other suitable object. Also, it is important for him to learn how the wrist should be turned when hitting a back-hander. An experienced friend can help him not only in these points, but can also prevent him from acquiring bad methods of play, which, when once learnt, are very difficult to rectify.

Practice on a wooden horse.—By far the best method for a novice to learn to hit the ball, even before he ventures to handle a stick on a pony, is for him to practise on a wooden horse (Fig. 1), which can be roughly made by any carpenter. No saddle is required, and side bars as foot rests can take the place of stirrups. The height of the seat should be about two inches less than the height, at the withers, of the pony which is to be ridden. For instance, for a 14.2 pony, the seat of the wooden horse should be about 14 hands high.

A few hours' practice under a competent instructor

Fig. 1.—Wooden Horse.

and with a couple of boys to bowl balls, will greatly help the beginner in learning how to make each stroke correctly, and has the further advantage of saving a living mount from injury; because a man in his first attempts almost always hits his pony's off fore leg more or less severely with stick or ball, or

with both. Every description of stroke, forward or
back, stationary or in movement, on either side of
the pony, can be successfully practised with this
contrivance. I would extend the recommendation
of its use to any player (even a first-class one) who
wanted to get his eye in, or to bring the muscles
of his right arm into proper trim. Practice on it
is particularly useful ; because a man can hit the ball
as often in twenty minutes on a wooden horse as
he would do in a couple of hours if he had to ride
a pony after the ball. The best plan is to have
several dozens of old polo balls lying about the
ground ; to get a couple of boys to bowl and retrieve
them ; and to put up goals at different angles, so
that each stroke may be practised for accurate
direction.

HOW TO HIT THE BALL.

In learning, we should start at a walk, and when
able to hit perfectly at that pace, we should proceed
to the slow canter, and end with the fast gallop.
We should hit always with a straight arm, with a
good swing, either for a forward or for a back-handed
stroke, and in a true direction, though not always
as hard as we can. Accuracy is the great object
to attain ; for pace will give strength. Consequently,
when going fast, we should refrain from hitting too
hard, in attempting to do which we are apt to raise
our elbow and miss the ball. It is always well to
have several balls to practise with, so that we shall
not have to pull our ponies about more than we
want, by having to turn round every time we miss
a ball.

FORWARD STROKES.

There are four kinds of forward strokes.

1. *Straight forward.*—When hitting this stroke, which is the first one of all to practise, we should sit square in the saddle, and ride the pony up to the ball, so as to bring him in such a position that the arm may come down straight with full force on to the ball. The ball when struck should be about a

Photo by]   [M. H. HAYES.

Fig. 2.—Finishing out straight-
forward stroke.

foot in front of our right knee, and about six inches to the right of it. We should be very careful not to hit the pony's fore legs with either stick or ball ; and in finishing out a stroke (Fig. 2) should, if anything, hit away from the pony, and not towards him. For manner of holding the stick in this stroke, see Figs. 3 and 4.

2. *To the off (or right) front.*—This is a very difficult stroke to do with accuracy ; but it must be learned by all who aspire to be good players ; for it is the one by which the ball is centred by the player who makes a run down the side of the

ground with the adversary's goal to his right front.
If he cannot do this, he is sure to hit behind the goal
line. A certain amount of "cut" must be put on
by turning the head of the stick sideways, with
the inside or short end of the head slightly to the
front ; and the ball must be hit later than for the
ordinary forward stroke, *i.e.*, a trifle behind the knee.
At the moment of hitting, we should turn the pony's

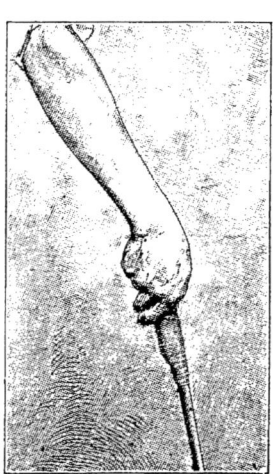

Fig. 3.—Forward drive,
view from front.

Fig. 4.—Forward drive,
view from behind.

hind-quarters a little to the left by a strong pressure
of the drawn-back right leg, so that the stick may not
strike the off quarter.

This stroke should be very frequently practised at
some object ; the angle made by the direction of
the ball with the direction in which the pony is
ridden being gradually increased according as dexterity
is acquired ; for the greater is the angle, the more
difficult will be the stroke. Like all other strokes,

it must first be tried at a walk, and afterwards at the canter and gallop.

3. *To the near side, or under the pony's neck.*— The difficulty of this stroke, like that of the preceding one, increases with the angle at which the ball is hit. When wishing to hit at or nearly at right angles to the direction in which we are riding, we can make the stroke much easier, if we have got time to do

Fig. 5.—Hitting under pony's neck, to save goal.

so, by turning the pony slightly to the left, in which case it will merely be a modification of the forward stroke. The difficulty of hitting at, or nearly at a right angle, consists in clearing the pony's fore legs, to do which we have got to lean very far forward. Even the best players are apt to fail by hitting the pony's fore legs with stick or ball, or with both. It is, however, a useful stroke when the ball is in front of goal (Fig. 5), and when we are unable to turn our pony's hind quarters to the left, in order to hit a back-hander under his tail to that side (Fig. 10). The latter, being much the easier stroke, should, when practicable, be always tried in preference to the former. Under no circumstances, when the ball is in front of the goal, should a back-hander be hit straight back ; for in that case, by leaving the ball in the line of danger, we violate the

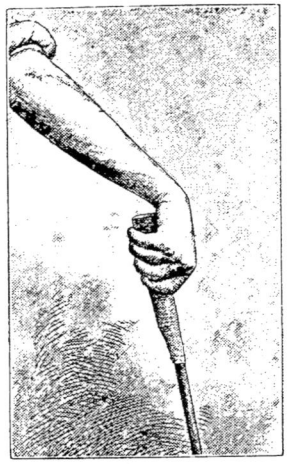

Fig. 6.—Hitting forward on near
side, view from front.

essential principle of placing the ball in such a position that from it the opposite side cannot make a goal.

4. *On near side.*—This is a most useful stroke for straightening the ball towards the centre of the ground, or for hitting it forward, or for a shot at goal, when being hustled on the off side. We should be careful to finish up the stroke a little away from the pony, so as not to hit his fore legs. The way to hold the stick is shown in Fig. 6.

BACK-HANDERS.

When hitting a back-hander, careful attention must be paid to the correct way of turning the wrist. The hand should be slightly turned, so as to bring the thumb down the front of the handle with the knuckles outwards (Figs. 7 and 8), and the stick still held in such a position that the long end of the head will be away from the pony. Additional

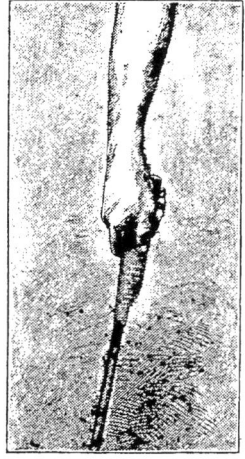
Fig. 7.—Ordinary back-hander,
view from front.

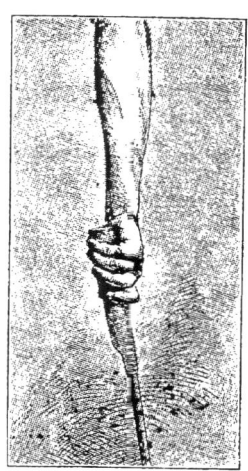
Fig. 8.—Ordinary back-hander,
view from behind.

strength can be put into the stroke by the support which the thumb gives by being held down the handle. The arm must be straight and kept as close to the side as possible.

There are four kinds of back-handed strokes.

1. *Straight back.*—When hitting straight back, the ball should be struck when about one foot behind the rider's knee (Fig. 9).

2. *To the left rear, or under the pony's tail.*—The ball must be in such a position that even when it is struck at right angles, it will go clear of the pony's hind legs.   It will therefore have to be a foot or more behind the rider's knee, and the pony's hind quarters

Photo by]   [M. H. HAYES.
Fig. 9.—Back-hander straight back.

must be turned to the left by a strong pressure of the drawn-back right leg (Figs. 10 and 11).

3. *To the off or right rear.*—The ball must be struck either level with or slightly in front of the rider's knee, and the pony's head turned to the left, so as to give room for the stick to come down.   Or the ball must be hit when at a distance of at least two feet from the pony.   This is much the most difficult

Fig. 10.—Hitting back-hander under pony's tail, to save goal.

.

stroke to do hard and well, and it is impossible to put as much strength into it as into the two preceding

Fig. 11.—Hitting back-hander under pony's tail, to save goal.

kinds of back-handers. It is very useful especially for the purpose of placing a ball for a comrade to take on, and is the best stroke to use in defending goal, when the No. 1 is riding the Back very close, on the near side. It should be well practised.

4. *On near side.*—This is a valuable stroke for getting one out of a difficulty, especially when one plays Back. For position of hand, see Fig. 12.

When a player who is expert at this stroke is being hustled on the off side, he can often, especially if he has a slight advantage in pace, lean to the

Fig. 12.—Back-hander on near side, view from front.

2*

right, push his opponent away, and get a clear shot at
the ball on the near side (Fig. 13).

A good deal of practice should be devoted to this
stroke, which is very useful for saving a goal. It
is much easier to do well, than a forward stroke on

Photo by]   [M. H. HAYES.
Fig. 13.—Back-hander on near side.

the near side; although it is harder than a back-
hander on the off side, which, when practicable, should
always be preferred in a match.

RIDING AT POLO.

Under this heading I shall confine my remarks
on horsemanship solely with reference to its connection
with polo.

Most good polo players ride with shorter stirrups at polo than they do at any other time, because they find that the fact of their doing so increases their power when stretching out to reach a ball, or when riding off an opponent.

A pony's head should invariably be left absolutely alone when the ball is being struck,

As the best polo ponies are those which play with a slack rein, stop dead at a touch on the mouth, and turn to the slightest indication of the leg, or weight of the rein on the neck ; our object should be to ride our ponies in such a way that they may obey these indications readily. If a man, when hitting at the ball, keeps hold of the pony's head, he is certain by the movement cf his body to give a jerk to the mouth. Therefcre, even if a pony be a puller, and it be necessary to keep a tight hold of his head when galloping, the reins should be invariably loosened at the moment the ball is being struck. The reason that very many ponies check over the ball, or shy off it, is owing to the neglect of this rule. A large number of ponies shy off the ball, or lean away from it ; because they are not properly ridden up to it, and kept in the right direction by a strong pressure of the drawn-back left leg. Instead of doing this, many players ride their ponies carelessly to within about four feet of the ball, and then lean out to reach it, which is a method that is open to two serious objections : First, the ball when far away from the pony cannot be hit with the same strength and accuracy as when at close quarters ; second, the fact of the weight of the rider being shifted to the right makes the pony lean away or shy off to the left.

The reins should be held rather shorter, and the left hand carried somewhat higher, at polo than on other occasions ; so that we may be able to apply the rein well forward on the neck in turning the pony, and stop him quickly even when we are a bit forward in the saddle. We should bear in mind that the flexibility of the neck increases according to its distance from the withers. If the hand is held low, the lateral pressure of the rein can be employed only against that portion of the neck which is immediately in front of the withers.

A fine polo player should be able, like a capable jockey when finishing a close race, to get the greatest possible speed out of his mount, and like a good school rider, to keep his animal at the same time under absolute control ; so that when going at full speed, he is able to stop or turn and hit the ball where he wishes.

We require a tight seat in order to be able to hustle, to keep firm in the saddle, to get the best pace out of the pony, and to stop him by force, if he won't stop by any other means. The question of hands is too difficult a one for me to discuss here ; although I am aware that there are a few riders, perfect artists at the game, who can hold pullers simply owing to their having perfect hands. Again, many men, otherwise good horsemen, seem to make all their ponies pull, on account of their bad hands. I have no great faith, as a general rule, in the efficacy, at polo, of that magic touch on the mouth which is a gift possessed by many of our best jockeys, riders to hounds, and horse-breakers, and which makes hot horses go kindly. Polo is such a rough and tumble game that one has not time to put in practice the niceties of such a fine art. I think the following leading directions are sufficient for general purposes : Ride with a loose rein ; stop your pony with a light touch on the mouth, if possible ; but stop him.

We should remember that the pony must be made to do his turns by the properly applied pressure of the legs (see remarks on school riding in Chapter V.) and that the reins are not meant to hold the rider in the saddle.

CHAPTER II.

THEORY AND PRACTICE OF POLO.

Combination—Duties of No. 1—Duties of No. 2—Duties of No. 3—Duties of
Back—Captaining a side—Umpiring—Hitting out from between the goal
posts in consequence of an exacted penalty—Dangers of Polo—Cruelty in
Polo Playing—Fair Play.

COMBINATION.

POLO is one of the most scientific of outdoor games,
although an uninstructed observer may be able to see
in it only a medley of galloping ponies, and the ball
hit here and there, apparently without system or
combination. Some people, even many of those who
frequently watch the game played, take this view of
it. I once overheard a lady in India say, " I don't
see much in polo. It is nothing but a cloud of dust
and bad language." Fortunately we have no dust on
English polo grounds. Strong words are, as a rule,
used only by a few extra energetic Captains, are
generally taken in good part by the players, and would
not signify much, if we were always able to restrict the
expression of our feelings to particular parts of the
ground. Unluckily, the strongest expletives have an
unhappy knack of escaping from our control just
under the Ladies' Stand. I am glad to say that of late
years as great an improvement has taken place in
" language," as in other departments of the game.

W. McCreery. F. M. Freake. W. S. Buckmaster. L. McCreery.

Photo by] [W. Rouch.

Fig. 14.—Old Cantab Team, winners of the Champion Cup, Hurlingham, and the Ranelagh Open Challenge Cup, 1900.

Before discussing in detail the science of polo, I must impress on young players the necessity of learning the rules. Although it is manifest that we should have at our fingers' ends the rules under which we play, many, even good players who have played the game for years, are marvellously ignorant on the subject of rules, on account of being too lazy or too indifferent to learn them from the book, which is the only accurate way by which to acquire that knowledge.

Four a side is the recognised number in all games and matches. In club games, when the full complement cannot be obtained, three a side will often afford plenty of sport ; but the diminution in number will, as a rule, entail too much galloping work on the ponies, and will render it impossible to carry out the principles of the game in their entirety. Three a side is, however, much better than five a side, for which there is not sufficient room in the present galloping game.

The places in the game are, Nos. 1, 2, 3, and 4 ; or, First Forward, Second Forward, Half-back and Back.

The rough idea of the duties of the different players in the Combination game, is that the main object of No. 1 is to interfere with the Back of the opposing side, to clear the way for his No. 2, and to hit as many goals as possible. No. 2's first duty is to attack hard, stop the opposing No. 3, and hit goals. No. 3 should assist in the defence of his own goal, and serve up the ball to the forwards. Back must defend his own goal. In practice this rough idea is, of course, subject to endless modifications ; for as the game changes, all the players in turn will attack and defend. No. 1

can assist in the defence of his own goal by preventing the opposing Back from coming up into the
game.   No. 2 can often save a goal with a back-

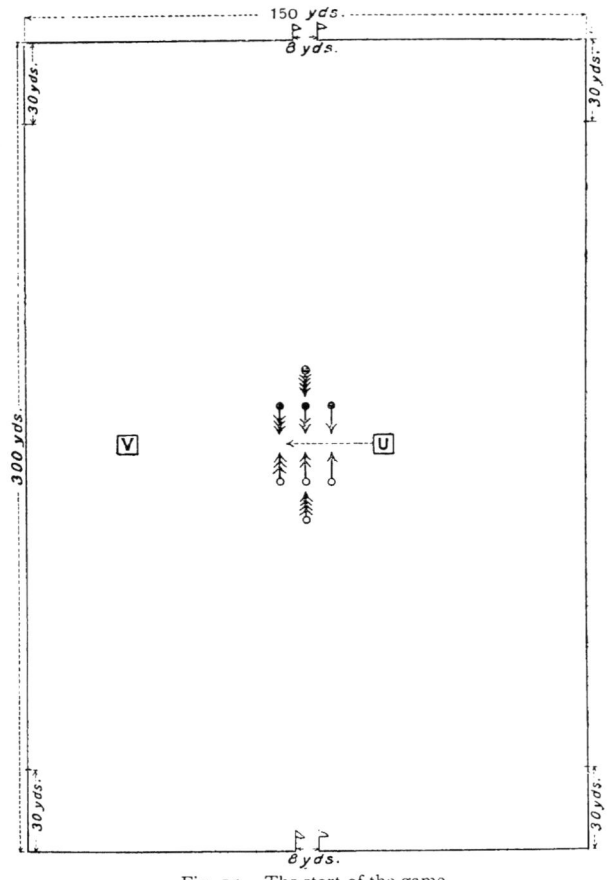

Fig. 15.—The start of the game.

U, Umpire ready to throw in ball.   V, Second Umpire.   Players' numbers are shown by arrow-heads.

hander or by hitting to the side.   No. 3 and Back
will get many chances of scoring on their own
account.

The start of the game is shown in Fig. 15.

The beginner should have the idea firmly impressed on his mind that he should play for his side and not

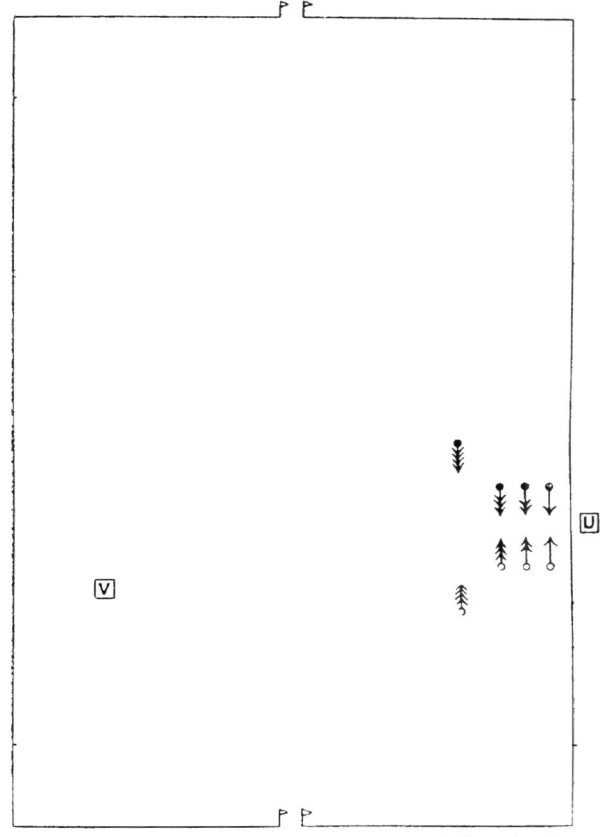

Fig. 16.—Ball out of play, Umpire U throwing it in from the side.

for himself; for unless he learns to play entirely for the success of his side, his presence will do more harm than good in a first-class team, no matter how brilliant his individual strokes may be. Besides,

the game is much more enjoyable when all the
members of a team are trying to help each other, than
when the whole aim and object of each player is to hit
the ball as often as possible himself.

I am sure many players do not obey orders, and do
not try to learn the scientific and unselfish game
because they think that they will get more fun if they

Photo by]   [M. H. HAYES.

Fig. 17.—Back galloping for back-
hander, hustled by No. 1.

play entirely for themselves, and always have a hit
at the ball when they get a chance, regardless of
instructions or exhortations from comrades or Captain.
I can assure these gentlemen that they make the
greatest mistake, and that, by being too eager, they
override the line, and spoil their own sport. Thus, by
ignoring the grand principle of give and take, each
man, instead of having only four opponents, will have

six or seven to contend against in his jostle for the ball. Such a player should remember that if he plays an unselfish game, and leaves the ball to a comrade when asked to do so, that comrade will in his turn accommodate him. Consequently, if all the side play unselfishly and for each other, not only is the game as a whole enormously improved, but each player will get far more fun out of it.

Only a few years ago, polo was taught, especially in

Photo by]   [J. WOOD.
Fig. 18.—Blue pulls up, instead of hustling white.

regiments, on rigid, not to say wooden, lines. No. 1 was often made to play without a stick at all, or even if he had one, he was not allowed to use it; and was told that his sole object was to nurse the opposing Back, and ride him off (Fig. 17) to clear the way for his No. 2, who had a real good time, and was frequently what we would now call a "loafer." That is to say, he hung about in the wake of his No. 1, or outside a scrimmage, did no real work, except when he got an opening, and would then probably make a most brilliant run, and thus earn all the *kudos* from the on-lookers. Only his own side, and perhaps his opponents, would know that he was really the most useless man in the team. When I speak of a man who does no real work, I refer to one who is always on the look-out for openings, and who, when he cannot dash in at the ball, canters about and does not try to hinder an opponent (Fig. 18). He ought, on the contrary, to be always busy, and should never lose a chance of hustling any opponent who has the remotest chance of getting to the ball. He should be constantly on the move, particularly when he occupies the place of 2 or 3, in which case he should almost invariably gallop. No. 1 has to adapt his pace to that of the opposing Back. Back has a more cautious game to play; for while defending his own goal, and watching for his opportunity, he must necessarily be often standing still or moving slowly. The duties of No. 3 in the old game were to stick to his own place at all hazards, to back up his No. 2, to support his Back, and to stop the opposing No. 2. The Back used to play the part of a sort of modified goal-keeper, and hardly ever went up into the game. These arrangements were good as far as they went, and were undoubtedly a great improvement on the ancient game of every one for himself. We have now made a still further advance by recognising the fact that to play polo in the best manner, we must do so on more elastic lines. In the hurry of a hard-fought galloping game it is absolutely impossible to always keep our exact place. For example, No. 1 temporarily gets into the place of No. 2, and No. 2 into that of No. 1. If, in such a case, they are attacking hard, and the ball is travelling towards the adversaries' goal, what can be more absurd than (as we may frequently see done) for No. 2 to slow up and shout for No. 1 to come on past him and ride the Back? That is what a selfish, ignorant player often does ; but it would be directly opposed to the interest of the side ; for the only man who has a chance of catching the opposing Back is No. 2, who throws it away. It is evident that if No. 2 finds himself temporarily in the place of No. 1, he should act the part of No. 1 until the circumstances of the game allow these two players to resume their own proper places. This remark applies to every other place in the game. Not only should Nos. 1 and 2 be ready to interchange when necessary, but Nos. 2 and 3 should also be similarly prepared to act, and No. 3 must be ready to instantly take the place of Back.

A man need not be a brilliant player to play a cool game, to be always ready to obey directions, and to seize opportunities with intelligence. Besides, an individually moderate side, which is well captained and perfectly drilled, will, by superior tactics, often beat four players who, man for man, are far better than their opponents, but who do not help each other. The remarks I have made about interchanging places, apply only to teams of which the members are all up to a fairly good standard of play. It may, however, happen that the Captain, who is probably the Back, is the only fine player of the side. Let us suppose that No. 3 is too moderate to be trusted to hit a back-hander with any degree of certainty ; that No. 2 is fair ; and that No. 1 is a good man at riding off, but is of no use on the ball. If they meet a stronger team with a very capable No. 2, the Back dare not go up into the game ; for he knows that he cannot rely on his No. 3. Interchanging places in a game like this would do more harm than good ; for if No. 1 gets into No. 2's place, he would probably fail to hit the ball, and if No. 3 takes Back's place, he would very likely make some disastrous blunder. Although we cannot lay down hard and fast rules as to how every game should be played, we may take for granted that the ideal team would be one in which the four players are equally at home in any position in the game. It is evident that when the members of a team have arrived at this pitch of excellence, it does not matter how often they interchange, so long as there is one man in each place. As such a team has never yet been seen on any Polo Ground, I am of opinion that, for practical purposes, the interchanging of places should be worked by the Nos. 1, 2 and 3 ; and that the Back should only come up into the game when he is certain of having the next hit, and of consequently keeping the ball in front of him.

Though I lay great stress on the fact that Back's chief duty is to defend his goal, it must be borne in mind that the best method of defence is a strong attack, and that the more the Back can force the game with strong forward strokes, the better chance will he have of keeping the ball out of his own half of the ground. So long as Back can keep the ball beyond the half-way line, his position remains an easy and comfortable one : his troubles never begin till he gets near his own goal.

The polo tactics of defence differ entirely from

those of attack. If the order of the day is to attack strongly, every effort should be made to hit the ball in the right direction, that is, towards the adversaries' goal. Wild hitting is of no use, and accuracy and direction are of far more importance than strength. For instance, we may often see a man make a fine run down the side of the ground and then smack the ball behind, instead of taking a pull, as he often has time to do, and either making a careful shot at goal, or middling it to a comrade by means of a back-hander.

In defence, exactly the opposite tactics should be employed. Although hitting round generally spoils the game, there is nothing for saving a goal like a good hard back-hander under one's pony's tail, so as to send the ball right out to the side of the ground (Fig. 10). A clever Back often turns defence into attack by hitting under his pony's neck from near his own goal to the side (Fig. 5). This is a very difficult and risky stroke for any one who has not an accurate eye, but it has the advantage over a back-hander that it cannot be stopped by the legs of the ponies which are galloping behind. It is a particularly paying stroke when, as often happens, the ball has come from one side of the ground towards goal, and the Back hits it under his pony's neck towards the other side, but away from his own goal (Fig. 5). If he does this successfully, he will probably get the next hit at the ball, which would save his goal for the time being, even if it does not result, as would not be unlikely, in a run the whole length of the ground. The objection to a man hitting round, is that the other members of his team, not

3*

knowing where the ball is about to go, will be apt to get spread-eagled, and the opposite side, by cutting off a corner, can usually stop a run.

In attack, if the ball be near both the side and the end of the ground, one member of the team, who will usually be the Back, should hang about near the centre of the ground, handy for a shot at goal, while the remainder of the side should use every endeavour to centre the ball out to him. Under these circumstances, if the Back is in the centre of the ground, No. 3 must keep ready to take Back's place, and after middling the ball to him by means of a backhander, should gallop towards the centre of the ground to such a position that he is able to take up the duties of defence. Certain risks may be taken—especially in the adversaries' quarter of the ground—which would not be allowable in defence. For instance, the Back, when close to the opposing goal, may dash in for a shot at goal and meet the ball ; because if he misses it, he will have the whole length of the ground in which to retrieve his error. But before doing this, he must warn No. 3 to cover him. Again, in defence it is never correct for No. 3 to let two of the opposing side get on to the Back ; because if No. 1 hustles the Back off the ball, No. 2 will have a free shot. When close to the adversaries' goal, however, No. 3 can often see where the back-hander will be likely to come, and may turn his pony before the stroke, in anticipation of a shot at goal.

If players will keep their eyes open and their wits about them, they will often be able to anticipate what is going to happen. For instance, No. 3 sees that his Back is about to hit a back-hander under his pony's tail, so by turning his pony to the left and moving in that direction, he will probably get on to the ball before any of the opposing side can do so. This principle applies to every phase of the game. By careful observation, a player can frequently tell by the way the stick is held, and by the angle at which a man rides at the ball, where he is going to hit it, and can thus save time and get a start. It is well to act on the supposition that an adversary will always hit the ball. It is not wise to anticipate a back-hander from a comrade when defending one's own goal; for if he misses it, the chances are that the fact of having one's pony turned for the back-hander, will let an adversary loose to have a free hit at the ball. With this exception, it is best to take for granted that the ball will always be hit, and to try to anticipate future events. The player most useful to his side is he who is most busy, who is always galloping hard, and who, if he cannot hit the ball, is always trying to hinder some opponent or the other in every way he lawfully can.

Except in the very best teams, the back-hand stroke is not used nearly often enough ; the passing of the ball from the side of the ground to the centre should almost invariably be done by this means.

When one member of the team takes the ball out to the side of the ground, one or more of his comrades should make for the centre in anticipation of this stroke, which should be made hard and true and towards the goal.

The secret of perfect combination is the accurate passing of the ball from one player to another. Every stroke should be studied in order to attain this result.

A ball hit twenty or thirty yards by one player, so that a comrade can get it, and in his turn either keep possession or pass it again, is much more likely to reach the goal than if the striker had sent it double or treble the distance, but into the possession of an opponent.

By these remarks, I must not, however, give the impression that I undervalue the importance of hard hitting. When a team is hitting out from behind, or to get the ball out of a position of danger, hard hitting is invaluable. Still, accuracy is more important than hard hitting. By combining strength with accuracy, perfection is attained.

DUTIES OF NO. 1.

It is a great pity that more players do not make a study of this position, which is unpopular, because it demands much self-denial. (Figs. 19 and 20.) Most men think that for the first year or two of their polo career, they must play No. 1 a certain number of times, and they try to avoid doing so, as often as they can. Afterwards, they will never play No. 1 if they can possibly help it. Nos. 2, 3, and Back should do their best to make No. 1's duties agreeable, and should remember that one reason why they themselves dislike the position of No. 1, is the unpleasantness of having such directions as " Gallop, No. 1," " Ride the Back, and leave the ball," constantly shouted at them, with frequent abuse, and with but few words of encouragement for their well-meant efforts. Therefore, in ordinary games they should refrain from what they know they would resent if applied to themselves. Even in matches, loudly shouted directions should be left to the Captain, and the other members should restrict themselves to instructions given in a quiet tone, and to words of encouragement.

A selfish No. 2 may often destroy the enjoyment of a young player for . the whole afternoon, by continually giving him directions to " ride the Back " and

Photo by]   [M. H. HAYES.

Fig. 19.   Fig. 20.

No. 1 (blue) hustling the Back (white).

" leave the ball alone." If, on the contrary, he were to allow the No. 1 to hit the ball whenever he got a fair chance, and were to take his own share of riding the Back out of the way of the No. 1 ; the young player would go off the ground encouraged and pleased with himself, and ready to play No. 1 whenever he was desired to do so.

Players should also guard against the too common

fault of asking No. 1 to do impossibilities. Men who have seldom if ever played there, do not know how much to expect from even a good No. 1, and they frequently shout at him to do things which are quite beyond his power. We all have often seen No. 2 pull up, look wildly round, and exclaim in agonising accents "Where is that No. 1?" when some exigency of the game has made No. 1 turn his pony in a direction which has brought him behind No. 2. Under these circumstances, a good No. 2 would, without wasting his breath, gallop on and tackle the Back, leaving No. 1 to fall into his place for the time being.

· Good and experienced players and also players who are experienced, but not good, should try to make a game of Polo as pleasant as possible for everyone, and particularly for beginners.

In ordinary club games, the position of No. 1 is usually given to a young player, or to the worst hitter, who, even though he does his best, will generally get all the abuse and no credit. Such a practice is altogether wrong ; for each player has an equal right to enjoy the game. Besides, it is very hard on a beginner to be always given a position in which he can get but little practice in hitting the ball, and will very likely have his young or imperfectly trained ponies spoiled. Unless a man has a natural aptitude for the place of No. 1, and likes it, he should be allowed from time to time an opportunity of playing in other positions of the game, both for the sake of his own practice, and with the object of preventing his ponies from becoming sick of the game. It is, of course, different when practising a team for a match ; for then the men should keep to the places they will occupy in the actual contest. Although No. 1 is not an enviable position for a young player on not the best of ponies, there is no better place in the game for a fine horseman who is a strong hitter, a good shot at goal, and who has plenty of big, blood, handy ponies ; provided always that his No. 2 hits the ball well up to him, and is ready to take his turn at hustling and jostling the Back if he finds himself in No. 1's place.

As Back almost always gets a start, he has a great advantage over No. 1, who has to adapt his movements to those of Back. For this reason the ponies of No. 1 are particularly liable to get spoiled. No. 1 will have to exercise great vigilance to remain onside, especially with an experienced and tricky Back. The chief thing for him to remember is that the only way for him to get off as quickly as Back, is to continually watch him, to start at the same moment and in the same direction as Back, and not to look over his shoulder for the ball. If he watches the ball, the Back will be certain to slip him. Another great advantage which Back has is that, when two players are galloping level for a ball, it is much easier while being hustled, to hit a back-hander than a forward stroke. For these reasons, and also because the ponies of a No. 1 frequently get cunning after a time and will not go in and face a back-hander, or jostle unless they are well alongside, every allowance should be made and abuse withheld from the luckless No. 1, who often incurs it because he fails to make much impression on a slippery Back. No. 1 should always try to come up on the stick side of the back (Fig. 21), and, if he can, should ride him off and get the ball, unless one of his own side behind him shouts out "Leave it!" On hearing this order, which means that the man behind has the best chance at the ball, No. 1 must at once devote his energies to riding Back off and must on no account try to hit the ball.

For two reasons he should if possible come up on his adversary's stick side. Firstly, because if he succeeds in this, the Back will be forced to hit on the near side, and it is much harder to place a near side back-hander where one wants to, than an off side one. Secondly, if he rides his opponent over the ball, his No. 2, who ought to be backing him up, can hit the ball to No. 1's right hand, and very likely give him a good opening (Fig. 21). But if No. 1 was on the other side, he would have to make his own hitting on the near side, which is much more difficult.

When the ball is hit out from behind his own goal line, he should be as close as possible to the Back, and ready to interfere with him if necessary (Fig. 23). If the ball, on being hit forward, does not quite reach the opposing Back, who may be afraid to dash in, No. 1 must go for the ball, if no one else of his side can get it. He should, however, if he has the opportunity, delay hitting his back-hander, and should shout to one of his own side to gallop past him. He will thus be able to place the ball for him If, on the other hand, he hits a back-hander at once, the opposing Back would be sure to get the ball without any difficulty. It is quite an exploded idea that it is not necessary for No. 1 to be a fine hitter. If he has good ponies, he will have as many openings as any other member of the team, and will probably get more chances of hitting goals than any of them. In

the final of the Open Cup at Ranelagh, 1901,
Mr. Walter Jones hit five goals out of the six
secured by his side.   No. 1 must, however, remember that, as the man behind him can see better
than he does how the game is going, he must on no
account touch the ball if he is told to leave it.   The
main thing for him to do, is to gallop and to keep the
Back galloping.   Even if he has not the remotest
chance of catching him, or of stopping the back-

Photo by]   [J. WOOD.

Fig. 21.—White No. 1 hustles blue, leaving his No. 2 to bring on the ball.

hander, he ought to gallop on after the Back ; because
in doing so he will hurry him, and will thus render the
direction of his stroke more or less uncertain.   If
Back were, on the contrary, left to himself, he would
have time to look round and place his back-hander
exactly where he wished.   If kept at the gallop,
especially if the ground is bumpy, the Back may miss
the ball altogether, or, if he manages to hit it, he may
probably succeed only in hitting it straight back, in

which case it will very likely be stopped by the legs of
ponies coming up behind.

As a rule, just as the Back is going to hit his back-
hander, No. 1 is about half a length to the bad, and
cannot stop the Back from hitting it. Under these
circumstances, we constantly see a player ride straight
at the ball, in the hope that it may be stopped by his
pony's legs or other part of the animal. If the pony
escapes being hit by the ball, he will probably be hit
on the legs or face by the stick, while the stroke is
being finished. This practice is unfair and cruel to
ponies, and nothing spoils them so quickly. After
they have been hit two or three times, they will
probably either cut it and not try to gallop, or will shy
away from the stick, when they see the stroke coming.
The No. 1 should ride about two feet away from the
line of the ball, when he finds he cannot get alongside, and hit at the ball on the near side, timing his
stroke to come a fraction of a second later than his
opponent's back-hander. By this means, if the Back
hits the ball, the No. 1 will often meet it, when it has
gone only a foot or so, and will either drive it forward
or stop it. With very little practice a player will learn
to time his stroke properly. This method will be
found more successful than the plan of riding straight
into the stroke and trusting to luck for the ball to hit
the pony, and it will not spoil the animal, which thus
will escape being hit either by stick or ball.

If the ball has been hit some way past the Back,
and No. 1 has succeeded in getting alongside him, but
cannot ride him off the ball on account of being
slightly behind, it will not be much good for him to
try to do so; because Back will simply let No. 1

ride him on to the ball, and will then get his back-
hander in on one side or the other without any
trouble.   It will be much better for No. 1 to pull away
about two feet from Back, and come in with a hard
bump, just as he is going to hit the ball (Fig. 13).   If
this bump is accurately timed, it will seriously inconvenience the opponent, and very likely put him off his

Fig. 22.—No. 1 (blue) keeping out Back (white), who is attempting to
dash through.

stroke.   But if the two are locked together, the
amount of shoving No. 1 can do, will not prevent
Back from coming on to the ball at the right moment.

In the foregoing directions, I have tried to instruct
a No. 1 how he should play when his own side is
attacking, and the opposing Back is employed in
defending.   I will now try to explain what he should
do when his own side is on the defence.

No. 1 has a very much better chance of interfering with the Back, when the opposite side is attacking, in which case his chief business is to constantly try to prevent the Back from coming up and forcing the game with forward strokes (Fig. 22). Provided he has handy, good ponies, he should nearly always be able to do this, and will thereby greatly assist his side, although he may not get much applause for it, as it is not a showy game. He will, however, win many a match for his side, and will be fully appreciated, if his Captain understands polo.

To succeed, he must stay close to the Back and watch him all the time. If he is watching the Back, as soon as he sees him try to dart in, he can intercept his pony and prevent him doing it. If the game is going fast towards his own goal, No. 1 should be riding alongside the Back, but with two feet the best of it, *i.e.*, with his knee against the shoulder of his opponent's pony. In this position, if the Back wants to dash in and get the ball, No. 1 can always ride him out towards the side, even if the Back is a much heavier man than himself. No. 1 should not do unnecessary hustling, when the ball is not near, and there is no object to be gained.

When the ball is hit behind the opposite back line, No. 1 should place himself for the hit out, facing the man who hits out, rather away from the goal, where he thinks the ball will be hit (Fig. 23 and 24). Here, his business is to meet the ball if possible, and prevent his opponent from dribbling out, by galloping straight in immediately the ball is hit over the back line. He should always remember, directly the ball is hit behind, to at once get to his place, and not stand about and talk, as is too often done. Often through the player's slackness, the ball is hit off before he is ready and while he has his back turned to the ball.

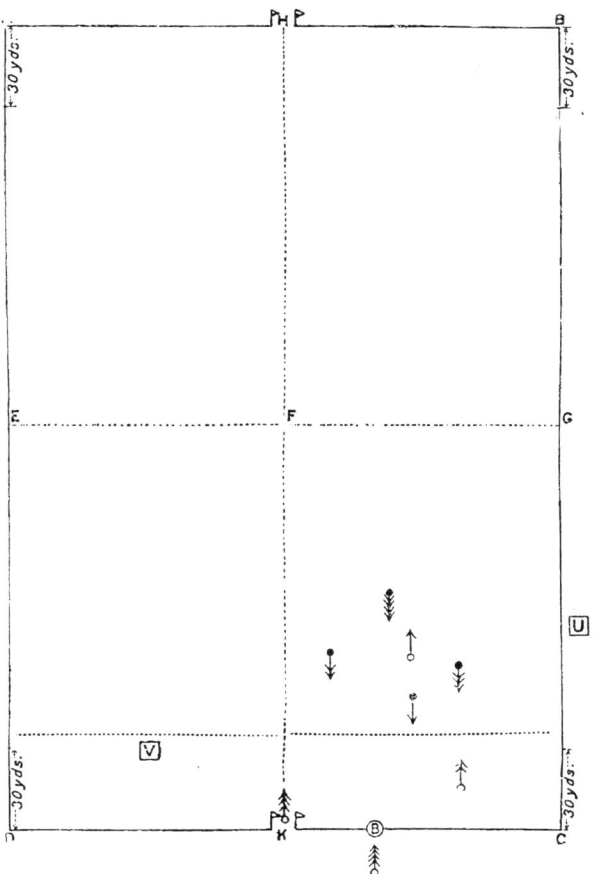

Fig. 23.—Hitting out from behind.

When all the opposing side are behind and hit out from between the goal posts, the No. 1 should face the goal on the left of the circle, so as to be able to meet the man who hits out stick to stick, with no danger of crossing him.

In both these cases, it is well for No. 1 to have his

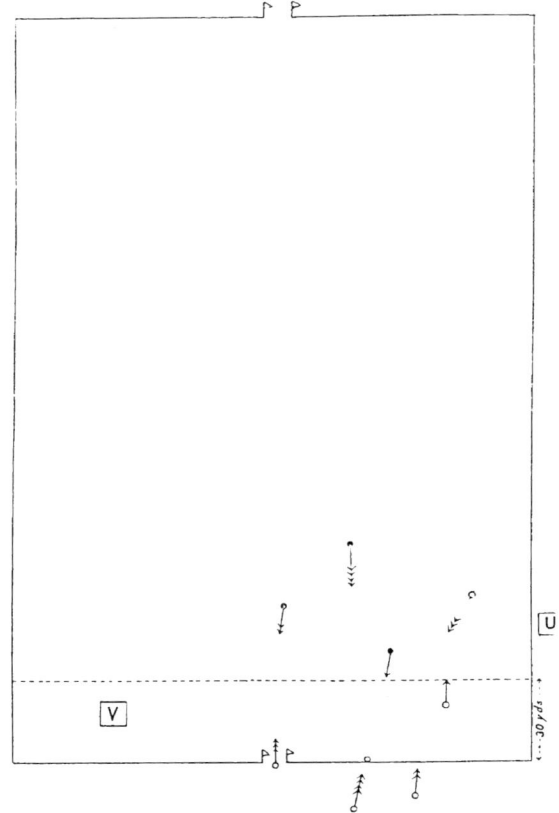

Fig. 24.—A method of placing the side for the hit out, if the hitter out be a weak striker.

pony on the move and well in hand, timing it so as to cross the line just as his opponent hits the ball. In this way, when the opposite side hits out between the goal posts, he should be able to prevent the man who hits off from making a short dribble, before he hits out hard. (Fig. 27.)

As I have already explained, No. 1 must watch the Back and not look behind for the ball. He should therefore rely on his No. 2 to give him instructions, and be always listening and ready to at once do what he is told. If the ball is near enough to his adversaries' goal for his own side to have a shot, he must try and clear the Back away from the goal, so as to leave it open. In any case, he should get himself out of the way, so that he may not interfere with the shot ; because goals are often stopped by the ball hitting a pony.

If No. 1 gets a chance of hitting the ball and receives no instructions from his own side to leave it, he should always take his chance and hit it.

If No. 1 finds himself temporarily in No. 2's place, he should do No. 2's work for the time being, and take the first favourable opportunity of changing back into his proper position.

When one of his own side is hitting out from behind, No. 1 should place himself close to the opposing Back, with his pony's head turned in the direction of the adversaries' goal. When the ball is being hit out, all the players should have their ponies in hand and collected, as if they were going to start for a five-furlong scurry, so that they may get off at the gallop with the least possible delay.

Finally, I would point out to young players that it is easier to become good enough to play No. 1 in first-class matches, than to play No. 2, No. 3 or Back ; and that there are so few who are really clever in this position, that a young player ambitious of getting into a good team, ought to cultivate that place.

DUTIES OF NO. 2.

It is a great mistake for a man to invariably play No. 2. No matter how brilliant a player he may be, he should occasionally play No. 1, by doing which he will appreciate the difficulties No. 1 labours under, and will learn what No. 1 can and cannot do. If he knows this thoroughly, he will be fully capable of helping his No. 1 with instructions and encouragement.

A No. 2 has to look after the oppposing No. 3, and his object both in attack and defence should be to get the best of him, and always try to be in front of him. If he cannot get the ball, he should try to stop any of his opponents obtaining possession of it. He must be a "busy" player, and constantly on the gallop. He must be always on the look out, and try to anticipate where the ball is going to be hit, and get there before his opponents. If he can rely on his No. 3 or on his Back hitting a back-hander, he should check his pace and prepare to turn before the ball is hit, when he has made up his mind where it is coming to. He should, however, not do this when the ball is close to his own goal; because he should then devote his attention to defending, and preventing the opposing No. 3 getting a shot at goal. When, his own side is attacking, and the ball is in his opponents' quarter of the ground, he may take more liberties and turn sooner in the hope of getting a shot at goal.

One of the chief duties of No. 2 is to give his

No. 1 constant instructions, for which No. 1 relies entirely on him, because he cannot see behind him. No. 2 should give as short and plain instructions as possible, such as, "leave it," and "take it," and should never use an ambiguous expression, such as, "all right," or "go on." The former, which is frequently used, may mean almost anything; and the latter may mean that No. 1 is to go on with the ball, or to go on and leave it to No. 2. If No. 2 wants No. 1 to hang over the ball until he can get there, the best expression to use is "keep it," by which No. 1 will know that he has to prevent anyone else getting it until his No. 2 can do so, and then clear out of the way.

No. 2 should be very careful about the direction of each stroke, and when his No. 1 and the opposing Back are in front, he should always hit the ball to whichever side his No. 1 is riding. No. 1 may then get a good opening, and may be able to drive the ball forward; but if No. 1 only succeeds in preventing the opposing Back from getting in a back-hander, the ball will still be left there for the No. 2 to have another chance at it. If No. 2 hits it to the other side, the Back is almost sure to get it. This is a most important point, and is not nearly enough studied by most men who play No. 2.

Above all things, No. 2 should not hit round or across the ground, except to defend his own goal; but should keep the ball towards the centre of the ground and always hit towards his opponents' goal when possible. If he finds himself near the boards in his adversaries' half of the ground, he should hit towards the centre at once, the easiest way

4*

to do which is to screw the pony round and hit a back-hander under his pony's tail. In a good team, the Back and No. 3 will be always on the look-out for this stroke, which will give them many an opening down the centre of the ground ; unless their opponents succeed in frustrating these tactics, by taking charge of any player who goes to the centre, before the ball arrives. It is most important for everyone on the side, when attacking, to hit to the centre and not along the boards, and not to wait until close to the back line, to send the ball to the centre.

No. 2 should be a dashing player, a hard and accurate hitter, and a good shot at goal. Above all things, he must do a great deal of work, and must devote himself as much to helping his Nos. 1 and 3 as to hitting. In attack, he should often clear the way for No. 3 in exactly the same way as No. 1 does for him. He should play quite as unselfish a game as No. 1, and if told by the man behind him to leave the ball, he should invariably do so, and should gallop on to ride off his next opponent, so as to keep the way clear. He must never let an opponent ride loose in front -of him, and it will generally be his business to look after the No. 3 of the opposing side. In attack, he must always try to be on the ball before him ; and in defence, he must prevent him getting a dash in at goal, to succeed in .which he should always endeavour, both in attack and defence, to be in front of the opposing No. 3—never behind him. Occasionally we see a No. 2 who, instead of doing a lot of real work, waits about to make runs, and when he ought to be hustling an opponent, in order to give a comrade an opening, he hangs back on the chance of getting the ball himself. And yet, because he makes several brilliant runs in a match, the on-lookers who do not understand the game will probably regard him as the best player on his side. I need hardly say he is not the sort of man we require when we want to win an important match. Moreover, he should thoroughly understand the duties of Nos. 1 and 3, and should be able to do their work equally as well as his own, if he finds himself temporarily in either of their places.

No. 2 is often too anxious to try for a goal, however difficult the shot may be. He might learn a valuable lesson on this subject by observing the fact that in a crack football match, no one shoots at the goal until a good opportunity arrives. The ball is invariably passed rapidly to the centre before the shot is tried. The finer the hitter, the greater is the temptation to make very long shots at goal. Many goals are lost by this practice, for no one can make a certainty of a goal at 80 or 100 yards; and even if the ball is sent in exactly the right direction, a quick Back will probably overtake it and save the goal. It is, as a rule, better to straighten the ball with the first stroke and then try with a second stroke to put it through the posts.

When the ball is hit out from behind No. 2's goal line (Fig. 23), he should place himself about 10 or 15 yards farther away from the goal and about 20 yards in front of the back line, and should have his pony on the move, as soon as Back starts to hit the ball, so as to have his pony cantering when the ball is hit up to him. As soon as the ball is past him, he can gallop on the line of it, and he will then be in possession. It is a great mistake for him to stand too far away, and be obliged to wait standing still for the ball to come up to him ; and he must be well on the outside, so as to enable the Back to hit past him without danger of being struck by the ball.

When the opposing side is hitting out, he should place himself facing his adversary's line, and on the goal side of where the ball is placed (Figs. 23 and 24). If they are hitting out near goal, he should be right in front of his adversary's goal. There are two reasons for this position : firstly, if his adversary hits the ball across his own goal, he should be able to get to it first, and prevent the opposing side getting a clear opening ; and secondly, if it is hit out to the side, he will be ready in front for his own side to pass to him. When the opposing side is hitting out from between the goal posts, No. 2 should place himself as in Fig. 27.

DUTIES OF NO. 3.

No. 3 is perhaps the busiest man on his side, whether for attack or defence. In defence he must never let the opposing No. 2 gallop loose ; because, if he does so, and the opposing No. 1 rides his Back off, No. 2 will have the chance of a clear run. It is No. 3's duty to attend to the carrying out of the rule that, in defence, two opponents should never be allowed on to the Back. In attack, and especially when very close to goal, liberties in this respect are, of course, allowable. In attack, it is No. 3's business to back up his No. 2, and if necessary, to make both No. 1 and No. 2 clear the way for him. He must be very quick, and, especially in a sticky game, must be always on the turn. If Back goes up into the game, he must drop into Back's place like clockwork, particularly if he sees Back attempting a risky stroke, such as meeting the ball.

In attack, No. 3 will get many openings, but he must remember that his first duty is to prevent the opposite side from hitting goals, and, bearing this in mind, he should always try to keep the ball in front of him. This result cannot be attained unless on every possible occasion he passes the ball to the right hand of his No. 1 or No. 2, and resists the temptation of making runs himself, unless he can make a certainty of hitting the ball next. If No. 3 sees the opposing No. 2 going to hit a back-hander, he should turn where he sees the ball is coming, and should not dash in to try to put No. 2 off his stroke, unless he sees that his own No. 2 is coming back into his place When No. 3 dashes in for an opening, he may often get into No. 2's place, in which case he should take the first opportunity of changing back into his proper place. Though he should make No. 2 clear the way for him, his chief object should be to hit in the right direction, and place the ball for his No. 2, and not merely hit forward, leaving it to chance who may get it next. When No. 3 dashes in to get a run, which he will frequently do, No. 2 should promptly drop back and take his place, so that, if No. 3 fails to get the ball or the game turns the other way, there may be a man in No. 3's place, ready to defend

As No. 3 is generally in the middle of the game, a side can be captained from his place nearly as well as from that of Back.

If No. 3 can hit out from behind equally as well as the Back, it is best for him to do so, and to follow the ball up, backing up No. 2, so that the advantage of having the players in their proper places to begin with may be secured. If, however, Back be the stronger hitter, No. 3 should place himself slightly in front of goal, so as to be able to defend it, if the hit out be not successful (Fig. 23).

When his opponents are hitting out, he should be about fifty yards out away from goal, where he thinks the ball will be hit, and should not be tempted to meet the ball, unless it is stationary and he is certain of getting it. His duty is to try to get it before the opposing No. 2, and hit a back-hander towards goal to his own No. 2. If the opposite side are hitting out from between the goal posts, No. 3 places himself as in Fig. 24.

DUTIES OF BACK.

Back, whose place is the most important one in the game, is as a rule the Captain of the side. A first-class Back must not only be a fine player, but must also be a master of the tactics of polo, cool, resourceful, never liable to throw a chance away, and always ready to profit by the error of an adversary. He must be mounted on perfectly trained and very handy ponies. Although great speed is always an advantage in polo ponies, it is not so essential to Back as to No. 1 or No. 2 ; for he will almost invariably get the start of the opposing No. 1.

He should not stay too far out of the game, and especially in attack, when close to the adversaries' goal, he should be close up, ready to make a dash at goal.

As a general rule, he should not meet the ball when it is travelling towards him ; because, if he misses it, he will be going the wrong way, and his opponents will get a fine opening. As an exception to this rule, we may suppose a case in which a smart No. 3 turns when the ball was hit towards his own Back, who will have only to shout to his No. 3, " Look out, Back ! " and can then dash in and meet the ball without risk. This is very often the only way to save a goal. The maxim that accuracy of direction and knowledge of tactics are of more importance in every position of the game than powerful hitting, applies particularly to Back, whose great object should always be to place the ball so that his side can get it. A hard, clean back-hander right through the players and up to the opposing Back, is a grand stroke to see ; but if the opposing Back repeats the performance, not much is gained, and there is always the risk of the ball being stopped by its hitting a pony's legs. As a rule, it is best to hit a back-hander slightly sideways. A good Back generally hits the ball slightly under his pony's tail, that is, towards his left rear ; the object being that No. 3 may turn to the left and get to the ball right-handed, unless there is some particular reason for hitting the ball elsewhere. Back should make a habit of hitting his back-handers in this direction, because his Nos. 3 and 2 will then know where to go. Hitting a ball back-handed in this way is easier than hitting it away from one's pony, and has the further advantage that No. 3 gets to it better ; because if he has to turn to the right after the ball, he will very likely have to take it on the near side, in order to prevent having his stick caught. Also, if No. 1 is in hot pursuit, a ball hit slightly sideways one way or the other will probably miss No. 1's pony ; but if hit straight back, it may not unlikely get stopped by the legs of that animal.

If we watch the play of one or two of our most celebrated Backs, we shall not be as much impressed by the brilliancy and strength of their strokes, as by the extraordinary accuracy with which they place the ball so that their own side can get it. Although we may often hear remarks about the bad luck of a back-hander hitting a pony, the accident in many cases is due to the faulty play of the man who hit it. In attack the Back should let the No. 1 get close to him, though not so close as to run the risk of having his back-hander stopped by the pony. Having got the No. 1 well on the gallop, he can back-hand the ball, turn round sharply and have him off-side. It is not a bad plan when near the adversaries' goal for No. 3, particularly if he has confidence in the Back, to let No. 2 of the opposing side on to him also, and prepare to turn for the back-hander. Then if the Back is very nippy, and if he can get them both galloping, he can turn quickly, and may be able to dart in and put both No. 1 and No. 2 off-side, in which case there will for the moment be four against two. These tactics can of course be employed only when a side is attacking strongly. In defence no risks of this kind should be incurred.

The Back should be able to hit back-handers on the near side, which is not so easy to do as on the off, although it is not difficult by diligent practice to acquire the desired ability. If No. 1, who should always try to come up on the stick side, succeeds

in getting level, the Back will have no option but
to ride him away to the right, in which case he will
come in on the ball at the last moment possible,
in order to hit a back-hander on the near side
(Fig. 13).   Back has here the further advantage that
he cannot have his stick crooked, as the ball is on the
far side of his pony from his opponent.   The Back
requires very handy ponies in order to put, as

Fig. 25.—Blue put off-side by six inches
by Back (white).

he should be always trying to do, No. 1 off-side
(Fig. 25).   The Back should always be on the move,
popping here and there, and twisting and turning ; if
he stands still he will be collared by the No. 1 and be
unable to take any advantage of an opportunity when
it presents itself.

From playing in second class polo or against inferior
Nos. 1, many Backs acquire the bad habit of slowing
up to hit a back-hander.   Although, when going slow,

a much stronger and more accurate stroke can be
made ; the temptation, which I know is strong, should
be avoided, because the practice of this habit will
probably make a man miss when going fast. Mr.
John Watson is the finest exponent I have seen
of the art of defending goal by, to use his own
expression, " playing close." When hard pressed
near goal, he can, by a twist of his wrist, get the ball
away at right angles, in front of the fore legs of the
No. 1's pony, towards the side of the ground, and
can place it in such a position, that it will be almost
impossible to hit a goal. Ten yards in a direction
of this kind will probably be worth more than one
hundred yards in front of goal. Finally, the best
Back is he who has fewest goals hit against him. A
Back who defends his goal consistently and well, will,
off his own bat, win far more matches for his side than
any other individual member of the team. He must
always bear in mind that it is his duty to defend his
goal, and to send the ball up to his Forwards, in such
a manner that they may be able to hit it through their
opponents' goal, and he must therefore try always to
keep the ball in front of him. By this I mean, he
must not dash in on the chance of hitting the ball,
in which case he may find himself on the wrong side
of the ball and unable to defend his goal.

CAPTAINING A SIDE.

For a Captain of a team to be successful, it is
essential that his word should be absolute law. There
should be no arguing or quarrelling in the game, even
if he makes an error. A good deal of latitude as
to speaking should be allowed in a match ; but no one

should shout so as to interfere with the Captain's directions. Every member of a team should carefully listen for instructions, which, except those given by the Captain, may be restricted to, " Ride the man and leave the ball," " Back-hander here," " Look out, Back," " Leave it," " Take the ball," and a few more of the same sort. The phrases used cannot be too distinctly uttered, and should be free from all ambiguity. As an instance to the contrary, I may mention that when a man shouts " All right!" probably meaning that he can get the ball himself, and wishes a comrade in front of him to leave it, the said comrade may not unlikely imagine that he himself is all right to go on and take the ball. Again, the shout " Ride him off " means either that the man is only to ride the opponent off, or that he is also to try and hit the ball. " Leave it " is the best expression for general use, as it is short, clear and emphatic. Every good player knows that, if he is told to " leave it," his duty is to gallop on at once and ride the next man. Many opportunities are lost by a player leaving the ball and pulling to one side in order to allow the man to whom he leaves the ball to take it on past him. On the contrary, he should gallop on at once, so as to ride the next man off, and in this way to get to the ball before his opponent.

A good Captain, by his energetic directions, by the force of his example, and, above all things, by his ability to play a losing game, wins many a match which has appeared impossible to retrieve. The best instance which I can give of such a leader is Mr. John Watson (Fig. 26), to whom we are indebted for the modern development of polo.. He has the rare gift of being able to animate the most moderate team with his own enthusiasm, and to make them play up, almost in spite of themselves. In addition to being one of the best players ever seen on a polo ground, he has the secret of making his team, no matter who they are, do their utmost from start to finish, and in this way he has pulled more matches out of the metaphorical fire than anyone else. He is a consummate master of the tactics of polo, and, in addition to being the best Captain of a side I have ever seen, is a wonderful instructor to anyone with or against whom he plays. Moreover, he plays up just as hard and as keenly in an ordinary practice game, as in a tight match.

UMPIRING.

An Umpire must not only have the rules at his fingers' ends and be in constant practice, but must also have quickness of eye, decision of character, application to his work, confidence in the correctness of his own opinion, and determination enough to stick to it. He should ride a good polo pony, work hard, never for a moment take his eyes off the game, and give his decisions promptly and clearly. His verdict is final, and should be received in absolute silence, no matter what the opinion of the players may be. To question his decision, either openly or aside, is the height of bad form. Even if we think that he has made a mistake, we should loyally keep that opinion to ourselves ; for we must give him the credit of doing his best, and must remember that the smartest of umpires

Fig. 26.—Mr. John Watson.

cannot always correctly decide a close thing. Indeed, in many cases of off-side, when the question is one only of inches, no one, except the Back and perhaps No. 1, can tell who is right and who is wrong. Besides, infallibility cannot be expected from mortals. If umpires be not treated with consideration, and always given the credit of doing their best, it will become very difficult to find men who will accept the office ; in fact, as it is, we have very few really good ones. A new rule has been passed, that it is the umpire's business to stop the game without being appealed to, in case of any dangerous riding ; but it is by no means enforced often enough. Backs, especially, are often allowed to cross time after time with the utmost impunity. Many Backs continually cross in front of the opposing No. 1 to hit an ordinary back-hander instead of leaving the line of the ball clear, and taking it on the near side.

Two umpires are necessary, as it is impossible for one man to cover the whole ground in a good match. The best way to divide the work of umpiring is to quarter the ground in the manner shown in Fig. 23. The umpires should keep to their own respective sides of the ground ; the one remaining more or less in quarter H B G F, the other in quarter E F K D, so that neither will go near the other's goal line. In this manner they can both obtain a good view of the game and there will always be an umpire handy to give a reliable decision on a close point. If, on the contrary, the two umpires get down to one end of the ground, and the ball is kept travelling up and down, cases needing their decision may occur at points too

5

distant for them to accurately observe what happens ;
for it is impossible for both of them to keep pace
with the ball.

In important matches a referee (see Hurlingham
Rule, No 4) may be appointed ; but his services
are really never required except to decide a knotty
point upon which the umpires have disagreed.

HITTING OUT FROM BETWEEN THE GOAL POSTS, IN CONSEQUENCE OF AN EXACTED PENALTY.

When hitting out from between the goal posts,
the hitting out side should arrange themselves to
the best advantage, according to the direction in
which the hitter out means to send the ball (Fig. 27).

Either Back or No. 3 will hit out, and which ever
of them makes the stroke, the other should follow
him up, in case of a miss-hit. The striker should
tell his No. 1 and No. 2 to which side he
intends to hit the ball ; for he should never hit it
down the centre of the ground. Nos. 1 and 2 should
have their ponies well in hand, about ten yards
behind the line, and should gallop up, when the
striker starts to gallop at the ball, so as to pass the
line at full speed a fraction of a second later than
the ball is struck. The Captain of the side will
make up his mind whether he hits the ball for No. 1
or No. 2 to follow. In Fig. 27, No. 1 is shown
on the left, and No. 2 on the right ; but this entirely
depends on the Captain's wishes.

The attacking side should divide themselves, so
that No. 1 and No. 2 are near the semi-circular line,
and No. 3 and Back farther out in the centre. It
is the duty of the opposing No. 1 to dash in and

prevent the striker from dribbling out, which is most important ; because the defending side may gallop out, if the ball is sent ever such a small distance over the line. No. 1 will place himself so as to be

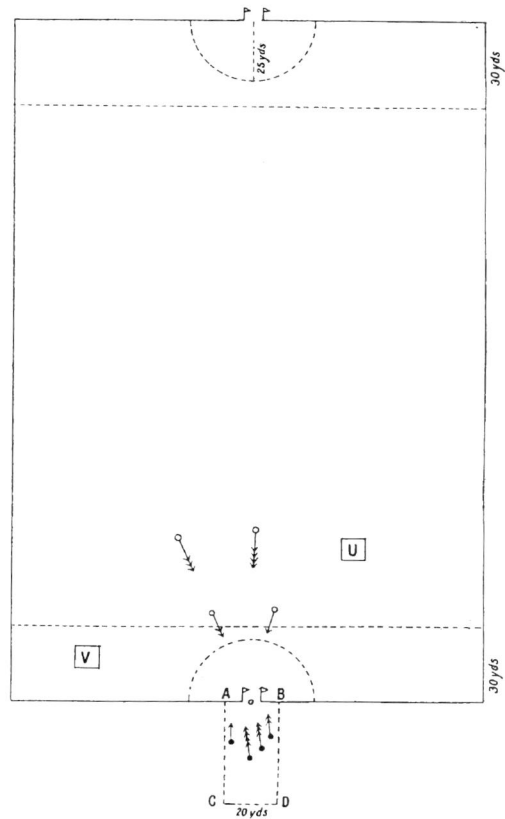

Fig. 27.—Hitting out from between the goal posts.

on the stick side of the hitter out, and then he will not cross him. He should adapt himself to circumstances, and must be very sharp at moving about, so as to frustrate the striker. He will

5*

generally be able to see in what direction his opponent means to send the ball, as soon as he starts to
hit it. Back and No. 3 will place themselves more
or less as in Fig. 27, so as to be ready to go to
either side.

The defending team must be inside the parallel
lines A C and B D, and must not advance over the
back line till the ball has been hit.

The attacking side are free to place themselves
anywhere they like, except within the twenty-five yards
semi-circle, until the ball has been hit.

DANGERS OF POLO.

The ordinary idea held by people who have
only seen polo played, that it is a very dangerous
amusement, is entirely wrong ; provided that the
ponies are suitable, that the players adhere to the
rules, and that they observe ordinary precautions for
the safety of others, as well as for themselves.
There is very little danger in polo, no matter
how hard the match, if the eight players are good
horsemen, the ponies well trained, and the men
play fair, which unfortunately they do not always do.
Then it is that a strong, determined umpire, a man
who is no respecter of persons, is required. I regret
to say that the foulest riders are not always found
among the worst players. The severe Indian penalty,
namely, a free shot at goal at fifty yards' distance,
would not be a bad addition to the Hurlingham rules.
Well-known Indian players have told me this year,
that the game, as played in England, is not nearly as
fair a one as it is in India. I am inclined to agree
with them.

The causes of the accidents which occur in polo may be summed up as follows :

1. *Faulty ponies.*—A polo pony should be under his rider's control, should be up to his rider's weight, should be thoroughly trained to the game, should have good shoulders, and should not be liable to cross his legs or speedy cut. Many ponies, however, are played in fast games before they know their work, and even before they are properly broken. Consequently they pull, get out of control, and will neither stop nor turn. The well-trained ones, on the contrary, will stop dead to avoid a collision, will turn, as the saying is, on a sixpenny-piece, and, like clever Irish hunters, will have a spare leg for every emergency. Besides, they will use their weight to such advantage that it will be exceedingly difficult to knock them over, even if they be charged almost at right angles.

Some people aver that it is more dangerous to play on big ponies than on small ones. This, I think is wrong ; for apart from the question of hardness of ground (see following paragraph), we cannot get over the fact that falls from colliding and crossing are more frequent in India than in England. Besides, big ponies are stronger than little ones, bumps take less effect on them, they are up to more weight, and consequently they are less likely to fall. The old idea that big ponies cannot be made as handy as little ones has been entirely exploded. In fact many leading English players hardly ever ride a pony less than 14.2, and yet I have never seen handier ones in India than some of them. Still, I am prepared to admit that big ponies take more time and trouble to train, and are not so easy to ride as little ones.

2. *Hard ground.*—The danger from falls, which, with every precaution, will sometimes occur, is proportionate to the hardness of the ground, a fact which I think will account for the many sad accidents that have happened at Polo in India. Luckily in England, where the turf is comparatively soft, there have been few serious mishaps. There has never been a better regulation framed than the one which enacts that players in India must wear sun helmets. Considering the hardness of the ground in the East, players there should be particular to use only ponies which are perfectly trained, well up to the weight they have got to carry, and possessed of good shoulders and true front action.

3. *Dangerous and reckless riding.*—For this there is no excuse, as the rule about crossing is so clear that its meaning cannot be misunderstood. Some men, who are generally the cause of these accidents, get so excited that, as soon as they start off galloping, they lose their heads, and do not know what they are doing. Neither they nor bolting ponies should be allowed on a polo ground.

The whole question of crossing (see No. 16 Hurlingham Rules) turns on the words : " at such a distance that the said player shall not be compelled to check his pony to avoid a collision." This is a vast improvement on the old wording of the rule, under which a great deal of the game of bluff was played. Now a smart umpire will give a cross if a man, from reasonable fear of collision, is obliged to check his pony ever so little. It must be borne in mind that the faster the pace, the more dangerous will be a cross, and the more distance will have to be allowed.

4. *Wild hitting.*—I regret to say that there have been lately one or two very serious accidents from blows of sticks. Players should be extremely careful about the manner in which they wave their sticks, and about hitting hard in a scrimmage. On such occasions, dribbling is much more effective, and obviates the risk of giving a fearful blow to a man on the face, possibly resulting in the loss of an eye, or other serious injury. Some men appear to make a practice of hitting as hard as they can in a scrimmage, with total disregard of what may happen to comrade or adversary ; and they finish every stroke right up in the air, whether or not there happens to be a man or pony within striking distance. Such wild, dangerous strikers are usually found among second or third class players. The umpire should certainly give a foul for any accident caused by such practices. Players as a rule are not half considerate enough about the legs of other people's ponies.

No man should let drive recklessly, and hit as hard as he can, when there is another player in front of him. I know some players who are most dangerous, on account of acting in this manner. They seem to think that they may hit where they like, and that they are in no way to blame, if they knock a man off his pony by a blow on the head at 10 yards distance. I maintain that if they look where they are hitting, the risk of such an accident is reduced to a minimum.

When riding along with an adversary on one's left, one is very apt to hit him in the face if one tries the stroke under one's pony's neck, especially with a whippy stick. If this occurs, a foul should always be given against the striker.

5. *Blows from a ball.*—This cause of danger is not nearly so fruitful of accident as the other four, although the ball occasionally inflicts unpleasant blows. A player can obtain great protection from the New Polo Cap, which was invented by Mr. Gerald Hardy, and can be obtained from Mr. Walter Barnard, of 97, Jermyn Street, who has patented it. It should be used by every polo player. The Indian helmet is even better than the polo cap, as it affords more protection if a man falls on his head. As regards blows, the cap serves its purpose perfectly.

CRUELTY IN POLO PLAYING.

From time to time, ignorant people have talked a great deal of nonsense about the cruelty to ponies at polo. In well managed stables, there is no description of horse which has such a good time as a polo pony. He gets just enough work to keep him fit ; he is fed on the best ; if in tip-top condition, he is seldom much distressed by the severest of matches ; and he probably has six months' rest out of twelve. If my readers will compare his lot with that of a hunter which has to go through long hours of exposure, hunger and fatigue, with a heavy weight on his back, from early morning to late in the evening, in every description of bleak weather, they will I think admit that the pony has the best of it. I am certain that many ponies like the game ; in fact I have had several which always gave me the impression that they enjoyed it as much as I did.

There is one way in which a pony can be tortured
unmercifully, and his game of polo converted from an
amusement into agony, and that is by his mouth being
wrenched about with a severe bridle, by a heavy fisted
rider. The cause which makes a large number of
ponies pull is simply pain ; for the more they are hurt,

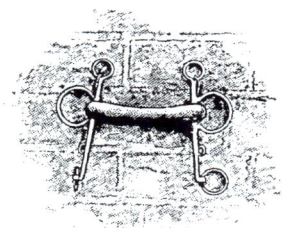

Fig. 28.—India-rubber Pelham.

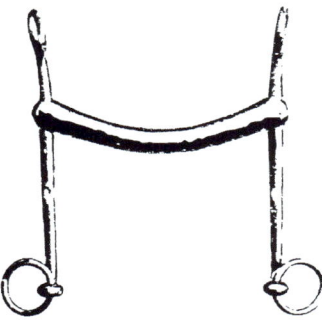

Fig. 29.—Ben Morgan bit.

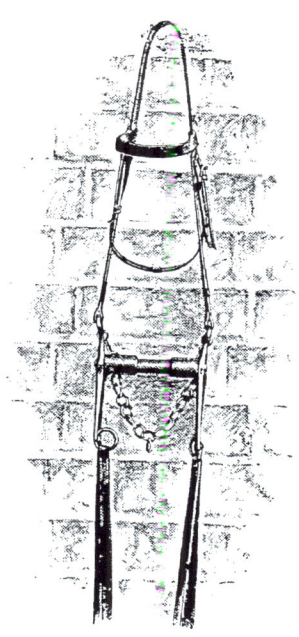

Fig. 30.—Kerro bridle.

the more will they pull, until they are driven almost
mad. Every polo player, if he cannot trust his groom
to do it, should examine his pony's mouth after every
game of polo, and should specially look at the bars of
the mouth and under the root of the tongue. Any
pony which bleeds at the mouth is wrongly bitted, and

under such circumstances, immediate steps should be taken to prevent a recurrence of this mishap. A new and easier bit should be tried, such as an India-rubber Pelham (Fig. 28), Ben Morgan (Fig. 29), Kerro bit (Fig. 30), or half-moon Pelham (Figs. 31 and 32), or the bit may be wrapped round with sponge or wash-leather. No player should knowingly continue to ride a pony which bleeds at the mouth. In most cases, the seat of the injury will be found on the bars of the lower jaw, just in front of the first back tooth.

Many ponies which will pull desperately in severe bits, will play kindly in light ones.

Men with loose seats should never use severe bridles at polo ; because they hang on to their horses' heads, and consequently have bad hands. Although the effects of sharp spurs, cutting whips and blows on the legs from sticks, are far less painful than those of severe bits, we should remember that ponies have feelings. Reckless hitting into a scrimmage, regardless of ponies' legs, causes quite as much cruelty as sharp spurs, which are not allowed at polo. Also, a young player should carefully accustom himself not to hit his own pony's legs with stick or ball.

As a good pony is worth a vast amount of trouble, the owner should consider his comfort in and out of the stable, and should see that he is sound and fit, and properly bitted and saddled, before playing him. The animal will then last for many years, and will become as fond of the game as his master. The long lease of playing life enjoyed by the majority of polo ponies, is one reason for the enormous prices fetched by first class ponies during late years. It is by no means uncommon for a pony of fifteen years of age to be playing as well as ever he did. Most ponies are not at their best until they are nine or ten. If a man buys a sound, good, six years old polo pony, he will in all probability get ten years' play out of him. Mr. Rawlinson's pony Redskin, which was registered at Hurlingham as an aged pony in 1881, was playing in 1897, and was consequently at least 23 years of age at that time.

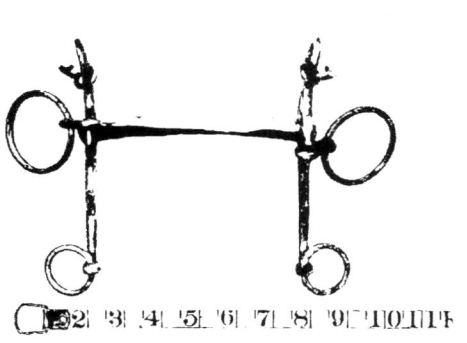 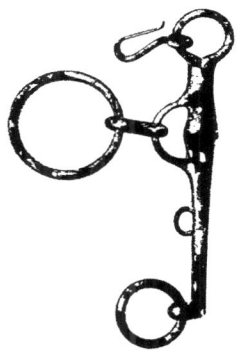

Fig. 31.—Half-moon Pelham.

Fig. 32.—Side view of half-moon Pelham (Fig. 31).

FAIR PLAY.

I have sometimes heard the question discussed, whether polo is a sport or a game. There is no doubt that it is a sporting game, and should therefore be played in a sportsmanlike manner. Anything in the least unfair should be rigidly excluded.

Such tactics as wasting time in hitting out from behind the line, when one goal ahead near the finish of a match, or in hitting the ball out at the side with the same object, is the very worst of form.

A deliberate foul, even to save a goal in a close match, because the umpire is not in a position to see, or because he is known to be inexperienced and may be bluffed with impunity, is utterly opposed to all the principles of fair play. Appeals for off-side or for a foul should not be made, unless the player is honestly of opinion that the appeal ought to be answered in his favour.

There can be no greater feather in the cap of a team, than for the members of it to be able to say that they have won a good cup, without having had a single foul given against them.

For polo to be a good game, every player should try his hardest to win ; but nothing should ever be done contrary either to the spirit or letter of the Rules. There should be no quarrelling, no grumbling at the Umpire's decision, and none of the " win, tie or wrangle " element. If played in this spirit, there is no game in the world like polo.

CHAPTER III.

POLO APPLIANCES.

Polo grounds—Goal posts—Sticks—Polo dress.

POLO GROUNDS.

A FULL-SIZED ground is 300 yards by 200 yards, but as a matter of fact, there are few full-sized grounds in England. A width of 150 yards on a boarded ground is big enough for any game, but a short ground spoils the game, and consequently no ground should be shorter than 275 yards. Boards, which generally vary from 9 to 11 inches in height, are a great advantage in making a game fast, by preventing a ball from going out of play. They save many hard hits, and many strokes which would cause the ball to just trickle over the line. Hitting round too much, because of the presence of the boards, is not advisable, and hitting for the rebound off the boards is nearly always bad play. The annoyance often experienced in an unboarded ground of having a good, hard, straight hit down the edge of the ground from the side roll a few inches out of play, owing, very possibly, to some inequality on the surface, is saved by the boards.

A good plan to prevent the ball hanging under the boards, is to raise the turf close to them two or three inches, and slope it inwards, so that if the ball touches them, no matter how gently, it will roll out again, and permit of a clear hit being obtained.

Great pains should be taken with the turf, which, even if not very good at first, will improve in a few years to an extraordinary extent, if well manured in the winter. Old cattle straw manure is better than horse manure for ordinary soils ; but the best of all is bone dust, which, unfortunately, is expensive. A fair dressing of bone dust is 3 cwt. to the acre ; but for the encouragement of turf suitable for polo, we need not scruple to spend 5 cwt. on each acre. A similar quantity of basic slag, which is excellent for producing good turf, may be employed.

If it is desired to improve an ordinary ground on which turf does not wear well, the following process may be carried out : Harrow and cross-harrow the ground at the end of August or early in September ; sow from 1 to 1½ bushel per acre of Sutton and Son's mixture of seeds for grasses for recreation grounds ; lightly bush-harrow the seeds in, and well roll down twice in different directions. A top-dressing in November will greatly help the seeds. Grass seeds may be sown at any time between the middle of March and the end of September ; but from the latter half of May to the beginning of August, dry or hot weather often proves destructive to the young plants. From the middle of March to the first week in May is the best time for spring sowing ; from the first week in August to the middle of September, for summer or autumn sowing. Should there be failure from any cause, more seed should be sown the following spring. The seed will probably be more evenly distributed by two sowings than by one, however skilful and practised the sower may be ; and the second sowing should cross the first one at right angles. If it is desired to seed down fresh land, about four bushels per acre will be required.

The best time for rolling is generally during the first week in March, after about two days of the east winds coming on top of the February rains, before the wind has had time to make the worm casts dusty. Ground should never be rolled when the worm casts would make a wet paste on the young grass blades, as that would weaken their growth.

Water well laid on is a grand thing to keep a ground in good order, but its application in England is seldom possible ; for an enormous quantity is required to produce a marked effect. When a ground has been cut up by play, it should be carefully trodden in before being rolled. Rolling will be useless unless the pieces of turf which have been cut out are first replaced. A ground which is well looked after will stand an extraordinary amount of play.

GOAL POSTS.

The best kind of goal posts are made of Willesden paper, and can be obtained from the Willesden Paper and Canvas Works, Willesden Junction, N.W., at a cost of £4 for the set, with a few shillings extra for painting in any desired colours. They should be erected with a thin post of wood in the centre, and a socket of thin iron or zinc for the lower extremities of the paper posts to slip into. They can then be easily put up or taken down as may be required. If broken, they can be repaired with a thin band of zinc at the break by any carpenter. Goal posts (Fig. 5)

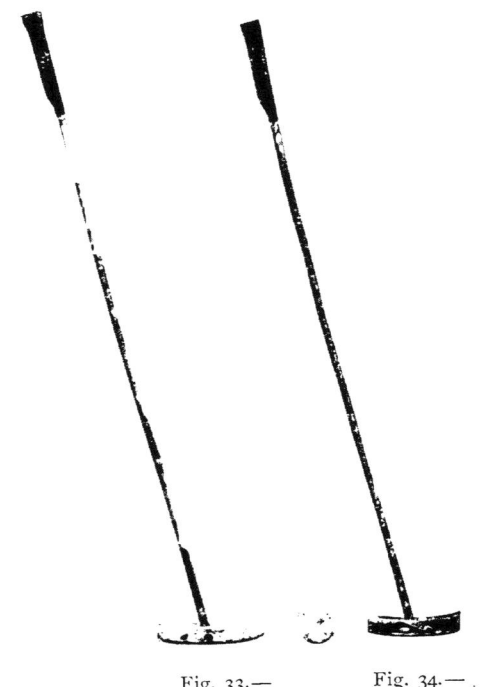

Fig. 33.—
Rugby polo stick
(Salter).

Fig. 34.— .
Stick with 4a head
(Salter).

thus looked after will last a long time. The advantages of these posts are immunity from danger to player or pony, in the event of colliding against them, and the fact that they can be readily seen, either by the umpire, when he tries to note on which side of the post the ball goes, or by the player, who has time only for a hurried glance before making a shot at goal. It is evident that thin wooden posts are difficult to see, and that thick ones are dangerous to knock up against.

STICKS.

A good stick is almost as necessary to the polo player as a good pony. As different players require

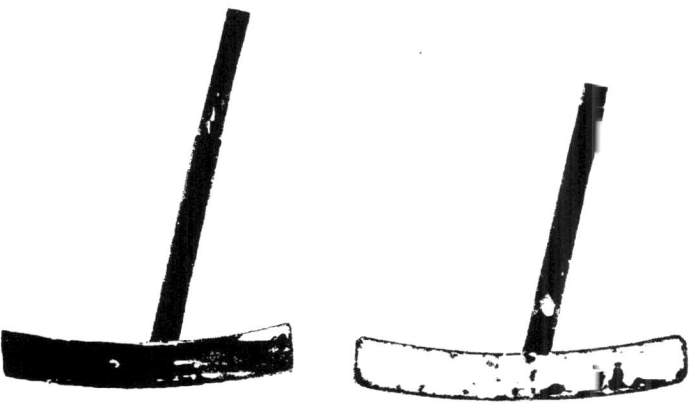

Fig. 35.—Head of stick shown in Fig. 34.   Fig. 36.—Head of stick shown in Fig. 33.

different sorts of sticks, no hard and fast rules can be laid down as to their length, weight, and shape ; hence, each player must find out for himself what kind of stick suits him best (Figs. 33, 34, 35, 36 and 37). A man with a muscular arm and a strong wrist can obtain the advantage of using a stick with a heavy head ; and a man with a long arm can get increased

6

command by using a short one.   Also, the shorter
the stick, the heavier can the head be made without
altering the balance, and, consequently, the more
driving power can be obtained.   For every inch taken
off the length of the stick, about half an ounce can be
added to the weight of the head.

Care must be taken that the weight of the head is
proportionate to the strength of the stick.   Although
a certain amount of spring in the cane is necessary
for the stick to drive well, very whippy sticks are

Fig. 37.—Different kinds of heads for polo sticks.

dangerous, as they are apt to curl round and hit an
opponent in the face, especially if the hit be made
under the pony's neck.   Above all things a stick
must be well balanced.   Fifty-two inches for a 14.1
pony is a good average length, the limit being about
two inches either way.   The best plan for a
beginner in search of a good stick is to make a
collection of the different kinds of sticks which the
best players of his acquaintance use, and having
tried them, to find out what sort suits him best.
He can then order his own sticks from the maker,

taking the greatest care that he obtains an exactly similar article. He need not think that a stick made by Salter, Holbrow, or Buchanan can be successfully copied by the village carpenter. A tape loop on the handle, to put round the wrist, will often save a player from dropping a stick, which accident might cause the loss of a match. The loop should readily yield (which a strong leather one might not do) to a severe pull, so that there may be no risk of hurting the wrist, if, for instance, the head of the stick is caught in a pony's bridle, and the stick is thus violently pulled out of the hand.

The Back as a rule requires a longer stick than a forward player ; because he has often to hit a backhander at some distance from his pony. He also needs a stick with a light head, in order to be able to play close, and to put in a lot of wrist work when being hustled by an opponent.

The shape of the head of the various sticks in ordinary use is shown in Fig. 37. The cigar-shaped head has somewhat gone out of fashion of late years, though a few of the best players still use it. It is, however, generally believed that a ball can be hit better with a square-headed stick out of heavy ground than with a round one. Cigar-shaped heads are greatly used in India, where the ground is hard and level. The handle of the stick should be oval, not round, so that it may not be liable to turn in the hand or slip, and in size it must fit the hand of the player. To still further prevent such an accident occurring, Mr. Salter has invented his " India-rubber grip." Besides, a stick with an oval-shaped handle can always be held in the right position for the head

6*

to strike the ball without the player having to look
at it.

POLO DRESS.

For the sake of spectators as well as players,
it is very important that distinctive colours should be
worn by opposing teams. The best plan, especially
when the players are not well known to each other, is
for one side to wear white, and the other some dark
colour. Sashes are not distinctive enough, and are
uncomfortable to wear, unless they fit well and are
pinned under the left arm. I have found that the
best thing for the dark side to put on is a linen or
silk waistcoat of some dark colour. These waistcoats
are light, do not impede one's movements in the
slightest, and show, even the spectators, at a glance
how the game is going. Decided colours, such as dark
blue, bright red, and bright yellow, are better than
light shades, which are not very different from white
at a distance.

CHAPTER IV.

CHOOSING A POLO PONY.

THE questions here are : what to buy, and how to buy. This problem is greatly simplified if money be no object. The best advice for an intending purchaser is for him to be always ready to buy a really first-class, trained pony. A small number of such animals come into the market every year ; but to get the real article, a man must be just as ready to buy in November or January, as in May or July. A first-class pony is of more importance to an ambitious polo player than is a first-class hunter to a man who means riding in the first flight in the Shires ; for many faults of mouth and manners may be overlooked in a brilliant cross-country horse, but not in a polo pony, which must be perfection itself in a game. For instance, a fine horseman on a puller which is able to gallop and jump, can get across Leicestershire with a fair amount of comfort to himself and safety to others ; but a pony which pulls at polo, although it may do well enough in a slow game, is perfectly useless, even to the best of horsemen, in a first-class match. A single fault, such as being a slow starter, shying off the ball, refusing to try when alongside another pony, or a little want of pluck when facing a back-hander, or when jostling

another pony, immediately puts a polo pony out of
the first class.   Again, on a slow hunter, though perfect jumper, a man who means going the shortest way
to hounds can, five days out of six, see a lot of fun
even in the grass counties; but a slow pony is
absolutely useless in a first-class polo match.   As perfection, without any credit being allowed for compensating merit, is demanded in a first-class polo pony,
I do not think that men who have never played polo,
and polo players who have never ridden a good pony,
are justified in the remarks they often make about the
—what they call—absurdly high prices some polo
ponies fetch.   A rich man who means to play polo
should, however, keep his eyes open, and should never
miss the chance of buying a pony of this class, if he
hears of one for sale.   He will be much mistaken if
he thinks that he can provide himself at a moment's
notice with a stud of first-class polo ponies at the
commencement of the polo season.

If a man cannot afford to play on the best of ponies,
he can, however, get his fun on moderate ones; but
in that case must forego the pleasures of first-class
matches.   It is true to a certain extent that price prevents men playing polo, especially when good ponies
are wanted all in a moment; but the fact that training
greatly enhances the value of a pony, enables many a
man to play polo who could not otherwise do so.   A
fair player, who is also a fine horseman, need spend
very little on his polo, if he looks about for likely
young animals, and if he takes the time and trouble
to train them when found.   More and more good
ponies are being bred every season, and the number
of breeders is steadily increasing.   Doubtless, the

efforts of the Polo Pony Stud Book Society will
have a good effect in this direction. As the method
of training raw ponies is described in Chapter V.,
I will now pass on to discuss the kind of pony we
ought to select. The recently made limit of 14.2
answers admirably in England. Experience shows
that, as a rule, the increase of strength, speed and

Photo by]   [M. H. HAYES.
Fig. 38.—Mr. W. J. Jones' "Luna."

weight in ponies over 14.2 does not compensate for
the loss of handiness, although it is undoubtedly
possible to make some horses of 15 hands, and even
more, perfectly handy for polo. Besides, as I have
already said, it takes far longer to train the average
big pony than the average small one.

Not long ago, the Hurlingham Committee dis-

covered that the old rule of challenging a pony by any
playing member was a failure ; because ponies which
were known to be over-height were constantly played,
and there was not a single instance of a pony being
challenged.   The   rule   was   therefore   altered,   and
now   all   ponies   which   have   not   played   in   certain
tournaments   must   be   measured.   During   the   last
few seasons I have been fortunate to ride in many
matches   two   wonderfully   good   big   ponies,   Luna
(Fig. 38) and Matchbox (Fig. 39), which measured
nearly 14.3, and were admitted under the rule of
existing polo ponies.   Both of these   animals   have
won champion prizes as polo ponies.   My experience
on them compelled me to change my opinion as to the
height I prefer for my own riding.   They are both
as handy as any 13.3 pony I have ever ridden.   They
are beautifully shaped, up to any weight, and fast.
I therefore say that for a big man there is nothing like
a good big pony.   On the other hand, animals much
above 14.2 would give a big man an undue advantage
over light men on smaller mounts.   It is a sound rule
to strictly limit the height to 14.2, which is the best
all-round compromise.   I am here writing in general
terms ; for I am well aware that many a 14-hand pony
is really bigger and heavier than others of 14.2 which
attain this height, simply on account of their withers
being unusually high.   The ideal weight-carrying polo
pony is the miniature 14-stone blood hunter, standing
· on short legs.   Provided that he has shape, substance,
power and scope, it does not matter much whether he
measures 14.1 or 14.2.

The objection to 14 hands as a limit is not that
ponies of that height are too small, but that they

are too difficult to get of suitable kind. English ponies which are fit for polo, have almost invariably at least one parent (generally the sire) a full-sized horse, and are consequently chance "gets" of a size much smaller than the average height of their respective

Photo by] [M. H. HAYES.

Fig. 39.—Lieut.-Colonel Fenwick's "Matchbox."

parents. They are seldom as small as 14 hands. Arabs, Syrians, and Egyptians, on the contrary, are a race of ponies whose average height may be put down at about 14.1½. Hence, a very much larger proportion of them than of English horses will be 14 hands and under. Also in America, owing to the severe climate, there are, I believe, many very good cow ponies not over 14 hands, although they may be at least three-quarters clean bred from English stock. In Ireland, which, according to my experience, is far the best country for ponies, the majority of those that are suitable for polo are by thorough-bred hunting sires out of well-bred hunting mares, or out of well-bred pony mares. The fact that they are ponies and not horses is generally due to their growth having been arrested by starvation, especially during the first winter, too early weaning, parental idiosyncrasy, or to their being first foals. Plenty of good 14.2 English ponies can be found, but only a few 14.1, and hardly any 14 hands. When speaking of English ponies, I of course include Irish, Scotch, and Welsh ponies.

If the would-be purchaser meets a likely unbroken pony, such as that in Fig. 40, I would advise him, unless he is anxious to try experiments, not to buy it until it is broken, so that he might feel how the animal would move under him. If, however, he is willing to take the chance of the pony turning out well, being probably stimulated thereto by the fact that unbroken ponies are cheaper than "made" ones, he should not conclude to purchase without looking into the pony's pedigree, and, if possible, seeing the dam. If she is well-bred and of the proper stamp for a polo pony, and if the sire is thorough-bred English or Arab, our friend will not do wrong to buy the youngster at a fair price ; but if the dam is a commoner and the sire half-bred, he should have nothing to do with the pony, no matter how good-looking it may be. In fact, I would go further, and say that if either the sire or dam was under-bred, the pony would not be worth training, although I might be wrong in a few exceptional cases. Nothing is more annoying than to take a lot of trouble with a pony, and then find out that he is too slow for polo. Most of the failures which I have had with polo ponies, have been due to the fact of my not following out the rule which I here lay down. I have never found a pony too slow for polo if its pedigree was all right.

Fig. 40.—Four-year-old Weight Carrier.

The nearer thorough-bred, the better; but a pony by a thorough-bred out of a dam by a thorough-bred will be quite good enough. Breeders in Ireland are very particular about pedigrees; so it will not be difficult, if one buys straight from them, to verify the accuracy of the breeding.

The great test by which to judge if a raw pony is likely to do well at polo, is the manner in which he moves when ridden. If he goes strong and well, has good shoulders and a nice mouth and manners, and is sound, there need not be much doubt about him. If he pulls or shows signs of bad temper, it will be long odds against him turning out satisfactorily, and he should therefore be avoided.

The chief points of *conformation* to look for in a polo pony are :

1. Good shoulders which will ride well, and which the pony can use with perfect freedom. The best way to judge if a polo pony or hunter has good shoulders is to gallop him down a sharp incline. If he gives us confidence when doing this, we may be certain there is nothing wrong with his shoulders. If, on the other hand, he travels down hill in stilty fashion, and gives us the impression that he may come down on his head at any moment, we may conclude that his shoulders are faulty, no matter how good they may look. We should never judge a pony's shoulders simply by their appearance.

2. A fairly long neck properly set on. The possession of this desirable point reduces liability to pull. I have found that a short thick neck is one of the most fatal defects a polo pony can have ; for, as a rule, such a pony will be difficult to turn, and will have a bad mouth.

3. A short strong back, with the best of loins, and plenty of depth in the middle of the back. The strength of the loins can best be judged by their width and flatness. Ponies long in the back are seldom able to turn quickly or to carry weight.

4. Good hocks well let down right under him. Sickle hocks are no disadvantage, as they enable the pony to turn quickly.

5. Not too heavy a body for his legs.

6. The best of fore legs, with plenty of bone in proportion to the size of the body. The shorter the cannon bone is, the better. The fore legs should be straight from elbow to fetlock (that is to say, the pony should be neither " over " nor " back " at the knees) ; the back tendons should be as nearly as possible parallel to the cannon bone ; and the suspensory ligament should stand out in a sharply-defined manner between the cannon bone and back tendons. With these conditions, the thicker the cannon bone, suspensory ligament and back tendons are, the stronger will be the leg and the better able will :t be to stand work. Any increased thickness due to injury will be accompanied in the case of the suspensory ligament, by the filling up, to a greater or less extent, of the spaces between it and the cannon bone and back tendons ; and in the case of the back tendons, by a more or less puffy condition of the part. The broader the fetlock is, compared to the width of the leg just below the knee, the less able will the animal be to stand fast work. We may see the correctness of this remark, if we compare the shape of the fore leg of a thorough-bred with that of a cart horse.

7. Strong, well-sloped pasterns, not too short. The shorter and more upright the pasterns are, the worse will the pony stand work on hard ground.

8. The hoofs should be strong, the soles concave, and the frogs well developed.

9. Plenty of quality, combined with substance.

10. A good kind eye. A pony with a wild staring eye seldom makes a good polo pony.

[The weight borne by the fore legs as compared to

that sustained by the hind limbs, varies in proportion to the weight of the rider. Hence, a *weight-carrier* should be proportionately lighter in front than a light-weight pony, and on this account will require to have his shoulders particularly well sloped, which is a point of conformation that will give his back the appearance of being very short. For the same reason, he should have a comparatively light head and neck. As the weight on the fore legs also varies according as the height at the withers is greater than that at the croup, a pony which has to carry a heavy man should not be low in front. This reasoning is supported by the fact that the height at the withers as compared to that at the croup, is greater in steeplechase horses, and especially in hunters, than in racehorses.—*Editor.*]

There are two distinct types of weight-carrying polo ponies, namely, the miniature 14-stone blood hunter, such as Sunshine (Fig. 41), Luna (Fig. 38), Matchbox (Fig. 39), Siren (Fig. 42), Charlton (Fig. 43) and Mademoiselle (Fig. 44) ; and the miniature weight-carrying steeplechaser, such as Dynamite (Fig. 45), Little Fairy (Fig. 46), the Californian pony Rex (Fig. 47) and Conceit (Fig. 48), all of which are up to 14 stone. All these ponies are superlatively good ; but as there are ten good ones of the former type, to every one of the latter, I strongly recommend an intending purchaser to keep the former in his mind's eye as his idea of perfection.

The three following types of handsome ponies should be avoided :—

The *first type* is very beautiful, but is more suitable for hacking than polo, as he is a thorough-bred weed, long in the leg, light of bone, narrow between the rider's

Photo by]   [M. H. HAYES.
Fig. 41.—Mr. W. S. Buckmaster on "Sunshine."

Photo by]   [M. H. HAYES.
Fig. 42.—"Siren."

Fig. 43.—The late Mr. W. J. Drybrough on " Charlton."

Fig. 44.—Comte J. de Madre's "Mademoiselle."

Fig. 45.—Mr. J. Peat's "Dynamite."

Fig. 46.—Mr. Walter Jones' "Little Fairy."

7*

legs, and deficient of weight and substance (Fig. 49).
We see this type, but of larger size, on every racecourse, and many of this kind are bred which are not
big enough for racing.   They are seldom fit for polo,
because, even if they play well, which they rarely do,
they are usually not placid enough, and are too light

Photo by]   [M. H. HAYES.
Fig. 47.—Mr. F. J. Mackey's " Rex."

to hold their own among the heavy ponies they will
have to meet.

The *second type* is the long-striding, awkward, but
generally well-bred galloping pony which gives a rider
who mounts him for the first time the impression that
the animal requires a forty-acre field to turn in.   Even
if trained to stop and turn, he takes too much out of
himself when performing these movements, and will

very rarely become a quick and handy polo pony.   He
is of the horse, and not of the pony type.   Even if
his shape and make is all that is required, a good
judge will find out his defects the moment he
rides him.

The *third type* is the good-looking coachy pony with
shoulders which we do not discover to be more suitable
for the collar than the saddle, until we sit over them.
I know many such ponies, and have seen some of them
honoured in the show ring by judges who did not ride
them.   Such ponies are seldom sufficiently fast for
polo, and even if they have the requisite speed, their
conformation prevents them turning quickly enough.

We should bear in mind that substance and weight-
carrying power are essential in a first-class polo pony,
even for a light man.   Weight and strength are
required to withstand the knocking about and riding
off by heavy men on heavy ponies.   Although a
light weight may hunt brilliantly on light-weight
horses, he must have ponies with strength and substance if he wants to take his place in good polo.

The defect which should above all be avoided in a
polo pony, is the possession of a bad or impetuous
temper ; because an animal which has this defect
hardly ever turns out satisfactorily, and is therefore
not worth the trouble of training.   Although it is frequently impossible to be certain that a pony has this
vice before feeding him well on corn, we may often
get a reliable intimation of it, in the first instance,
by the appearance of the animal's eye, which is his
most tell-tale feature.   When buying a trained polo
pony or one which has done other kinds of work, the
intending purchaser will do well to carefully examine

Photo by]

Fig. 48.—Lord Shrewsbury on " Conceit."

[W. ROUCH.

the animal's mouth and lower jaw, in order to find marks of old scars on the chin-groove or bruises or sores on the corners of the lips, bars of the mouth and under the tongue, all of which are generally sure signs of pulling, and should therefore be regarded with the greatest suspicion.

Good *action* is most important, because it means

Fig. 49.—The wrong type of thoroughbred pony.

speed and weight-carrying power, and is obtained when the movement in all paces is true, straight and not too high. We should never buy a pony which turns its toes out ; because this defect will probably give rise to brushing, and will more or less detract from the animal's weight-carrying power. A pony that steps high can seldom gallop. A quick striding galloper generally makes a better polo pony than one which goes in racehorse style ; because he is quicker at starting and turning. Many long striding thoroughbreds, however, soon learn to shorten their stride as occasion may demand, and thus adapt themselves to the game.

Of course, the purchaser must be guided by his own requirements. If he is buying several for himself, he should try to get them as much as possible of the same height and character.

As a rule, suitable foreigners (see Chapter VIII.) are not difficult to buy, and are comparatively easy to train.

The would-be purchaser may also buy well-known ponies at Tattersall's. There is no place like an auction for a pony to fetch its real value, although fancy prices are sometimes given, when more than one man is anxious to get· the same animal. Polo ponies, if properly advertised, will almost invariably fetch their full value at Tattersall's in the months of March, April, May, June and July. The fact that many terrible brutes are sold by auction during the summer, under the description of "good polo ponies," should make us very careful, before bidding, to find out all we can about the animal which we are thinking of buying.

The guarantee at Albert Gate is that "a good polo pony must be sound in wind and eyes, quiet to ride, go to a ball, and be capable of being played." This is a great protection to purchasers. To be on the safe side, a man should never buy a pony which has been trained and played, unless he can trust the seller to tell him the truth, or unless he knows all about the pony himself or through a friend. Personal trial, if possible, in a game is of course the best means of finding out the animal's merits and defects ; for what will suit one man will not always suit another, and even with the best intentions, the seller or friend may recommend an entirely unsuitable pony. Besides, if the purchaser, after having tried the pony, finds that he has made a mistake, he will have no one but himself to blame.

A great many good ponies are missed owing to veterinary certificates. By all means I would advise that a pony should be examined, particularly for its eyes ; but after that ordeal . has been gone through, the intending purchaser should personally consult his veterinary surgeon, and then act on his own judgment in the event of an absolutely sound certificate not having been given ; for he must remember that the veterinary surgeon must state everything that is amiss, and that technical unsoundnesses, which do not materially affect the animal's working capabilities, may be passed over in the polo pony. Very few ponies which have been played for two or three seasons would pass a veterinary examination, although, for all practical purposes, they might be as sound as a bell. In May, 1893, I sold at Tattersall's, for an aggregate price of 450 guineas, two ponies which were examined by several veterinary surgeons, according to some of whose certificates there was hardly one sound leg between the two ponies, and yet both of them have played for many years without going lame.

It must be remembered that polo ponies have to gallop only for ten minutes on end, and are not subjected to nearly so much strain and fatigue as hunters. An animal which would be considered an absolute screw as a hunter, might play polo for years without going wrong.

CHAPTER V.

TRAINING THE POLO PONY.

General remarks—Long rein driving—Turning—Reining back—To stop dead—
To start into the gallop from the halt—To turn right about or left about at
the canter or gallop—To change legs before and behind at the canter or
gallop—Figure of 8—To go with a loose rein in all paces—To meet other
ponies—To hustle other ponies—Breaking the pony to stick and ball.

GENERAL REMARKS.

I PROPOSE in this chapter to describe a pony's education, from the time he is taken up from grass, until
he is fit to take his part in a good polo match.

It is advisable as a rule to break ponies to ride at the
age of three years ; to have them quietly ridden about
for from three to six months ; and then to turn them
out till the autumn of their fourth year. At that time
their education will have to be begun over again, and
they should be carefully trained for at least six months,
in order to make them fit to play hard polo at the commencement of their five-year-old season. In Ireland,
many men play four-year-olds, but I do not think it is
generally good policy to put them into fast matches at
such an early age. Having a large number of ponies,
I do not break my young ones until the autumn of
their fourth year, so as to save the trouble and expense of doing the work twice over ; but all the same,
I think it is a great advantage to break ponies to ride

at the age of three; because the younger they are taken in hand, the more tractable will they become.

It is best to start with an unbroken animal in an enclosed space; a riding school for choice. If a school be not available, a walled-in enclosure, such as a cattle yard, or any place from which a pony can neither see the ground outside, nor jump out of, will do.

To begin with, put a plain snaffle in the animal's mouth, buckle on a roller or old saddle, lead him quietly about, get him accustomed to be petted and handled, and in a couple of days he will probably let himself be led without any trouble. On the third or fourth day a sack of earth may be strapped on the saddle, and the rope twitch can be applied, if the pony plays up.

The method of using this twitch is to jerk it and at the same moment shout "steady!" in a reproving tone of voice, which the pony will mentally connect with the painful jerk, and in nine cases out of ten he will become immediately cowed. This is the best twitch I know; because it does not hurt the animal except at the moment of the application of the jerk, the severity of the punishment can be regulated with exactness, and the pony can be taught to obey the voice. When the pony has become quiet with the twitch, the sack may be taken off and a man put on his back. At first it is best to use a saddle without stirrups, and give the man a leg up. In a couple of days it will be found that the pony is quiet to ride inside the enclosure, and he may then be taken outside on a leading rein, and exercised either by leading or lungeing him. In a fortnight he should be fit to go by himself on quiet country roads.

Keeping in view the sound principle that the education of a polo pony should be progressive, we may divide it into the following stages :—

1. Making him quiet to ride.
2. Mouthing him.
3. Making him handy in his slow paces.
4. Making him handy in his quick paces.

Photo by]   [M. H. HAYES.
Fig. 50.— Circling with long reins.

5. Breaking him to stick and ball.
6. Teaching him polo.

By the statement that each step should be progressive, I mean that we should pay particular attention to each lesson, so as to thoroughly prepare him for the next one. A good horseman will of course start making the pony's mouth from the time he first gets on his back, and ponies may be broken to stick and ball at a walk, as soon as they are quiet to ride, and while they are still low in condition.

LONG REIN DRIVING.

The quickest method of making a pony handy, is with the "long reins" (Figs. 50 and 51). A perfect horseman may dispense with their use ; but I would recommend a few lessons with them in all cases. If the long reins, which are about twenty-two feet in length and are attached to the rings of the snaffle, are

Photo by] [M. H. HAYES.

Fig. 51.—Circling with long reins.

used three or four times on a pony which has never been ridden, it is long odds that by the end of that time he will be so quiet and tractable that he may be ridden without any risk. Their use, and that of the rope twitch, are fully described in *Illustrated Horse-Breaking.*

Our object with the long reins is to make the pony handy, and to prepare him to obey the indications of rein and leg. By this method of mounting, we are

able to teach a pony to answer a feeling of either rein
with his hind-quarters, as well as with his head and
neck, so that we can get him to turn "all in one piece,"
by the reins alone.   We all know that when a badly
broken horse "runs out" at a fence, the fact of the
rider being able to pull his head round towards the
obstacle, will have little or no effect in straightening
him, unless he is made at the same time to bring his
hind-quarters round, which is a difficulty that is readily
overcome by the long-rein method.   For instance, if
the breaker who is in a position similar to that of the
man in Fig. 50, wishes to turn his pony to the right,
he will take a long step forward with the right foot ;
will slide the right hand forward on the off rein, while
holding both reins in the left hand ; and will take a
steady pull of the off rein with the right hand, by
which means the animal's head will be drawn round
to the right and his hind-quarters will be pushed over
to the left, by the pressure of the rein on them.   As
soon as the turn has been completed, the breaker will
check the further revolution of the hind quarters by
feeling the left rein, which will then act in a manner
similar to that of the drawn-back outward leg of a
skilful horseman.   To obtain a good result with the
long reins, it is of course necessary that the employer
of this method should thoroughly understand its
principles and practice, which he can do only by
intelligent and assiduous study, and which will be
greatly facilitated by competent instruction.

One of the most important lessons to teach a pony
is to make him rein back collectedly, which can be
done more easily with long reins, than by any other
system.   If the pupil fights against this movement,

I would recommend the breaker to get an assistant to stand in front of the pony with a long cane in his hand, and, as the pressure of the reins is applied, to wave the stick slowly in front of the animal's face, and to keep repeating in a drawling tone of voice, the word "back!" If the pony continues to fight, the reins may be buckled to the nose-band, so as not to hurt the mouth, and the assistant may tap the legs of the pony alternately before and behind, taking care to select the leg which should be the next to move.

When the pony is quiet at a walk on both circles, will turn both ways, and rein back at word of command, an assistant may mount him, and the breaker may continue to circle, turn and rein him back as before, by means of the long reins.

The pony may now be taught to strike off into the canter in circles of gradually decreasing size, until he is rendered sufficiently handy and collected. Cantering a pony in small circles, whether with the long reins or mounted, is an admirable practice for calming down excitable animals, and for teaching awkward ones to go collectedly. We must not consider our pupil perfect with the long reins, until we can make him change from one circle to the other, whether the outward rein be round the quarter, as in Fig. 50, or only on the pad, as in Fig. 51. We do this by slackening out the outer rein, and pulling on the inner one, after having first shortened it.

It must be borne in mind that in all breaking, the voice is of great use, and that ponies soon learn to know and obey these three simple words of command : "whoa !" "back !" "hup !"

The word "whoa !" should be pronounced sharply

8

and loudly, and followed by a feeling on both reins, which should not be done before the word is finished, so as to give the pony a chance of stopping of his own accord, a thing that he will as a rule very quickly learn to do.

The word "back" is used only for reining back, and should be pronounced slowly in a drawling tone of voice, while at the same time the pony's mouth should be felt with both reins.

"Hup!" should be used in a loud cheery tone, in order to make a pony start into a gallop from the rein back, halt, walk, or trot. At the same time, the rider should use the pressure of both legs.

These three are the most important words of command, although others may be employed with advantage. The same tone of voice should be used for each respective word.

We need only see old troop horses at work in a riding school, to recognise the fact that they know several words of command.

After a month or so of the practice I have described, we may take for granted that the pony is quiet to ride, and that his polo education may commence.

The pony may now be worked daily for about an hour and a half, and should not be given more than about 5 lbs. or 6 lbs. of corn, but he may have as much hay as he likes to eat. Although under-feeding does not pay, it is not advisable to give ponies in training much corn. The pony's education will be greatly simplified by having a riding school, which, however, is not essential, because all the exercises I shall describe can be done in the open, or between unjumpable fences in a field.

It is so very much easier to control a horse in an enclosed space than in the open, that I would recommend any one who trains many young animals and has not a riding school, to rail off in the corner of a field a rectangular space about thirty-six yards by twelve yards, in which to teach them to turn, stop, and

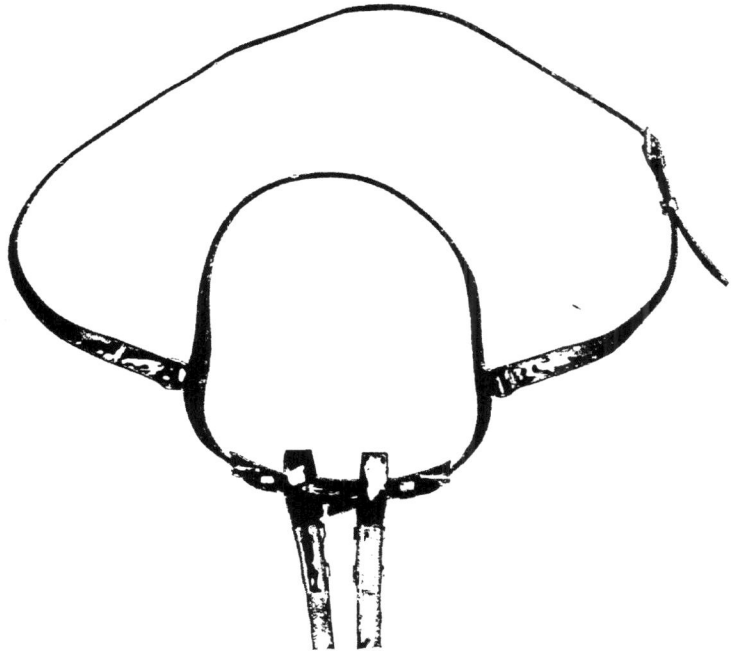

Fig. 52.—Standing Martingale on nose-band.

canter in small circles; but the enclosing fences must be unjumpable and solid.

The programme for the first week may be a lesson in the riding school for half an hour, and riding about the roads at a walk for an hour.

8*

TURNING.

The first object to aim at is to make the pupil obey the rein and leg; to turn to the right or left; and to rein back collectedly. To begin with, I would recommend a plain smooth jointed snaffle, and a long standing martingale on the nose-band (Fig. 52).

It must be remembered that horses turn in three different ways.

    1. On the forehand.

    2. On the centre.

    3. On the hocks.

When a pony, which is going fast, turns to the right on his forehand, his hind-quarters will have a strong inclination to turn out to the left; and *vice versâ*. The result of this will be that he will not be firm on his legs, and through not being collected, will very likely slip up and fall. Many ponies turn well on the centre, but when turning in this manner, it can easily be understood that, if turning to the right, the fore legs must come towards the right, and the hind legs go towards the left, and *vice versâ* if turning to the left; thus there is no fixed pivot on which to turn. But in turning on the hocks, the weight of the pony and that of the rider is thrown back on to the hocks, and a fixed pivot is made by the inward hind leg. This enables a pony to turn in the smallest possible space without going on the circle at all, and has the double advantage of saving time in the turn and of gaining firmness on the legs.

From the above it may be assumed that a polo pony should never turn on his forehand; that when turning on a circle, no matter how small, he should turn collectedly on his centre; and that when it is desired to turn really quickly, and to go in the opposite direction, the pony must be stopped dead, swung round on his hocks and started again at full gallop from the halt. It must be remembered that to turn on the hocks, a halt must be made, if only for the fraction of a second.

To turn to the right, take the reins in both hands, gently feel the right rein, press the left rein on the side of the neck, and apply the drawn back left leg behind the girth. For the *left turn*, the reversed aids are to be applied.

By making the pony describe circles gradually decreasing in size, we may get him to turn on his centre. We may then take the reins in the left hand, and make him go through the same movements by simply pressing the right rein on the right side of the neck, if we wish him to turn to the left ; and the left rein on the left side of the neck, if we wish him to turn to the right. At first, the drawn-back outward leg should be applied as before described ; but this pressure may be gradually withdrawn, according as the pony learns to turn in equally good form, by the simple pressure of the rein on the neck, which is technically called " the weight of the rein on the neck."

The right leg is " the outward leg " in the turn or circle to the left ; and the " inward leg " in a turn or circle to the right.

The object of the pressure of the outward leg in turning or circling, is to prevent the animal's hind quarters swinging round, which they are inclined to do, owing to the fact that the fore legs bear more weight than the hind ones, especially at fast paces—another reason why ponies are apt to turn on the forehand instead of on the hocks.

REINING BACK.

The rider should lean forward, in order to lighten the hind quarters ; and should gently feel the reins alternately, according to the fore foot which is in advance. For instance, if the off fore is farther in front than the near fore, the right rein should be felt ; and *vice versâ.* At the same time, the leg of the side opposite to that of the rein should be drawn back and applied ; the hands should be kept low on each side of the withers ; and the word "back" should be used in a drawling monotonous tone of voice. Too much should not be tried at once ; for it sometimes takes several days to make a pony rein back even a couple of yards. As soon as an animal goes back kindly, he will as a rule give no further trouble.

I do not believe in any pony being first-class at polo, if he will not rein back, which is a practice that balances ponies to an extraordinary extent. It teaches them to use their hocks, to turn on them, and to stop more quickly at fast paces, than they would otherwise be able to do.

To make our pupil a perfect polo pony, we must try to teach him all the following evolutions, especially the first two, because a pony cannot be good unless he will quickly start and stop. Most polo players turn their ponies to the right-about or left-about on a more or less big circle ; whereas a first-class player stops his pony, turns him round on his hocks, gallops back on his own track, and thus takes the lead of an antagonist who turns on a circle.

TO STOP DEAD.

Shout "whoa!" in a loud sharp voice; close both legs; feel both reins; and throw the weight of the body back. The reins should not be tightened till the word has been shouted, so as to give the pony the chance of stopping of his own accord at the word of command.

TO START INTO THE GALLOP FROM THE HALT.

As a preliminary to this lesson, it is best to begin by teaching the pony to break into a canter from the trot, then from the walk, and finally from the halt. When he has learnt, on receiving the order "whoa!" to stop collectedly at the end of a small canter, we may quicken the pace, and by using the same aids, teach him to gallop instead of canter from the halt. Suppose we wish him to strike off from the trot into the canter with the off fore leading, we may begin by trotting him on a circle to the right, with the reins loose. When we wish him to perform the desired change of pace, we should (1) sit down in the saddle; (2) turn his head slightly to the left; (3) feel both reins; (4) lean a little back and to the right; and (5) apply the drawn-back left heel (more or less sharply, as may be required) and shout "hup!" the moment he places the near fore on the ground, because at that instant the near hind is in the act of being brought forward, and a touch of the heel and the sound of the rider's voice will tend to quicken its advance, so that it may come down before the off fore, and immediately after the near fore and off hind are raised. With the near hind foot on the ground and under the body, and the other three feet off the ground, all four legs will be in the correct order of movement for the canter. As soon as he is in the canter, we should let the reins loose. When the pony has learned to answer these aids accurately and promptly, the reversed aids can be employed to get him to strike off into a canter, with the near fore leading, when trotting on a circle to the left. As soon as he has attained proficiency in this, we may make him change from the trot into the canter, with whichever fore leg we wish, when going in a straight direction. And then we can teach him to change from the walk into the canter, in the same way as before, except that the indications of heel and voice should be given at the moment the near fore is being extended to the front, if we wish him to lead with the off fore and off hind ; and *vice versâ.* When he can do all these movements properly, we may teach him to start into the canter from the halt, and finally convert the canter into the gallop, by practice.

TO TURN RIGHT ABOUT OR LEFT ABOUT AT THE CANTER OR GALLOP.

To turn to the right about, begin with both hands on the reins and apply the aids for stopping the pony dead. Separate the hands and feel the right rein, by drawing the right hand back to the right knee ; press the left rein against the left side of the pony's neck ; strongly apply the drawn-back left heel, so as to make him swing round on his hocks and be ready to strike off with his hind legs well under him ; bring the weight of the body back and to the off side, in order to fix the off hind leg, which should be his pivot ; and start him off as before described. To turn to the left about, the reversed aids are applied.

Turning to the right about at one end of a riding school, and to the left about at the other end, while keeping as close as possible to one of the long sides of the school, makes an elongated figure of 8. By turning the pony towards the side of the school, it will be found that he can be made to go right and left about with very little trouble, as he will not like to run his head against the boards. When he makes these turns well, he should be taught to do them, by simply pressing the rein on the neck, without applying the outward leg ; and the reins can be held in one hand. In doing this figure of 8, great attention should be paid to make the pony come round with the inward hind as well as the inward fore leg leading. He should change his legs at the moment of the turn about, and he can be made to do this by a sharp kick of the drawn-back outward heel.

TO CHANGE LEGS BEFORE AND BEHIND AT THE CANTER OR GALLOP.

This can be taught in the same way as the last exercise ; in fact, the aids are the same as those for turning. The canter and gallop differ from the other paces, by the fact that the leading fore leg, during each stride, is extended much more to the front than the non-leading one ; and consequently it is impossible for a pony to cross his leading fore with the non-leading one. Also, it stands to reason that one or both inward legs should be the pivot on which he should

turn, circle, and change direction.   If he makes any of
these movements with the outward fore leg leading,
he will be liable not only to cross his legs, but also to
overbalance himself, especially on slippery ground, in
either of which cases a fall will be the probable result.
In fact, more falls occur at polo by ponies thus "going
false," than from any other cause.   The change in
question is made by the hind legs as well as the fore
ones.   Therefore, when a pony is leading with the
right fore, he should change all four legs the instant
he is circled or even slightly turned to the left ; and
vice versâ.   Practice at the figure of 8 is the best
means for teaching him to make these indispensable
changes.

FIGURE OF 8.

As I have already explained how to make a pony
lead off with either fore leg, we will suppose that he is
started leading with the off fore and off hind on the
right circle.   He will remain on the right circle until
he completes it, when a change is made by collecting
him with both reins, applying a strong pressure of
the drawn-back right heel behind the girth, pressing
the right rein on the right side of the neck, and
throwing the weight of the body to the left, in which
direction the pony will now proceed, and will form
the other loop of the figure of 8 by circling to the
left.   The next change is made at the same place
by reversing the aids.   If he will not change, we
may pull him back into a trot, and make the change
in one of the corners, by starting him into the canter at
that spot.

In doing the figure of 8 with a young pony, it will

be advisable to canter him in several circles at one end of the school, before making him change, as before explained ; and when the change has been made, to give him several circles on the other rein at the other end of the school, before changing him back to the original rein. Before trying the figure of 8, a pony should be well practised in cantering round the school, so that he may get accustomed to lead with the correct leg. Ponies very soon learn to lead with the inward leg when going round the school ; because they find that they can turn much more easily on it than on the out-ward leg. If a pony is leading falsely when going along the side of the school, a corner will be the easiest spot at which to make the correction.

TO GO WITH A LOOSE REIN IN ALL PACES.

I cannot give much advice on this point, beyond recommending the rider to accustom the pupil at first to walk about with the reins hanging loosely. The pony then be gently trotted, and the pace gradually increased, so that he may understand that he has to go at any pace with the reins loose ; and that when they are tightened, he has to reduce his pace proportion-ately to the tension exerted by them on the mouth-piece of the bit.

TO MEET OTHER PONIES.

This may be easily taught by riding the pony to-wards two others coming in an opposite direction, and passing between them. We should begin at a walk, and gradually increase the pace, until the pupil will go through the narrowest practicable opening at full pace without flinching.   When he is perfect at stick and ball, he should be taught to face other ponies whose riders are waving sticks in his face.

TO HUSTLE OTHER PONIES.

This can be taught in a field, simply by making the pony push against another one, at first at a walk, and gradually increasing the pace, until he will do it at full gallop, when he is at a disadvantage (*i.e.*, when the other pony's head is in front of his) ; when he has the advantage ; and when the two ponies are level.

If what I have written on riding school work is too technical for an ordinary beginner who has never been within the walls of a *manège*, I would advise him to go through two or three times the instructions I have laid down, so as to get a general idea of the figures, and if no riding school is available, to take his pony into some rectangular place, enclosed by mud walls, if in India, or by fences, if in England, and devote himself to teaching his pony to stop dead at the word "whoa!" shouted very loudly ; to start at a gallop at the word "hup!" ; to turn quickly both ways at any pace ; and to turn right and left about, while riding all the time with a loose rein.

The aids for turning may be briefly summed up as follows :   To turn to the right, apply a strong pressure of the drawn-back left leg, feel the right rein, press the left rein against the side of the neck, and shift the weight of the body to the right.   To turn to the left the aids are reversed.   Ponies soon learn what these aids mean, and will then readily obey them.   By carrying out these elementary instructions, the beginner will find that although he may not ride in artistic riding school fashion, his pony will become a more handy and more comfortable mount, which, after all, is the object required.

BREAKING THE PONY TO STICK AND BALL.

For this purpose we should employ as large a piece of open ground as possible (for choice, a common in England, or a *maidan* in India); for if the work is given in a small field or paddock, the pony will be very apt to get so sick of it that he will show temper, and constantly try to bore away in the direction of the gate. If more than one field be available, we should, if possible, never take him to the same field two days running. If our only practice field be close to the stable, we should always take the animal to and from it by a circuitous route, so that he may not associate in his mind the pleasurable idea of home with the stoppage of work. I feel certain that the bad habit displayed by many polo ponies, of bearing away towards the spot at which they are accustomed to stand during the intervals between the periods of play, has generally been acquired in the early stages of their education by their having been allowed to go straight to their stables after practice. Every pony should be thoroughly broken to the stick before he is tried with a ball. We may begin with a stick, when riding along the roads or anywhere else, and waving it about in every direction, so as to convince the pony that it will not hurt him.

When he is perfectly quiet with the stick, we may commence hitting the ball about at a walk. If the pony shows signs of nervousness, it may be necessary to go on for some days quietly tapping the ball along, without raising the hand to make a hit. We may gradually use more strength, and try back-handers and strokes on the near side. When the pony has been thoroughly broken to all this at a walk, we may put him through the same process, at first at a slow trot, then at a gentle canter, and increase the speed proportionately to the progress made. When teaching the pony to go straight, we shall be greatly assisted by having another man on a pony or horse to canter steadily about the field in front of the pony upon which we are mounted, so that he may follow the leader on his own account, with but little assistance from us, while we try to accurately hit the ball (not a very easy matter in a rough field) in the direction taken. We should be very careful to leave the reins loose when hitting the ball ; for a job in the mouth at that moment will do much to make him "ball-shy." Another fruitful cause of making ponies shy off the ball, is the habit some riders adopt of not drawing back the left leg and pressing it against the pony's side (so as to prevent the hind-quarters from swinging round to the left) at the moment when they lean to the off side and forward, in the act of striking the ball. Others, again, make a pony shy off by pulling his head round with the right hand on the right rein instead of using the weight of the rein on the neck with the left hand ; and some always touch the pony with the right heel when in the act of striking the ball, and thereby cause him to carry his hind-quarters away from the ball, and to contract the vice of shying off. During the preliminary stages of training, we should, when hitting the ball, sit straight in the saddle,

and ride the pony right up to the spot from which we
can hit the ball without shifting our seat; for if we lean
to the right and forward, the displacement of weight
will have a greater or less tendency to cause the hind-
quarters to revolve round the forehand to the left.   It
is most important to observe this precaution in training
a pony, so that afterwards, in a game, he may not be
inclined to shy off, no matter how much the rider's
weight gets shifted in the saddle.

After hitting a back-hander, we should be careful to
turn right about and left about alternately, so that the
pony will learn to turn equally well both ways, and will
not acquire the bad habit of beginning to stop and turn
before the ball is hit.   This practically constitutes an
elongated figure 8; the turns being made at the
extremities of the loops, where the back-hander is
struck.

Ponies which have been previously handled and
ridden, generally turn more readily to the left than to
the right, on account of the custom of handling and
leading horses on the near side, and of riding them
more with the left hand than with the right.   No
matter how good a pony may otherwise be, he cannot
be considered first-class at polo unless he will turn
equally well on both sides.   The best method of
making a pony turn well to the right on the ball, is to
canter him in small circles to the right, while the rider
keeps gently tapping the ball in the same direction.
If we happen to miss the ball, which we cannot help
doing sometimes, especially in a rough field, we should
take the pony a little way past it, before halting and
turning him; for if we pull him suddenly over it, we
will get him into the habit of slowing up and stopping

over the ball, which is almost as bad a fault as shying off the ball.

After a pony has been thoroughly broken to stick and ball, he should be played, if possible, in a cantering game ; but should on no account be played in a fast match until he is fairly perfect in company at a canter. As all ponies go better in company than by themselves, it is much better for two or three men to train their ponies together than singly. When this cannot be done, the owner will find that the education of his pupil will be greatly accelerated by getting, for instance, a stable boy to canter about with him, even if he cannot trust the lad with a stick.

When training my own young ponies to stick and ball, I always practise several of them at a time, hitting a ball round and round a big field, and make them pass and repass one another, the different riders taking their turns to hit the ball. This practice checks the tendency which the ponies might otherwise have of racing against each other and of pulling. When my youngsters are steady at this kind of work, I put them into a cantering game, two or three a side, taking great care that they do not go out of a collected canter, and that they are not frightened by being hit by ball or stick. As their education progresses, I increase the speed of the games. By being brought on gradually like this, they have but little inducement to become pullers, or to learn tricks like shying off the ball, being afraid to face other ponies, etc.

When breaking a pony to stick and ball, it is most important to devote all one's attention to the pony, and not to one's own practice at the pony's expense.

I have made the foregoing remarks with reference

to the training of ordinary English ponies. Some exceptional ponies require hardly any training, and will play right off; others will take months and months of care and patience, and a few will never learn to play at all. By adopting the directions I have given, the percentage of unplayable ponies will be found to be very small. Foreign ponies, such as Arabs, Barbs, Egyptians, Argentines, Africans and Americans, do not, as a rule, take nearly so much trouble to train as English ponies. Generally, they have better mouths, and are not so high couraged, or, at least, possess more placid tempers. The majority of them play polo with very little training. Many Americans and Argentines have been used as cow ponies, which is about the best training a polo pony can have— any good cow pony makes a polo pony at once. Geldings, as a rule, are more amenable to discipline than stallions, and have just as much, if not more, pluck. Entires, particularly Barbs, have often an annoying trick of looking round and trying to bite any pony which may be alongside, instead of galloping their best.

Ponies which have advanced to a certain extent in their polo education, but which are addicted to some awkward tricks, such as pulling and shying off the ball, will, if turned to grass during the winter, often forget their tricks of the previous season, although they will remember the valuable lessons they received. I think the reason of this is that ponies frequently get sick and tired of being pulled about and trained to polo, and that the tricks they pick up are merely signs of temper, or because their mouths get hurt, their legs and feet sore, and their health upset. After a winter's

9

run at grass, they come up cool and sound, and are ready to start fair with their lessons, which were previously a source of irritation and discomfort. The success of this plan, especially in the case of a puller, will be greatly promoted by remouthing the pony in a light bridle, such as a snaffle or half-moon Pelham, when he comes into work again

CHAPTER VI.

POLO PONY GEAR.

Bits and bridles—Saddles—Whip—Spurs—Bandages and boots.

BITS AND BRIDLES.

THERE is perhaps some truth in the saying, when applied to bits, that "there is a key to every horse's mouth," although there are some hot-headed and spoiled animals which no bit ever invented could stop, if they really mean pulling. Most ponies, I think, will go kindly if we can only find the bit which suits them; but therein lies the difficulty. My editor, in "Illustrated Horse-Breaking," points out that the cause of pulling and other bridle faults lies in the brain, and not in the mouth; and that we would employ our time better by trying to remove it by breaking, than by seeking after a particular kind of bit. The two principal causes which make ponies pull at polo are excitability and pain. We see these causes at work in a pony which, having got excited in a gallop, for instance, gets pulled up short by a job in the mouth, the pain of which adds to the pony's excitement and prompts him to fight against the bit. In the selection of a bridle, our object should be to find one which will be powerful enough to stop the pony,

9*

but which will accomplish its purpose with as little pain
as possible.   There are many ponies which will pull
desperately in severe bridles, but which will go easily
in light ones.   A pony with a perfect mouth can be
ridden in almost any bridle by a man with perfect
hands ; the latter, however, being as difficult to find as
the former.   A pony to have a perfect mouth for polo
must, when going at full speed, be capable of being
readily turned with a loose rein, and of being halted in
a stride or two.   A pony with an ordinary mouth for
hacking purposes will be a puller according to the polo
acceptation of the term ; for although he may bend
nicely to the rein when going slow, he will catch hold a
bit (which he ought not to do if intended for polo) at
top speed.   If we cannot get him to go as temperately
as we wish, it is evident that we must put something in
his mouth which will stop him.

The most difficult kind of pony to cure of pulling is
the hot-headed animal which gets excited whenever he
goes fast.   There are many such ponies which are
good hacks and are quiet in harness, but which are
perfectly useless for polo ; because pace has such an
exciting effect on them that it drives them almost mad.
Although I have had many hot-headed animals
through my hands, I have never succeeded in making
any of them into decent polo ponies ; and consequently
nothing would now induce me to buy a pony, no
matter how good-looking he was, if I had any
suspicion that he was hot-headed.   The use of a
severe bit is of no avail for curing this vice, which in
extremely rare cases may be conquered by time and
patience.   Defects of the teeth are another cause of
pulling.   A pony's upper grinders often get too long

and rough at the outside edges, which causes them to cut the inside of the cheeks, and makes the animal irritable, inclined to throw his head about, and pull. In such cases, the outside edges of the upper grinders require only filing, and when that is done, all irritable symptoms will cease.

Every day, after playing polo, we should carefully

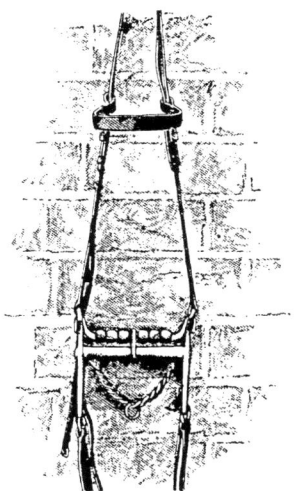

Fig. 53.—Mohawk bridle.

examine our ponies' mouths, particularly the bars of the mouth and the parts under the tongue, which by rough handling are apt to be cut severely, with the possible result of an abscess or diseased bone. We should also look at the chin-groove, to see if it has been hurt by the curb chain ; and at the corners of the lips, which are apt to get cut by the snaffle.

Having, on one occasion, cut the bars of a pony's mouth under the tongue by the use of the bit shown in Fig. 53, I substituted for it a Kerro bit (Fig. 30),

in which I continued to play the pony, and had him
well in a week.   An animal with a sore chin should be

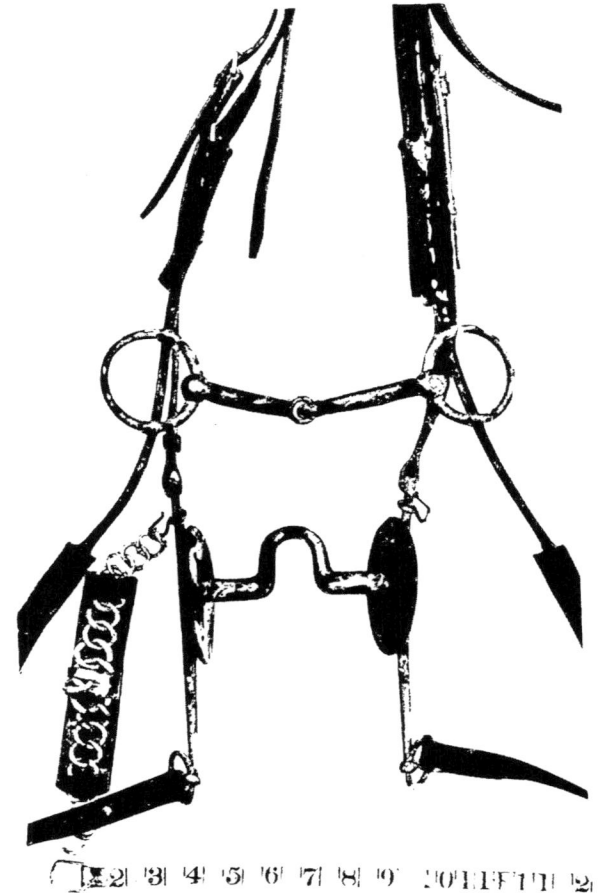

Fig. 54.—Curb with gag snaffle and leather guards.

played without a curb chain, or, if that is not practicable, the curb chain should be provided with a leather
or felt guard, or passed through an india-rubber tube

about 4 inches long. If the corners of the lips become chafed, I would recommend a half-moon Pelham to be substituted for the double bridle, or leather guards, as in Fig. 54, to be used, in order to protect the corners of the lips from contact with the rings of the bridoon. The curb chain must always hang outside the rings of the Pelham (Fig. 31). Besides, this method of adjustment has the effect of making the curb chain lie in the right place. All half-moon Pelhams should be made in this manner.

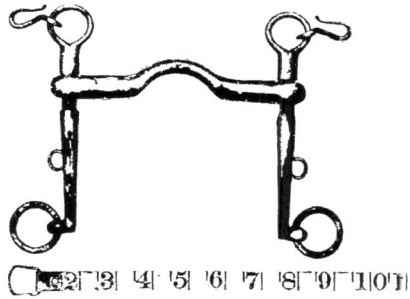

Fig. 55.—Ward Union bit.

The height of the port should be limited to that which would be sufficient to relieve the tongue of pressure ; and should on no account be so high as to touch, let alone hurt, the roof of the mouth. The only three legitimate ways for increasing the severity of a curb are : (1) tightening the curb chain ; (2) lengthening the lower arm of the cheek-piece ; and (3) using a nose band. With a double bridle, we may increase its severity by using a twisted bridoon instead of a plain one.

We should make a careful study of each case, and may not improbably have to try half-a-dozen bridles before the right one is found. The bridle which I find most useful, in all ordinary cases, is a bit and bridoon, heavy and smooth, with a sliding bar and a low port (Fig. 55). It is commonly called a " Ward Union Bridle." Care should be taken that its mouthpiece is not too narrow ; for the animal's lips are more apt to be pinched by a sliding bar than by a fixed mouthpiece. Large leather cheek-pieces (Fig. 54) are as a rule

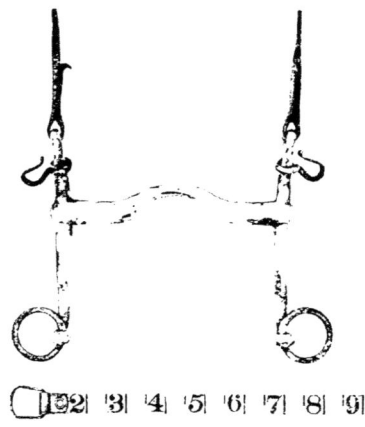

Fig. 56.—Short cheek Curb bit.

advisable. The length of the lower arm of the cheek-piece of the bit may vary from 3 to 6 inches ; that of the upper arm should not exceed 1¾ inches. In almost every bridle, the upper arm of the cheek-piece is made too long, the effect of which is that the curb chain when tightened, is pressed against the sharp edges of the lower jaw, instead of lying in the chin groove, as it will do if the upper arm of the cheek-piece is short (Figs. 56 and 57). The height of the port should be about 1½ inches as a maximum ; and the width of the mouthpiece from 4½ to 5½ inches, according to the size of the pony's mouth. The mouthpiece should on no account be too narrow; for it would then be apt to hurt the animal's lips. A pony from 14 hands to 14.2 seldom requires a bit narrower than 5 inches (inside measurement). The curb chain should be heavy, flat and smooth, and will be all the better if covered with an india-rubber tube, or a leather

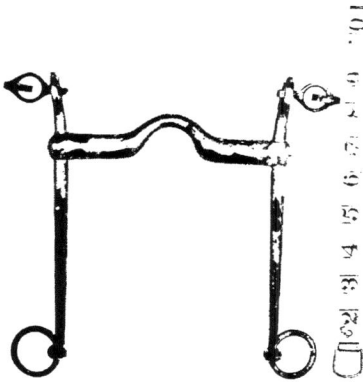

Fig. 57.—Long cheek Curb bit.

guard (Fig. 58). Thin curb chains are an abomination. We should always employ a lip strap to keep the curb chain in its place, and should have the lip strap rings placed about 1¾ inches below the mouthpiece in all bridles, so as to prevent the curb chain slipping over the chin and into the mouth of the pony. The bridoon should be smooth, round and heavy, and should be placed just high enough to touch, but not to wrinkle, the corners of the mouth. Thin snaffles are very irritating to ponies. A nose band, placed low down and tight enough to prevent the

animal from opening his mouth too wide, should be
used with every pony which is the least inclined to
pull; for its presence will give us control over the
entire of his head, and not only over his lower jaw, as
we would have without it. With a bridle made and
applied as I have described, we can obtain great power
over a pony, especially if we add a standing martingale
fixed to the nose band, or to the rings of the snaffle.

The most generally useful bridle for a puller is

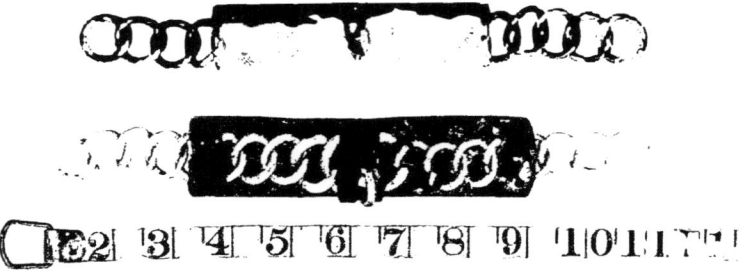

Fig. 58.—Curb chain protected by india-rubber tube ; ditto, by leather guard.

that shown in Fig. 54. It is used with a gag and
is called the " Stansted Bridle."

In the first edition of this book I recommended the
Mohawk bridle (Fig. 53) for polo ; but I regret to say
that I have been compelled to alter my opinion. My
remarks had been based on the fact that I had used
this bit with great success on one or two hard-mouthed
ponies ; but, later on, I was obliged to discontinue it,
because I found it cut their mouths badly under the
tongue and on the bars of the mouth, an injury which I
found this bit caused to a large number of ponies
ridden in it. Although it may be a very good bridle
for hacking and driving, it is too severe for polo, at

which game ponies have often to be pulled about very sharply. If it is employed as a last resource, its lower bar should be covered with india-rubber.

An india-rubber Pelham (Fig. 28) and the " Kerro" bridle (Fig. 30) will be found useful for light mouthed, excitable ponies. The india-rubber Pelham will wear better if covered with leather, for ponies are apt to bite through the unprotected rubber very soon. The leather after a short time becomes soft from the saliva of the mouth, and will then prevent the bars from becoming bruised, or the lips pinched. The " Kerro" bridle is a Pelham. I have not been able to find out the name of its inventor. It consists of a roller of wood which revolves on a steel bar, and is covered with either leather or india-rubber. It gives the rider, by reason of its thickness, great power over a pony. Besides being a useful bridle for some excitable pullers, it is excellent for a pony whose mouth has been cut or bruised by a severe bit.

The Ben Morgan bit (Fig. 29), which consists of a half-moon mouthpiece turned downwards, is a most useful bit for many pullers ; seemingly because it bears on a different part of the pony's mouth to that pressed on by the ordinary curb bit This bit is particularly useful, when the bars of a pony's mouth have become sore through the action of an ordinary curb.

The half-moon Pelham (Fig. 31), in conjunction with a leather curb chain, is especially good for forming the mouth of a young pony, or for riding a very light-mouthed pony at polo. A curb bridle of some kind is almost invariably necessary for a pony at polo.

Besides the bits I have described, which will be

quite sufficient for the needs of an ordinary steed,
there are many others that may be used with advantage.   We may often suit a pony's mouth by
altering the height of port and length of cheek of
the ordinary hunting curb, or by covering the bit
with india-rubber or leather.   Such cruel bits as
the Segundo and Chifney, should not be used ;
for although they may be employed, hacking or

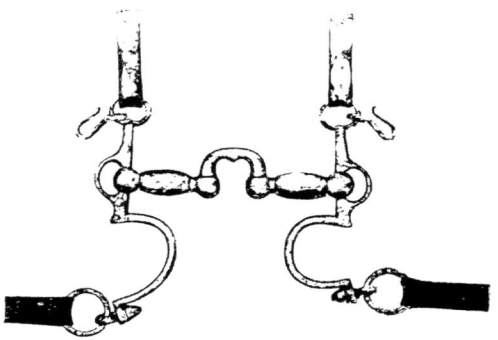

Fig. 59.—Hanoverian Pelham.

hunting, by a man who has very good hands ; they
are too severe for polo, at which game a pony's
mouth is unavoidably wrenched and pulled about
a good deal at times.   In India, I used severe
bits a good deal, until, on one occasion, I broke the
lower jaw of the pony I was riding, and then gave
them up for ever.   After this pony, which was a
hard puller, had recovered from the fracture, I tried
him with such success in a short-cheeked hunting
bridle, with both bit and bridoon wrapped round
with wash-leather, that he gave up pulling.   This is

only one of many instances of ponies pulling from pain. The Hanoverian Pelham with a low port (Fig. 59), is a useful bit for a pony that gets his head too low.

One of the worst tricks a polo pony can have is that of getting his tongue over the bit, which then acts solely on the sensitive bars of the mouth. I have never known a pony addicted to this abominable trick with a decent mouth. Besides, it is one of the

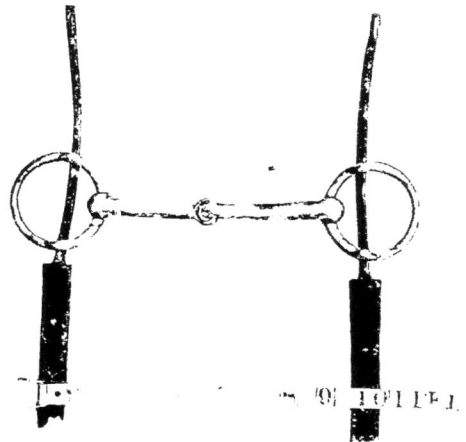

Fig. 60.—Gag snaffle.

most difficult of all vices to cure. Of the many contrivances I have tried, including ladder bits and tongue layers, the most successful have been an ordinary gag (Fig. 60), and tying the tongue. The gag has the disadvantage of being too severe for some really hot-headed ponies. Tying the tongue is done by means of a piece of tape passed over the tongue and under the chin. It should be made just tight enough not to slip off the tongue. The knot used is a single knot on the upper surface of the tongue, and a double bow knot in the chin groove.

The most generally useful bits for ponies with good mouths are shown in Figs. 28, 29, 30, and particularly 31, 55, 56 and 57.

The standing martingale may be dispensed with at polo when the animal is perfectly trained, and, consequently, carries his head in the right position. Without this useful contrivance, very many good polo ponies, especially Arabs, would star-gaze, and be found difficult to stop or keep under control. With ponies which raise and bring back their heads when they stop suddenly at full gallop, so as to throw their weight on to the hind quarters, this martingale, if used at all, should be long enough to allow them the free use of their heads for the purpose just mentioned, but no longer.

In breaking a pony, a standing martingale will be found useful, except for those which have such perfectly shaped necks that they always carry their heads in the right position. For this purpose the martingale should be of such a length as to prevent the muzzle being raised higher than on a level with the top of the withers.

Many good players in England never use a martingale at all; but, as a rule, they are the happy possessors of ponies with good mouths and with beautifully shaped heads, necks, and shoulders. On the other hand, in India most of the best players use a standing martingale on every pony, because, as far as I can see, they ride Arabs, which, unlike well-bred English ponies, seldom have their heads and necks well put on, or their shoulders sufficiently sloping.

The inference to be drawn from this is that the necessity for the use of a standing martingale depends on the conformation of the forehand.

The rule I have laid down about allowing ponies which stop best with their heads in the air a long standing martingale, cannot be of universal application, because such wonderful performers as the famous team in India captained by the Maharajah of Jodhpur play their ponies with very short standing martingales, tied on to the nose band. The bridles they use have only a curb rein, and are without bridoons. They ride with a slack rein. Their method as regards Arabs must be sound ; for no ponies in the world are handier or more perfectly trained.

No definite rule as to the length of a martingale can be laid down ; so an intelligent study must be made of each pony's requirements, and the owner must find out for himself what will best suit particular cases. If his pony star-gazes with a long martingale, he must shorten it. If, as may often occur, the pony will not go up to his bit with a short martingale, it must be lengthened. As far as my own experience goes with English ponies, I find that I have to ride the majority of young ones with a short martingale when training them. I lengthen it to play them in a game, and, as a rule, dispense with it altogether when they are thoroughly trained.

I have seen very few Arabs which do not go better with a standing martingale than without one. I once possessed an Arab which I could not keep on a polo ground at all until his former owner told me that the animal's muzzle had to be strapped to within six inches of his chest. I followed his directions, and was then able to ride the pony in good matches with moderate comfort.

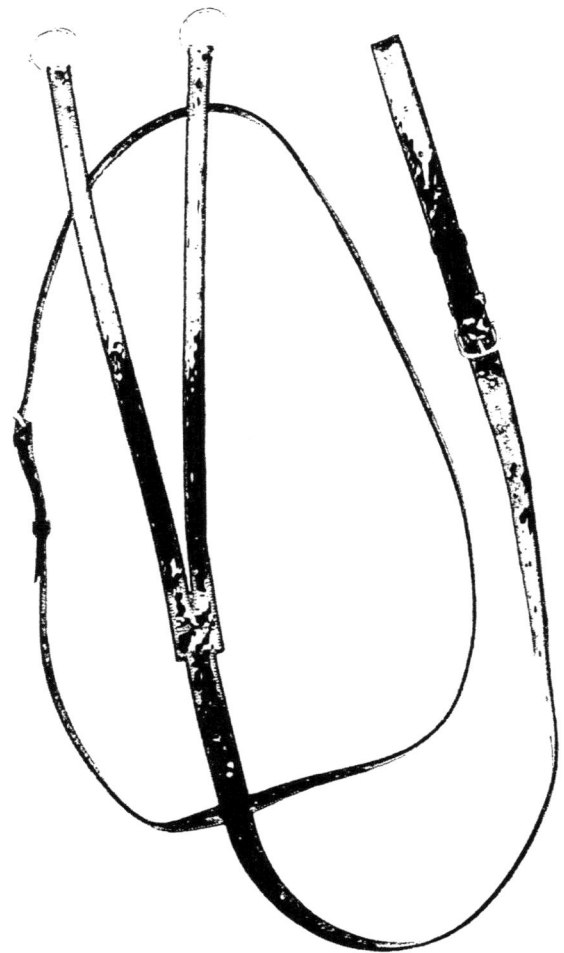

Fig. 61.—Lord Lonsdale's running martingale.

When driving with "the long reins" (page 95), or when riding either in the school or hacking, this martingale may be buckled on to the rings of the bridoon, which plan is especially useful with a puller; but when playing polo, it is always better to fasten it

Fig. 62.—Nose band with pad removed.

Fig. 63.—Nose band and pad.

to the nose band; for we thereby save the pony's mouth from being hurt in the rough and tumble of the game.

I have not discussed the question of the running

10

martingale (Fig. 61), as I do not as a rule advocate its use for polo; the standing one being much more effective in every way.

Nose bands (Figs. 62 and 63) should be made about 2½ inches broad in front, so that the nose may not become chafed ; and should have a pad, or india-rubber tube (Fig. 64), behind to protect the sensitive edges of the bones of the lower jaw, and buckles at each side, so that the nose band may be tightened or

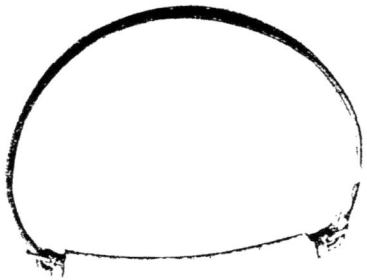

Fig. 64.—Nose band with india-rubber tube to protect pony's lower jaw.

loosened, as may be required, without altering the position of the pad.

A standing martingale should be made with large long billets, so that it can be buckled comfortably over the nose band pad, or to the rings of the snaffle. The strap should be 1½ inches wide, and made the same shape all along to the division, so that it may pass through the buckle, which should be a strong one. This arrangement will enable the martingale to be let out to such an extent as to prevent a star-gazer hitting his rider in the face, or to be taken in so far that the pony's head will be practically strapped to his chest.

SADDLES.

I think that players as a rule have a tendency to use too small saddles. I like a roomy hunting saddle (weighing, say, 12 lbs.) in which I can move about, when hustling or reaching out for a ball. Besides, a big saddle is a great comfort to an indifferent horseman, and the increase in weight of, say, 5 lbs., will be more than made up to the pony by the extra bearing surface. Every pony should have his own saddle specially fitted for him. A leather-covered panel is excellent, as it stands wear well, does not soak up the perspiration, and does not require renewing so often as a serge or linen covered one. A leather numnah is a good protection to the back, and saves the lining of the panel from wear, and the stuffing from becoming wet and caked by sweat.

WHIP.

Every polo player should learn to use a whip in his left hand while playing ; for the simple fact that the rider carries one will make many ponies jump quickly into their bridles and gallop kindly. Its presence in his hand is no inconvenience if he does not wish to use it.

SPURS.

Sharp spurs are never allowed in games, but are occasionally useful in training a regular slug. Spurs without rowels are generally an advantage with ordinary ponies for making them start quickly. Keen, first-class ponies do not need them, and they often

10*

cause an excitable one to pull. They are usually an assistance to a weak horseman.

We can afford protection to the legs of our ponies from blows of stick or ball by means of bandages or boots. There are two objections to the use of the former: first, they require special care in putting on, so that they will neither become undone during play nor hurt the legs by being too tight; and, secondly, they cannot be arranged so as to effectively protect the fetlocks without incurring the risk of their working loose. If a bandage on a fore leg becomes undone, it will remain attached to the leg by the tapes, and there will then be great risk of the pony putting a hind foot on it, and thus tripping himself up. To obviate this danger, in the event of our electing to employ a bandage for work, we should begin applying it by leaving the end loose, either at the knee or fetlock (according as we wish to commence from above or from below), and after having taken two or three turns, we should take hold of the loose end, lay it over the portion of the bandage which has been already applied, and then continue the turns until the bandage is ready to be tied on. If a bandage is put on too tightly, it is very apt to hurt the back tendons, and give the pony a big leg. Boots, made of thin felt, are in every way preferable to bandages. They can be put on quickly and easily by any stable lad; and, if they are properly made, they will protect the fet-locks without interfering with the action of these joints, and without lessening the closeness of their adhesion to their respective legs. Those I use on my ponies are the Rugby Club Polo Boots, made and invented by Mr. T. U. Clarke, of Rugby (Figs. 65, 66 and 67). I would advise that each pony

Fig. 65.—Rugby polo boot; inside view.

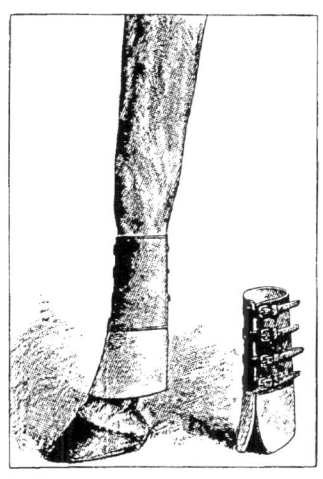

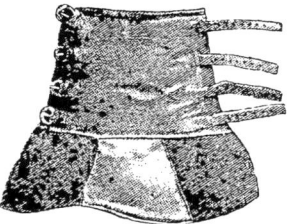

Fig. 66.—Rugby polo boot; outside view.

Fig 67.—Rugby polo boot.

should have his own boots, the holes in the straps of which should be so marked that anyone can see at a glance at what length they ought to be buckled up.

Boots should not be put on till the pony reaches the polo ground, and should be taken off as soon as play is over; ponies should never be walked home any distance in boots.

Photo by]   [M. H. HAYES.

Fig. 68.—Wintering ponies.

CHAPTER VII.

POLO PONY MANAGEMENT.

Wintering ponies—Conditioning ponies—Stable routine, feeding, and watering—Bedding—Stables—Using polo ponies in harness—Racing and chasing polo ponies—Treatment of a polo pony on the polo ground after a period of play—Saddlery.

WINTERING PONIES.

THE first question here is, what shall we do with our ponies from, say, the 1st September to the time it will be necessary to begin getting them fit for the 1st April? Although their welfare will be our chief consideration, economy and convenience may also have to be studied. Assuming that a pony has been in hard work during the preceding season, and that he does not require to be kept in a sick box for veterinary

treatment, the best thing for his general health, and
for the soundness of his legs and feet, is to turn him
out to grass for September and October, during which
months the grass will be still growing and the dews
will be heavy. For that time, supposing the grass is
plentiful, he will do all the better for having no corn or
hay, unless he is old (especially if he has not been
turned out the previous autumn), delicate, or, if a
foreigner, unacclimatised, in which cases he may get a
couple of feeds of corn daily. The owner should see
that the supply of grass is plentiful and good, and
should remember that the larger the run is, the better.
If the fields or paddocks are small, he should arrange
to have the pasture grounds changed from time to
time. He should on no account try the dangerous
experiment of leaving the ponies to the tender mercies
of an ordinary farmer, who, generally, has other work
to attend to, is short handed, and is not well acquainted
with the requirements of valuable horseflesh.

Having given our ponies a two months' run at grass,
we have next to decide what to do with them in the
winter. We must remember that ponies, as a rule,
are hardier, sounder, and less liable to go wrong in
their wind than big horses, and that they do well in
the open, no matter how cold it may be, provided they
have plenty of good grass to eat, and enough space in
which to roam freely about. At the same time we
must bear in mind that our ultimate object is to have
our ponies perfectly fit by the 1st of April. We are
here placed in a different position to that which we
occupied six months previously, when deciding the
question of summering our hunters, which we were
able, if we had chosen, to bring gradually into work

during cub-hunting time, and in the early part of the season, when the blindness of the ditches may be an excuse for going slow and prudently. Polo ponies, however, have to be as fit as the proverbial fiddle, from the very first day of the season ; for in play we cannot, without spoiling the game for our comrades, spare our animals, beyond playing them for only one ten minutes instead of for two or three. Therefore, the wintering must be so arranged that any loss in hard muscle and wind may be regained, with a large increase of health and soundness, before the 1st of April. After their autumn run of two months, we may take them into the stable and have them regularly exercised, which is a method to be adopted only by those to whom expense is no object ; or we may keep them at grass until it is time to get them again into condition. I do not at all approve of turning them into loose boxes, as I think they would do much better at grass, especially in the way of exercise. Whichever method we adopt, we must remember that our animals will not thrive as well as they ought to do, unless we give them personal supervision, or unless we can leave them in charge of some perfectly trustworthy person. If we find that one or more of the ponies at grass cannot stand the cold and exposure, we should put them in a shed or stable and have them regularly exercised. Supposing that we adopt the sound and economical policy of keeping our ponies at grass during the winter, we must not forget that, although they will remain in health on grass alone, it is not sufficient in itself to enable them to keep their muscles in well-developed condition, and that the recovery of muscular development will cost more than its retention. Undoubtedly the best plan

of managing ponies which are turned out in the winter
is to shut them up in a shed at night, and give them a
feed of corn and a liberal supply of good hay ; another
feed in the morning ; and at noon a third feed put into
feeding boxes in the field. Ponies done like this
during the winter months, should be fit for any kind of
polo on the 1st of April, if taken up on the 22nd of
February, and put into work on the 1st of March. If
economy be a great object, the owner can use his
discretion whether to begin feeding with corn on the
1st of November, or to wait till later on. In this he
should be guided by the amount of "keep" there is in
the fields, and on the severity of the season. He
should bear in mind that the earlier he begins to do
his ponies well, the less corn and time will they require
to get fit when taken up and put into work. Feeding
is of more importance than shelter. Even when open
sheds exist in the fields, ponies will not, as a rule, use
them. Consequently, these buildings are not of much
advantage, unless the ponies are shut up in them at
night. It is a curious fact that even in the coldest and
roughest nights in mid-winter, the majority of ponies
seem to prefer lying out under a hedge or tree, even
in the snow, to using the most comfortable shelter
provided for them. During the very severe winter of
1892-3, I put six valuable ponies into loose boxes, and
fed them on the best of hay and oats. At the same
time I turned six other ponies which I did not care so
much about into some big grass fields without sheds,
and gave them nothing in addition to what they could
pick up, beyond a little rough hay and oat straw. For
a whole month they had to get their food by shoving
away the snow with their noses and fore feet, and

yet they came up in better condition and with more
flesh and muscle on them than the ponies which had
been in loose boxes, but which had not been exercised.
All these twelve ponies, however, took a long time,
quite two-and-a-half months, to get into polo condition.
Had the six turned-out ones been well fed during the
months of December, January and February, they
would not have taken half that time to have got fit.
It is really extraordinary how well ponies will condition
themselves when turned out, if they are fed as liberally
and as regularly as they would be when in the stable.
We obtain an excellent proof of the good effect of corn
on turned-out ponies, from the fact that after the
morning feed, they will almost invariably have a gallop
about together; but if they are not fed, they will seldom
go out of a walk. It is evident that this morning
gallop is a capital means for maintaining their muscle,
and keeping their wind clear.

I have found that the best food for ponies when
turned out is crushed maize. All the corn should
be crushed and mixed with a liberal allowance of
old hay cut up into chaff. A good daily ration for
a pony during November, December, January and
February, would be 7 lbs. of maize and 10 lbs. of hay.
If there is plenty of keep in the fields, the ration can
be cut down in quantity.

CONDITIONING PONIES.

When the ponies come up from grass, I like to give
them a mild dose of physic, say three drachms of aloes,
after which they will be ready to start regular long
exercise in about a week's time. Taking a month's
work as sufficient to get them ready to play on the

1st April, I would, therefore, advise that they should be taken up about the 22nd February. Long walking exercise on roads is the best thing for conditioning ponies, especially as regards their legs and feet, which, if the animals are gross, will take longer to get hard and fit than their bodies. Half the sprains and lamenesses which occur at the beginning of a season arise from ligaments, tendons, and bones being put to unaccustomed work. Besides, when a pony's legs have been hardened by exercise, blows take little effect on them, whereas a comparatively trivial knock may give a pony that is out of condition a big leg, which may necessitate the animal being rested and put on soft food for about a week, with the result that he may get thrown back so much that he will take a long time to get fit again. Here we may adopt my editor's axiom, that the more work a horse or pony gets, the better, so long as his appetite and condition continue good, and his legs and feet remain sound. The average hunting-stud groom loves to have all his work done by nine o'clock in the morning, and then shut up his animals in their stable for the remainder of the day. His idea of daily exercise is doing about eight or nine miles, principally at a walk, with a little trotting. The first day the owner goes out, he will perhaps ride (or have his horse ridden) ten miles to the meet, hunt him three hours, covering, say, sixteen miles, and have him ridden back another ten miles. This not immoderate amount of walking, trotting, galloping, and jumping, which on occasions may be easily increased to a total of fifty miles, will be more than equivalent to a whole week's work given by the stud groom; and then the owner will be astonished to find next morning that the horse's legs are filled all round, and that the animal is stiff and sore in every joint. The same remarks apply to ponies, except that the polo pony groom is, as a rule, inclined to give his animals one hour's work instead of two. Previous to playing, ponies should do from three to four hours' work a day, with a lot of trotting during the third week, and should wind up the last week with two or three good canters a day. Ponies conditioned like this will be well fortified against sprains, blows, and other accidents from which they would be very liable to suffer during the season if they had begun to play in an unfit state. I have taken for granted that the ponies have continued in lusty health all through. If they are thin and poor to start with, it will probably take about three months to get them up to concert pitch.

Work, and plenty of it, in addition to that at polo, is necessary to keep a pony fit, especially if he is not played regularly. Many men who play polo never see their ponies, except to ride them, at most four times, sometimes only once or twice, a week, for two periods of ten minutes each day. Besides the question of fitness, the fact remains that many ponies are uncomfortable mounts at polo from being too fresh. We have, therefore, three good reasons for giving our ponies lots of work, namely, to make them fit, to keep them sound, and to render them comfortable to ride. Ponies which are somewhat infirm will, of course, require more lenient treatment; but even they should be given as much work as they can safely stand. Many young, high-couraged ponies are often spoiled by being played when too fresh. I have often heard men complain that they could not play their ponies because their animals were too impetuous, which was entirely the fault of the respective owners, who, if they had given their ponies three or four hours' walking exercise in the morning before playing, would have had far pleasanter rides. The fact of many ponies having to go from six to ten miles to the polo ground, has a most beneficial effect on their spirits and temper. I always give my own young ponies from two to four hours' walking and slow trotting exercise every morning up and down a hilly grass field, except on the day after playing, when I allot them only sufficient to remove their stiffness, for which one hour will be quite enough. The good effect on legs and feet of this hour's work will be greatly increased if the exercise can be given early in the morning in a grass field where the herbage is long, and while the dew is still on it. Even a better plan, if practicable, is to have them first walked about up to their knees and hocks in water.

STABLE ROUTINE, FEEDING, AND WATERING.

Strict regularity should be observed in the feeding of ponies, and the requirements of each of them should be separately studied ; for what will suit one, may not answer with another. The following arrangement of hours and diet will be found applicable to the average pony in hard polo work :—

6 a.m. : The stable should be opened at this hour, and the ponies should get a few go-downs of water, (say, a third of a bucket full) and half a feed of oats (which, if good, will weigh 1¼ lbs.), and a little chaff. If a full feed be given, the ponies, as a rule,

will not have time to eat it while the stable is being roughly cleaned and the bedding swept to one side, before they are taken out to exercise. Even if they are allowed to finish it, they cannot usually digest it properly while being worked, as we may see by their tendency to scour at this time under such circumstances. Too much water in the early morning will also increase their liability to diarrhœa during exercise given shortly afterwards.

6.30 a.m.: Exercise till 9 a.m. or 9.30 a.m. on ordinary days, and till 7.30 a.m. on days after playing polo. When they come in from exercise, they should first of all get as much water as they will drink, and then have a feed (2½ lbs.) of corn, and 4 or 5 lbs. of good old hay. When the groom has given this, he should go and have his breakfast, and leave the ponies in peace to feed. After he returns from breakfast, the ponies should be well dressed, and the stable put right.

12 noon: A full supply of water, a feed of oats; but no hay. The groom can now clean his saddlery, and hang it up ready to put on before 1 p.m., at which hour he will go to dinner. He can have his ponies ready on the polo ground at 3 o'clock, even if he has to go four miles to it. If the distance is much further than this, he must clean his saddles and bridles overnight, and finish his dinner earlier. On non-polo days, between 2 p.m. and 6 p.m., the man should give his ponies a second good dressing, and exercise any of them which have not had sufficient work in the morning, or clean his saddlery.

At 6 p.m. · Full allowance of water, a feed of oats, and about 8 lbs. of hay.

In this way, a good groom can look after three ponies well during the polo season. Plenty of work will keep the men out of mischief, especially if they are by themselves in a livery stable. It is much better to have one man to three ponies, provided he rides well, and to hire a boy every polo day to help to hold the ponies on the ground, than to employ two men to look after three ponies, and thus encourage idleness. Two men will, however, be necessary for four ponies which are regularly played. A groom who is in charge of three ponies can, at exercise, ride one and lead the other two, one on each side, in a field.

Some ponies do well on 9 lbs. (3½ feeds) of the best old oats a day ; others require more ; but 12 lbs. is sufficient for the biggest-framed and hungriest pony. From 10 to 12 lbs. of hay, most of it to be given at night, is a good allowance. We can give the oats mixed with a couple of double handfuls of chaff (hay cut up short in a chaff cutter).

If oats have an undue tendency to make a pony's dung loose, we may with advantage bruise the oats, and before giving them, allow the pony some hay to eat. The precaution of giving hay before feeding, giving it at feeding time, mixing it in the form of chaff in the corn, and bruising the oats, are adopted with the object of making the horse eat more slowly and masticate his corn more thoroughly than he would otherwise do. We can be certain that a pony bolts his corn, only by the fact that he does not digest it, which we can see if it passes out in the dung without having been fully acted upon by the digestive fluids, or if it produces diarrhœa. Dry bran, say a couple of pounds a day, mixed in the corn, will help to check a tendency to looseness in the bowels, probably on account of the presence of the bran obliging the animal to chew his oats better than he would do if the bran was absent. Bran prepared in India contains a larger amount of flour than English bran, and appears, apparently for this reason, to be more nutritious. The good results obtained by giving remounts a large proportion of bran in their corn, when sending them to South Africa on board ship, shows that bran is a valuable food. Its mode of administration, and that of other feeding stuffs for use in the East, are fully discussed in *Training and Horse Management in India.*

A little meadow or rye grass, clover, lucerne, comfrey or carrots may be regularly given with advantage, even when a pony is in the hardest work ; but the amount should be kept within such moderate limits that the green food or roots may not have any tendency to unduly distend the stomach and intestines of the ponies which eat it, or to make them scour. On Saturday nights all the ponies may get a mash made of bran, bran and linseed, or boiled barley mixed with them.

It is a good general rule always to leave water with the ponies, so that they can take it when they want it. There will then be no doubt about their getting enough. In this case, the bucket should be left in a corner of the stable away from the manger ; for some horses will slop the water all over their corn if the bucket is kept close to it. If it is not convenient to have a bucket of water always within their reach, they should be invariably given as much water as they choose to drink before every feed, and whenever they come in from exercise.

Some ponies, like many of ourselves, are fond of taking an occasional sip of fluid with their food, which they will not relish unless they are allowed to do so. I need hardly say that such ponies should always have water within reach.

BEDDING.

The best kind of bedding is undoubtedly good wheaten straw. When economy has to be studied, sawdust and moss litter are excellent substitutes. Against the use of both of these kinds of bedding there is the slight objection that contact with them removes the gloss off the coat ; a fact which is not of much importance in the case of ponies that are clothed when in the stable. Moss litter, and probably sawdust to a less extent, are apt to injuriously affect the soles and frogs, unless the feet are frequently (at least, three times a day) picked out, and unless the bed is kept dry. Neither of these economical substitutes look so well in the stable as straw. As they are very absorbent, their fouled portions should be removed every morning and evening. Moss litter (peat moss) makes an excellent manure, especially for grass land, and, unlike straw manure, need not be kept to rot. Mixing it with wood shavings, which can be procured very cheaply, if not for the mere carting away, from the yard of any builder or carpenter, is a good way for keeping it dry without much attention, and consequently may be practised with ponies which are wintered, or horses which are summered on it. Sawdust is almost useless for manure unless kept for a long time to rot, when it should be mixed with some other kind of manure. The bedding, whatever material is used, should be removed, and the floor of the stall or box swept clean and dry every morning when the stable is mucked out. I like to let my ponies stand on the bare floor for two or three hours a day, as I think this practice helps to harden their feet. The use of peat moss or sawdust is an excellent preventive against ponies eating their bedding.

Apart from the question of gloss on the coat, it is a mistake to suppose that a pony dirties himself more on peat moss than on straw. The contrary is, I think, the case, if we may judge by the fact that a white horse does not stain so easily when kept on it, as when bedded down on straw.

STABLES

Can hardly be too cold, provided there is no draught, and that the ponies have plenty of clothing. The ventilation should be at the roof or high up in the walls. Colds, coughs, influenza, roaring, cracked heels and other diseases are far more rare in cold stables than in hot ones. It is best for stables to have no drains, which, if they exist, should be flushed out with water from time to time, and kept clean. As a disinfectant, we may use one part of either crude carbolic acid or phenyle in twenty parts of water, or dry gypsum. Whitewashing the walls, ceiling and floor will keep them in a sanitary condition.

USING POLO PONIES IN HARNESS.

Although circling a pony with the long reins on foot (Figs. 50 and 51) is much the better plan for keeping him in exercise ; still, if it is a matter of covenience, we may occasionally use him between the shafts. We should remember that harness work is apt to spoil his action (particularly if breast harness is employed instead of a collar), teach him to pull, and make him heavy in front. No young polo pony should be put into harness until he has been thoroughly broken in to polo, so that he may not acquire too much knee action from trotting, and may not become heavy on his fore hand. Unambitious polo players, who have only second or third class ponies, need not of course be so particular about the question of action and mouth as men who aspire to play with distinction in first-class matches. There are, however, some rare and invaluable treasures in pony flesh which no kind of work seems to hurt, and which can be moderately driven both winter and summer without impairing their efficiency at polo. Even their power of resisting deterioration has its limits.

RACING AND CHASING POLO PONIES.

As a great rule, nothing spoils polo ponies so much as racing or steeplechasing them ; for both these sports teaches them to pull and to extend themselves in a manner which is totally different to that which is required even in the fastest gallop at polo, it makes them excitable, and diverts their attention from the game. Even here, as at harness work, we may meet with some exceptionally intelligent ponies which recognise the fact that different kinds of games require different methods of play, and accordingly regulate their movements to suit the nature of the work at which they are engaged. The best instance of this that I can call to mind is the

11*

pony Charlton (Fig. 43), which used to play polo equally well the day after a severe race as the day before it.

TREATMENT OF A PONY ON THE POLO GROUND AFTER A PERIOD OF PLAY.

A pony, after ten minutes of hard play, wants careful treatment, in order to bring him up fresh again for his next turn.

A couple of quarts of water should be given him, especially on a hot day. This will be just sufficient to wash his mouth out, quench his thirst, and freshen him up. His head, mouth, and nostrils should be carefully sponged over, also his dock and sheath.

The girths must be loosened at once, and a second man, if possible, should set to work and scrape him all over. He may be then rubbed dry with chamois leathers, and should be walked about for a few minutes till cool. When cool he should be wiped over with a clean cloth, and got ready for his turn.

This can all be done in twelve minutes, but it is of course advisable on ordinary occasions that a pony should only play two periods in a match, which will give him more than twenty-five minutes' rest.

After the match he may be freely watered. When the pony goes back to his stable, he may have as much water as he likes to drink, and should be given a feed of hay ; he may be then well dressed and made comfortable for the night, and be fed an hour after his arrival in the stable. A mash once a week on Saturday night is quite sufficient for polo ponies in ordinary hard work.

SADDLERY.

All girths and linings to saddles for polo should be of leather, which can be kept soft and in good condition with soap and neatsfoot oil.

The best stuffing for saddles is felt, which, though too hard for hunting, acts better than anything else for polo.

CHAPTER VIII.

VARIOUS BREEDS OF POLO PONIES.

General remarks — English ponies — Arabs — Egyptians — Syrians — Barbs — Argentines — North Americans — Californian ponies — Mexicans — Montana ponies—Gulf Arabs or Persians—Indian country-breds—South African ponies —Australasians—Canadians—Importation of ponies.

GENERAL REMARKS.

THE different breeds of ponies have their respective merits, which may be profitably studied by the intending purchaser, the nature of whose weight, strength, horsemanship or pocket may be better suited by one class of animal than by another. Besides, the demand for well-bred galloping ponies so far exceeds the supply, that various foreign countries are drawn upon to meet it. Not only has the number of players increased, but the improvement in the game necessitates the use of a class of pony which will be always comparatively difficult to find.

The principal breeds of ponies now played in England are :—(1) English, by which term I wish to include Irish, Welsh and Scotch ; and (2) Americans, including those from the Argentine Republic, Mexico, Texas and Montana. There are also a few instances of Arabs, Australians, Barbs, Syrians, Egyptians,

Canadians and South Africans or Cape ponies being used for the English game.

During the last few years, Eastern ponies have gone very much out of fashion among English players, and I have lately noticed an increasing tendency to augment the undoubtedly insufficient supply of polo ponies, by importations from the Argentine Republic, and from the United States, instead of from Algeria, Tunis, Gibraltar, Malta, Egypt and India. The principal reasons for this change are as follows.

The number of good well-trained English ponies has greatly increased during late years, on account of the growing popularity of polo in country parts, where the members of the new clubs are constantly on the look-out for likely ponies, many of which, when trained, come into the market. Also, the raising of the height to 14.2 is all in favour of the English pony, which as a rule is heavier for his height than foreigners ; and besides, the bigger he is, the easier it is to get him of a high-class blood type. Hence, at 14.2, an Arab has little or no chance with him ; although there might not be so much difference between them at 14 hands. Few Eastern ponies can go through dirt, carry weight, or stay ; and it has been found by experience that a team mounted on them has but a poor chance against another team on English ponies, especially in the final twenty minutes of a tight match and on heavy ground. They become worn down more by the superior weight and staying power, than by the greater speed of the English-bred animals. At present, there are extremely few Arabs playing in England. In 1891, there were more than a dozen times the number of men looking out for Eastern

ponies than there are now.   These animals are regarded simply as useful ponies for beginners and for
riders who cannot play English ponies properly.

Probably the chief reason which has brought
Eastern ponies into disrepute, is the reputation they
have acquired of being liable to fall on the slightest
provocation.   As a rule they are light and weedy,
have inferior shoulders, and when they fall, they come
down all of a heap, with scarcely an effort to save
themselves.   On the contrary, English ponies, like
Irish hunters, seem to have always a spare leg, re-
cover themselves, and get out of difficulties with
extraordinary cleverness.   Men who have ridden
Eastern ponies during the last few years, have had
more than their proper share of bad falls.   As the demand for good polo ponies far exceeds the supply,
ponies from North and South America have largely
taken the place of Eastern animals, which is a move
in the right direction ; because, owing to their large
infusion of English blood, they more nearly approach
the home type than any other breed, except Australian
ponies, which have not yet come into the English
market in large numbers.   The American ponies
we have seen, are sure-footed and can carry weight;
but with a few brilliant exceptions, they cannot gallop
as fast or stay as well as English ponies, especially
with a heavy weight or in deep ground.

ENGLISH PONIES.

The English polo pony is essentially a dwarf hunter
or dwarf steeplechaser ; and, consequently, he is
entirely different from the general utility pony or

cob. He is without doubt better than any foreign breed now used for polo in England.

The only ponies of foreign blood that I know in England from personal experience to be of the same class as the best English ponies, are

Photo by] [M. H. HAYES.
Fig. 69.—Mr. W. S. Buckmaster's Canadian pony, " Bendigo."

Mr. Mackey's Californian Rex (Fig. 47), Mr. W. McCreery's Follow Me, also a Californian, Mr. Buckmaster's Canadian Bendigo (Fig. 69), Mr Foxhall Keene's American Texina (Fig. 102), Captain Haig's grey Australian pony, and my own Argentine, Langosta II. Probably between two and three hundred ponies are imported for polo into England every year, and this has been going on for several years, so I think the superiority of the English pony is fairly established.

Any of the old breeds of ponies belonging to these islands, whether Shetland, Welsh, New Forest, Exmoor, or Dartmoor, are perfectly useless for polo by reason of their small size and want of pace. I would extend the same remark to all common-bred ponies of larger size, especially those of Hackney blood. The great love of blood entertained by breeders in Ireland makes that country the best in the world for finding ponies suitable for polo ; although I have known but few that have been specially bred for the game in that country. As a rule, an Irish breeder tries to get a hunter, or failing that, a smart trapper ; for his countrymen love to drive a bit of blood. From the Irish animals which are too small for hunters, we get the large majority of our polo ponies. Fortunately, for many generations back in Ireland there have been few sires which were not practically, if not actually, thoroughbred. Even the large majority of the so-called half-bred sires, had the letters "h.b." after their respective names, only because they or one or more of their ancestors, though thoroughbred, were not entered in the stud book, in order to get the 7 lbs. allowance at racing, when that rule was in force. Although several Hackney stallions have been introduced into Ireland, there is not much danger of their contaminating the hunter class ; for the Irish breeders know their business, and are very conservative in their ideas as regards the value of good blood. Up to the present, the majority of attempts at breeding ponies within narrow limits of height have failed, on account of the tendency sires and dams have of "throwing back"; the fillies frequently being too small for polo; the colts, too big. For instance, I have known a filly by a Barb out of a well-bred English mare to be 13.2, and her own brother 14.3; both parents being 14 hands.

Another great difficulty our breeders have to contend with, is the tendency to increase in size which all breeds that are placed under favourable conditions of feeding and health in England manifest. Many sportsmen, led by Mr. Hill, the originator of the Polo Pony Stud Book, are endeavouring by careful selection to establish a breed of ponies fit for high-class polo. If the attempt be possible, these gentlemen are certainly making it in the right way.

The following are instances of first-class English polo ponies :—

Matchbox (Fig. 39), Luna (Fig. 38), Mademoiselle (Fig. 44), Siren (Fig. 42), Nipcat (Fig. 70), Wig (Fig. 71), Sunshine (Fig. 41), Charlton (Fig. 43), Dennis (Fig. 72), and Mickey (Fig. 73), which are miniature 14-stone blood hunters; and Dynamite (Fig. 45), Sailor (Fig. 74), Conceit (Fig, 48), and Little Fairy (Fig. 46), which belong to the miniature steeplechase type.

We all have our own ideas of what is the type for a perfect polo pony, but the best polo judges in England are agreed that the hunter stamp is the right one; because experience has shown us that, though there are some ponies of the miniature steeplechase stamp quite as good as those of the miniature hunter type, there are twenty first-class ponies of the latter type for every one of the former.

We have seen on page 101 that the blood hack is "The Wrong Sort" (Fig. 49).

Matchbox (Fig. 39) and Mademoiselle (Fig. 44) are admitted by common consent to be the best show ponies of the present time, and next to them probably comes Luna (Fig. 38). In 1898 Luna, when younger and fresher, beat Matchbox for championship honours. These three ponies are of the same type, and combine

Fig. 70.—Mr. G. A. Miller's "Nipcat."

the highest quality with substance. They have perfect mouths and manners, and that combination of elasticity and strength which makes a perfect mount. Matchbox's polo performances are of the highest class. She has played in the winning team of seven open cups, four times at Hurlingham, twice at Ranelagh, and once in Dublin, and in many other less important tournaments. Luna has won six open cups, besides many smaller events. Both of them can stay, and

Photo by] [ELLIOTT & FRY.

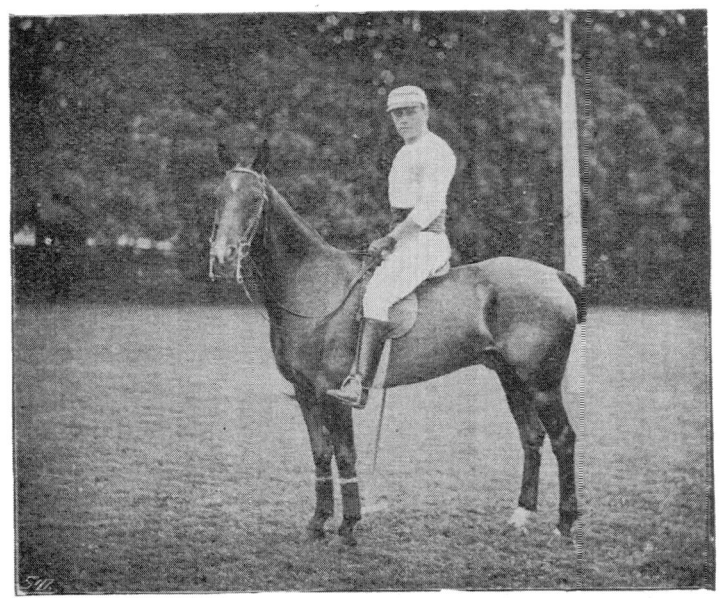

Fig. 71.—Captain Daly's "Wig."

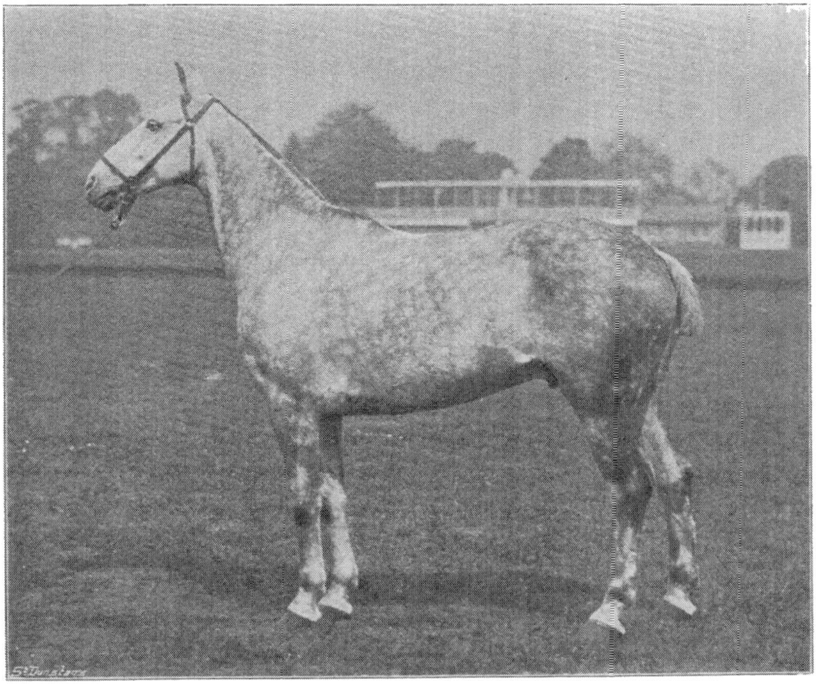

Photo by] [M. H. HAYES.

Fig. 72.—Mr. L. McCreery's "Dennis."

Photo by]   [M. H. HAYES.

Fig. 73.—Mr. L. McCreery's "Mickey."

Fig. 74.—Mr. Harold Brassey's "Sailor."

they always have been ridden for thirty minutes out of the sixty in a tight match.

Siren (Fig. 42) and Nipcat (Fig. 70) are ponies of the same class and stamp as the three just mentioned, but they are not so good from a show point of view, because they are a trifle short in front and carry their saddles a little forward. They have been ridden in all the matches played by the Rugby team for several years. Nipcat's performances are quite unique. I rode her as a four-year-old in the winning team of the Open Cup in Paris in 1894; she has played in four winning Champion Cups at Hurlingham, in two Open Cups at Ranelagh, and in three Open Cups in Dublin. Altogether she has helped to win ten Open Cups. In 1901 she played for thirty minutes in the final of the Champion Cup at Hurlingham, in the Open Cup at Ranelagh, and in the Open Cup at Dublin. Siren's performances are as good, but she has not been as long at the game. In my opinion she is the best forward pony I have ever ridden, as she has more pace than those that I have just mentioned, and is quite as handy. It is a great pity that we know so little about the breeding of these flyers. The pedigrees of Matchbox and Luna are quite unknown; Siren is believed to be by Loved One out of a pony mare; Mademoiselle is by Loved One out of Madame Angot, a favourite old hunter mare belonging to Mr. L'Estrange, of Sligo. Madame Angot was by Munster Blazer, grand dam by Woodpecker, by Birdcatcher. Nipcat is by Buckshot (the sire of Swanshot, Ardcarn, and many other good horses) out of a 14-hand pony mare. Luna, Siren, Mademoiselle, and Nipcat are Irish. Mickey (Fig. 73) and Dennis

(Fig. 72) are two other ponies of exactly the right stamp for polo. They are short, thick, strong ponies, with great pace combined with perfect handiness. It is a mistake to suppose that, because a pony is short and thick, he has not the same good blood in his veins as the long-tailed galloping sort. My experience is that these short, thick ponies often gallop just as fast, and their conformation enables them to start, stop, and turn more quickly than their less closely-put together brethren. In a race of half a mile the cobby-built animal will probably not have a chance against the long-striding thoroughbred; but at polo, where ponies are always turning, stopping, and starting, the compactly-built pony does all these movements with less fatigue. Also, the harder the game and the longer it is continued, the more easily will he turn inside the long striding pony, and will repeatedly gallop quicker for 50 or 100 yards. Mickey and Dennis are very well known as having carried their owner, Mr. Lawrence McCrery, in all the important tournaments of the last few years, including the winning team of the Champion Cup at Hurlingham and of the Open Cup at Ranelagh in 1900. Dennis had previously distinguished himself in the Regimental Tournament when he was the property of Captain Pedder, 13th Hussars. Wig (Fig. 71), Sunshine (Fig. 41), and Charlton (Fig. 43) are heroes of days gone by. Wig and Sunshine were perfect types of the miniature 14 stone blood hunter, but Charlton was perhaps more of the steeplechase type; in fact, she won several races, and distinguished herself in many hard-fought tournaments under the welter weight of the late Mr. "Jack" Drybrough. Wig was the property of Captain Daly, who rode him in the winning team of the Champion Cup in 1894 and 1895. Sunshine was the first pony to help Mr. Buckmaster to make his present reputation as a polo player.

Among ponies of the steeplechase type, Sailor (Fig. 74) is perhaps the best known living example. He won the Champion prize at Ranelagh for the best polo pony in 1897. When he was the property of Mr. Gerald Hardy, he carried the late Lieut.-Colonel le Gallais for the Freebooters, when they won their celebrated victory over Sussex in 1894; in fact, Sailor helped to secure the winning goal by his extraordinary speed and dash. Since 1894, he has been continually playing in first-class polo. In 1898 he fetched the record price of 750 guineas for a polo pony when he was sold by auction. More money has changed hands over him than over any other polo pony. His breeder was Captain Cecil Featherstonhaugh of the Royal Dragoons. Mr. Grogan bought him for £30, and he subsequently fetched on different occasions £250, £400, 750 guineas, 460 guineas, and 410 guineas, making a total of £2,351. He is by Lurgan out of a polo pony which won many races. His own sister is 15 hands high, and his breeder told me that she was never worth more than £25. Sailor is now 12 years old.

Conceit (Fig. 48), who is by Brag, and was bred by a tenant of Mr. L. de Rothschild, is one of the most shapely animals playing. She is perhaps the best of an extraordinary stud belonging to Lord Shrewsbury, who hardly ever buys a short tailed pony. All his ponies are of the steeplechase stamp, and he never rides a racing weed. His animals

12*

have substance as well as quality, and are well up to 13 stone.

Little Fairy (Fig. 46) is one of the few racing ponies I have known to be a success. I bought her at Tattersall's for the Champion Cup of 1897, and she has played in all the big matches for Rugby since, and in the Open Cup at Dublin in 1901, for the "Nomads." Her history is curious. She is by Glen Dale out of Leonora, and her racing name was Tessie. She won a selling race at Newmarket, as a two-year-old, and at four and five she bred foals. After that she was used as a hack, and was once sold at Aldridge's for 16 guineas. I gave 300 guineas for her when she was 13 years old. She is now 17, and although she has been a roarer for some years, she is still able to take her place in the best of polo. She has the temper of an angel, and as she is up to 14 stone, she is very different to the ordinary cast-off from a racing stable.

Dynamite (Fig. 45) is now long past her best days. When she belonged to Mr. J. Peat, she was generally considered to be the best forward pony in England. Certainly I have never seen any No. 1 player as good, or even in the same class as Mr. J. Peat, especially when he was riding his favourite. Dynamite was never the same pony in other hands, probably because of the rule that a pony could not be changed, unless at the owner's risk, at any time, except the intervals between the 10 minutes' periods of play. When Dynamite was at her best, a pony could be changed, and ten minutes were allowed whenever the ball went out of play. Under the old rules, a pony that could not stay was as valuable as a pony that could hold out, but nowadays no pony is in the first class unless he can go from end to end of a ten minutes' period without tiring or pulling. An absolutely first class pony never pulls. The large majority of ponies begin to pull when they are tired, because they cannot stand the constant stopping, turning, and starting afresh.

Photo by]   [M. H. HAYES.

Fig. 75.—A good stamp of light weight thoroughbred up to 12 stone.

Fig. 75 is a good stamp of a light weight pony, and Fig. 76 of a middle weight pony. Snipe (Fig. 77) is a nice type of a 14-hand pony.

Nancy (Fig. 78), the property of Mr. Leaf, is a beautiful Welsh mare, and is a very favourable specimen of her breed. Though her pedigree is unknown, she looks thoroughbred. I know nothing personally about Wales as a place for breeding ponies. The few which I have bought out of Welsh droves have not been a success. Welsh ponies are undoubtedly very hardy, and they would produce suitable polo ponies if sufficiently crossed with thoroughbred blood. I would advise anyone who intended to purchase young ponies in Wales for polo, to be very careful about pedigree, and to have nothing to say to under-bred blood.

Spruce (Fig. 79), the property of Mr. J. R. Walker, is by Saracen, an imported Syrian; dam, Sprightly, by Awfully Jolly (or The Barb), out of the English polo pony, Lady Golightly. Spruce is inter-esting from a breeder's point of view, as he shows the effect of crossing English pony mares with Barb and Syrian blood. His dam's sire, Awfully Jolly, is a celebrated polo-playing Barb, which was imported by the Earl of Harrington, and lately sold by him to the Irish Congested Districts Board, which has sent him to stand in the West of Ireland. While standing at Elvaston, he got many good ponies; among others, Ali Baba, Aunt Sally, which sold for £200; Ally Sloper, £200; Abbott, £150; Antelope, Arthur Roberts, Abbess, and many others.

Spruce is a marvellously speedy pony. He stands about 14 hands; has nice shoulders and plenty of substance.

Saracen, the sire of Spruce, is a handsome Syrian Arab which Mr. John Walker used for stud purposes at Barton, and which he gave me in 1893. I sent him to stand in County Sligo. Both Sprightly and Lady Golightly were good polo ponies.

[M. H. HAYES.
Fig. 76.—A good stamp of a pony up to 12 stone 7 lbs.

Fig. 77.—14 hand pony, "Snipe."

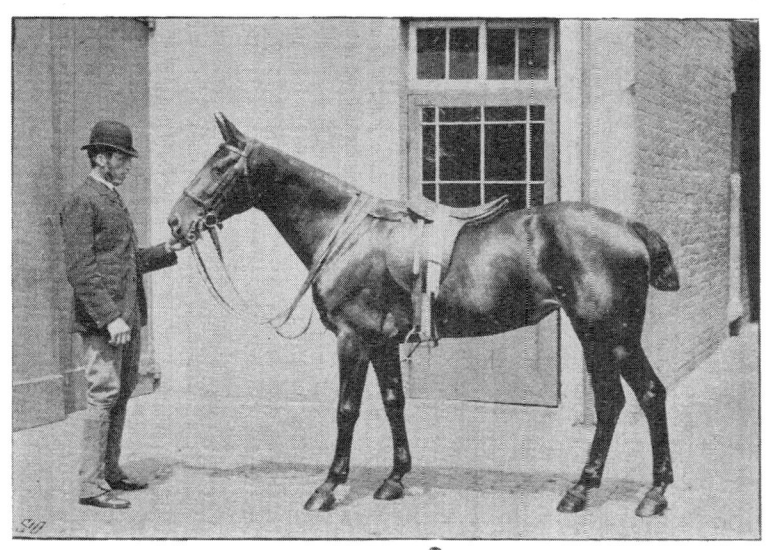

Fig. 78.—Mr. Leaf's Welsh mare "Nancy."

Fig. 79.—Mr. J. R. Walker's "Spruce."

ARABS.

We get almost all our Arabs from India, Bombay being their port of disembarkation from Bagdad, *viâ* the Persian Gulf. They generally arrive in Bombay during the months of September and October, at which time high prices are asked by the Arab dealers for anything of good class. In fact, it would be difficult to get a newly-imported pony, with bone, good shoulders and quality, for less than £50.

During November, 1894, I bought ten ponies in Bombay, after having had about 500 animals paraded before me, and having ridden at least 150. I bought every pony between 14 hands and 14.2 which I could find with good shoulders and sufficient bone. My speculation was not a success from a pecuniary point of view, because I got only two really good ponies out of the ten I brought home. The vast majority of animals in Bombay would not be worth £10 apiece at home; most of them being coarse and leggy, and having bad shoulders and ewe necks. As a rule, these brutes have only a small dash of Desert blood. The best time for buying cheaply in Bombay, though naturally at a large sacrifice of power of selection, is during the months of February and March, when the dealers, with the prospect of their customers flitting to the hills or England, are anxious to sell off, lest their horses be left on their hands during the long hot weather.

Johnnie (Fig. 80) is a chestnut Arab horse which was bought in Bombay by the late Lieut.-Colonel le Gallais in July, 1891. Unlike most Arabs, he was not easy

to train.   Although he played in the winning team
of the tournaments of 1891 and 1892, his owner did
not consider him to be a first-class player until the
following year, when he played him at Hurlingham.
While in India, he grew over height for polo in that
country ; but coming under the Indian rule for " Existing Polo Ponies," he obtained a certificate and was
allowed to play.   After Captain le Gallais had put
him on board the troopship, in which the pony went
with him to England, he received a telegram containing an offer for the pony of 2,500 rupees, which
he refused.   Johnnie now measures 14.1¼.   He has
beautiful shoulders, well-set-on head and neck, sound
legs, sloping pasterns, and good feet.   He looks a
trifle narrow behind, but his quarters are long and
strong, his gaskins muscular, and his hocks well
shaped.   Though by no means a showy pony, he is
a capital type of a well-bred, wear and tear Arab.   He
played in the winning team of the Paris International Tournament, 1894, and of the Champion
Cup of the same year.   I bought him on the day
of the final of the County Cup, and rode him in
that match.   I afterwards sold him to Mr. John
Walker.   Captain Tilney's Royal, which is one of
the best Arab polo ponies that ever came to
England, has had an exceptionally long career at
the game.   I played him in his first tournament at
Calcutta, in 1888, for the 17th Lancers, which we
won.   He has taken part in almost every match
played by the regiment since that date, and is
now (February, 1902) taking his ease in Ireland,
while his owner is in South Africa.   In the last
match in which I saw him take part, he carried his

owner in the winning team of the Irish Regimental Cup of 1899. Although he is now 18 years old, I hear he is sound and well, and that there is no reason why he should not again play.

Grey Dawn, the property of the late Mr. Kennedy, is the best Arab I have ever known in England.

Photo by]   [ELLIOTT & FRY.
Fig. 80.—The late Lieut.-Colonel le Gallais on his Arab pony "Johnnie."

For substance and weight-carrying power, he is more like an English pony than an Arab, although he clearly shows all the characteristics of his Desert origin. In 1894 he unfortunately broke a pastern bone and has been sent by Lord Harrington to the stud at Elaston.

Mr. Tilney's Royal, Captain Daly's Cheeky Boy, Mr. Kennedy's Umpire, Captain Wise's Seagull,

Mr. Nickall's No Name, Captain Burns' Blue Blood, and some which Lord Milton imported in 1893, are very good specimens of Arab blood.

Probably the best Arab pony which has played in India for some years, is Snow (Fig. 81), who belonged to Captain de Lisle, of the Durham Light Infantry. He won thirty-one races all over India, including the biggest pony steeplechases. He won four first prizes in the Bombay Horse Show in 1895, including the pony-jumping prize and that for heavy-weight polo ponies. He played in the winning team of many polo tournaments, and is, moreover, one of the best-looking Arabs I have ever seen. He is now at the stud in Australia.

The chief characteristics of the high-caste Arab are :—

1. Long, strong and sloping pasterns.
2. Long back ribs.
3. Roundness of barrel behind the girths.
4. High setting on of tail.
5. Width of forehead and jowl.
6. Large eyes and nostrils.
7. Flat, muscular loins.
8. Fineness of the hair of the mane and tail.
9. Thin growth of the hair on the tail.
10. Habit of carrying the tail in one fixed position and generally to one side.

Their chief defects are :—

1. Short and heavy shoulders.
2. Calf knees.
3. Sickle hocks.
4. High on the leg.

However great a fault the possession of sickle

hocks may be in a racehorse, I do not object to them in a polo pony ; for though it may detract from speed, the fact remains that ponies with sickle hocks are usually very handy.

The best Arabs are bred in the Desert, and gener-ally bear rope marks just above the hocks. The well-

Fig. 81.—Lieut.-Colonel de Lisle on his Arab pony "Snow."

bred ones as a rule belong to the large district of Anezah, where are found Humdani Somree, Saklowi, Khailan Krush, Yenidji Shumarr, and other castes. I may remark that Nejid is a part of Anezah. Usually, the name of a caste is taken from that of the foundation stallion of that breed. If it be a double name, the second one is that of the foundation mare. Many so-called Arabs have never seen the

Desert, and are really Persians, or natives of the Euphrates Valley. In India, these animals generally go by the name of Gulf (Persian) Arabs.

EGYPTIANS.

There are many ponies bred in Egypt, where they are called Bellady ponies, to distinguish them from Syrians, which are imported in large numbers for remount and other purposes. They are so interbred with Syrians that it is not always easy to tell one from the other. The Syrians, among which we may often see Arabs of the highest caste, all conform more or less to the Desert type, although some of them are coarse. The Egyptian ponies are of all sorts and shapes, without any special characteristics of a well-defined breed. Egyptian dealers call all their ponies Syrians, so as to get more money for them.

Mr. T. B. Drybrough tells me that each of the six Egyptians which he had in his stables at one time, differed altogether in type and conformation from the other five; an experience which is similar to that which I have had with these animals. He informs me that their special characteristic, leaving out exceptional cases, is their lithe, flexible style of going, and that they glide along in their gallop with the smooth motion of a thoroughbred, but without the sharp, steel-like spring of the three-quarter bred English pony. Many of them drag their hind legs behind them, which causes them to lose time in their stride. This, which is their most common fault, is due to their being weak in the loins. Although they vary just as much as other breeds, they are, as a rule, bold enough, and when taught, will hustle well. Their individual power of going through deep ground depends, of course, on their respective conformation. In the Delta they are accustomed to travel through very deep sand. Egyptian ponies may not compare favourably with high-caste Arabs as regards bone, shortness of legs, roundness of barrel and flatness of loins; but they have, as a rule, better shoulders. As the Egyptian authorities found that the purchases of the English sojourners removed out of the country their best horseflesh, and enhanced the increased difficulty of obtaining remounts, they issued such stringent regulations respecting the export of horses, that it is now very hard to get horses out of Egypt, although an odd one or two may be exported by judicious management.

In the winter of 1890-91, the ordinary price for Egyptians was from £12 to £18; and for Syrians, from £5 to £10 more. Those which had shown any racing pretensions fetched from £40 to £60; but prices have gone up since those days. Raw ponies used to cost just as much as trained ones; for in nine cases out of ten, neither Syrian nor Egyptians gave any trouble to train. In 1891, my brother officers and I sent home about twenty-five ponies, not one of which turned out badly. The majority of them were Syrians; but of those which I know were Egyptians, the best were Spring, Magnet, Lancet and Modena.

Spring, in 1892, unfortunately died. He was the best light-weight Egyptian I have ever seen, and was an extraordinarily good jumper. Captain Renton owned and played him for two seasons at Hurlingham.

Lancet I bought originally for £5. He has been through many hands since then, and is a good pony. He fetched £175 when sold in 1894.

Modena, who was only 13.3, was a wonderfully good little light-weight pony.

The Rake, a bay pony, 14.0¾, was the property of Mr. T. B. Drybrough, who imported him in 1892. He won races at Cairo. He was a smart, handy pony, had excellent bone, and strong, well let-down hocks. Although his hind legs were inclined to stream out behind him, this habit did not appear to affect his pace or powers of turning. He carried his tail high, and looked very like a Syrian.

Khalifa (Fig. 82) is a chestnut pony 14.1, owned by Mr. T. B. Drybrough, who imported him at the same time as The Rake. Khalifa cost £13 up country in 1892, in which year he won over hurdles at Cairo. He goes well in all his paces, has wonderfully good shoulders, clean, well-shaped legs, and is very quick. His Egyptian origin is chiefly betrayed by his hocks being very close together. He is rather slackly coupled, is a trifle long on the leg, and is shaped rather like a mule.

Both The Rake and Khalifa have carried their owner in three County Cup Tournaments, and have been on two occasions in the winning team. They carried their fourteen stone with ease, and went through deep ground well. Hurlingham was like a slough in 1893, and was by no means light going in 1894.

All the Egyptian ponies I have mentioned were great successes in their time; but I do not believe that any of them would be of much use in first-class polo nowadays. The class of pony in ordinary use has enormously improved, and I believe there are quite twenty good English ponies at present for every one that was playing in 1895.

SYRIANS.

All the Syrians now in England have been imported from Egypt, to which country they are brought from

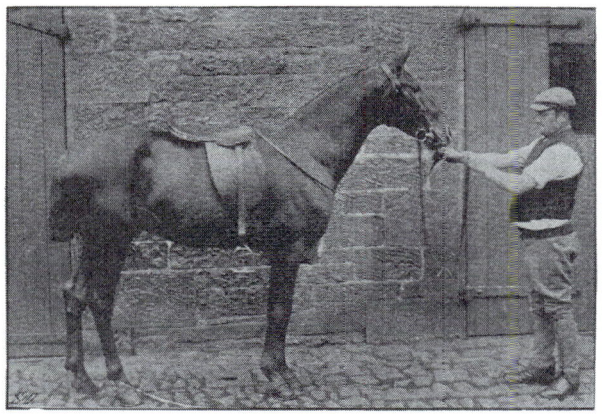

Fig. 82.—Mr. T. B. Drybrough's Egyptian pony " Khalifa."

Beyroot. As the exportation of horses, except to Egypt, is prohibited by the Syrian authorities, and as the Egyptian Government will not allow them to be sent out of their country, the market for Syrians, as well as for Egyptians, is closed to English importers, unless in exceptional cases, worked by interest or bribery. The only feasible way of getting horses or ponies out of Syria is *viâ* Bagdad, which is far too roundabout a route for practical purposes.

The term " Syrian " includes Desert-born Arabs which

13*

have been brought into Syria, as well as the horses, or rather ponies (for they seldom exceed 14.2 in height) which have been bred in that country.   The true Arabs which figure as Syrians, come from the same tribes as do those which are shipped to Bombay.   In fact, an Arab dealer, from whom I bought two ponies in Bombay, in November, 1894, swore to me that they had been marched from Syria to the Persian Gulf, from whence they were shipped to Bombay.   Representatives of the Yenidji and Saklowi breeds are to be found, though not very frequently, in Egypt, where we may sometimes see as high-caste Arabs, particularly in the possession of rich natives, as in India.   The Syrian proper is a coarser animal than the Desert Arab, upon whose management and breeding more care is expended.   As far as polo is concerned, I put the Syrians proper on a par with true Arabs; as I have found just as large a proportion of good players among the former as among the latter.   They are, as a rule, easier to train than Arabs.   Most Syrians show the characteristic points of the Arab fairly well, except that their heads are bigger, their ears longer, their tails set on lower and not carried in such a flag-like manner, and they lack quality.   As far as looks go, they are about half-way between Barbs and Arabs, though they are longer from the hip to the hock than Barbs, which are inclined to be goose-rumped.

Sinbad (Fig. 83), having come from Syria to Egypt, whence he was imported to England by Mr. J. R. Walker, is classed as a Syrian, although it is more than probable that he is a true high-caste Arab. When the ground was hard, he was one of the best light-weight ponies in England ; but, like most of his breed, he was not so good under a heavy burden and in deep ground. In his day he was a brilliant player, fast, had a mouth of silk, and was wonderfully quick to get an opening, as he was round and off before many other ponies would have begun to stop. His only defective point is that, like many other Arabs, he is

Photo by]   [M. H. HAYES.
Fig. 83.—Mr. J. R. Walker's Syrian pony " Sinbad."

a little short in front ; but this is redeemed by the perfect freedom with which he moves his shoulders.

Peter (Fig. 84) is of a totally different stamp from Sinbad, his Arab origin being betrayed only by his long, strong pasterns, round barrel, wide forehead, large, intelligent eyes, wide nostrils, and well-shaped sensible-looking head. He is rather high on the leg and long in the back. In the gallop he sprawls somewhat, and goes much higher than Arabs usually do at this pace ; but he has capital shoulders, long quarters,

big, well-shaped hocks, perfect fore legs, and plenty
of bone.   I bought him in 1890, at Cairo, for £21,
and without any preliminary training took him
straight on to the polo ground, where he played
perfectly, in a snaffle bridle, on the very first occasion.   I knew him to be an exceptionally hard, good
animal, and a perfect player ; but as I considered him
too slow to be first-class at the game, I kept him. as
the slave of the establishment.   He often carried me
six miles down the hard high road in less than half-
an-hour to the racecourse in the morning, and played
polo on the same afternoon.   I took him home in
1891, after having added him to the list before starting.
Thinking that he was not of much value for polo, I
lent him to a child to hunt all the following winter, and
sold him early in the spring for £60.   As he proved
unsuitable to his buyer, he was returned to me, so I
began to play him again, and soon discovered that, in
the meanwhile, he had acquired the one thing, namely,
speed, which he had before lacked to make him a polo
pony of the highest class.   His great improvement in
pace appears to have been undoubtedly due to his
having been " well done " all the winter on the best of
English hay and oats, and having been galloped with a
light-weight on his back.   The practice which he had
through heavy ground enabled him to go faster on our
soft English turf.   Purchasers of foreign ponies should
remember that these animals greatly improve on good
English food, and that they are seldom at their best
until they have been a year or two in this country.
The same remark applies to Arab horses in India
which get into the hands of careful owners.

In the following spring, Peter fetched 250 guineas at

auction. He is one of the few foreign ponies I have known to be equally good whether the ground is hard or soft, and to be able to stay. I have seen him play for fifty minutes out of an hour in a tight match, and I have ridden him on more than one occasion for thirty minutes on end. Although he is not exceptionally

Photo by]   [M. H. HAYES.

Fig. 84.—Syrian pony "Peter."

speedy, he goes quite fast enough for his rider to be able to hold his own, even now in ordinary games and in second-class matches. His chief merit, however, is that he knows the game thoroughly, that he can play it perfectly by himself, and that he always does his best, no matter who is on his back.

Although Syrian ponies as a rule are not able to carry a heavy weight, say fourteen stone, fast and well at polo through heavy ground, with strength to hustle

and to resist the bumps of big, strong English ponies ;
they are able, as remounts, to travel under enormous
burdens in their own country.   I used Peter in Egypt
as second charger, all the squadron being mounted on
similar animals.   Our men in full marching order
weighed, on an average, 18 st. 7 lbs.

BARBS.

Under the term " Barbs " is included all the ponies
which are bred along the northern coast of Africa
(especially Algiers and Morocco), excepting Egypt.
Large numbers are imported from Tunis to Malta, and
from Algiers and Tangiers to Gibraltar.   Almost all
the ponies at these two English stations are Barbs.
My experience of ponies of this breed, both personally
and with those belonging to other people, is that they
are a good deal inferior to either Arabs or Syrians.
Out of all the Barbs I have played and seen played in
1894-95, amounting probably to about seventy, Mr.
John Walker's Sherry, M. Boussod's Trappist, Lord
Charles Bentinck's Algiers and Tangiers, and Captain
Barclay's (10th Hussars) Abdullah are the only five
which could be called first-class.   Among others which
I saw were the ponies of the Spanish Polo Team of
the Brothers Larios, who were mounted entirely on
Barbs in the International Tournament at Paris in
1894.   As they were allowed to be the best team on
the Rock, we may presume that they were mounted
on the pick of that place.   We had four Barbs in our
stable in 1893, and six in 1894 ; but out of all of
them Trappist was the only first-class player.   He
was imported from Gibraltar by Captain C. Gordon
Mackenzie, and now belongs to Mr. Ashton of the

2nd Life Guards, who was playing him in 1901. My Editor, who broke in a large number of ponies at Gibraltar and Malta, and who made particular inquiries respecting the galloping powers of Barbs, shares my opinion as to their inferiority to Arabs. He regards them to be, on an average, about three stone worse on the flat, say, for a mile, than Arabs of the same height ; and looks upon them, in comparison to the sons of the Desert, as a particularly sulky,

Fig. 85.—Mr. J. R. Walker's Barb pony "Sherry."

spiritless breed. Mr. T. B. Drybrough (and so did the late Mr. Moray Brown) thinks highly of Barbs. Mr. Drybrough maintains that the reason why few Barbs are exported, is that the dealers cannot afford to buy really good ones, which the rich natives keep for themselves.

In my opinion the faults of Barbs for polo are :—

1. Want of speed.

2. Inability to go through deep ground, stay, or carry weight.

3. The possession of at least one, if not several, vices, such as refusing to face a scrimmage or a back-hander, refusing to hustle, looking round and trying to savage other ponies instead of doing their best in the game, and being sluggish.

4. Want of courage, and tendency to become jady if hurt by ball or stick.

5. Softheartedness, which is often shown by their doing well enough in ordinary games ; but cutting it when forced to go faster than they like, and against better ponies than themselves.

6. Lastly and worst of all faults : their liability to cross their legs, or be knocked over by heavy English ponies.

Their merits are :—

1. Soundness, and ability to stand with impunity the ill effects of galloping on hard ground.

2. Handiness, quickness in learning the game, and the possession of good mouths.

3. Cheapness.

4. Facility for being played by weak or indifferent horsemen.

The Barb is essentially a pony for an unambitious player, and does well enough for ordinary club games, or in places like Malta and Gibraltar, where they are not called upon to meet animals of good class, or heavier ponies than themselves.

Barb blood, for instance, Lord Harrington's Awfully Jolly, has nicked with our English mares. I think, however, that equally satisfactory results could be obtained by a cross with a high-caste Arab.

The points of Barbs are much the same as Syrians, except that they are more goose-rumped. They are frequently high on the leg. As a rule, they are cow-hocked, narrow, and split up. They have almost always excellent legs and feet.

Sherry (Fig. 85), a bay gelding, is the best and fastest Barb I have ever seen. Mr. John Walker, who still owns him, bought him from Major Peters (4th Hussars), in 1892. He has good shoulders, perfect mouth, is marvellously handy, and quick at starting.

Fig. 86.—Argentine pony.

ARGENTINES.

In 1896 and 1897, we had the pleasure of two visits, from Buenos Ayres, of polo teams mounted on Argentine ponies. As almost every year players come over for a holiday from that place, and bring their ponies with them, our knowledge of these animals has been considerably enlarged. In London and elsewhere, these teams earned a good reputation for play, dash and combination in the game ; but their ponies, with a few exceptions, were too slow to allow them to compete on even terms with well-mounted English teams.   Mr. Scott Robson, the Back of both Argentine teams, always has big, strong 14.2 ponies, which have to be really good to carry their owner, who walks nearly sixteen stone.   Among his large stud, I liked Langosta and Bismarck best.   Langosta thoroughly justified the high opinion formed of him ; for he turned out by far the best Argentine pony we have seen. My brother and I played him in the winning team of the Champion Cup and Ranelagh Open Cup of 1897, after which I sold him to Captain Renton, who has ridden him in all the first-class tournaments played in London since that time.   Langosta has now, in 1901, for the second time, come into my possession and has played in all the matches of the Rugby team this year. I sold Bismarck to the late Mr. " Jack " Drybrough, who played him in the Champion Cup in 1898, and in many other first-class tournaments.   Moloch, a black gelding, turned out well, although he is not as speedy as the other two.   Mr. Spender Clay played him for three years in good company.   Orsino was another good one.   He was landed in 1896, was subsequently well known as the property of the late Lord Kensington, and is still playing well with Mr. Brassey.

In 1897, Mr. Balfour imported a large number of ponies, among which were Slavin and Sandow, that were played by my brother in the winning team of the Champion Cup of that year.   There were many other good ponies in that lot, but few of them were fast enough to compete against first-class English ponies.

I look upon Argentines as really good useful animals in second class company, especially for a beginner ; but with the exception of Langosta and Bismarck, I have not found them up to Champion Cup form. Their chief drawback, particularly for a weak rider, is that they take a great deal of driving. Fig. 86 is a good type of an Argentine pony.

NORTH AMERICANS.

After English and Australian ponies, North Americans are probably the best. Australians are of nearly pure English blood, and are reared in a splendid horse-breeding country. Consequently, there is probably little or no difference between them and our home stock. The average North American pony seems to have more pace than the Argentine, but not so much stamina as the English pony. Only the very best of them are up to first-class form. Although a large number of them has been imported during the last two or three years, very few have gained a high reputation.

Mr. Mackey has brought over several of which I think the best are the Californian Rex (Fig. 47), Cap, Tom and Brady ; Mr. Mackey has played all these ponies continually in first-class matches and they seem, with their owner up, to be able to compete with the best of English ponies. Mr. Mackey used to own some very good English ponies, but he has given them up, as he finds the Americans easier to ride. Mr. Foxhall Keene has a fine stud of American ponies, of which the best are probably Texina (Fig. 102) and Chief (Fig. 103). Express (Fig. 104) is also good.

Although few American ponies are up to tip-top
form, they are really useful, hardy, handy animals,
especially those which have been employed after cows,
as it is almost impossible to knock them off their
legs.

Mr. Thorn used to get all his ponies from Texas,
and is invariably well mounted. He tells me that

Fig. 87.—Texan pony " Ronald."

many of the ponies there are very well bred, owing
to the presence of a large number of thorough-bred
sires. He finds that the best ponies are three-
quarter pure blood (by a thorough-bred out of a
dam by a thorough-bred), as in Ireland, or by a
thorough-bred out of a good broncho. In Texas,
there is a good deal of racing over short distances,
and we accordingly find many of these ponies to be

extraordinarily speedy. Baron le Jeune is beautifully mounted on Texan ponies.

Rondo (Fig. 87), the property of the Hon. William Anson, of Coleman, Texas, is· one of the best and cleverest ponies ever seen in that country.

Manita (Fig. 88) is a Texan cow-pony, which was imported in 1895 by Mr. George P. Millen. My brother and I played her in several matches and

Fig. 88.—Mr. F. Menzies' Texan pony " Manita."

tournaments that season. She is a perfect polo pony, and is very easy to play. Though not as fast as some English ponies, her extreme handiness makes up for a good deal of her deficiency in speed. She is good enough to play Back on in ordinary company.

I wrote the above description of Manita in 1896. She now belongs to Mr. Menzies, who has owned her for the last two or three years. He finds her quick enough to play No. 2 in any company. He is very

well mounted, and I am inclined to think that Manita
is his favourite pony ; I suppose she has got faster
with age ; anyhow I saw her playing well in the
Champion Cup, Ranelagh Open Cup and Dublin
Open Cup of 1901.

CALIFORNIAN PONIES.

There must be many good ponies in California, when
we see such examples of the breed over here as Rex
(Fig. 47), Follow Me, and Santa Romona (Fig.
89). As a rule, it is not easy to find out from what
part of the continent American ponies come, but I
should think it not unlikely that California sup-
plies a fair proportion. They probably keep most
of their best ponies for their own use, as Mr. Charles
Raoul Duval told me he had sold a pony in
California for £300, and that he knew another which
fetched £600.

Rex and Follow Me, I believe to be about as good
as any English ponies, and I have had plenty of
opportunities of judging, for I have played against
them very often.

Santa Romona, which now belongs to my youngest
brother, is a marvellously handy pony. She has been
through many hands ; on one occasion she was sold at
Tattersall's for fourteen guineas, and on another she
fetched twenty-six guineas. Her record for 1901,
however, is a good one. Between May 15th and
September 7th, she played in 40 matches, in 35 of
which she was on the winning side ; that is, she
played on an average five matches every fortnight.
She played in the winning team of the Champion Cup
at Hurlingham, the Open Cup at Ranelagh, the Open

Cup in Dublin, and the Public Schools Cup at Ranelagh in 1901.

MEXICANS

are very handy, and as a rule have perfect mouths ; but they are generally deficient in speed. Mr. Escandon kindly lent me two very good ones in Paris

Fig. 89.—Mr. C. D. Miller's Californian pony "Santa Romona."

in 1895. They were easy to play, quick and handy, but hardly up to my weight, which, with a comfortable saddle, is about twelve stone.

MONTANA PONIES

are, in Mr. Thorn's opinion, handy and good-looking ; but from having been reared in an alkaline district

14

(how that fact affects them, I cannot say), they are
not good stayers.   It is very difficult to get the
best ones.   Mr. T. B. Drybrough, who imported a
batch, says the same thing about the difficulty of
obtaining a satisfactory selection.   They are generally
spoiled in breaking.   The young ones, being out on
the ranche, cannot be measured and examined.
Owners do not like selling a picked one, but expect
purchasers to take a car load of eighteen or more at
an average price.   On open ranches they are
handled only once a year.   With the thermometer
at —40° F., early spring shipments are hard to
effect.   The greatest difficulty is to get on the
other side a friend who can be trusted to buy the
proper article.   My brother once bought in the
North of Ireland a pony (Paddy, late Buffalo Bill)
which was known to be an American only on account
of the brand on his quarter, and which, in appearance, speed, and every other requirement, was just
as good as an English pony.   It is therefore probable
that he comes from Texas, and that he is three-
quarters thoroughbred.   I am certain that out of
a batch of raw American ponies, the proportion of
good ones would not be large enough to make the
speculation profitable.   I am told that really good
cow-ponies are so rare that their owners will not part
with them, even at long prices.

I daresay there are many other districts in the vast
continent of North and South America where ponies
are bred ; but the foregoing countries are the only
pony-breeding ones of which I had been able to get
any information.

Before the year 1894, very few American ponies

appeared on English polo grounds ; but during the last few years, Americans and Argentines have come in large numbers, and have completely cut out all other foreign breeds in the estimation of our players, on account of their nearer approach to the attributes of English ponies. They are sure-footed, and many are up to weight and fairly fast. For further remarks on American ponies, see pages 306 to 308.

Fig. 90.—Gulf Arab "Spec."

GULF ARABS OR PERSIANS

are not as good as Arabs, and in no way suitable for importation into England. Spec (Fig. 90) was a good pony in his day, but would be of no use now.

INDIAN COUNTRY-BREDS.

I know only of three Indian country-breds which have been imported into England for polo. One was

14*

a tiny little 12.2 animal which Captain McLaren brought home and played during several seasons. Several years ago, he used to play him in good games and matches, and it was simply marvellous how well this pony used to carry him. This little wonder was so clever that it could play the game without a bit in his mouth. Another animal of the same nationality was the mare Nettle, which Captain Tilney, 17th Lancers, imported in 1891, and which had played polo in India, though too big for tournaments. She was very narrow and leggy; but though perfect in a slow game on hard ground, was not fast enough for good company, and was no use in heavy ground with any weight on her back. The third was the chestnut mare Namouna (Fig. 91), which the late Lieut.-Colonel le Gallais brought home early in 1893, and which he played at Hurlingham for two seasons. She was a handsome light-weight, and was not unlike a very slight, well-bred English pony, but narrower.

In India I have known a few country-breds just as good as Arabs. Indeed, two of the best polo ponies I have ever seen in India were the country-breds, Joe and Marguerite, the property of Captain Renton. This breed are much more difficult to train than Arabs, being frequently tricky, nervous, bad-tempered, or pullers. Their vices are, I think, chiefly due to the cruel treatment which they receive from the natives before they come into English hands.

In 1889 I owned a couple of exceptionally good country-bred ponies, named New Guinea and Pole Star. I believe that nowadays it is very difficult to get a country-bred which can compete with a good Arab at polo.

Among the distinctive breeds in India we find the Kathiawar ponies, which are light-weight, well-bred animals, with very little bone. They are usually dun in colour, with a dark stripe down the back. The Deccan ponies are smart, hardy little animals, but very small, being seldom more than 13 hands high. The Cutch ponies were the best of the indigenous breeds ;

Fig. 91.—Indian Country-bred pony " Namouna."

but their original type has been almost entirely altered by the introduction of a large number of Arab and English sires into the country. They are very strong, tough animals, with plenty of weight-carrying power and endurance. The best country-bred racing ponies have been bred in the Meerut district, and have had a large dash of English thoroughbred blood.

As a rule country-breds are narrow and very light of bone, and would not be of much use in England, as they cannot carry weight through heavy ground, and few of them are fast enough.

SOUTH AFRICAN PONIES.

Very few South African ponies are worth bringing to this country ; for they are, as a rule, slow, weedy,

Photo by]   [M. H. HAYES.
Fig. 92.—Captain Renton's South African pony "Jess."

and have bad shoulders. From time to time a few good ones have come over, such as Idgit, who made a name for himself when owned by Colonel Rimington of the Inniskilling Dragoons, and Jess (Fig. 92), the property of Captain Renton, was good for a small pony, though slow. The 7th Hussars owned a couple of useful ones.

AUSTRALASIANS.

In Australia, New Zealand, and Tasmania there are a large number of well-bred galloping ponies, which are essentially of English blood, and which differ but little from the home product. They are generally well up to weight, and are coming into fashion enormously

Photo by]   [M. H. HAYES.
Fig. 93.—Colonel Kuper's Australasian pony ' Ophir.''

in India, where they have quite superseded Arabs as first-class tournament ponies.

Colonel de Lisle, a great Indian polo player, and Captain of the Durham Light Infantry Polo Team, is a warm admirer of Australasian ponies, and prefers them to all others for polo in the East. He owned a pair of beauties, and tells me that they were quicker starters, and faster, than Arabs. These Australasian ponies, with all the good points of English ponies, have legs and feet able to stand galloping on hard ground. As a rule, Australasian ponies have less bone than English ponies ; but they can carry weight. The white pony belonging to Captain Neil Haig is probably the best Australian pony in England. She shows great quality, and can carry her owner's welter weight with ease. Ophir (Fig. 93) is an Australian pony which Colonel Kuper, R.A., imported in 1901. This pony played in India, but will not commence his polo career in England until the coming season (1902).

In 1895 the best racing pony in India was Comewell, an Australian, who beat out there all the English ponies, which are the pick of the finest English racing ponies ; for good racing ponies fetch immense sums in India. The best Australian pony Captain de Lisle owned was a bay mare called Mary Morrison (Fig. 94), a winner of twelve races. She played in the winning team of five polo tournaments, and was imported by Colonel St. Quintin, of the 8th Hussars, for the Civil Service Cup. Her pedigree is unknown, but from her performances she must have been nearly, if not quite thoroughbred.

CANADIANS.

Among the very few Canadians which have been imported into this country, the only good one I know is Mr. Buckmaster's Bendigo (Fig. 69), who is a perfect marvel, and is by an imported English thorough-bred. Mr. Buckmaster bought him early in 1898, since which date he has played him in the finals of nearly every important tournament that has taken place in England.

In the final of the Rugby tournament of 1900, he did not get off this pony's back for half an hour ; and he makes a rule of always playing him for three periods of ten minutes in every important match. Bendigo's chief merits are great pace, handiness, and a perfect mouth. He is so easy to play that he never tires his rider. Mr. Lawson brought him to England after having won with him, in Canada, 22 races, most of

Fig. 94.—Colonel de Lisle's Australian pony "Mary Morrison."

which were steeplechases : in fact, he is a perfect type of a miniature steeplechase horse. Mr. Buckmaster got several other ponies from Canada, but none of them was of any use. They were good-looking ponies, but slow, and had bad tempers as a rule. It would not be fair to judge Canadians by one or two small batches, and perhaps in the next few years some enterprising sportsmen will pay us a visit from Canada and bring their ponies with them. We shall then have a fair chance of forming a correct opinion on their merits.

IMPORTATION OF PONIES.

As a last word of advice on the subject of bringing ponies of any breed into England, I can safely say that such a speculation can never pay, unless the shipment consists of the best-trained ponies which the country of exportation can produce. The risks and expenses of travelling and of keep, while raw ponies are being acclimatised and trained, would swallow up all the profits. Only a small proportion of raw imported ponies could possibly turn out good for polo ; and only well-trained, capable ponies fetch a remunerative price in this country. I have seen batches of green ponies brought from India, Australia, the Argentine Republic and America ; but I have never heard of such a consignment doing more than pay very moderate interest on outlay. In most instances, the result was a considerable loss.

For polo in England, English ponies are admittedly the best in the world. Therefore, to compete with them, only the best tried ponies should be brought from other countries.

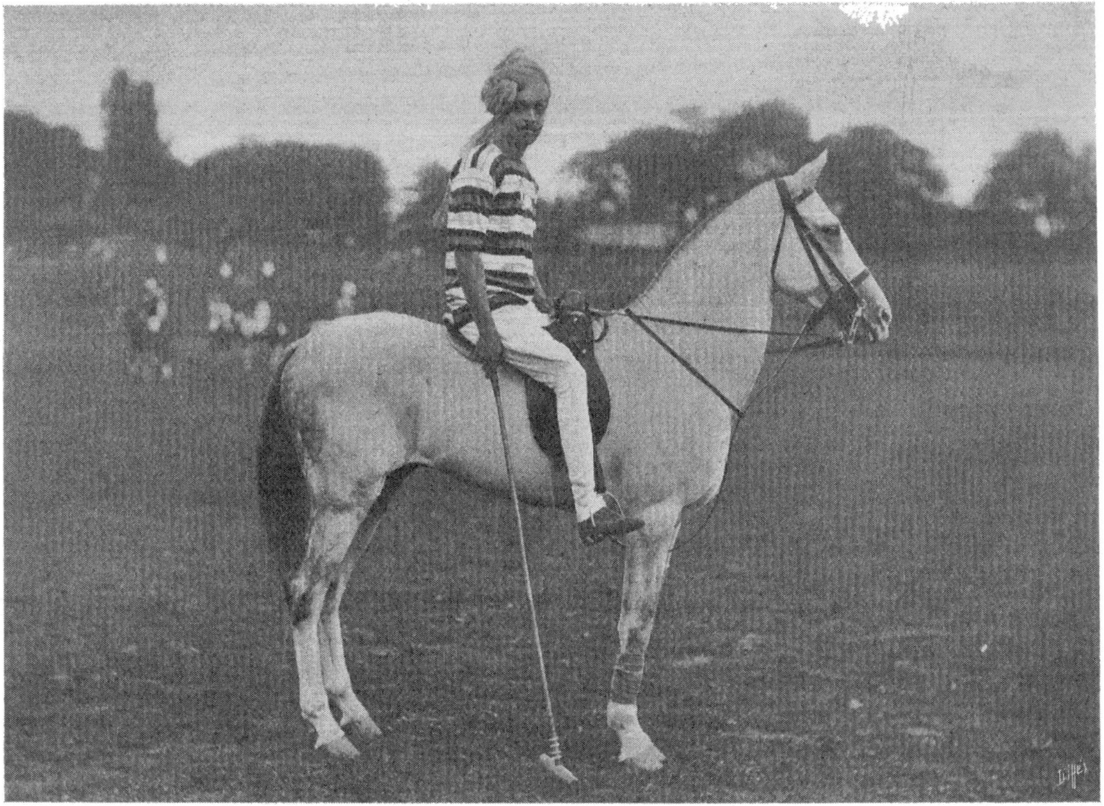

Fig. 95.—Maharajah of Jodhpur.

CHAPTER IX.

POLO IN INDIA.

Remarks on polo in India—Polo ponies—Stable management—The bitting of polo ponies—Indian polo rules—Subsidiary goals—Necessity for the better training of ponies in India—Polo pony club—Polo saddlery required for India.

REMARKS ON POLO IN INDIA.

In India, polo is far more general than in England, and enjoys many advantages that cannot be obtained in this country. There, ponies are more plentiful, cheaper, and easier to train. Polo is played all the year round, and is as popular among Anglo-Indians ·as cricket is among Englishmen at home.

Life in an Indian station must have been very dull thirty years ago, before the introduction of polo, lawn tennis and golf, which are now played all over the country. No wonder that our Indian predecessors were afflicted with liver and shortness of temper in the piping times of peace.

To a large section of His Majesty's servants, polo in India is not merely an amusement and a game, but is also a serious occupation, to which a great deal of time, money and trouble are devoted. Polo is now recognised by the majority of our military authorities as one of the most important parts of the training of an officer ; for there is no better riding school than the polo ground, and there is no game or sport which calls into play so many different good qualities, such as coolness, decision, command of temper, pluck, horsemanship, strength, condition, tactics, drill and organisation. The Captain of a regimental polo team should be endowed with all these qualities in no small degree, and the remainder of the team should back him up well, if they are to take a forward position in the annual tournaments.

There are many more fairly good players in India than in England, and faster games can generally be obtained there than on the majority of country grounds in this country. I think the reason for this is that the game is easier to play in India than here ; because the grounds are hard, true and level, and the ponies are smaller and easier to ride than English ponies. In England the grounds when hard are often rough and bumpy, owing to their having been cut up in wet weather. After rain they are frequently so heavy, that it requires much strength and skill to hit the ball well. Therefore, although our English ponies have more speed than the Indian ones, the ball travels faster and easier in India, and players are continually trying to overtake the ball at full pace there, in-stead of steadying for it as in England. Conse-quently there are fewer pauses and scrimmages, the ball is not so often missed, and the game as a rule is faster and better. I here refer to second-class polo, which, after all, is what one usually meets with in both countries. With respect to first-class polo, I can state that I have had equally good games in both countries, and there are on an average just as good players in India as at home. Indeed, many of our best English players began their polo education in the East.

The Indian game is a looser one than the English, and there is much more riding off and hustling in it. Indeed, Indian country-breds and Arabs would have difficulty in standing up against the bumps of which a strong English pony takes no notice, a fact that explains why Arabs and country-breds are unsuitable for English polo. A few authorities have from time to time advocated the abolition of riding off, but the riding off game requires more skill than one in which riding off would be prohibited. It is self-evident that it is easier to hit a goal when we are not interfered with, than when we have a man pushing against our side with all his strength. Again, if I was playing Back and riding off was not permitted, I should say to the No. 1, "Don't touch me," and I should hit a back-hander on the off side, if he came up on my near side, and *vice versâ*. As the game is now played, the Back, if as well mounted as the No. 1, has the best of it ; but if riding off was abolished, he would have very much more in his favour. I once heard a distinguished general officer give his opinion on riding off in a speech at an Indian polo dinner as follows : " I think the man on the ball is like a man after a pig : he should be left alone till he misses it." If this gentleman's ideas were carried out, the game would often degenerate into a tame procession up and down the ground ; for a clever dribbler under such circumstances, if he avoided having his stick crooked, would be able to carry the ball the whole length of the ground, and our present dashing, exciting pastime would become about as lively as a

funeral. Strange to say, this officer's opinions should
have been entitled to some weight; for he was a fine
horseman, very good after pig, and a first-rate all-
round sportsman; but he didn't like being ridden off
at polo. Once when he was playing in a regimental
game, an excited subaltern, who was coming up behind
with the ball, shouted : " Ride the General!" A
furious voice was heard in reply : " Ride the General ?
By Jove, ride the General ! And what next ? " In
Station games, and in second-class polo in England,
the very wrong plan, as I have already pointed
out, is frequently adopted of not allowing a No. 1
to hit the ball at all ; whereas I maintain that No. 1
should hit the ball whenever he can, unless he is told
by the man behind him "to leave it." The No. 2 is
frequently a selfish player who tells the No. 1 to "leave
it," only because he wants to hit the ball himself: a
man who is guilty of such conduct does not deserve
to play in a good team. This restriction of No. 1's
duties is entirely opposed to the principle of interchange of places, which is a marked feature of
scientific polo. It stands to reason that a team in
which each of the four men will be able in all probability to hit a goal, if they get anything like an easy
shot, will have an advantage over one that contains
only three men capable of doing so. If a man is
always playing No. 1 and is never allowed to hit the
ball, he will, from want of practice, be unable to hit a
goal with any certainty when he gets the chance.
Besides, if the No. 1 be a better player, a finer horseman, and better mounted than the Back, he will very
likely get more chances and openings (which it would
be folly not to take advantage of) than those behind him.

A writer who carries great weight and whose name will always be specially connected with Indian polo, is Colonel de Lisle. Indian polo players owe him a debt of gratitude, for having proved to them the possibility of playing on first-class ponies in first-class company for almost nothing. He has shown them that a team of novices can by practice, care, keenness and discipline, be brought into the very front rank ; and he has also written exhaustively for their benefit on subjects connected with stable management and the training of ponies.

POLO PONIES.

The six usual ways of buying a trained pony in India are :

1. When a regiment is going home.

2. After a tournament.

3. When the opportunity of buying a pony which one knows well, is offered. If a trial is given, so much the better.

4. By advertisement, and by going to see the adver- ˙ tised pony.

5. Sending a competent friend to buy an advertised pony.

6. Buying an advertised pony by reputation or by the owner's description.

The first four of these methods are undoubtedly the best. If the intending purchaser knows nothing about horses, he ought to abide by the advice of a competent friend. The sixth method is to be recommended only when reliance can be placed on the accuracy of the description, or when there is no doubt that the pony's reputation has not been overrated.

15

If the man in search of a raw pony likes the appearance of the animal, the first thing for him to do, supposing that either he or his friend is a fairly good judge, is to get a ride on it. He should, therefore, always take a saddle, bridle and martingale with him, if he goes to a fair, and having selected the ponies by their appearance, he should mount them in order to try their paces, mouths, and tempers; for many of the best-looking ones are the greatest brutes to ride. These remarks apply just as much to Arab stables in Bombay as to up-country fairs. I have ridden thirty ponies in a single day in the Bombay stables, and have frequently had to reject a beautiful-looking animal, only because he could not use his shoulders, which is a fault that cannot be ascertained without riding the animal. I may here refer my readers to page 190 for information about the points of an Arab. With regard to country-breds, see my remarks respectively on them and on English ponies; for the ideal country-bred is a miniature 13-stone English hunter. Though such animals are few and far between, I have seen them, and have owned more than one. They are to be found in India; because there is a great deal of thoroughbred English and Arab blood in that country. As regards the respective merits of country-breds and Arabs for polo in India, I unhesitatingly plump for Arabs. Although some of the best ponies I have ever seen in India were country-breds, their average of fair polo ponies is much smaller than that of Arabs, the majority of which will make really good ones. We may find country-breds better than any Arab; but such animals are rare exceptions; and, as a rule, Arabs have more weight, bone, and substance than country-breds, and last much longer. Colonel de Lisle and most other first-class players prefer Australians to anything else for polo in India, and very naturally too ; as they seem to me to combine all the virtues of the English pony, with better legs and feet. Indeed, the best pony I saw in India was an Australian belonging to the Maharajah of Cooch Behar ; and now that the height has been raised to 14.1 I fully expect to see the Australian supersede the Arab in first-class India polo, to almost as great an extent as the Arab has superseded the country-bred. I think I am right in saying that when I played for the 17th Lancers at Meerut in 1888, there was only one Arab pony playing in our team ; all the rest being country-breds. In 1895 I played at Lucknow against the 16th Lancers, who were mounted almost entirely on Arabs, there being only one or two country-breds. The only reason that Arabs may still continue to hold their own, is that Australians are far harder to train ; so that moderate horsemen, who constitute by far the majority of polo players, will always find that Arabs suit them best. Australians have the great advantage over Arabs, of not being nearly so likely to fall. On the whole, I would strongly recommend beginners, if they can do so, to stick entirely to Arabs.

When passing through Bombay, as nearly every newcomer does, the intending polo player should buy, or get a friend to buy for him, an Arab pony. Although Arabs are more expensive than country-breds, the increased cost will be more than made up by the greater probability of success. I am here alluding of course to untrained ponies. Arabs

15*

take a long time to get fit and to learn to gallop ; but they are such sensible, hard, sound animals, and so easy to train, that it is a real pleasure to own them.   Country-breds, though sound and tough, are often fidgety, excitable, and possessed with a pain in their tempers.   Regimental polo clubs, if buying a batch of raw ponies for different men to train, should never touch country-breds ; but should buy Arabs, which will pay better, even at double the cost.   I attribute the great improvement during the last few years in the class of ponies played up-country in India by good teams, to the employment of Arabs.

STABLE MANAGEMENT.

As regards stable management, I cannot do better than refer my reader to *Training and Horse Management in India*, by my Editor, and will limit myself to the following hints :—

1. Ponies should get enough regular work.   If a pony has only one or two days' play at polo in a week, he will require faster work than being merely led about by a syce at a walk.   I always made my syces ride, instead of lead—as is usually the custom in India—their ponies ; for I knew that they could not, on foot, give them a sufficiency of smart walking exercise, which should occupy daily about three hours (say, two in the morning and one in the evening), when the animals are not ridden on off days by the owner.   If ponies are not playing polo regularly, they should have trotting and cantering exercise, as well as walking ; because it puts muscle on, and keeps the wind right.

2. It is well in India to crush the corn, the best mixture of which is quarter gram, quarter bran and half

oats. If oats cannot be obtained, we may give equal quantities of gram, bran, Indian corn, and parched barley. Boiled barley may be given with advantage as an evening feed after a game of polo. Indeed, whether the pony is playing or not, a feed of boiled barley, two or three evenings a week, will be found excellent for the animal's coat and general condition.

3. Lucerne grass should be grown and given by every horse owner in India. Sick horses will eat it when they will touch nothing else. It is far better as a rule than cooling medicine, for horses which are laid up from accidents or other causes. Even when in fast work a little of it does a deal of good. Several crops of it can be grown in the year, and, when once planted, it requires only to be irrigated, in order to make it last several years.

4. Doob (called *hurryalee* in Madras) grass is the most important factor in keeping a pony in good condition, and getting flesh on him. Care should be taken that the grass cutters bring in a sufficient supply of it.

5. Ponies should get every day in their food about 3 ozs. of salt, or a lump of rock salt should be left constantly in their mangers.

6. Chopped rice straw is a good addition to a horse's corn, as it helps him to digest it, and makes him eat slower than he otherwise would do. It is given like hay chaff in England.

7. Unlimited water should be given to every pony. The best plan is to leave a bucket of water in the stall. If we find it empty, we shall know that the syce is to blame.

8. In the cold weather we should see that the

animals have plenty of bedding and clothing.   Nothing knocks off their condition more than to be short of these necessaries ; for they feel cold severely, and Indian stables are draughty.

9. As drainage is difficult to manage in India, mud floors to stables are better than solid ones, which are seldom well made in that country.   The great advantage of the mud flooring is that it can be constantly renewed, the foul portions being removed every morning, and replaced by fresh earth.   In damp climates, such as the indigo districts, that awful scourge "kumry" (paralysis of the loins) would be to a great extent avoided if the floors of the stables were raised about three feet above the level of the ground.

10. Syces should be allowed to exercise ponies only with big, smooth, unjointed snaffles ; not with the thin abominations in ordinary use.   When the ponies are being led, the mouthpiece should be a smooth, round ring, so that, in all cases, more pressure will not be put on one side of the mouth than on the other.   The leading reins should be short enough to obviate the danger of the ponies stepping on them, and getting tripped up, in the . event of the ponies breaking away from their syces, as they are often apt to do.

The following would be a good daily programme of work, grooming and feeding in an Indian polo stable during the hot weather.   The only difference I would advise for the cold weather, would be that the work should begin at daylight.   It should be remembered that too much attention cannot be paid to regularity in the hours of feeding and exercise. If the same thing is done every day at the same hour, syces will soon get into the way of doing the work methodically, which is of great importance ; because regularity of hours has a very beneficial effect on the condition of all horses.

4.45 a.m. Water ; feed with about 1 lb. of grain ; pick out the feet ; remove all dung and other foul matter from the floor ; take up the bedding and put it outside the stable ; remove the clothing ; and rub down lightly.

5.30 to 7 a.m. Exercise ; syces riding.

7 to 8 a.m. Water on coming in, and give an hour's grooming, which should be real hard work for the syces. Vigorous grooming is one of the most important matters in keeping a pony in condition and muscle. If the syces are not looked after, they will simply pretend to work, and will only lightly rub the animal over with a damp cloth. There should on no account be any washing. The syces should be made to pay particular attention to picking out the feet clean and drying them. The grooming should be done systematically with brush and curry comb, supplemented by energetic hand and elbow rubbing, which natives can do well, if they like.

8 a.m. Feed with from 2 to 2½ lbs. of grain, and a small supply of the previous day's grass, which should have been very carefully cleaned. Bed down ; clear the syces out of the stable ; and leave the ponies perfectly quiet, with the chicks down, and the stable darkened.

12 noon. Water and feed with from 2 to 2½ lbs of grain.

At an hour and a half before the time to start polo or for evening exercise, say about 2 o'clock, open the stables, put the bedding out again, and give the ponies another real good dressing.

As soon as the ponies return in the evening, they should be watered, dressed and made comfortable for the night. A big feed of grass may be left with them the last thing.

THE BITTING OF POLO PONIES.

I have been surprised, on inspecting the ponies on several polo grounds in India to find that the majority of them were ridden in Hanoverian Pelhams. I noticed, on one occasion, that out of eight ponies, six were thus bitted. The presumption from this is that such ponies are inclined to " catch hold " a bit, or, at least, that they would do so in lighter bridles. Among the eight ponies just mentioned, there was only one standing martingale, which was too long, and only one noseband, which was too loose to be of the slightest benefit. I am perfectly aware that a few ponies which would pull in any other bridle, go kindly in a Hanoverian Pelham ; but am convinced that, as a general rule, it is better first of all to try the effect of a lighter bit, with a properly applied standing martingale and noseband, than such a severe bit, without these useful adjuncts. The science of bitting is less studied in India than in England, although the need of it is greater in the former than in the latter country ; because, other things being equal, ponies are not under such control in India as at home. One great reason for this is that the ground does not give as good foot-hold for stopping and turning as springy English turf. Another is the smaller size of the ponies. It stands to reason that a big, strong

English pony, being much better up to his rider's weight, is able to stop more readily when going at full speed than a pony which is two or three inches smaller.

I would, therefore, recommend Indian polo players to pay the greatest attention to the question of bitting, which I may briefly define as the proper application of the standing martingale and noseband, and the intelligent selection and adjustment of a bit which gives ample control with the least possible pain.

These remarks of mine must not be taken as applicable to first-class polo in India ; for most of the good players I have seen out there, thoroughly understood the value of having their ponies properly under control, and went the right way to work to attain their object.

INDIAN POLO RULES.

The Indian Polo Rules are under the direction and management of the Indian Polo Association. The Hurlingham Rules and those of the Indian Polo Association are, as regards general principles, almost identical, with the following important exceptions :—

1. Height of ponies.

2. Penalties for fouls and dangerous riding.

3. Time occupied by a match, and rules for changing ponies.

4. Riding off.

5. Subsidiary goals.

6. Rules for left-handed players, and a few minor differences.

On account of many serious and some fatal accidents having taken place, the Indian authorities, headed by the Commander-in-Chief, drew attention to the necessity of making the game less dangerous ; the result being the establishment of the Indian Polo Association and the enforcement of stricter rules.

Under the Indian Rules, the penalties for fouls and dangerous riding are more severe than under the Hurlingham code.

Height of Ponies :—The height of polo ponies in England is 14.2. In India, no pony is allowed to play in a tournament until it has been measured by stewards appointed by the Indian Polo Association, which publishes a register of all ponies that have successfully passed that ordeal. The height has been raised to 14.1.

The rule as regards riding off is, usually, taken in a very much more liberal spirit by umpires acting under Hurlingham Rules, No. 16, than those guided by the Indian Rules. What at home-would be looked upon as "a fair bump ; a bit of an angle perhaps ; but quite safe," would most unhesitatingly be given as a foul by any umpire in India ; and quite right too. English ponies are so big and strong, and so well able to carry their riders' weights, that it is, happily, almost impossible to upset them.

As regards the prevalence of bad accidents, allowance must of course be made for the hardness of an Indian ground, on which a fall is a much more serious business than at home. I have seen some bad falls in India, and have no hesitation in saying that they were caused by the ponies not being up to their riders' weight ; by being blown or tired ; by the fact of the animals being badly trained, wrongly bitted, or out of hand ; or by the riders being bad or reckless horsemen. I am perfectly convinced, and am by no means alone in my opinion, that these are the most fruitful causes of accidents wherever polo is played. But I do not believe that an accident has ever been due to the fact of a pony being an inch or so too big, unless, perhaps, the pony collided with some weak little animal which was greatly over-weighted.

Strict limitation of height, not to exceed 13.3, made the game much more expensive, as it reduced the choice of ponies. There was a very large number of animals which were just over the height, and which, otherwise, would have been suitable for polo. I know nothing more maddening than to take a great deal of time and trouble to make a nice pony perfect at polo, and then to find that it has, in the meantime, grown half an inch too big. The smaller size of the ponies handicapped a heavy-weight in India. In England, it is rather an advantage at polo to be heavy, provided the man can afford to pay for the best of ponies. Some of our very best players ride well over 14 stone on ponies which are able to carry them with the greatest ease; and can gallop even with the light-weights. It was different in India; for small ponies cannot gallop or stop quickly with a welter-weight in the saddle.

With the limit now raised to 14.1, these objections no longer exist, and the game will, I think, be safer and better for men of all weights. I believe that the raising of the height was chiefly due to the good influence of the Inspector-General of Cavalry in India, General Locke Elliot. He knew that 14.1 animals would be of far more use than smaller ones, for military purposes, especially as native cavalry and mounted infantry remounts and chargers ; and that the army would consequently be benefitted by giving encouragement to the importation of Arabs and Australians of that height.   Also, every Indian polo player will be able to ride his ponies hunting, pig-sticking, paper-chasing, or in any other amusement or sport which may turn up.   I know from experience that 14.1 ponies are quite big enough for chargers in South Africa.

Time occupied by a match.—In India, a match is limited to forty minutes' actual play ; in England, to one hour, including all stoppages, except the intervals for changing ponies.   In India, a timekeeper with a stop-watch must be appointed at every match, in order to deduct the odd seconds every time the ball goes out of play, and to time the longer delays when a goal is hit. The result of this is, that matches in India generally last longer than in England, where umpires are responsible for hurrying up the players without waiting for any-one, and where players who change ponies do so at their own risk, except at the end of the ten-minute periods.   In England, no time is deducted except the authorised intervals between the periods of play, or when a man or a pony is disabled from an accident. This plan is certain to be adopted in India before long, with modifications as regards time, and limits to suit the different conditions of play.

In India, a match is often protracted to an unconscionable length ; whereas in England, if men do not take too long to change ponies, it will be over in an hour and sixteen minutes, or thereabouts.   I think it would be a much better plan in India to deduct no time except the specified intervals between the periods of play. In order to allow for the extra time required by this proposed method, an alteration in the length of time occupied by a match would have to be made. For instance, instead of play occupying forty minutes, as is now the rule, sixteen minutes more might be given, or fifty-six minutes in all, split up into eight periods of seven minutes each. This would result in no more actual play than under the present arrangement, but matches would be played off in less time; for a great deal more than sixteen minutes (in addition to the regular three-minute intervals now allowed) is wasted in every match at present. Under the existing rule, it is no uncommon thing to see a match which, including stoppages, should last but little more than an hour, drag itself out into a matter of two hours. It must be remembered that in India the ball goes out of play much more frequently than on an English ground, where, as a rule, there are boards, and where the "going" is not so hard, and is consequently not so fast. If it were found that seven minutes is too long for a pony to play at one time in a really fast match, the whole might be divided up into shorter periods of play; or it might be left, as a matter of private arrangement, to the Captains of sides in an ordinary match, or to the Committee in a tournament, to decide into how many periods of play the match, or series of matches, should be divided. I feel convinced it would make a match more enjoyable both to players and spectators, if no time were deducted when the ball goes out of play; because we would no longer see players strolling up to the middle after a goa is hit, or casually taking their places, when the ball goes out at the side ; because they know that the Umpire will not throw the ball in until every player is in his place. This plan would have the further advantage of removing the uncertainty as to how long a match would last, which is no unimportant matter in a country of brief twilight. Besides, one official less would be required, namely, the man with the stop-watch. At present, to manage a match properly on any Indian ground, four goal referees, owing to the existence of subsidiary goals, are needed : two umpires, a scorer, and a timekeeper, amounting in all to seven officials, which is a number of kind, un-selfish men that is not always easy to find. If the stop-watch could be dispensed with, the duties of scoring and keeping time could be performed without the slightest trouble by one man. At present, it takes all the time and attention of one man to keep the time accurately.

SUBSIDIARY GOALS.

I have no hesitation in saying that subsidiary goals are a mistake, and should be abolished. The primary object in all polo is to hit goals, and the team which cannot do this ought to lose the match. Subsidiary goals are a premium on bad goal shooting. We often see a stronger side make a score of, say, two goals and seven subsidiary ones, against two goals by the weaker side, who evidently took advantage of the few opportu-nities they received, while their opponents made a mess of the numerous chances which their superiority gave them. In such cases, it would only be fair that the weaker side should have a chance of winning the match by playing it out. It may even happen that a match may be won by subsidiaries, without any goal being scored by either side. Surely this is not polo?

NECESSITY FOR THE BETTER TRAINING OF PONIES IN INDIA.

The bad training of the ponies and bad riding of the players is due to the fact that polo is a much more general game than in England. Very many men who go out to the East without ever having been on a horse, or with only very elementary ideas about equitation, immediately start, like good sportsmen as they are, to learn to ride by playing polo. Frequently, not being able to buy a trained pony, they begin on one which knows as little of the game as they do themselves. I know several grounds in India where no one dreams of taking the trouble even to break their ponies to stick and ball before putting them into a game ; nor do they even think of making their new purchases in the slightest degree handy before playing them. If they would take the trouble even to bit their ponies properly and to teach them to stop and turn, and to change their legs, they would make their games of polo a pleasanter and safer amusement for themselves and their friends.

In England, as a rule, polo is played by fairly rich men, who, if they are bad horsemen, can afford the luxury of a trained pony which will not need much riding. Those who have not sufficient money to buy a really good one, usually content themselves with an animal which knows the game, but which is perhaps a bit of a screw, or rather troubled with the slows. Owing to the absence, as a rule, of special training, such animals can rarely be got, particularly up country, in India.

One day, while riding to an up-country ground, on which I had been engaged to play, I apologised to a member of my side, by saying : " I fear I shall be of no use this time, as my pony has never played before." My friend replied : " He is sure to be all right ; *you* will have taken at least the trouble to knock a ball about on him." It amused me to find that I was regarded as an exception to the general rule in that part of India, of not doing anything with a pony to make him handy and reliable before attempting to play him.

My remarks on the bad training of ponies apply only to many station games. I am quite aware that the good polo-playing Rajahs and good polo regiments are just as particular about the training of their ponies, and have as good players, as one ever sees in England. By the Indian Polo Association Rules, in every station where polo is regularly played, a " Station Polo Committee " must be appointed ; their chief duties being to see that there is " no dangerous riding," and that " no pony is allowed to play except it be well broken, properly bitted, and under the maximum height." To judge by some of the ponies I have seen playing on Indian grounds, I do not think that all the Polo Committees are as stringent as they might be on the subject of training ponies. If they insisted on double bridles, standing martingales and nosebands being used on all ponies at all inclined to pull, and on all ponies with snaffles being ordered off the ground, except a few extraordinarily handy ones, they would make the game much safer than it is at present.   I am confident that there is not one pony in five hundred which does not play better in a double bridle than in a snaffle ; 75 per cent. go better with nosebands than without ; and the large majority of Arabs and country-breds should not be ridden without a standing martingale.   A noseband and martingale may be dispensed with, only when a pony is perfectly broken, and when his rider is a really fine horseman, but such a combination is rare in an ordinary station game.

An indifferent horseman can make an ordinary pony handy enough for safety on a polo ground, by teaching him to stop and turn in a riding school.   Almost any-one in India can get sufficient space for this in his "compound," or in some adjoining waste space, where he can enclose a piece of ground thirty yards long and ten yards wide, with a surrounding mud wall, five feet high.   Except in the rains, this will answer the purpose as well as the most elaborate riding school. The floor can be left alone, if it consists of ordinary soil, and will merely require to be occasionally raked over and levelled.

Chapter V. contains information on riding school work ; but if the instructions therein given are too elaborate for a beginner, he can do a great deal with a pony by galloping him round the improvised school, cutting figures of eight, turning about sharp both ways, and stopping dead, on the loudly-shouted word " whoa ! "   All the aids may be incorrect and the horsemanship bad ; but if the novice gets his pony to do all this with a slack snaffle rein, the practice will improve his mount in handiness and safety.

Many a man has said to me, " *My* pony won't play

16

in a double bridle." This may be quite true ; but the reason probably is that the curb chain is put on too tightly or twisted wrongly ; or because the pony has not been broken to it. The owner should break his pony to a double bridle by substituting a leather curb for the steel one, and by protecting the corners of the mouth with leather guards. Then in a few days he will see what a great improvement his pony will have made ; but he must ride him about, and break him in this bridle for some days, before taking him into a game. Arabs and country-breds are so much easier to train than English ponies, that there is really no excuse for the large majority of ponies in India not being handy enough to do away with the serious element of danger which, I am sorry to say, still exists on ordinary Indian grounds.

Another danger, which is by no means confined to India, is the reckless waving of sticks in a scrimmage or at other times, with criminal disregard of consequences to friend, adversary or pony. I know two cases, within the last year or two, of men who have lost an eye from blows of sticks at polo. It cannot be impressed too much on all players that they should keep their sticks low in a scrimmage, and that they should not hit about recklessly. No man should allow his stick to finish in the air, if there is another player within reach.

POLO PONY CLUBS.

The great drawback to polo as compared to every other game, is its expense ; because, in the majority of cases, it is undoubtedly a costly amusement. If a man is capable of training ponies well, there is no

reason why the game should cost him much, either in
India or England. The generality of players, however, are far more apt to spoil a young pony than to do
him good ; and besides, their judgment in the purchase
of animals is frequently at fault, which fact naturally
enhances the cost of the game to them. In order to
help the majority, various systems have been started
in regiments to lessen the heavy expense which polo
entails on individual players. I shall now discuss four
of these systems.

1st. A fund raised entirely by subscriptions, which
may vary from Rs. 2 to Rs. 10 a month for every
officer of the regiment who belongs to the Polo Pony
Club, in order to pay the travelling expenses of the
team to and from tournaments. The help thus given
to members of a team, may prove to be too small to
enable a poor man to play.

2nd. A fund raised in the same manner and with
the same object as the above, but from which in
addition, money may be borrowed without interest for
the purchase of ponies by members, subject to the
approval of the Committee, who have a claim on
such ponies for tournaments.

As a rule, this plan works well ; but although it
enables a man without money to mount himself, it
may be an inducement to get into debt.

3rd. The following is the system which has been
worked with great success by Colonel de Lisle in the
Durham Light Infantry :

A sum of money is borrowed for the purchase of
the first lot of ponies, which are bought raw in the
Bombay stables, and are distributed to the members of
the regiment. A monthly subscription of Rs. 2 is

charged to every officer, and each player is given two ponies, whose stable expenses he has to pay. The ponies are sold off annually, and the funds of the club, which are almost entirely derived from the profit made from these sales, are devoted to paying off borrowed capital, buying new ponies, and paying the expenses of the team to tournaments.

This system has worked admirably under Colonel de Lisle, to whom is due its entire success in the case of his team. It is however doubtful that in most regiments a man who is a fine judge of the raw article, a good buyer, sound organiser, and capable trainer, could be found. I think that in ordinary cases a subscription of Rs. 2 would be too small : because the success of a regimental club will generally depend on subscriptions, and not on the profit of ponies sold. Besides, ponies as a rule should be kept, and not sold annually.

4th. This system is more expensive than the last one, but will I think be found to cost players far less than if they had to buy their own ponies. Its details can vary according to circumstances. If a regiment can afford it, the subscriptions should be fairly high, and I would point out to any Committee which intends to start a club of this kind, that the more money they have at their disposal, the less trouble and anxiety will they experience.

Let us take as an example a regiment numbering twenty-five officers belonging to the Polo Pony Club, of whom fifteen are polo players, and that the club is formed with the idea of supplying each player with two ponies. Non-players can join, if they like, at a monthly subscription of Rs. 5, which will bring

in an annual income of Rs. 600, supposing that all
the ten non-players belong to the club. It is advisable that each player should pay an entrance fee
of Rs. 100 ; but in any case the subscription should
not be less than Rs. 10, with an additional Rs. 5 for
each pony supplied. The entrance fees would bring in
a lump sum of Rs. 1,500, and the subscriptions from
players and non-players and the monthly payments
for the ponies would bring in an annual income of
Rs. 4,200. If from this we deduct Rs. 1,200 as interest
at 8 per cent. on Rs. 15,000 borrowed, the yearly balance
to the good would be Rs. 3,000, a certain proportion of
which might go towards paying off capital, and the
remainder for the purchase of new ponies and tournament expenses. This co-operative polo society scheme
can be worked by any number of players, who would
find that they could thus play more cheaply than by
any other arrangement. It would be easier to carry
out this system in a regiment than elsewhere ; although
there is no reason why a smart Committee should not
work it for a county club in England, just as well as
for a regiment.

If three men can raise enough money to buy nine
ponies, and will carry out the system on exactly the
same lines, entrance fees and subscriptions varying
according to circumstances and the class of pony
required, it will be found that they can work it in the
same manner as if there were twenty or thirty members with fifty or sixty ponies. The only difference is
that the larger the number in the club, the more good
management, care and trouble will be required of the
Committee. One great advantage of this system is
that a man will know exactly how much his polo will

cost him.   If he has two ponies, their stable expenses will amount to about Rs. 50 a month, and he will know that he is spending under Rs. 800 per annum on the game.   If he cannot afford this, he cannot play ; but anyhow he will not be liable for more than this sum ; for the club takes all risk, and he has to find no capital for outlay.

Rich men in a regiment which has a club of this kind can help in a very substantial way, by means of money, and by making no demands on the club for ponies.   Every Polo Pony Club should be simply a co-operative society, solely for the benefit of its members.   It should be entirely self-supporting, and it should not be considered obligatory on any member of the regiment whether a polo player or not to join it.

I have heard that in some parts of India, Polo Pony Clubs are forbidden by the authorities, on the ground of running officers into extravagance, and of forcing them to pay unnecessary subscriptions.   If the above plan were adopted, I do not think that this argument could possibly hold good ; in fact, the tendency would be rather towards economy.

For the guidance of those who may wish to try this system, I append the following rules, which can be altered according to circumstances :—

1. The Committee shall consist of three members of the club, two of whom shall form a quorum.   Their decision shall be final on all points.

2. Entrance fee Rs. 100, and monthly subscription Rs. 10, with an additional Rs. 5 a month for each pony supplied by the club.

3. All the stable expenses of the ponies to be

borne by the respective members in whose possession they are.

4. The club ponies may not be hunted, ridden pig-sticking, or lent to anyone, without special permission from a member of the Committee.

5. All risks to the ponies while playing polo are taken by the club. But if the pony is injured or dies when not playing polo, his temporary owner may be held liable for his full value.

6. At the option of the Committee, any member of the club may purchase a pony from the club at cost price ; but such pony may not be sold out of the club, without being first offered to the Committee at a discount of 10 per cent. for each complete year the pony has been in his owner's possession.

7. Any member of the club having a pony for sale, is bound to offer it to the Committee before selling it to anyone else.

8. The Committee may apportion the ponies as they think best, and may take a pony away from one member at any time and give it to another, if they think fit.

9. The Committee may call on any pony's services, for any purpose which they may consider of advantage to the club.

10. The Committee may sell any club pony at any time.

11. Any member of the club who takes a pony for the purpose of training it for polo, is charged no sub-scription for it, until it has been passed by the Committee as a trained polo pony. If no one can be found to take ponies, the club bears all expenses of keep.

POLO SADDLERY REQUIRED FOR INDIA.

A man can play polo in India with only a small supply of saddlery and stable gear. If money be no object, nothing conduces more to one's comfort than a plentiful supply of stable kit; and if a man means to set up a large stud on his arrival in the country, he will find it a great advantage to have an ample assortment of bits for his ponies (see Chapter VI.).

At least the following articles of saddle and bridle gear will be necessary :—

Two saddles complete.
One snaffle bridle.
Two double bridles (Figs. 55 and 56).
One long-cheeked double bridle (Fig. 54).
Two nose-bands (Figs. 62 and 63).
Two standing martingales with buckles, so that they can be fixed to the nose-band or rings of snaffle (Fig. 52).
One leather saddle cloth.
One numnah (felt).
Two pairs of spare stirrup leathers.
Two curb-chains, with thick broad links, and leather guards.
Three pairs of spare girths.

For a man to whom money is no object, I give the following list, which includes all that is necessary for training ponies. Clothing can be obtained in India much cheaper than in England, but not nearly so good.

The following is a complete saddlery and bridle outfit for India :—Six saddles complete, suitable to the height and weight of the rider, and weighing not less than ten pounds each. For a man of more than twelve stone, I would recommend saddles of at least twelve pounds. It is a great convenience to have a saddle for each pony on the polo ground, so as to avoid changing kit.

Six pairs of spare stirrup leathers.

One punch for making holes of different sizes in leathers.

Two bridles as in Fig. 55.

Two bridles as in Fig. 56, with jointed snaffles in addition.

One bridle as in Fig. 54.

One bridle as in Fig. 57.

Two half-moon Pelhams as in Fig. 31.

One Ben Morgan bit (Fig. 29).

Six caveson nose-bands (Figs. 62 and 63).

One jointed snaffle bridle.

One gag snaffle (Fig. 60).

Six standing martingales with buckles for attachment to nose-band or rings of snaffle (Fig. 52).

One running martingale (Fig. 61).

One caveson with bit, etc., complete.

One driving pad (Figs. 50 and 51).

One pair of long web reins (Figs. 50 and 51).

One abscess lancet, similar to those used by veterinary surgeons.

One rasp for filing the teeth.

One hoof rasp.

One drawing knife.

One searcher.

One pair of pincers, same as used by blacksmiths.
One measuring standard.
One cutting whip.
One long whip for driving on foot.
One brass syringe.
One enema.
One muzzle.

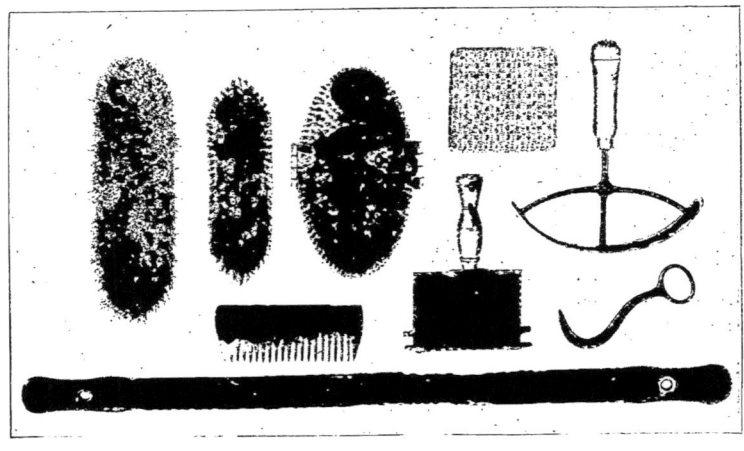

Fig. 96.—Grooming tools.

Three pairs of spare web girths.
Three pairs of spare leather girths.
One pair of Australian open work leather girths.
Grooming tools (Fig. 96).

The reins and cheek pieces of the bridles should be provided with studs (Figs. 97, 98 and 99), which have the advantage of allowing the bits to be removed for purposes of cleaning and change. If the bits are sewn on, the necessary washing will more or less rot the stitches, and will thus give rise to an element of danger.

The stud principle is very useful when a change of bit is required, and looks almost as neat as sewing. Buckles on a bridle are of course an eyesore from a fashionable point of view.

Fig. 97.   Fig. 98.   Fig. 99

Fig. 97.—Spring hook attachment.   Fig. 98 and 99.—Stud attachments.

CHAPTER X.

A RETROSPECT.

POLO is a game of recent and very rapid growth in England. We have seen (p. 1) that the first match in this land was played in 1871. The first organised polo tournament on record took place at Hurlingham, when the Royal Horse Guards won the first Champion Cup in 1876; and the first regimental tournament was played in 1878. Since then, the popularity of the game and the number of competitions have enormously increased. In 1891, when my regiment came home from India, the only polo club and the only ground in London was at Hurlingham, where polo was in full swing. Ranelagh was open, but there was no regular game there. Hurlingham players used sometimes to go to Ranelagh, in order to save their own ground after wet weather.

At Hurlingham there was always a match on Saturday, followed by a members' game, and sometimes a match on Wednesday; but at other times, only members' games were played, except during the progress of the Champion Cup, Regimental Tournament and the County Cup, which occupied three weeks of the season. The excellence of the members' games at Hurlingham was a great advantage which polo players had in those days, but which we seldom now enjoy. At present in London, it is a very rare occurrence to find eight good players in an ordinary game, and we generally take for granted that good polo can be found only in matches. But in 1892, I often took part in members' games with. such masters of polo as the Brothers Peat, Mr. John Watson, Lord Harrington, Mr. F. Mildmay, and that accomplished player, the late Mr. T. Kennedy. They and others of the same high class were regular attendants at members' games, with the addition of a few really good soldier players.

At the time in question, the only important polo events which were contested in England, were the three tournaments just mentioned, the annual Autumn Tournament at Barton, and an Open Tournament at Abergavenny, which is the headquarters of the Monmouthshire Club, and the home of the Herberts, who were the chief pioneers of English polo in its early days, before the Peats had made themselves known.

Within a radius of ten miles from Charing Cross, there are at present (1902) no less than ten well-patronised polo grounds : namely, two at Hurlingham, two at Ranelagh, two at Eden Park, one at Wimbledon, one at the Crystal Palace, one at Kingsbury, and one at Cricklewood.

In the season of 1901 at Ranelagh 132 members played at least once on the ground. Sometimes three matches and a members' game have been played there on one day. I have counted nearly forty players on the two grounds at Ranelagh on a Saturday. Hurlingham has similar difficulties to contend with, though to a somewhat lesser degree. Besides the crowds at Hurlingham and Ranelagh, polo was going on at the same time at the other six grounds already mentioned.

Although there were not more than twenty regular frequenters at Hurlingham, now, eleven years later, there are always over a hundred men playing at the different clubs, in and near London on a Saturday afternoon during the season. As a result of this overcrowding at Hurlingham and Ranelagh, the grounds are far too much cut up, and it is a great treat, when the London season is over, to play on smooth country grounds which have been comparatively at rest during the months of May, June and July. It is to be hoped that in future, polo players will have more room, and that London polo may be made still more attractive by the formation of a third big club at Roehampton, which is close to Ranelagh and which will provide three new grounds.

The constant change of opponents in a series of matches gives a charm to London polo which can be found nowhere else. All the best players in England and most of the best ponies congregate in London ; match succeeds match and tournament follows tournament to such an extent that, provided a player can get into good teams, his fun will be limited only by the endurance of his stud. The ball of tournaments is generally set rolling in May, with the Social Club Cup at Hurlingham, which is quickly followed by the Hunt Cup at Ranelagh, the Open Champion Cup, the Ranelagh Open Cup, the Regimental Tournament and the Subalterns' Cup for soldiers, the Novices' Cup for second-class players, the County Cup for county players, and finally in July, the Ladies' Cup and the Public Schools Tournament wind up the season of competitions, which some say is overdone. There is no doubt, however, that it is very difficult to get such a hard and exciting match at any time, as in a cup tie; and very few men play absolutely all cut, or at all events they do not ride only their best ponies, except in a near thing during a tournament.

As a rule, polo players are very slack about arranging their own matches, and leave too much to the polo managers. They ought to organise themselves into teams to constantly play together, and should ask the respective polo managers to give them a ground, and to get them an opposing side. The few men who act thus, and who take their teams to play matches at the different clubs, obtain far more fun out of the game, even if they are moderate performers, than others who simply ask for a place in a match, and day after day find themselves playing with different men whose methods they do not understand. In this respect, soldiers are much better off than civilians, for if they belong to their regimental team, or to their subalterns' team, they can get as many matches as they want.

When the season in London is drawing to a close, the honorary secretaries of county clubs now adopt the plan of arranging polo weeks on their own grounds. I venture to take the credit of having started this custom by inaugurating the Rugby tournament in 1894, which has been played every year since that time.

Nowadays, if a man likes to take a team on tour, he can go and play at St. Neots in the second week in July, at Stratford-on-Avon in the third week, at Leamington in the fourth week, and at Rugby in the first week in August. He can then proceed to Dublin and play in the Open Cup, which is always held at the same time as the great Annual Horse Show. In 1891 there were comparatively few polo clubs in England, and almost all the county grounds were to be found at Chester, Barton, Elvaston, Abergavenny, and the great military centres. The idea was then common that polo was too expensive for people of moderate means to take part in, and the game was practically confined to London, Liverpool, and Edinburgh. Now there are over fifty clubs where polo is regularly played, and nineteen of these clubs are affiliated to the County Polo Association, and compete for the County Cup, the preliminary ties of which are played off in their own districts : the semi-finals and finals taking place at Hurlingham. Men have found out that provincial polo is not a very expensive amusement, and young country gentlemen who ten years ago only thought of hunting, are now equally keen to play polo.

During the last few years, polo has made extraordinary progress in Ireland, thanks chiefly to that great polo player and organiser, Colonel Rimington of the Inniskilling Dragoons. I believe I am correct in saying that in 1897 there were not more than two men in Ireland who played polo regularly, besides the soldiers who were quartered there. Now, Irish players can be counted by dozens. The County Dublin Club started a ground of their own at Ashtown, and the only difficulty they had to encounter was the great number of players for whom they had to cater.

The Irish County Polo Club Union is supported by twelve county clubs, and it organises the following tournaments :—The County Cup, which, with the exception of the Inter-Regimental at Hurlingham, is in my opinion the best and hardest fought competition that takes place during the year ; the Novices' Cup ; and the Hunt Cup, which is played on the Kildare County Ground.

If polo increases in England and Ireland during the next ten years at the same rate as it has done since 1891, every county district will have its polo club like it has its pack of hounds.

258

CHAPTER XI.

POLO PONY BREEDING.

General remarks—Polo Pony Society—Experiences of breeders.

GENERAL REMARKS.

I APPROACH the subject of pony breeding with a certain amount of diffidence, and must ask my readers to bear in mind that I do not wish to pose as an authority on the subject; for any ideas I may have of my own about it are more or less theoretical.

I had a small breeding stud of some half-dozen mares in Ireland, but the young stock did not grow big enough on the poor land, and I disposed of the stud.

What I propose doing in this short chapter is to quote some of the best authorities, and to leave my readers to form their own opinions.

A good deal of interest has been taken during the last few years in the subject of the improvement of the breed of ponies, and I am certain that great strides have already been made in this direction, though much remains to be done. At the Royal Agricultural Show at Chester, on June 20th, 1893, the Polo Pony Stud Book Society was formed with the object of improving the breed of polo and riding ponies. The first volume came out in 1894. It contains the pedigrees and particulars of 57 stallions, 316 mares and their produce. There are now 6 volumes, no less than 210 stallions having been registered and 1,147 mares. The object is a great one, and the thanks and co-operation of all polo players are due to those energetic sportsmen who have worked hard to make the undertaking a success.

The society is also doing excellent work by having shows, at which valuable prizes are given for every class of riding pony. The information that can be gained by would-be breeders through these shows, and through the Society in general, should be the means of making vast improvements in the breeds of polo and riding ponies in the course of the next few years.

I presume that the real object of the Polo Pony Stud Book is to get a true breed of pony of a definite stamp, so that a man may be able, with a fair chance of success, to breed a pony of a certain size, quality, and appearance by mating a particular mare and stallion together. At present the usual theory is that there is no certainty as to the result of any particular alliance; most people imagining that the bigger class of pony is a manufactured breed, and that either sire or dam may throw back to a very much bigger ancestor. But men of experience have discovered that particular mares and stallions get offspring similar to themselves, which is another argument in favour of the Stud Book; for as the years go on and the produce of those animals already in the book are entered, we shall be able to see which are the stallions and mares that reproduce themselves.

17*

POLO PONY SOCIETY.

The Polo Pony Society has, during the past three years, made excellent progress in membership, and has largely extended its influence. Its supporters have increased from 200 to 450 ; it has registered 210 stallions and 1,147 mares and fillies, and its prizes and medals are now in evidence at twenty-three shows, besides its own London spring exhibition. This successful record dates from the transference of the Society's offices to 12, Hanover Square, London (in which congenial atmosphere flourish many notable examples of the British Breed Society), and is the natural outcome of the enthusiasm and determination of an energetic council, numbering, among others, Lord Arthur Cecil, Sir Walter Gilbey, Bart., Sir Humphrey de Trafford, Bart., Mr. John Barker, Mr. G. Norris Midwood, and Rev. D. B. Montefiore,

Following the example of the other horse-breeding societies located in London, they have organised a spring show comprising all classes of breeding stock and made ponies, securing entries of 102 and 141 in 1900 and 1901 respectively.

To associated shows offering definite amounts in prizes for polo ponies, they have awarded gold and silver medals, while the exhibitors of polo ponies at the Royal shows are under obligation to the Society for the schedule of prizes provided, as since 1897 they have raised the necessary funds. Their latest, and by no means least successful, movement was to offer a helping hand to the owners and breeders of mountain and moorland breeds of ponies, affording them opportunities of registering their best stallions and mares in separate sections in the Stud Book, and awarding silver medals to the best specimens of each sex. That this latest effort is appreciated may be seen by anyone who takes the trouble to attend any of the typical shows—the New Forest Pony Association, for instance.

The eagerness of the exhibitors to secure the recognition of the Polo Pony Society by taking their medal was evident, and the willingness to register their ponies placed on the record a score of new sires. In Scotland, at the recent Highland Show, the institution of a special section for the Highland pony in the Stud Book secured upon the spot some ten to twelve new members.

These facts speak for themselves and demonstrate the utility of the Society's work, though it is a pity that the support from polo players is so small, and that the additional money required to finance the London, Royal and subsidiary shows should have to be borne by the council. A membership of 450, even though annually increasing, does not suffice to provide prizes on the present year's scale—in London, to the extent of £455; and at the Royal amounting to a hundred guineas, with contributions to the associated shows totalling over £60. The deficiency has been made good by the liberally supported prize funds, with which the Society will dispense at the earliest possible moment.

The Stud Book, now in its sixth volume, has become practically self-supporting, and the rules for the seventh

volume have been drafted with a special view to the
all-important question of height.   That of type is being
satisfactorily solved, if the young stock presented for
competition during the last two years is any criterion.
The reports of the judges at the Spring Shows
emphatically endorse this view.   The Council have
now tackled the question of height and the new rules
for the Stud Book, and its annual Supplements are
appended in full.

ANNUAL SUPPLEMENT FOR 1901 TO THE POLO PONY STUD BOOK, VOL. 7.

CONDITIONS OF ENTRY.

Young Ponies (Colts and Fillies)—Foals, Yearlings, Two-and-Three-year-olds—
without any limit as to their height will be received for entry without a
number in this Supplement, to be annually issued to members, provided
they are :—

Pedigree.—(*a*) By a registered* Polo Pony Sire out of a registered* Polo Pony
Dam ; or

(*b*) By a Thorough-bred or Arab† Sire, out of a Registered* Polo
Pony Dam ; or

(*c*) By a registered* Polo Pony Sire, out of a Thorough-bred or
Arab† Dam.

Honours.—(*a*) Or if they have been awarded Honours in Polo Pony Classes at
the Associated Shows.

* The term "registered Polo Pony Sire or Dam" covers the Colts and
Fillies entered in the Supplements.

† Arab Sire or Dam must be registered either in General Stud Book or Polo
Pony Stud Book.

CONDITIONS OF ENTRY IN VOLS. 7, 8 AND 9 OF STUD BOOK.

POLO PONY SECTION.

CONDITIONS OF ENTRY FOR STALLIONS AND MARES.

1. *Age*—No Pony will be admitted to registration and a number in the Stud
Book until it is four years old,* when its

2. *Height*—Must not exceed 14·2, confirmed by the certificate of a qualified
Veterinary Surgeon, or by Hurlingham certificate.

3. *Pedigree*—To be specially considered by the Editing Committee in acceptance
or rejection of a Pony.

A Pony not fully qualified by pedigree shall, for final acceptance in the Stud Book, be in every respect a "high-class riding-pony," or one likely to breed such a Pony.

4. *Inspection*—When no pedigree is available such Pony must be inspected by a present or past Member of the Council, or by two Members of the Society appointed by the Member of Council in the district.

   * N.B.—Ponies, under four years old, are admitted into the Annual Supplement by pedigree and honours in Polo Pony Classes. Particulars on application to the Secretary.

MOUNTAIN AND MOORLAND SECTIONS.

CONDITIONS OF ENTRY FOR STALLIONS AND MARES.

1. *Inspection*—The inspection of Ponies from each breed is in the hands of the respective Local Committees, of which the Conveners (to whom all applications shall be addressed) are :—

> CONNEMARA.—Professor J. Cossar Ewart, The Bungalow, Penicuik, Midlothian.
> DARTMOOR.—T. H. O. Pease, Skaigh, Okehampton, Devon.
> EXMOOR.—Viscount Ebrington, Exmoor, South Molton, Devon.
> FELL.—W. W. Wingate-Saul, Fenton Cawthorne House, Lancaster.
> NEW FOREST.—Lord Arthur Cecil, Orchardmains, Torbridge.
> WELSH.— { J. Marshall Dugdale, Llwyn, Llanfyllin, Oswestry.
>   { John Jones, Dinarth Hall, Colwyn Bay, North Wales.
> HIGHLAND.—J. H. Munro Mackenzie, Calgary, Tobermory, N.B.

2. *Type*—These Committees are desired to register only Ponies of riding type and that, on the dam's side, are of pure pony blood.

   N.B.—The Society considers that the foundation stock of these breeds should not be registered unless they contain three-quarters pony blood.

3. *Height*—The following heights have been officially accepted by the respective Local Committees :—

> NEW FOREST : 12·2 to 13·2.
> DARTMOOR : Stallions, 14 ; Mares, 13·2.
> HIGHLAND : Up to 14·2.

   The other heights will be added as received, and incorporated in later editions of the Entry Form.

4. *Medals*—The Society, being anxious to encourage the breeds of native Ponies by giving Medals, instruct the Committees to make the conditions most suited to the breed they represent ; but }

   No pony may compete for a Medal unless already entered in its respective section, or passed as fit for entry by a Member or representative of the Polo Pony Society, either before or at the Show.

Briefly, the Supplement will provide an annual register of the foals bred from qualified parents, the

prizes awarded to the young stock, statistical state-
ments of the shows devoting classes and prizes to
Polo Ponies—in fact a yearly record of the Society's
work. The Stud Book will recognise and register with
numbers only ponies which at four years old comply as
regards height ; pedigree and type being specially
considered in their acceptance.

No person however much he may be out of sympathy
with the Society's work, can object to these rules. A
breeder can enter his young stock in the Supplement
with opportunities of submitting them at four years
old, if of proper height for full registry. Through
the Supplement it is hoped to fix the type In the
Stud Book it is proposed to register only animals of
the authorised height, thereby debarring all young
animals which exceed it.

These rules practically bring the rules of registration
of the Polo Pony Stud Book into line with those
governing the registration of polo ponies under
Hurlingham rules.

These rules aim at encouraging the production of
the highest type of riding ponies (the polo pony), but
if the ideal is not attained, the result must be the
improvement of the riding pony. The benefits to the
cart and harness breeds of horses, which have followed
the application of systematic registration by the Shire
and Hackney horse societies, apply equally to the
pony, and the increased interest in the riding pony at
country shows is the outcome of the Society's policy ;
and the importance of the pony to the Army has
been forcibly proved during the war in South Africa.
The Shire, Hackney and Hunter societies obtain the
support of those who, though not actually benefiting in

the work of these societies, are interested in the encouragement of the respective breeds, and surely the Polo Pony Society may equally claim the support of those gentlemen who are interested in the maintenance and improvement of the riding pony.

EXPERIENCES OF BREEDERS.

Lord Harrington, who is a practical and successful breeder, contributed a most able article to " The Polo Magazine," in which he gives his experience of breeding from the Barb, Awfully Jolly (a 14.1 pony), and English mares.   The following table of results is very instructive :—

	SIRE.	DAM.
Ali Baba, 14.1 :	Awfully Jolly, 14.1.	15.1
Jenny, 14.0 :	,,	13.0
Abbot, 14.1 :	,,	14.1
Abbess, 13.3 :	,,	14.1
Aunt Sally, 13.3 :	,,	Welsh, 15.0
Arthur Roberts, 14.0 :	,,	Welsh, 14.0
Cyclops, 14.2 :	,,	Thorough-bred, 15.3
Ally Sloper, 14.0 :	,,	Welsh, 13.2
Adventurer, 14.0	,,	Welsh, 14.2
Awfully Jolly II., 13.3 :	,,	Welsh, 13.2
Antelope, 14.1 :	,,	Thorough-bred, 14.1

Lord Harrington says : " My own experience is that you cannot have a better hunter than a clean thorough-bred one that has not been raced, but kept for hunting, and I have little doubt that, if it were possible to breed ponies which were quite thorough-bred, and had substance enough to carry weight, with good temper and polo action, it would be impossible to breed better polo ponies ; but I am afraid it would be impossible to carry out this idea.   Choose an ideal thorough-bred sire, say, Sir Humphrey de Trafford's Rosewater, put him to my thorough-bred mare Dancing Girl, or to the thorough-bred Tessie, you would, I think, get an animal much over the height. If either of these mares were put to the Barb pony Awfully Jolly, that used to belong to me, you would get a polo pony." Lord Harrington then proceeds to show by the above table how very successful Awfully Jolly has been when crossed with English and Welsh mares, and also says that "several of these ponies were sold for high prices, £200, £170, £200 and £150, and all except one, that is used up after playing for seven years, and Awfully Jolly II., whom I am keeping to take his sire's place, are playing polo now." He lays down the following rules for pony breeding :—

" 1. Use only the best pony mares, and see above all things that they have good polo action, that is to say, that they appear to go straight when they are trotted away from you and when you stand directly behind them : it is quite useless to breed from a mare or stallion that dishes : if you want a polo pony, see that the mare and stallion are well bred ; the more breeding they show, the better, so long as they have substance.

" 2. If possible, when choosing your stallion, see some of his stock. If he is inclined to throw large stock, put small mares to him, and, if possible, of pony blood (that is to say, by a pony out of a pony).

" 3. If your mare is an accident (that is to say, by a large horse out of a large mare), although she may be small herself, she is pretty sure to throw back, and produce animals larger than herself. For a mare of this sort choose a stallion of pony blood.

" 4. In choosing a mare or stallion for polo pony

breeding see that they have good shoulders but avoid those with high, narrow withers, as these ponies measure high, and do not carry weight.

"Some people think that by putting a small mare pony to a large thorough-bred, they may get polo ponies ; but this plan is very risky, and these small ponies will often throw animals much too large for polo ; but there is this advantage common to all misfits for polo that are bred from good animals on both sides, that you are sure to produce a good, hardy animal, that, be he too large or too small, will be available for some purpose."

All the above valuable information appeared in an article, written by Lord Harrington, in "The Polo Magazine," of March, 1895, and his opinions carry more weight than would those of any one that I can think of ; for he has been at the game for many years, breeding almost entirely his own hunters and polo ponies, and has been most successful with both.

Mr. Hill's opinion about breeding is that a foundation stock is required of pure pony blood, and in his Preface to Vol. I. of the "Polo Pony Stud Book," he writes : "I have no hesitation in saying that there is no safer or more appropriate foundation for the object which the Society has in view than this pure Welsh pony blood. There are several distinct types of these ponies. First, the small, hardy, mountain-bred ones, standing 11 to 12 hands high ; secondly, those bred on the lower grounds, and from 13.3 to 14.2 hands ; and thirdly, the cob of from 14.2 to 15 hands. Although quite distinct in appearance and height, still they have the same family likeness and true 'pony' character action, and hair, perfectly different to that of the

Hackney-bred pony or cob. Their action is remarkable for its freedom and dash. The second and third I named usually bend their knees, but at the same time throw out their legs with a swinging motion straight from the shoulder, distinct from the higher and rounder action of the Hackney. The hock movement is good, though in some instances they go a trifle too wide in their fast paces, and the hindquarter is often shorter than it should be. The little mountain ponies very much follow their larger cousins in action, but many breeders do not like too much bend of the knee, preferring rather a kind of darting movement, like a thorough-bred horse or an Arab. I must say I like to see every class of horse bend the knee in the trot, and this may be easily distinguished in the riding horse or pony, from the more extravagant high movement so valuable for those suitable for harness. The indomitable pluck, endurance, and good temper of the Welsh pony, together with his substance and dash, will be found an invaluable cross for the thorough-bred and Eastern-bred ponies.

"As one of the great difficulties in breeding polo ponies is to keep the height within limit, pure, small pony blood, especially as foundation stock, becomes the more valuable, so that the Dartmoor, Exmoor, New Forest, Church Stretton Hills, and Highland-bred ponies must not be overlooked, and the worth of these breeds cannot be well over-estimated in laying the foundation for the breed of the future."

From the above I understand Mr. Hill's opinion to be that a cross of thorough-bred or Eastern blood with one of our pure English breeds of ponies is what is required. But I very much doubt the possibility of any success on these lines within the lifetime of any one breeder.

Mr. J. Anderson, who was inspecting veterinary surgeon in the Bombay Presidency, had charge of the Government breeding studs in India for some years. He told me that many of the best racing ponies in India of which the great Mite was an instance, were sired by very old English thorough-bred stallions, out of big mares. So well was this fact known, that when the stallions became old, they were got rid of, because their stock would not be big enough for remounts. When I told him I had purchased a 14.1 thorough-bred to breed polo ponies, he told me that he believed it to be of no use ; that probably the pony would throw back ; and that he was convinced that the only way to breed racing and polo ponies by English sires was to select mares of the size required, and to put them to English thorough-bred stallions twenty years old or more. But this plan would not help us in any way to establish a breed of ponies which will reproduce themselves.

Breeding to height may be a pure lottery, but, like Lord Harrington, I feel pretty confident that the young stock will be valuable for some purpose, even if they are too big or too small for polo. This impetus to pony breeding must be an excellent thing for the country.

The fact that first-class ponies which are nearly thorough-bred, are, as a rule, accidents, proves, I think, that to get a real pony breed, we must use a stallion whose ancestors were small. The right animal, to my mind, is the high-caste Arab ; for he is just as well bred as our thorough-bred, and though his produce may

increase in size, owing to the nature of English food
and climate, they are more likely to be of the same size
as their sire than if they owed their parentage to a 14-
hand English thorough-bred, which, very likely, was
sired by a horse 15.2, out of an equally big mare.

Lord Harrington was very successful with the Barb
Awfully Jolly, which I believe was an excellent polo
pony in his day.   Personally I do not like Barbs,
though I would be the last to say there are no good
ones among them, as I do know a few.   Lord Harrington says that he has never been able to find another
one like Awfully Jolly, a fact I am not surprised at.
If one is going in for Eastern blood, I am quite certain
it would be better to use the pure, high-caste Arab than
any less aristocratic breed.   With respect to breeding
from an Arab, we must remember that not one Arab in
a thousand has good enough shoulders for the purpose ;
and that the defect of bad shoulders seems to be more
hereditary than any other fault.

Rosewater (Fig. 100) and his son Sandiway, out of
the polo pony mare Cuddington, both breed ponies,
and as far as I can hear, the former gets all his
stock of polo height, but it remains to be proved
if they will breed first-class performers at the game,
although I have no doubt that they will succeed.

Other considerations must be taken into account in
pony breeding, such as climate, feeding and soil.   A
pony bred on rough mountains, and forced to get his
living as he can, without care or shelter, is certain not
to grow as big as he would do, if he was brought
up on rich pasture, and given oats from the time he
was a yearling.

The real difficulty about pony breeding is that we

want to breed a pony as near 14.2 as possible. 14.0 is too small for polo, and 14.3 is too big, so the margin of height is practically only two inches, a consideration that does not come into the calculations of the breeder of any other kind of stock. At present the difficulties seem great; but by the light of experience, and

Fig. 100.—Champion Sire " Rosewater," late " Johnnie Day."

through the valuable information we hope to gain through the Society, these difficulties may vanish in a few years, and I shall hope to see a breed of polo ponies spring up that will reproduce themselves as surely as does the Thorough-bred, the Shire horse, or the Suffolk.

Of one thing I am sure, and that is that we cannot expect to get a really good breed of riding and polo

ponies unless we breed on both sides from riding stock.
There must be no admixture of any of the harness
breeds, such as the Hackney, or of any of the varieties of
the hairy-heeled cob.   Although there may have been
some good polo ponies owing part of their origin to one
or other of these strains, I am sure they were the
exceptions, and not the rule.   As I have already said,
when buying a raw young pony, I always like to get
him if possible, at least three parts clean bred, and
this of course means that at least three quarters of his
origin is derived from horse stock, and that only one
quarter can be from pony stock.   The main difficulty
which breeders have to contend with, is the fact that
nearly all the best ponies now playing are by big
thorough-bred horses.

To take two or three instances, Sailor is by Lurgan,
out of a polo pony mare which won many races when
she was the property of Captain Cecil Fetherstonhaugh,
of the Royal Dragoons.   Mademoiselle is, as we have
seen (p. 177), by Loved One out of a hunter mare,
Madame Angot by Munster Blazer, grandam by
Woodpecker by Birdcatcher.   This pedigree, which
has no pony blood in it, is good enough for a winner of
the Grand National.   Nipcat is by Buckshot out of
a pony.   Attack is by Munchausen out of a pony.   In
fact nine out of ten of the ponies I buy are supposed to
be by big thorough-bred horses.

CHAPTER XII.

POLO IN THE ARMY.

POLO is *par excellence* "the soldiers' game." They brought it into England from India, and for many years it was played almost exclusively by them. Had it not been for soldiers, polo would not now be the chief summer pursuit of hundreds of county gentlemen and civilians in all walks of life. It is in every way the most suitable form of amusement for regimental officers.

The following are a few of its advantages :—

1. No better riding school exists than the polo ground.

2. To be a successful polo player, a man must be to some extent a horsemaster ; for he must know a good deal about horses, in order to be able to buy his ponies, and to keep them sound and fit.

3. The qualities which make a soldier succeed in his profession, bring him to the front at polo, particularly if he has to organise and arrange the regimental polo.

4. Polo occupies only an hour or two in the afternoon, and in no way interferes with an officer's official work, provided the ground is not far from barracks. Cricket is a splendid regimental institution, but it

18

requires twenty-two men and a whole day for its performance. Hunting is as good or perhaps even a better educational amusement for soldiers than polo, because it teaches quickness of eye for a country, decision, and promptness to seize an opportunity; but hunting is possible only in a few places where soldiers are quartered. Even in England it can, as a rule, be indulged in only when an officer is on leave, and in any case it occupies the entire day. Well managed polo, on the contrary, can be played close to barracks in almost every part of the Empire. Besides, polo has the inestimable advantage, from a military point of view, that it promotes among officers enthusiasm and *esprit de corps*, which is not done by individual sports, such as hunting, shooting, pigsticking, or by any other game that can be played by the officers of a regiment. I do not think that anyone who has not belonged to a polo playing regiment can exactly understand how keen is this spirit. A polo playing officer looks on a place in his regimental team in the Hurlingham or Indian Inter-Regimental Tournament in the same light as a public school boy regards his colours in the school XI.; a cricketing university man, his position in the great match at Lord's; or a university rowing man, his seat in the contest from Putney to Mortlake. *Esprit de corps* is keener among officers than even among school boys and 'Varsity men; because the majority of officers look on their regiments as their home for life, whereas a sojourn at school or college seldom lasts more than five years.

Although the best polo playing regiments may not always be the best fighting regiments, they are certainly near the top of the tree in that respect ; and well organised polo has assuredly a great influence for good on the officers of any regiment.

The great advantage of polo over all other outdoor games is the fact that it can be played in late middle life. One of the best Backs in England is fifty years of age. Consequently, an officer can go on playing at his best throughout his whole career in a regiment. No better sight can be witnessed at polo than a colonel of a regiment playing Back, and urging his officers on to victory in a hard fought match, as I have seen done by Colonel Lawley of the 7th Hussars, Colonel Babington of the 16th Lancers, and Colonel Ridley of the Manchester Regiment. Equally good examples have occurred in other instances.

The only possible objection to polo as an amusement for officers is its expense, which, of course, is its great drawback as compared to other outdoor games. Owing to this cause, military authorities have been supposed for some years to have looked askance at polo, and many rumours have been current that hindrances will be placed with respect to officers playing it. One general officer in India has gone so far as to prohibit polo clubs in regiments under his command, owing to the mistaken idea that non-players have to subscribe for the benefit of members of the team ; whereas a well managed polo pony club, which is composed only of members of the regiment who wish to join it, works the other way, and puts the game within the reach of comparatively poor men who would otherwise be debarred from it (p. 242 *et seq.*).

Polo costs a good deal of money, but its expenses as regards the purchase of ponies, keep and wages can

18*

be ascertained beforehand, and the cost counted. I do not think that there is a single authentic case of an officer having to leave his regiment by reason of his having spent too much money on polo, although the high price of polo ponies is often the excuse given to parents and guardians for an additional allowance ; the truth probably being that the money went on amusements of a much less reputable nature which would not bear explanation. I came across the following instance of this kind a couple of years ago. An old gentleman who had formerly commanded an infantry regiment, put his son into a cavalry regiment, because the boy had passed too low to be able to get a commission into the infantry, and recruits at that time were badly wanted in the cavalry. The old colonel complained to a friend of mine that his son would be obliged to leave his regiment, as he had got into debt by trying to keep pace with his brother officers, and they had told him that if he could not mount himself better at polo, he must leave. The father was naturally very bitter about this, and as I knew the regiment and did not believe the story, I made enquiries. I discovered that the boy was a very bad horseman, could hardly keep his seat in the riding school, had never owned a polo pony or a hunter, and was in trouble with his commanding officer for not buying a second charger. I was told how his money had gone, but the details of its disappearance would not bear repetition here. It is probable that the old colonel still attributes the ruin of his son's career to his extravagance about polo.

Any opposition to polo which may exist in the higher ranks of the Army is probably due to the fact that the game is of recent growth, and that men who have never belonged to a polo playing regiment, often pay more attention to its drawbacks than to its more than compensating advantages. Fortunately the Commander-in-Chief has the interests of polo at heart, as we know by the wise legislation he instituted for the benefit of the game a few years ago when there was an outcry about the prevalence of bad accidents in India. He insisted on helmets being worn as a head protection, stricter umpiring, severer penalties for fouls, and he made the captains of clubs responsible for the warning off of dangerous and badly trained ponies. If any question concerning polo crops up at home during the next few years, officers may rest assured that Lord Roberts will deal with it as ably as he did in India.

I do not think that the Regimental Tournament at Hurlingham will be stopped ; but if it be forbidden, some officers will be largely to blame, for the following reason : It is well known that for a polo team to become expert at the game, especially if they have not played much together, it is necessary for them to get practice against good teams. Hence the temptation to allow a regimental team to go to London for a week or two before the tournament, because as a rule they can play only among themselves near their barracks. I have known cases of a regimental team being practically on leave for a month previous to the tournament, living in London, and amusing themselves, while their brother officers were doing their work, in the busiest time of the year. This of course is altogether wrong. Besides it gives such a team an undue advantage over other teams which go to London for the week, and it also has a very bad effect on regimental polo, because it deprives the regimental polo club of the four best players and very likely all the best ponies for a month or more. The other polo playing officers may thus find their fun spoiled, and may consider that the game is not worth the candle. If a team goes up for the Regimental Tournament and has perhaps one practice match on the previous Saturday, the services of the four officers will not be lost for long, expenses will not be heavy, and neither regimental work nor regimental polo will suffer.

Some years ago the Inspector-General of Cavalry in India had just grounds of complaint against certain regiments, because their chargers were by no means up to the mark, although they possessed the best of polo ponies. His impression was that some of these officers paid more attention to the interests of polo than to soldiering. Such cases, which are happily very rare, would do more harm to polo in the Army than almost anything else.

The most successful polo regiments of late years have been the 13th Hussars and the Inniskilling Dragoons, neither of which ride expensive ponies. The 13th Hussars have specially distinguished themselves, for they won the Cup in 1892, '94, and '95, and were beaten in the final only by one goal in each of the years 1896, '98, and '99. They had an exceptionally good team in 1897, but they scratched, owing to their being in mourning. The 7th Hussars won the Tournament in 1899, and bought four or five high-priced ponies just before the Tournament, in order to win. They had only recently come home from India, and had not had the opportunity of getting their ponies together. On this occasion they were extra keen to win the Cup the first year they were at home, having won it on the last occasion they had played for it, namely in 1886, in which year they left for India ; and they succeeded in their worthy ambition.

Few officers in the Army can afford to pay big sums for their ponies. Many have actually considered polo an economy, as it has caused them to give up racing and other expensive amusements. Polo can be played cheaply in regiments, by the system of Polo Pony Clubs (p. 242), if well managed, a fact which has been amply proved by Colonel de Lisle of the Durham Light Infantry, Captain Egerton Green of the 12th Lancers, and many others. I have never heard of officers in high positions object to polo, except on the ground of its expense. They often say that a polo pony should not cost more than £50, and that officers should be content to play among themselves in regimental games at the station where they are quartered. It is true that the regimental or station game is the backbone of polo in the Army ; but players would be no more content to go on playing day after day among the same set of players, than would a cricketer be to play always on the same ground in a pick-up game, with no prospect of matches against neighbouring clubs.

The Tournament is the culmination of the season's play, and it stimulates a regiment to work and improve themselves. The regimental team, especially in India, is often a tie which keeps a whole regiment together, and prevents them going away in search of individual amusements. In England it often keeps officers from attending every possible race meeting, where they would probably lose much more money than what polo would cost them, and prevents them seeking more expensive and less desirable distractions in London.

I think we may take for granted that polo has a good influence on the education of an officer. At all events, the same qualities which bring a man to the front at polo are required by anyone who aspires to lead men. I think this will be admitted by anyone who takes the trouble to read the following list of names of lovers of the game, some of them are very well known brilliant players, and nearly all have served with distinction in the war. These officers are of every rank from general to subaltern, and, alas! we shall never again see many of them :—

Major-General Elliot, C.B., D.S.O., Inspector-General of Cavalry in India, was, when I was soldiering there, one of the finest horsemen in that country, and could give weight to nearly every professional on the flat. He was a good polo player, but is specially known for the valuable work he did for the Indian Polo Association, and for raising the polo height to 14.1, which has had the effect of making polo ponies useful animals for Army purposes.

Colonel C. P. Ridley, C.B., has probably stuck more wild boar than any other white man in India, and polo held but a secondary place in his estimation ; yet when he commanded the Manchester Regiment at Dinapore, he got together a regimental team and captained it himself in many matches. Major Eustace Crawley, who is a well-known polo player, was Brigade Major to Colonel Ridley, and earned a brevet for his services.

Major-General Smith-Dorrien D.S.O., was a keen

polo player when serving with the Derbyshire regiment and on the Staff in India. After a successful term in South Africa, he has been made Adjutant-General in India.

Colonel Babington was quite in the first class of soldier players when he was in regular play. In recognition of his work in South Africa he has been given command of the Forces in New Zealand. I saw him play Back most brilliantly in 1895 at Lucknow. His polo record dates from 1880, when his regiment won for the first time at Hurlingham. He repeated his success in 1881, and also played in the winning team of the Champion Cup in 1882.

Major-General Lord Chesham, K.C.B., was well known as a Master of Hounds and one of the best men across country in England before this war brought him to the front as a military leader. When the 10th Hussars and 9th Lancers played in India during the late seventies and early eighties, he was one of the keenest among an exceptionally good lot of polo players.

Sir R. Pole-Carew, K.C.B., C.V.O., and Major-General Baden-Powell, C.B., who played for the 13th Hussars in India, are two other distinguished generals who have been keen on polo.

Brigadier-General Alderson, C.B., A.D.C., is another military commander who is fond of polo, and had as his A.D.C. Charlie Beatty, D.S.O., who is better known as a fine steeplechase rider, although he was one of the six original members of the Rugby Club, and has played many matches for it during the last few years. General Alderson played in the winning team of the County Cup for Kent in 1880.

That very successful Brigadier of Cavalry, Colonel
Broadwood, C.B., A.D.C., has always been fond of
polo, although he devoted his attention chiefly to
hunting and steeplechasing, at which he distinguished
himself by riding his mare Frigate in the Grand
National. He chose for his staff officers two first-
class players in Brand, who earned a brevet and was
the Back of the 10th Hussars team which won the Cup
at Hurlingham in 1893, and in Aldridge, who got the
D.S.O., the Back of the Royal Artillery team.
Aldridge played many times in the Gunner team with
Major Schofield, who gallantly earned the Victoria
Cross at Colenso, poor Jack Hanwell and C. G.
McKenzie, two among many gallant sportsmen whom
the Army and the polo world can ill spare.

Colonel Mahon, C.B., D.S.O., like Ridley and
Baden-Powell, is perhaps better known for his prowess
with the spear and big game rifle than as a polo
player ; yet he often played for the 8th Hussars at
Meerut, Umballa and Hurlingham, with the gallant
le Gallais, Henderson, and their commanding officer,
Lieut.-Colonel Duff. The 8th Hussars have supplied
for service in South Africa several other good players,
among them their late commanding officer, Colonel
Clowes, C.B., and Major Wood, than whom no better
judge or trainer of a polo pony can be found anywhere.
Mahon has not been seen on English polo grounds
lately, because he has spent but little time at home
since he took to active soldiering about seven years
ago in the Egyptian Army.

Lieut.-Colonels Rimington, C.B., and de Lisle,
D.S.O., are admirable instances of enthusiastic Army
polo players who have never allowed the game to

interfere with their military duties or ambitions. They are both men of ceaseless energy, who have won their way to the front in their profession in exactly the same dogged and determined manner by which they brought their regiments into first-class polo with very little outlay of money.

Rimington has never let a chance slip. In 1898 he disappeared from everyone's sight for six months and turned up again in London only just in time to steer his regiment to victory in the Regimental Polo Tournament of that year. The experience gained during those six months has been turned to good account during the last two years. Colonel Sir Henry Rawlinson, C.B., who has greatly distinguished himself both in Egypt and South Africa, is one of the best Back players, although he has not lately had much time for polo.

General French has had several polo players on his staff. First of all is that brilliant cavalry officer, Colonel Douglas Haig, C.B., who is as clever a chief of the staff as even General French could wish to have. As a polo player his record is exceedingly good. He played for the 7th Hussars when they won the Tournament at Hurlingham in 1885 and 1886 ; and in India, when they won it in 1891. Among other polo playing staff officers who were with General French at different periods of this war, are Brevet Lieut.-Colonel the Hon. H. Lawrence, of the 17th Lancers, the General's Chief Intelligence Officer ; Brevet Major Kenna, who with poor Montmorency won the V.C. in the celebrated 21st Lancer charge ; the Hon. R. Ward of the Blues ; and Captain Barry, D.S.O., of the 10th Hussars.

Lieut.-Colonel Lawrence was captain of the 17th Lancer team when we won the Cup at Meerut in 1889. During recent years, soldiering has monopolised his time too much to allow him a chance of indulging in his favourite pursuit of ten years ago. Kenna and Montmorency played together in the 21st Lancer team. Kenna, though a very brilliant Forward player, is better known in India as a first-class steeplechase rider.

"Reggie" Ward is equally well known in the English polo and steeplechasing world. He always plays No. 2 in the Blues team.

Barry is as keen a polo player as there is in the 10th Hussars.

Colonel Little, C.B., who commanded the 9th Lancers with marked success, was severely wounded when in command of the 3rd Cavalry Brigade. He was well known for many years as a good and successful polo player. His polo record includes many triumphs. He formed one of the four who won the American Challenge Cup in 1886, the others being Lieut.-Colonel the Hon. R. Lawley, now in command of the 7th Hussars, Captain T. Hone, late of the same regiment, and John Watson. He played in the winning team of the 9th Lancers at Hurlingham in 1889 and 1890, and in Ireland in 1892 and 1893.

The 9th have distinguished themselves on many a hard-fought field, and in many a tight polo match. In their ranks are included several fine soldiers and good polo players. Their best player is Brevet Major Lord Charles Bentinck, who was mentioned repeatedly during the defence of Mafeking. Major MacLaren, D.S.O., of the 13th Hussars, who was badly wounded after doing invaluable work for months under Plumer in his gallant attempts to get into Mafeking, Colonel Rimington, Lord Charles Bentinck, and Major Poore, D.S.O., are four of the best Back players in the Army.

When the 9th Lancers won the Cup at Hurlingham in 1896, the team consisted of David Campbell, Captain Jenner (now Major Sir W. K. Jenner, D.A.A.G. at the Curragh), G. Ellison and Lord C. Bentinck. Poor Ellison, who was a fine polo player and good sportsman, has played his last game, and his place is hard to fill. Campbell is best known for having reached the height of every steeplechase rider's ambition, by winning the Grand National on Soarer. He rides at polo with the same dash and determination as he does over a country. Sir W. K. Jenner has more regimental polo triumphs to his credit than probably any other man, as, for instance, the Inter-Regimental at Hurlingham in 1889, '90, '91 and '96, and the Indian Inter-Regimental of 1883, '84 and '85. His brother officer, Brevet Lieut.-Colonel F. Colvin, runs him close in this respect.

There are many other good players in the 9th, namely, Captain Allhusen, who won the Kadir Cup ; Captain Hon. C. Willoughby, who played for his regiment when they won at Hurlingham in 1891, and in the final in 1893 ; Lord Douglas Compton, who obtained a Brevet Majority ; and younger players, such as Lord F. Blackwood, D.S.O., and Sadleir Jackson, D.S.O. The 9th sustained a sad loss in that dashing polo player, P. Brassey, who was killed on the relief of Kimberley.

Like the 9th, almost all the 17th, from colonel to last-joined subaltern, play polo. Sad to say, they have suffered very heavily during this war. No one who has read the account of the splendid fight and heroic resistance made by the 150 men under Sandeman in September, 1901, when rushed at Elands River Poort by Smuts' Commando, can wonder that I am proud of having belonged to that distinguished regiment. Lieutenants Sheridan, Morrit and Russel were killed ; Major Sandeman and Lord Vivian were wounded ; over 30 N.C.O.'s and men killed, and 31 wounded, out of a total of 150. Sandeman was an excellent polo player in 1888, but he has not played much in late years. Sheridan was a promising and dashing player. Major Nickalls is a very fine Back player, and has played for the regiment several times. He was particularly good in India and Egypt, despite his welter weight. Captain W. A. Tilney, who has done invaluable work in Ladysmith, and subsequently on Lord Methuen's staff, is the captain of the 17th Lancers' polo team, and he won the Open Cup in Dublin with a team consisting of himself, Major Portal, R. S. Carden, and A. F. Fletcher, all of whom have served in this campaign. The deeply lamented Lord Ava, who was killed in Ladysmith, was another well-known player that got his education in this regiment. Poor Brinsley Sheridan was his cousin, and joined the regiment through his advice and influence.

The Household Cavalry sent many polo players to the war. The 1st Life Guards contributed Colonel Calley, who won his Brevet Colonelcy ; Captain G. F. Milner, who, when he was in the 17th, played in the winning team at Meerut in 1889 ; the Duke of Teck, who played for the 17th in India in 1889, and who earned a Brevet Majority ; Captains E. W. Clowes,

D.S.O., J. S. Cavendish, D.S.O., Lloyd Phillips and Cookson ; the Hon. G. Ward and W. Waring. Lord Lovat, late of the 1st Life Guards, greatly distinguished himself by raising and commanding the invaluable Lovat Scouts.

The 2nd Life Guards' polo players were represented by Lord Longford, Captain Brinton, D.S.O., Captain de Crespigny, D.S.O., Captain Spender Clay, Lord Wicklow, Hon. A. O'Neill, Sir G. Prescott, the late Captain R. Peel, and the late Lord Kensington.

The Royal Horse Guards sent to the war many officers, all of whom were polo players, as, for instance, Lieut.-Colonel Fenwick, D.S.O., Captains Villiers FitzGerald, Mann-Thomson, Hon. R. Ward, Ricardo, Lord Tullibardine, D.S.O., the Duke of Roxburghe, H. E. Brassey, Hon. D. Marjoribanks, D.S.O., and A. Rose, and Vet.-Captain F. E. Drage. Marjoribanks, Ward and Drage won the Subalterns' Cup at Ranelagh in 1897 and 1898, their captain being poor Ernest Rose, who was the only officer the Blues lost during this campaign, and who was shot at the head of his men.

Major Bell-Smyth, Captain Lockett, D.S.O., D. A. Rasbotham, and many other officers of the K.D.G.'s, are keen polo players.

The Bays, who are on their way to South Africa while these lines are being written, have many well-known polo players, such as Kirk, Persse, and Wilberforce, who won the Indian Regimental Tournament in 1892, '93 and '94, and Major V. G. Whitla, now of the 3rd Hussars, and Captains C. K. Bush and Sykes.

The 4th Dragoon Guards had lately an excellent

polo team, and are rapidly improving in their play. Captains J. H. Lloyd, Sellar, Gaunt and Mathew-Lannowe are all good players.   Lloyd is a particularly brilliant player.

The 5th Dragoon Guards, like the 4th, has only lately been much heard of in the polo world, probably because neither of these regiments were formerly on the foreign roster, and consequently they did not get the advantage of playing in India.   Their Adjutant, Captain Winwood, D.S.O., Captain Darbyshire and Major Eustace are some of their best players.

Since the Carabiniers were in India in 1887, they have also not been known as a polo playing regiment till lately; but they have a good prospect before them, with Major Leader, Captain Collis, D.S.O., W. E. Watson, D.S.O., and other good players.   Mr. Godfrey Heseltine, who is a brilliant player, has been given a Captain's commission in the regiment in recognition of his services with the Yeomanry in South Africa.

Captain Makins, of the Royals and Captain Lafone of the 4th Hussars, were known as good polo players when their respective regiments were quartered at Hounslow.   Major Hoare, Captain Barnes, Mr. Winston Churchill, and poor Savory, who was killed in Natal, were the members of the 4th Hussars team which won the Inter-Regimental Tournament in India in 1899.   Captain Barnes earned the D.S.O. in South Africa, and obtained command of a Yeomanry regiment.

Among the Scots Greys, the names of Lieut.-Colonel W. H. Hippisley (their commanding officer) and Brevet Lieut.-Colonel Middleton appear as long ago as 1880, in the winning team of the Irish Open Cup. Major Adams, Captain Bulkeley-Johnson, and the late Tom Conolly were well-known players.

Among polo playing officers of the 5th Lancers, past and present, who have been in this war, are Major C. Little and Captain L. H. Jones, of the Lancashire Yeomanry who played in the winning team of the Regimental Tournament at Hurlingham in 1878 and '79, which were its first two years, and in 1882. Captain Jones also won the Champion Cup with the Freebooters in 1884, '86 and '87, and the All-Ireland Open Cup in 1881. Other well-known polo players in the regiment are Major A. C. King, whom I remember as an expert at the game when he was in the 23rd Fusiliers ; Major Graham, D.S.O. ; Major Bailey ; and Captain Collis, who with Captain Daniell, of the Cheshire Yeomanry, won the Indian Inter-Regimental at Meerut in 1890. F. B. Dugdale, of the 5th Lancers, who is a young recruit to polo, won the V.C. most gallantly in Natal.

The Inniskilling Dragoons is one of the best regiments at polo ; their three most celebrated players being their commanding officer, Lieut.-Colonel Rimington, Neil Haig, and G. K. Ansell, with C. H. Higgin, Major Paynter, Captain F. A. Fryer, Captain E. C. Holland, E. Paterson, D S.O., and others to fall back on. Major Yardley rejoined them for the war, and was promoted Major for his services. Their triumphs include the Regimental at Hurlingham in 1897 and '98, the All-Ireland Open Cup in 1899, the Irish Regimental in 1897 and '98, and the Irish Subalterns' Cup in 1897, '98, and '99.

The 7th Hussars won the Inter-Regimental at

Hurlingham in 1883, '84, '85, '86 and '99 ; the Indian Regimental in 1891 ; and the Subalterns' Cup at Ranelagh in 1899.   Their commanding officer, Lieut.-Colonel Hon. R. Lawley, appears to have first played in 1883, and he played for his regiment in 1901.   His example is followed by all his officers.   Their finest players are perhaps Colonel Haig, to whom I have already referred, Major Carew, D.S.O., Major Poore, D.S.O., Major Vaughan, Captain Hon. J. Beresford, who represented England *v.* America in 1900, Major Brooke, D.S.O., and Captain Wormald, D.S.O. ; but there are many others, such as Major Nicholson, D.S.O., Lieut.-Colonel Holdsworth, and Captains Norton, Fielden, D.S.O., Holford D.S.O., and Johnstone.

Colonel Fisher, who commanded the 10th in South Africa, played for his regiment when they won the Cup in India in 1881 and '82.   Lord Airlie, who died at the head of the 12th Lancers, was one of this team.   In late years, the men who represented the regiment when they won at Hurlingham in 1888 and '93, and are still serving with it, are Major Hughes-Onslow, Captain Lord G. Scott, Major Hon. T. Brand, Lord W. Bentinck, D.S.O., and Brevet Lieut.-Colonel Kavanagh, Captain Hon. J. Dawnay, D.S.O., R. Chaplin, S. L. Barry, D.S.O., Major Hon. E. Baring and Captain C. Barclay.

The chief polo players of the 12th Lancers are Majors Crawley, Wormald, and H. Clifton-Brown, all of whom are Brevet Majors for their services in this war ; and Captain Hobson.   The best known player in the regiment was Captain Egerton Green, who was formerly Captain of the team, and served in the South African war.

The 13th Hussars have always been there or thereabouts in the final of the Tournament at Hurlingham during the last few years, and they secured this coveted trophy in 1892, '94, and '95. Their most celebrated team was composed of Captain Pedder, J. F. Church, F. H. Wise, and Captain MacLaren. J. T. Wigan, Captain Taylor, D.S.O., and A. Symons are also well-known players.

The 14th Hussars were very keen on polo when they were in Ireland, and had Captains Murray, Eley, Brooksbank, Tottenham, D.S.O., and Stephen, besides other good players.

The 15th Hussars are a very keen polo regiment in India. Major de Crespigny and Captain Hambro were their best known polo players in England. Lord Kensington, who is a member of their present team, earned the D.S.O. in this campaign.

The 16th Lancers have been a polo regiment for the last twenty-two years. Their team, which won the Cup at Hurlingham in 1880, was composed of H. R. L. Howard, J. M. Babington, F. G. Blair, J. G. A. Baird and W. H. Wyndham Quin. Howard and Blair earned the C.B. and Wyndham Quin obtained the D.S.O. in this campaign with the Yeomanry. Poor Orr-Ewing, who was killed at Kheiss, was an old 16th Lancer man, who, though fond of polo, was better known in the racing world. Major Gough is a particularly good polo player. Lord Fincastle, V.C., C. E. Harris, D.S.O., Captain Campbell and Captain Tuson formed the 16th Lancer team in 1899.

The 18th Hussars have several good polo players, such as Captain Wood, D.S.O., Captain Burnett, and A. C. McLachlan.

19*

Perhaps the best polo team ever seen in India was that of the Durham Light Infantry, who carried all before them from 1894 to 1898. They won the Infantry Tournament four times, the Regimental three times, and the Championship. Their best teams were those in which L. F. Ashburner and W. J. Ainsworth played with Captains Wilkinson, Luard and de Lisle. The Durham Light Infantry polo players have come well to the front in this war, as for instance, Lieut.-Colonel de Lisle, whose performances are well known ; Major Ross, C.B. ; Captain Ainsworth, D.S.O. ; Captain Ashburner, D.S.O. ; Captain Mathew, D.S.O. ; Captain Elwes, D.S.O. ; and poor R. E. Rasbotham, who was awarded the D.S.O. after he was killed. Captains Wilkinson and Luard, and P. W. Nickalls, were also in this campaign.

Brevet Colonel Pilcher, C.B., and A.D.C. to the King, of the Bedfordshire Regiment, and Colonel Henry used to play for the 5th Fusiliers.

Brevet Colonel Hon. C. Lambton, D.S.O., of the 5th Fusiliers, was 5th man for England v. America in 1886, and captained his regimental team when they won the Infantry Tournament at Hurlingham. He twice rode the winner of the Grand Military.

The Rifle Brigade have always been fond of polo. Their 3rd Battalion team (E. W. Bell, G. B. Gosling, Hon. G. H. Morris and P. R. Creed) won the Indian Tournament in 1900. Rifle Brigade teams were in the finals of the Indian Regimental Tournament in 1881, '82 and '83. One of their teams, which I saw playing well in Dublin and at Rugby in 1899, consisted of A. D. Boden, Lieut.-Colonel A. V. Jenner, D.S.O., Major A. E. Jenkins, and Captain H. E. Vernon,

D.S.O., all of whom were in South Africa. Captain Congreve, who won the V.C. at Colenso, is another keen Rifle Brigade polo player.

The Yeomanry have furnished us with many fine polo players, such as Major F. B. Mildmay, M.P., who won the Champion Cup with the Peats no less than seven times; Major Jenkinson, D.S.O., late of the Derbyshire Regiment, who was a well-known Lucknow expert in 1885; Lord Valentia, C.B., who began his polo career in the 10th Hussars, and for many years has been one of the chief members of the Hurlingham Polo Committee; both he and Colonel St. Quintin, also of the 10th Hussars, played in the first English match (p. 3); Lord Alwynne Compton, who played for the 10th Hussars in 1882; Colonel F. Meyrick, C.B., who played for the 15th Hussars in 1890; Colonel Burn, C.B. who played for the Royals in the final at Hurlingham in 1890; Major Gascoigne, D.S.O., late of the Blues, where his name appears in the Regimental team of 1877; Lieut.-Colonel Harrison, D.S.O., late of the Scots Greys; Herbert Wilson, D.S.O.; Clive Wilson; U. O. Thynne, D.S.O.; Godfrey Heseltine, the well-known No. 1 of the Old Cantabs; Clarence Wilson; C. G. M. Adam; F. and J. Bellville; Banbury; the brothers Gold; G. B. Milne; and many others.

The Indian Army has sent many good players to this war, as, for instance, Colonel Beatson, C.B., who taught the great Jodhpur team how to play; Colonel Younghusband, C.B., who wrote a capital book on Polo many years ago; poor Brazier Creagh, whom I knew as a fine player in 1887, when he was in the 9th B.L.; Captain F. A. Maxwell, V.C. and

D.S.O., of the 18th B.L., who played for his regiment when they won the Bengal Cavalry Tournament
in 1899.

The Indian Volunteers furnished a grand contingent of Polo players with Lumsden's Horse,
among whom were Captain Rutherfoord, D.S.O.,
Captain Taylor, of the Bengal Cavalry, Sergeant-
Major Marsham, who earned the Distinguished
Conduct Medal, his brother H. Marsham, who is
a very brilliant player, Percy Jones and Sergeant F.
Macnamara. I have had many good games with
them in Behar (India).

The Egyptian Army furnished a strong contingent,
among them Colonel Maxwell, D.S.O., whom I
remember as a brilliant player at Cairo in 1890 ;
Major J. K. Watson, C.M.G., D.S.O., Lieut.-Colonel
C. G. Martyr, D.S.O. ; and several others.

The gallant General Penn Symons, who was beloved
by every officer and man that served under him, did a
great deal for polo in India, and at the time of his
death was President of the Indian Polo Association.
The late Major Sherston, who soon followed him, was
Honorary Secretary of this Association. Indian polo
players owe him a deep debt of gratitude for having
brought Indian polo, including the revision of the rules,
into its present state of business-like efficiency.

The late Colonel Chisholm was well known as a
brilliant polo player in India and at Hurlingham when
he was in the 9th Lancers. His name first appears in
the winning team of that regiment at Meerut in 1878.

The late Lord Ava, who was the best of sportsmen,
comrades, and friends, was well known in the Indian
polo world when he was in the 17th Lancers, and

he played in the Regimental team when we won the Tournament at Meerut in 1889. He greatly promoted the success of the Ranelagh Club by taking up the secretaryship in 1895.

The late Lieut.-Colonel le Gallais was probably the best polo player who met his death in this war. I never played with or against a better No. 3. He played in the winning team of the 8th Hussars at Umballa in 1886 and '87, and was captain of his regimental team for several years. He also won the Paris Open Cup in 1895; and for the Freebooters in the same year, he helped to lower the colours of the hitherto invincible brothers Peat at Hurlingham, in the Champion Cup. If he was a good polo player, he was a still better soldier, and when he fell one of the finest young cavalry leaders in the Army was lost to the country.

Among many other good polo players whose loss during this war we have to regret, are Ellison, of the 9th Lancers, who won the Inter-Regimental at Hurlingham in 1897; C. G. Mackenzie, of the Royal Artillery, who did much for the Gunners' polo at Woolwich; "Jack" Hanwell, R.H.A., who was an excellent polo pony trainer, organiser, and captain of a polo team; Rose, of the Blues, who was No. 3 for many years of his regimental team; Kensington, of the 2nd Life Guards, keenest of sportsmen, best of friends; Tom Conolly, of the Scots Greys; Montmorency, V.C., of the 21st Lancers; Charles Cavendish, of the 17th Lancers; Lieut.-Colonel Vandeleur, D.S.O. a most distinguished young soldier; Bellew, of the 16th Lancers; Captain Legge, D.S.O., of the 20th Hussars, and Eyre Lloyd, of the Coldstreams, who was well known at Hurlingham for many years.

The above list by no means includes all the Polo players who have distinguished themselves in this campaign. There must be scores of others, especially in the Infantry and Royal Artillery, who have done most of their polo abroad. I have only mentioned those whom I have either played with, or have seen playing, or whose names I have found in the records. I think I have mentioned enough to show, if only by the extraordinary large proportion of decorations, and Brevets awarded to Polo players, that the game has some influence for good in the training of an officer, and should therefore be encouraged by our military authorities in every possible way.

Photo by]   [M. H. Hayes.

Fig. 101.—The late Lord Ava.

CHAPTER XIII.

POLO ABROAD.

United States of America—California—Argentina—The Colonies—France—Russia.

UNITED STATES OF AMERICA.

POLO was started in America by Mr. James Gordon Bennett in 1876. I see in *The Boston Herald*, that " he and Messrs. Herman Oelrichs, Frederick Bronson, Col. William Jay, Fairman Rogers, F. Gray Griswold, G. R. Fearing, W. P. Douglas, Sir Bach Cunard, Lord Mandeville, S. S. Howland, Hollis Hunnewell, John Mott, W. K. Thorn and others practised first in the old Dickel Riding Academy, and later on Mr. Bennett's private grounds near Jerome Park, Fordham. These gentlemen organised the Westchester Polo Club and played at Newport the following season, while Mr. H. L. Herbert and Messrs. Howard Stokes, W. W. Robbins, C. A. Robbins, Arthur Sewell, H. J. Montague, Capt. Grierson, G. W. Elder and Adolph Ladenburg established the New Brighton Polo Club at Long Branch. The last mentioned organisation played also at the Fair Grounds, Freehold, N.J., before an audience of some 5,000 people. Next the members of the Narragansett

Gun Club took up the game, Messrs. Pierre Lorillard, jun., E. W. Davis and Carroll Bryce being associated with Mr. James Gordon Bennett and others. The Messrs. Cary and Hamlin, of Buffalo, then organised a club, and a branch of the Westchester organisation played under the name of the Queen's County Club on Long Island, Messrs. August Belmont, F. Gray Griswold, Herman Oelrichs, Elliott Zobrowski and others being among the first to play.

" The first match between clubs in public was that which took place June 21, 1879, in Prospect Park, Brooklyn, members of the Westchester and Queen's County Clubs participating. The game was witnessed by upwards of 10,000 persons. The Westchester team, which won, consisted of Messrs. Harry Oelrichs, August Belmont, Carroll Bryce, William C. Sanford and H. L. Herbert. The Queen's County players were Messrs. F. Gray Griswold, Herman Oelrichs, F. T. Iselin, Pierre Lorillard, jun., and Center Hitchcock.

" The following year saw the opening of the Manhattan Polo Club grounds at Sixth Avenue and One Hundred and Tenth Street, New York. This field took the place of the old Jerome Park ground for a couple of seasons, but this in turn was also given up, and local interest in polo, so far as public matches were concerned, seems to have ceased for a time. At Meadow Brook and Rockaway Country Clubs the game had, however, become a great favourite with the members, who organised teams and practised assiduously. A club was also formed at Pelham. Among the players at these clubs were August Belmont, jun., Thomas Hitchcock, jun., Foxhall P. Keene, Winthrop

Fig. 102.—Mr. Foxhall Keene on his American pony "Texina."

Rutherford, J. D. Cheever, E. La Montague, Albert Francke, R. T. Francke, A. C. Tower, Farley Clark, J. S. Stevens, H. L. Herbert, W. K. Thorn, Oliver W. Bird, R. D. Winthrop, J. L. Kernochan, Stanley Mortimer, Sidney Dillon Ripley, E. D. Morgan, F. O. Beach, James M. Waterbury E. C. Potter, C. Oliver Iselin and the writer of these lines.

" Thus the sport in the East stood during the seasons immediately prior to 1885, when a team was organised at Harvard College by Messrs. Raymond Belmont, Edgerton Winthrop, Oliver Bird and Amos French. Yale College does not appear to have organised a team.

" It was during the summer of 1885 that polo found a footing in the West, the first club being established at Lemars, Ia., by Messrs. Maclagan, Watson, Grayson, Moreton, Pardoe and Richards. Mr. Maclagan later assisted Messrs. Benson, Dodsworth, Orde and Gray to organise a club at Sibley, Ia., and this was followed by the formation of a club at Colorado Springs, Col., by Mr. J. S. Stevens, of the Rockaway team, assisted by Messrs. Lyle, Braggiotti, and others. In 1886 Mr. H. L. Herbert organised a team at Orange, N.J. This club formed the nucleus of the Essex County organisation.

" It was in 1886 that the international match occurred at Newport between members of the English Hurlingham Club and a quartet of American players. On the English team were Mr. John Watson, Hon. R. Lawley, Messrs. T. Hone and Malcolm Little, with Mr. C. Lambton as umpire. The American players were Messrs. Thomas Hitchcock, jun., W. K. Thorn, jun., Raymond Belmont and Foxhall Keene, their umpire being Mr.

E. C. Winthrop, ·jun. Mr. S. Sands, jun., was time-
keeper and Mr. S. H. Robbins the referee. If anything,
the American players displayed more dash and spirit than
their competitors, but the superior strategy and combination play of the visitors so outclassed the work
of the home team that the result was a victory for the
former, the Englishmen registering ten goals as against
four scored by the American players. This game
demonstrated the necessity of an entire change in the
character of American polo, and the players, recognising the advantage of sustained combined effort over
brilliant individual play, quickly adopted that style and
have practised it ever since.

" Players soon became so numerous and so expert
that the introduction of a system of handicapping was
deemed expedient. This was distinctly an American
innovation, and, as events have proved, is decidedly
beneficial. It is a very simple arrangement, and consists of penalising players with a certain number of
goals commensurate with the degree of dexterity they
evince in actual play. When the system was inaugu-
rated in 1888 Mr. H. L. Herbert was, by mutual consent of the players in the East, appointed official
handicapper, and for several seasons arranged the lists
to the satisfaction of all concerned. But as new clubs
were started and the system extended it was too much
to expect that one player should be burdened with all
the work, and so, after a time, the duties of the office
devolved upon a committee made up of delegates of
the Eastern polo clubs, who now agree upon the
handicap changes which, at intervals during every
season, are deemed necessary.

" Following the introduction of the handicap system,

the offering of prizes became general, and the formation of new clubs took on the nature of an epidemic. In the neighbourhood of Boston the Myopia and Dedham Clubs were, during 1889, organised respectively by Messrs. R. M. Appleton, R. L. Agassiz, Robert G. Shaw, 2d. G. L. Peabody, A. P. Gardner, Samuel D. Warren, C. H. W. Foster, Allan Forbes, W. Cameron Forbes and their associates. On the Pacific coast the Santa Monica or Southern California Polo Club was organised by Messrs. E. Gorham, H. A. Winslow, G. L. Waring, J. B. Proctor, W. H. Young, J. E. Hoy, Captain Bolton, R. P. Carter, J. A. Parker, J. Machell, W. R. Ward and P. Martin.

" In 1890 the Philadelphia Club organised, with Messrs. J. S. Groom, H. P. McKean, jun., H. G. Groom and others.

" This year also saw the inauguration of the Oyster Bay, L. I., Club, with Messrs. Theodore Roosevelt, Francis G. Underhill, W. C. Tuckerman, Elliott and others.

" The year 1890 is notable as that in which the American Polo Association was organised. The members of a committee, which was formed on the 21st May, 1890, were Mr. H. L. Herbert, chairman; Messrs. Douglas Robinson, Oliver W. Bird, E. C. Potter and John C. Cowdin. The result was the formation of the Polo Association and the adoption of rules and regulations and bye-laws. At the first meeting held in New York, Friday, June 6, 1890, the American Polo Association was duly organised, embracing, as a nucleus, the country clubs of Westchester, Essex County, Meadow Brook, Morris County, Rockaway, Philadelphia, and Oyster Bay Polo Clubs,

Rules governing play were revised, dimensions of grounds agreed upon, implements used in the game defined and Association prizes offered.

" The American Polo Association has accomplished wonders during the decade just closed in the matter of its membership, clubs having been organised under the Association's auspices in almost every State in the Union. Its influence has been far reaching, and the tournaments held on the grounds of the several clubs as mutually agreed upon by delegates at the annual conventions have brought about a degree of public approval of the sport far greater than its most ardent sponsors ever anticipated. Counting the active participants at present included on the handicap lists, and the many club members who take part in occasional games only, and therefore have expressed a desire to be dropped from club schedules, and adding to these the many players who are not attached to any regular organisation, it is safe to say that fully five hundred polo players could, if necessary, be got together in this country."

Mr. W. A. Hazard, of 29, Broadway, N. Y., is now the Honorary Secretary of the American Polo Association.

During the season 1901 American polo players took part in tournaments held on the grounds of twenty clubs for thirty-five sets of cups and other special prizes, involving one hundred contests.

" In many respects the season just closed has been a most remarkable one. The schedule of one hundred games actually played shows an increase of ten over what were negotiated last year, and twenty-five more than were decided in 1899. Seventy games were played under the handicap system, the novices and young players thus being afforded unusual opportunities to try their strength against experts. Twenty contests were conducted regardless of handicap penalties, and in ten instances teams were rated evenly. Ample scope was therefore afforded followers of the sport to gauge the ability of individual players as well as regularly assigned combinations.

" Of the meetings which were the most successful, that held on Mr. George J. Gould's estate, Georgian Court, near Lakewood, N.J., and which practically opened the season in the East, so far as public attendance was concerned, must be accorded first place by reason of the diversity of sport presented, though in the matter of actual number of contests decided, the Rockaway tournament ranks highest with sixteen, next come Jersey, Point Judith, Newport, Westchester, Philadelphia, Meadowbrook, Bryn Mawr, ranking in the order named, and so on through the list down to Myopia, that wound up the season with a single combat."

For records of championship matches see page 329.

There are two important differences between the rules of American polo and those of English polo. In the States there is no off-side, and hooking sticks is not allowed ; the result being that in America the game is much looser, more brilliant runs are made, and more goals are hit than on English grounds.

On account of the system of blocking, a man in a first-class English match is lucky if he hits the ball more than twice running ; but in America, if he gets away with a clear run, which often happens owing to the absence of the off-side rule, his pursuer must overtake him in order to get the ball away from him, and is not allowed to put on a short spurt and hook his stick. No. 1 is of course much better off in the American game, and competes on even terms with the Back, instead of being at a great disadvantage, as in the English game.

Several American players are well known in this country as first-class performers, and it is greatly to be hoped that a representative international match will be played before long. We shall find the Lakewood team to be far superior to the one which Hurlingham easily defeated in 1886. We should remember that Americans, when trying to take the cup back to their own country, labour under the great disadvantage of having to play under Hurlingham rules, and they will have all the more credit, if they win.

The best known American players in England are Messrs. Foxhall Keene, Lawrence and Walter McCreery, F. J. Mackey, and the brothers Eustis, all of whom are fine players and good horsemen. The more that come, the better pleased will be their brother polo players on this side of the Atlantic.

In a letter which I recently had the pleasure of receiving from Mr. Foxhall Keene, he tells me that we English polo players are inclined to underrate American ponies, which he thinks are as fast as our animals, a trifle more handy, and more consistent in their form. He considers that superiority in weight is a decided advantage in favour of English ponies. To my question, " Can America produce as good ponies as the best in England ? " he replies as follows : " I do not think, even with the hundreds of ponies that are sent to us every year from Texas, Colorado, California and elsewhere, we have yet been able to find the very best ponies which our country produces, because very few of our men are willing to take the trouble and time to seek out these great individuals. There are many 'quarter horses' (14.2 and 14.2½ ponies) that are raced through our West for a quarter or three-eighths

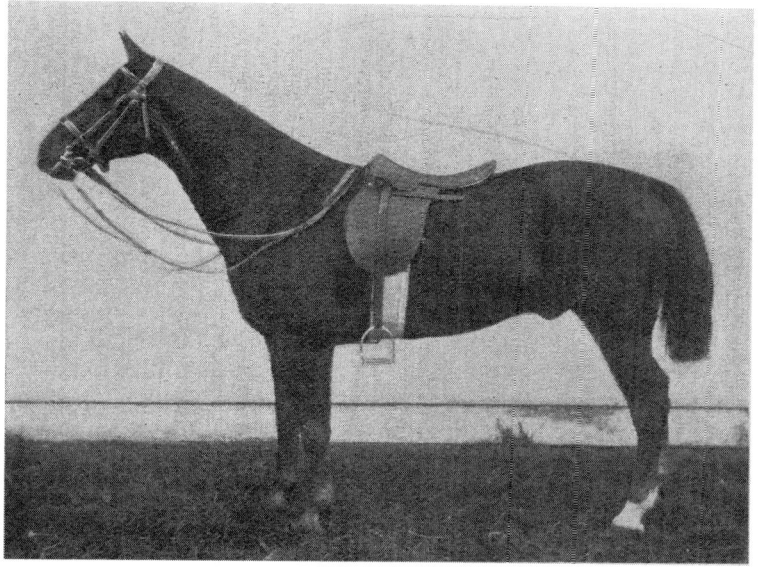

- *Photo by*]   [C. F. DE MOTT.
Fig. 103.—Mr. Foxhall Keene's chestnut American pory "Chief."

of a mile, which would make perfect polo ponies, if they were properly trained and schooled for four or five months. As a rule we do everything over here in such a hurry, that the large majority of our players prefer inferior ready-made ponies to these flyers."

The bay mare, Texina, on which Mr. Keene is mounted in Fig. 102, is a typical American pony, and

20*

is generally regarded as the best polo pony in that country. The chestnut pony Chief (Fig. 103) is also a typical American, and is of the highest class. Express (Fig. 104), though not quite as good as his two stable companions, is bad to beat.

CALIFORNIA.

In California, the Burlinghame Club is the headquarters of polo, although there are many other good clubs. Ponies are plentiful and good, as we may see from Figs. 47 and 89. Englishmen started polo in California, where the game is played under Hurlingham rules, which fact is, I think, a proof of the superiority of the English over the American game, because Californian players had the opportunity of judging which was the better of the two.

ARGENTINA.

The Hurlingham Club at Buenos Ayres is the leading polo club in the Argentine Republic, where the game is vigorously supported whenever eight Englishmen can get together. Even a dearth of our countrymen does not always stop the game in that part of the world ; for some of the owners of *estancias* have their own teams of natives, who play admirably.

An annual championship (p. 332), and many other good tournaments and matches take place. On many occasions we have had the pleasure of welcoming Argentine players on English grounds. H. Scott Robson, the ambidextrous welter weight, is the best player who has come from South America ; but we have seen many other good performers from that country, such as Frank Furber, Frank Balfour, and

H. Ravenscroft, the three of whom with Scott Robson formed a very successful team in 1897. F. E. Kinchant, an extraordinary hard hitter, is a very fine player, who came over in 1898. As a rule, teams from Argentina are greatly handicapped by the fact that their ponies take a long time to become acclimatised.

Englishmen who live in the Argentine Republic, like

Fig. 104.—Mr. Foxhall Keene's American pony "Express."

to spend their holidays in England, during which time they get lots of fun by bringing over with them their ponies, which they sell before returning. Although they do not make much pecuniary profit on the transaction, the sales somewhat help to pay the cost of the good polo which these fine sportsmen obtain.

THE COLONIES.

Polo flourishes at all the military stations, such as Gibraltar, Malta, Cairo, Alexandria, Wady Halfa, Suakim, Khartoum, Samoa, Jamaica, Aden, Singapore, Hong Kong and Shanghai; and soldiers and civilians play whenever they can. It is popular in Canada, Burma, the West Indies, and British Columbia. All over Australia and New Zealand flourishing clubs abound, and hold tournaments and matches.

The war has stopped polo to a great extent in South Africa, where it was played at Cape Town, Durban, Maritzburg, Harrismith, Johannesburg, Kimberley, Estcourt, Greytown, and many other places. Even now, in all standing camps, games are got up as a matter of course. An officer in a colonial corps told me that he had often taken part in a brush with the enemy in the morning, and played polo in the afternoon. In the near future South Africa will be a great polo country, because good and cheap grounds can be obtained in plenty, and the climate is perfect for the game all the year round.

FRANCE.

Mr. Réné Raòul Duval, who fell in love with the game when he was staying with the 7th Hussars in India, started polo in Paris in 1892 with a few other keen sportsmen, and an international tournament took place the following year (p. 328).

The early pioneers of polo in France were the three brothers Raoul Duval, Prince de Poix, Vicomte de la Rouchefoucauld, Duc de Luynes, M. Boussod, Marquis de Villaviega and his two brothers E. and P. d'Escandon, Luis d'Errazu, Baron le Jeune, Baron

E. de Rothschild, and a few others, nearly all of whom are still playing vigorously.

Polo is played five days a week during the Paris season, and there is no pleasanter place in or near the gay city than the charming little club-house and

Fig. 105.—Prince Serge Belosselsky on his half-bred Arab and Russian pony " Negress."

grounds at Bagatelle on the slopes of the Bois. Taking a polo team for the week between the Grand Prix and the big steeplechase at Auteuil is a most delightful experience. An International tournament then takes place ; amusement succeeds amusement with startling rapidity, and the hospitality accorded to English polo players is most cordial in every possible way.   Many of the French players are well known on English grounds, our most frequent visitors being the Escandons, Duvals, Baron Rothschild and L. de Errazu.   The Comte de Madre cannot now be regarded as a visitor, for he has taken up his residence in Rugby.

There are also grounds at Ferrières, Baron Rothschild's home, which has a perfect ground.   An annual tournament is held at Deauville in the autumn (p. 328).

The French cavalry officers have lately started for themselves a club near Paris, where they play together with great keenness.

RUSSIA.

Prince Serge Belosselsky (Fig. 105), who is well known at Paris, Pau, and Rugby, as an enthusiastic polo player, started the game at St. Petersburg about nine years ago, and was greatly helped in this laudable project by his father, Prince Belosselsky, who very generously presented the Polo Club with a beautiful ground on the island of Krestovsky.   Among other English residents of St. Petersburg, Mr. Tamplin, who was well known some years ago with the Brighton Harriers, rendered valuable aid to the good cause, both as a player and as a manager.   The keenest players at the Russia capital have been Prince Serge and English residents, including members of the British Embassy. Grand Duke Boris and Prince Kantacojène joined the ranks of keen players, and their good example will no doubt be followed by many other Russian gentlemen. In 1901, a tournament for an open cup took place, and the Hamburg Club, which is managed by Mr. Hasperg, of 36, Glasshüttenstrasse, sent a team in a most sporting manner. The following teams entered :—

HAMBURG.	BRITISH EMBASSY.	ST. PETERSBURG.
Mr. Beit.	Mr. P. de Bathe.	Count Kinsky.
Mr. Hasperg.	Mr. R. Graham.	Prince Serge Belosselsky.
Mr. Muller.	Mr. H. Beaumont.	Mr. Mouranyi.
Mr. Traum.	Hon. C. Hardinge.	Mr. Grabovsky.

The final was won by St. Petersburg by six goals to four, after a good game with the British Embassy. It is interesting to note that Count Kinsky, who won the Grand National on Zoedone, takes part in another British sport in a different part of the world.

Fig. 106 shows a half-bred Cossack pony.

Fig. 106.—Hon. C. Hardinge on his half-bred Cossack pony by a thorough-bred horse.

APPENDIX.

CHRONOLOGY OF MODERN POLO.

INTRODUCTION OF POLO.

1854. This year Major-General Sherar witnessed the game of Chaugan in the Munipoori Valley, and the tea planters of Cachar took it up shortly afterwards.

1859. Major-General Sherar introduced the game to Calcutta by bringing a Munipoori team to that city.

1861. Polo introduced in Punjaub and N.W.P. of India by British officers.

1867. Polo introduced to Madras and Ceylon; and became general throughout India.

1869. First polo match in England (*see* p. 2).

1872. Captain Herbert started polo at Lillie Bridge, in London.

1874. Hurlingham Club opened.

1876. Polo introduced to Australia.

1877. First year of Champion Cup, Hurlingham.

1877. First year of Indian Inter-Regimental Tournament.

1878. First year of Hurlingham Inter-Regimental Tournament.

1878. First year of Irish Open Cup.

1885. First year of County Cup, Hurlingham.

HURLINGHAM INTER-REGIMENTAL TOURNAMENT.

1878. 5th Lancers : J. Spicer, G. R. Tufton, Cosmo Little, L. H. Jones, Capt. R. St. L. Moore.

1879. 5th Lancers : G. R. Tufton, Cosmo Little, L. H. Jones, J. Spicer, Capt. R. St. L. Moore.

1880. 16th Lancers : J. G. A. Baird, W. H. Wyndham Quin, J. Babington, F. G. Blair, H. L. Howard.

1881. 16th Lancers : J. G. A. Baird, W. H. Wyndham Quin, J. Babington, H. L. Howard, J. Oswald, W. Browne.

1882. 5th Lancers : Cosmo Little, L. H. Jones, Capt. Tufton, Capt. J. Spicer.

1883. 7th Hussars : Hon. R. Lawley, T. Hone, Capt. Hunt, Capt. Roper.

1884. 7th Hussars : Hon. R. Lawley, T. Hone, Major Hunt, Capt. Roper.

1885. 7th Hussars : D. Haig, T. Hone, Major Hunt, Capt. Roper.

1886. 7th Hussars : Capt. T. Hone, G. A. Carew, D. Haig, Capt. Hon. R. Lawley.

1887. 5th Lancers : L. H. Jones, Capt. C. Little, B. Mundy, Capt. J. Spicer.

1888. 10th Hussars : A. Hughes Onslow, E. W. Baird, Capt. Greenwood, Capt. Allsop.

1889. 9th Lancers : Capt. W. K. Jenner, Capt. Malcolm Little, Capt. F. Colvin, Capt. Lamont.

1890. 9th Lancers : Capt. W. K. Jenner, Capt. Malcolm Little, Capt. F. Colvin, Capt. Lamont.

1891. 9th Lancers : Capt. W. K. Jenner, Capt. Hon. C. Willoughby, Capt. F. Colvin, Major Lamont.

1892. 13th Hussars : E. N. Pedder, D. Robertson Aikman, F. Wise, Capt. MacLaren.

1893. 10th Hussars : Lord G. Scott, Capt. Kavanagh, Lord W. Bentinck, Hon. T. Brand.

1894. 13th Hussars : Capt. E. N. Pedder, J. F. Church, F. Wise, Capt. MacLaren.

1895. 13th Hussars : Capt. E. N. Pedder, J. F. Church, F. Wise, Capt. MacLaren.

1896. 9th Lancers : D. Campbell, Capt. W. K. Jenner, G. Ellison, Lord C. Bentinck.

1897. Inniskillings : F. A. Fryer, G. K. Ansell, N. Haig, Major Rimington.

1898. Inniskillings : H. C. Higgin, G. K. Ansell, N. Haig, Major Rimington.

1899. 7th Hussars : J. Vaughan, Capt. Hon. J. Beresford, Major Carew, Major Poore.

1900 and 1901. No Tournament, on account of South African War.

HURLINGHAM OPEN CHAMPION CUP.

Conditions :—Open to any Polo Teams.

The entries, naming colours, to be made on or before 5 p.m., on the Saturday prior to the week of competition.

The respective Teams to be drawn, and the said draw to take place on Saturday, at 5 p.m., prior to the week of competition. The Captain of each Team to name his four players at time of entry.

In the contest for the Champion Cup, in case one or more of the players should be incapacitated from playing, one or more substitutes, not having already taken part in the Tournament, may be brought in.

Unless three Teams contend the Cup will not be given.

In case of a Tie between two Teams, it must be played off the same day till one Team obtain a Goal, always excepting both Teams electing to postpone.

1877. Monmouthshire and Tyros played a tie : F. Herbert, R. Herbert, H. Owen, J. Mellor, E. Curre ; C. de Murietta, A. de Murietta, Sir B. Cunard, E. Baldock, Hon. C. C. Cavendish.

1878. Monmouthshire : F. Herbert, R. Herbert, J. Mellor, E. Curre, Sir C. Wolseley.

1879. Hurlingham : E. Baldock, W. Ince Anderton, J. Peat, A. E. Peat, A. Peat.

1880. Sussex : Earl of Lewes, Phipps Hornby, J. Peat, A. E. Peat, A. Peat.

1881. Sussex : Earl of Lewes, A. Peyton, J.·Peat, A. E. Peat, A. Peat.

1882. Sussex : J. Peat, Kenyon Stow, A. Peyton, A. Peat, J. Babington.

1883. Sussex w.o. : Phipps Hornby, J. Peat, A. E. Peat, A. Peat.

1884. Freebooters : L. H. Jones, T. Hone, John Watson, J. Spicer.

1885. Sussex : J. Peat, F. Mildmay, A. E. Peat, A. Peat.

1886. Freebooters : Capt. B. Gough, L. H. Jones, J. Spicer, John Watson.

1887. Freebooters : Malcolm Little, L. H. Jones, K. MacLaren, John Watson.

1888. Sussex : J. Peat, F. Mildmay, A. E. Peat, A. Peat.

1889. Sussex : J. Peat, F. Mildmay, A. E. Peat, A. Peat.

1890. Sussex : J. Peat, F. Mildmay, A. E. Peat, A. Peat.

1891. Sussex : J. Peat, F. Mildmay, A. E. Peat, A. Peat.

1892. Sussex : J. Peat, F. Mildmay, Lord Harrington, A. E. Peat.

1893. Sussex w.o. : J. Peat, F. Mildmay, A. E. Peat, A. Peat.

1894. Freebooters : Gerald Hardy, Lord Southampton, Capt. le Gallais, Capt. Daly.

1895. Freebooters : Gerald Hardy, Lord Southampton, A. Rawlinson, Capt. Daly.

1896. Freebooters : Gerald Hardy, Lord Southampton, A. Rawlinson, W. S. Buckmaster.

1897. Rugby : G. A. Miller, Capt. Renton, E. D. Miller, W. J. Drybrough.

1898. Rugby : G. A. Miller, Capt. Renton, E. D. Miller (and Walter Jones), W. J. Drybrough.

1899. Rugby : Walter Jones, G. A. Miller, E. D. Miller, W. J. Drybrough.

1900. Old Cantabs : W. McCreery, F. M. Freake, W. S. Buckmaster, L. McCreery.

1901. Rugby : Walter Jones, G. A. Miller, E. D. Miller, C. D. Miller.

HURLINGHAM COUNTY CUP.

1885. Gloucestershire : E. Kenyon Stow, Lord Harrington, F. G. Matthews, T. S. Baxter.

1886. Gloucestershire : E. Kenyon Stow, Lord Harrington, F. G. Matthews, M. Little.

1887. Derbyshire w.o. : E. Kenyon Stow, Lord Harrington, Gerald Hardy, Capt. Herbert.

1888. Kent : R. Stewart Savile, Capt. Alderson, Major Peters, G. Russell.

1889. Barton : Gerald Hardy, J. Reid Walker, W. Hall Walker, Lord Harrington.

1890. Berkshire : Capt. V. Ferguson, H. T. Fenwick, Hon. W. Lambton, Capt. J. Spicer.

1891. Liverpool : G. H. Pilkington, C. E. Mason, A. Tyrer, W. Hall Walker.

1892. Meath : Gore Lambarde, F. Featherstonhaugh, J. O. Jameson, T. Hone, J. Watson.

1893. Edinburgh : W. Younger, C. G. Mackenzie, W. J. Drybrough, T. Drybrough.
1894. Edinburgh : W. Younger, Egerton Green, W. J. Drybrough, T. Drybrough.
1895. Rugby. Lord Shrewsbury, G. A. Miller, E. D. Miller, Capt. Daly.
1896. Stansted : Guy Gilbey, G. Gold, A. Gold, W. Buckmaster.
1897. Rugby : W. Neilson, F. J. Mackey, Lord Shrewsbury, Capt. Renton.
1898. Chislehurst : C. Nickalls, H. Savill, M. Nickalls, P. W. Nickalls.
1899. Stansted : P. Gold, Capt. Gosling, T. Gilbey, G. Gold.
1900. Rugby : J. Drage, Comte J. de Madre, K. Marsham, Sir H. de Trafford.
1901. Eden Park : H. Rich, P. Bullivant, H. Marsham, H. Cardwell.

HURLINGHAM SOCIAL CLUB CUP.

1897. White's Club : Capt. Fitzgerald, Capt. Renton, G. A. Miller, Sir H. de Trafford.
1898. Raleigh Club : Walter Jones, E. B. Sheppard, W. S. Buckmaster, W. J. Drybrough.
1899. Nimrod Club : Lord Shrewsbury, F. J. Mackey, A. Rawlinson, Capt. Renton.
1900. Pitt Club, Cambridge : W. McCreery, F. M. Freake, W. S. Buckmaster, L. McCreery, C. D. Miller.
1901. Orleans Club : F. Hargreaves, F. Menzies, F. M. Freake, L. McCreery.

RANELAGH LADIES' CUP.

N.B.—Entries close Wednesday previous to week of play.

Conditions :—Thirty-two ladies will be nominated by a committee appointed for the purpose.

Each lady will nominate one player. The nominator is responsible that her nominee is available to play on any day from July 1st to July 6th.

The players will be drawn together in teams.

The ladies nominating the winners will receive the prizes presented by the Ranelagh Club.

If a team cannot play at the time advertised, that team must scratch ; but the Polo Manager will do his best to meet the wishes of Competitors if informed before entries close of the most convenient hours.

1901. "B" Team : Lord Shrewsbury, M. Nickalls, F. M. Freake, Capt. Schreiber.

RANELAGH PUBLIC SCHOOLS' CUP.

N.B.—Entries close Wednesday previous to week of play.

Conditions :—Open to any team, the Members of which have been at the same Public School.

No player is eligible to represent his School unless he spent not less than two years there.

The Captain of each team to name his four players, in writing, at the time of entry.

For a Cup presented by the Ranelagh Club, which will be given to the School represented by the winning team.

An entrance fee of £4 must be paid for each team. The Sweepstakes to go to the winning team.

If a team cannot play at the time advertised, that team must scratch ; but the Polo Manager will do his best to meet the wishes of Competitors if informed before entries close of the most convenient hours.

1901. Old Marlburians : Capt. L. C. D. Jenner, E. B. Sheppard, G. A. Miller, C. D. Miller.

RANELAGH OPEN CHALLENGE CUP.

N.B.—Entries close Wednesday previous to week of play.

Conditions :—Open to any team, club, or regiment.

The preliminary ties to be played off by all the teams entered, the holders on giving notice to that effect before the closing of the entries need only defend the Cup in the final.

The Captain of each team to name his four players, in writing, at the time of entry.

After a team has once played no substitute for a member of the team will be allowed, without the consent of the Polo Manager ; under no circumstances may one man play in two teams.

An entrance fee of £5 must be paid for each team. This fee will be returned unless the team scratches, in which case the money thus collected will be given to the Ranelagh Club Servants' Christmas-Box Fund.

If a team cannot play at the time advertised, that team must scratch ; but the Polo Manager will do his best to meet the wishes of Competitors if informed before entries close of the most convenient hours.

1897. Rugby : Walter Jones, G. A. Miller, C. D. Miller, E. D. Miller.
1897. Ranelagh : A. Rawlinson, Dokhal Singh, W. S. Buckmaster, W. J. Drybrough.
1898. Freebooters : A. Rawlinson, F. M. Freake, W. S. Buckmaster, John Watson.
1899. Freebooters : J. Vaughan, G. K. Ansell, A. Rawlinson, Capt. Hon. J. Beresford.
1900. Old Cantabs : W. McCreery, F. M. Freake, W. S. Buckmaster, L. McCreery.
1901. Rugby : Walter Jones, G. A. Miller, Lord Shrewsbury (and E. D. Miller), C. D. Miller.

RANELAGH CLUB, NOVICES' CUP.

N.B.—Entries close Wednesday previous to week of play.

Conditions :—Open to any polo team, club, or regiment, with the following exceptions :—

No polo player is eligible who has played in the winning team of any of the following tournaments :—Champion Cup at Hurlingham ; the Ranelagh Open

Challenge Cup ; the Regimental Tournament, at Hurlingham ; the County Cup ; the Regimental Tournament, in Dublin ; the Open Cup, in Dublin ; International Tournament, in Paris ; Rugby Tournament ; the Regimental Tournament, in India ; the Subalterns' Cup, at Ranelagh ; the Subalterns' Cup, in Ireland ; the Hunt Cup, at Ranelagh ; the Social Club Cup, at Hurlingham ; the Champion Cup, in India ; the Hurlingham Tournament, in Buenos Ayres ; the Championship, in America ; the Public Schools Cup, at Ranelagh ; and the Novices Cup, at Ranelagh, in 1901, or subsequently.

The Novices Cup is confined to Members of Ranelagh, and to one team from each county belonging to the County Polo Association, and to one team from each regiment.

The Captain of each team to name his four players, in writing, at the time of entry.

After a team has once played no substitute for a member of the team will be allowed, without the consent of the Polo Manager ; under no circumstances may one man play in two teams.   The Captain of each team to name his four players, in writing, at time of entry.

An entrance fee of £5 must be paid for each team.   This fee will be returned unless the team scratches, in which case the money thus collected will be given to the Ranelagh Club Servants' Christmas-Box Fund.

If a team cannot play at the time advertised, that team must scratch ; but the Polo Manager will do his best to meet the wishes of Competitors if informed before entries close of the most convenient hours.

1896. Fulham Rovers : G. W. Hobson, W. R. Court, L. C. D. Jenner, A. Suart.
1897. Rovers : Capt. A. Jenner, L. C. D. Jenner, Dohlal Singh, Capt. Bruce.
1898. Trekkers : U. O. Thynne, J. Wormald, F. E. Kinchant, P. W. Nickalls.
1899. Trekkers : Capt. Schofield, L. C. D. Jenner, F. C. Menzies, U. O. Thynne.
1900. Trekkers : B. Wilson, L. C. D. Jenner, A. Stourton, F. Menzies.
1901. Eden Park : H. Rich, P. Bullivant, H. Marsham, L. Bucknall.

RANELAGH HUNT CHALLENGE CUP.

N.B.—Entries close Wednesday previous to week of play.

Conditions :—Open to any pack of Foxhounds or Staghounds in the United Kingdom, or abroad.

No player is eligible to compete unless he has, for the previous season, subscribed not less than £10 to the Hunt he represents, on or before the 1st of March of the same year.   He must also have hunted on not less than ten occasions the previous season with that Hunt.

No player may represent different Hunts in consecutive seasons unless he is no longer qualified for the Hunt he represented the previous season.

The Captain of each team to name his four players, in writing, at the time of entry.

The Captain must be responsible that each Member of his team is duly qualified.

An entrance fee of £5 must be paid for each team. This fee will be returned unless the team scratches, in which case the money thus collected will be given to the Hunt Servants' Benefit Fund.

After a team has once played no substitute will be allowed without the consent of the Polo Manager.

The Challenge Cup is held for one year by the Master of the winning Hunt.

Prizes will be presented to the Winners by the Ranelagh Hunt.

If a team cannot play at the time advertised, that team must scratch ; but the Polo Manager will do his best to meet the wishes of Competitors if informed before entries close of the most convenient hours.

1897. Muskerry : G. W. Hobson, Capt. Clifton Brown, Capt. Egerton Green, F. Wormald.

1898. Warwickshire : F. Hargreaves, F. J. Mackey, F. M. Freake, W. J. Drybrough.

1899. Pytchley : C. P. Nickalls, Capt. Renton,W. S. Buckmaster, P.W. Nickalls.

1900. Pytchley : G. W. McIvor, Capt. Renton, W. S. Buckmaster, Comte J. de Madre.

1901. Pytchley : C. P. Nickalls, M. Nickalls, W. S. Buckmaster, J. Drage.

RANELAGH CLUB, SUBALTERNS' CUP.

N.B.—Entries close Wednesday, July 17th.

Conditions :—Open to teams of Subalterns from any regiment of the Regular or Auxiliary Forces. Infantry Regiments of more than one Battalion may enter a combined team.

The Royal Artillery are eligible to enter as a team.

The Captain of each team to name his four players, in writing, at the time of entry.

The conditions are, with the above exception, the same as for the Inter Regimental Tournament, at Hurlingham.

If the team cannot play at the time advertised, that team must scratch ; but the Polo Manager will do his best to meet the wishes of Competitors if informed before entries close of the most convenient hours.

1896. 9th Lancers : F. H. Allhusen, G. Ellison, D. Campbell, Lord Charles Bentinck.

1897. Royal Horse Guards : } Hon. D. Marjoribanks, Hon. R. Ward, E. Rose,
1898. Royal Horse Guards : } F. E. Drage.

1899. 7th Hussars : H. Fielden, J. H. Holford, F. Wormald, J. Vaughan.

1900. }
1901. } Tournament did not take place owing to South African War.

ALL IRELAND COUNTY CUP.

Conditions :—See Rules of the Irish County Polo Club Union, 1901 ; page 351.

WINNERS.

1890. Fermanagh : }
1891. Fermanagh : } A Maude, C. C. D'Arcy Irvine, E. M. Archdale, J.
1892. Fermanagh : } Porter-Porter.

21*

1893. Meath : Shirley Ball, Capt. Steeds, J. O. Jameson, Capt. Hone.
1894. Sligo : }
1895. Sligo : } P. W. Connolly, C. O'Hara, G. M. Eccles, J. FitzGerald.
1896. Westmeath : Major Lewis, R. Hudson, Joyce, P. O'Reilly.
1897. Westmeath : J. H. Locke, R. Hudson, Major Lewis, P. P. O'Reilly.
1898. Sligo : {
1899. Sligo : } P. W. Connolly, H. G. L'Estrange, C. O'Hara, J. Fitz-
                Gerald.
1900. Sligo : P. W. Connolly, W. Campbell, C. O'Hara, J. FitzGerald.
1901. Sligo : G. M. Eccles, W. Campbell, C. O'Hara, J. FitzGerald.

ALL IRELAND HUNT CUP.

This Tournament was promoted by Co. Kildare, and is played on their ground at
Castletown.

Conditions :—Open to teams comprised of Members of any recognised Pack of
Fox or Staghounds in the United Kingdom.

1901. Meath Hunt : R. Houston, S. Watt, Capt. Steeds, Capt. Long (and John
      Watson.)

ALL IRELAND OPEN CHALLENGE CUP,
DUBLIN.

Conditions :—See page 39, Book of Rules.

1878. 7th Royal Fusiliers : Not recorded.
1879. 7th Hussars : Capt. Roper, Capt. Phillips, Hon. R. Lawley, Lord Lumley,
      J. Hunt.
1880. Scots Greys : W. C. Middleton, W. H. Hippisley, Torrens, Wolfe.
1881. 5th Lancers : Combe, Tufton, J. Spicer, L. H. Jones.
1882. All Ireland P.C. : Capt. Montague, Dugdale, G. B. Hone, J. Watson.
1883. Carlow : W. Edge, Wolfe, T. Hone, J. Watson.
1884. 5th Lancers : Mundy, Sinclair, Capt. L. H. Jones, Capt. Spicer.
1885. Freebooters : W. Edge, W. Anderson, J. O. Jameson, J. Watson.
1886. Freebooters : D. Haig, W. Edge, Capt. Hon. R. Lawley, J. Watson.
1887. All Ireland P.C. : J. D. Calley, Capt. Babington, J. Locke, J. Watson.
1888. All Ireland P.C. : J. Reilly, Capt. Middleton, J. O. Jameson, J. Watson.
1889. Freebooters : Capt. F. H. Featherstonhaugh, J. O. Jameson, H. T. Fen-
      wick, J. Watson.
1890. All Ireland P.C. : J. Reilly, Capt. Hone, J. O. Jameson, J. Watson.
1891. 13th Hussars : Capt. Pedder, F. Wise, D. Robertson Aikman, Capt.
      MacLaren.
1892. 9th Lancers : Capt. Jenner, Capt. Little, Capt. Colvin, Major Lamont.
1893. 13th Hussars : Capt. Pedder, F. Wise, D. Robertson Aikman, Capt. Mac-
      Laren.
1894. 15th Hussars : Capt. Dalgety, Capt. Dundas, Capt. Mundy, Captain de
      Crespigny.

1895. Freebooters : Lord Shrewsbury, A. Rawlinson, W. S. Buckmaster, Capt. Daly.

1896. 13th Hussars : Capt. Pedder, J. F. Church, F. Wise, Capt. MacLaren.

1897. Rugby : C. D. Miller, G. A. Miller, E. D. Miller, W. J. Drybrough.

1898. Rugby : F. Hargreaves, G. A. Miller, E. D. Miller, W. J. Drybrough.

1899. Inniskilling Dragoons : Capt. Paynter, G. K. Ansell, C. H. Higgin, Neil Haig.

1900. Freebooters : F. Hargreaves, Capt. Hon. J. Beresford (and O. Haig), F. M. Freake, John Watson.

1901. Nomads : P. W. Nickalls, Capt. Steeds, G. A. Miller, C. D. Miller.

ALL IRELAND NOVICES' CUP.

Conditions :—See Rules of the Irish County Polo Club Union, 1901 : page 351. See page 40—41, A. I. P. C. Rules, 1900.

1898. Derry : A. A. Watt, S. Watt, T. F. Cooke, R. P. Uniacke

1899. Curragh Rovers : T. G. Gibson, E. Carbutt, Dixon Johnson, Capt. Paynter.

1900. All Ireland P.C. (A Team) : H. Nutting, Capt. Gosling, T. Leonard, T. L. Moore.

1901. North Westmeath : A. M. Rotherham, H. Wilson, P O'Reilly, R. O'Reilly.

ALL IRELAND REGIMENTAL CHALLENGE CUP.

1886. 10th Hussars : E. W. Baird, Hon. G. Baring, A. Hughes Onslow, F. Bowlby.

1887. 16th Lancers : E. Beaumont, J. D. Calley, Orr Ewing, G. P. Windham, Capt. Babington.

1888. 3rd Hussars : J. W. Burns, Capt. Oswald, Capt. Pattor Bethuse, Capt. Chaloner.

1889. 4th Hussars : R. Hoare, Capt. Kincaid Smith, Majo Peters, Capt. Baillie.

1890. 4th Hussars : W. Wigson, R. Hoare, Major Peters, Capt. Baillie.

1891. 15th Hussars : J. Hargreaves, Dundas, Capt. de Crespigny, Bewicke.

1892. 13th Hussars : Capt. E. N. Pedder, F. Wise, D. Robertson Aikman, Capt. MacLaren.

1893. 9th Lancers : D. G. Campbell, Capt. M. Little, Capt. Covin, Capt. Hon. C. Willoughby.

1894. 10th Hussars : N. Curzon, Capt. Kavanagh, Lord W. Bentinck, Hon. T. Brand.

1895. 13th Hussars } Capt. E. N. Pedder, J. F. Church, F. Wise, Capt.
1896. 13th Hussars } MacLaren.

1897. 6th Inniskilling D. } Capt. Paynter, G. K. Ansell, Neil Haig, Major
1898. 6th Inniskilling D. } Rimington.

1899. 17th Lancers : A. F. Fletcher, Capt. W. A. Tilney, Capt. Portal, R. J. Carden.

1900. ⎫
1901. ⎭ No Tournament on account of South African War.

ALL IRELAND SUBALTERNS' CUP.

1896. 10th Hussars : N. Curzon, S. L. Barry, B. C. Meeking, Hon. T. Brand.

1897. Inniskilling Dragoons : C. H. Higgins, G. K. Ansell, Neil Haig, E. C. Holland.

1898. Inniskilling Dragoons : E. Patterson, G. K. Ansell, Neil Haig, E. C. Holland.

1899. Inniskilling Dragoons : E. Patterson, G. K. Ansell, C. F. D. Johnson, Neil Haig.

1900. ⎫
1901. ⎭ Tournament did not take place on account of South African War.

RUGBY TOURNAMENT.

Conditions :—For a Challenge Cup presented by the brothers MILLER, open to any Polo Club, Team, or Regiment, with the exception that not more than two players who have won the Champion Cup at Hurlingham, or the Ranelagh Open Challenge Cup, may play in the same team. Played during the first week in August.

1893. Rugby : R. Chaplin, J. Reid Walker, E. D. Miller, G. A. Miller.

1894. Cheshire : M. Walker, W. R. Court, W. H. Walker, Lord Harrington.

1895. Freebooters : Lord Shrewsbury, Lord Southampton, A. Rawlinson, Capt. Daly.

1896. Rugby : Walter Jones, G. A. Miller, E. D. Miller, Sir H. de Trafford.

1897. Winwick : C. D. Miller, F. M. Freake, A. Rawlinson, Sir H. Rawlinson.

1898. Old Cantabs : G. Heseltine, F. M. Freake, W. S. Buckmaster, L. McCreery.

1899. Not finished.

1900. Rugby : Walter Jones, M. Nickalls, G. A. Miller, P. W. Nickalls.

1901. Not finished.

RUGBY AUTUMN CHALLENGE CUP.

Conditions :—Open to any Polo Club, Team, or Regiment, with the exception that not more than one man who has played in the winning team of the Champion Cup at Hurlingham, or the Ranelagh Open Challenge Cup, or Inter-Regimental at Hurlingham, during the last five years, may play in the same team.

The COMTE J. DE MADRE presented a Challenge Cup to be played for every year, to be won three years consecutively by the same Club, Regiment, or Team, before becoming their absolute property. Played in September.

1900. Deauville : Baron E. de Rothschild, A. Rawlinson, F. A. Gill, Marquis de Villaviega.

1901. Handley Cross : H. Rich, F. J. Mackey, W. S. Buckmaster, F. O. Ellison.

WARWICKSHIRE TOURNAMENT.

Conditions :—Open to any Polo Club, Team, or Regiment, with the exception that not more than two players who have won the Champion Cup at Hurlingham, or the Ranelagh Open Challenge Cup, may play in the same team.   Played in July.

1894. E. D. Miller's team : J. Bellville, P. A. Leaf, H. J. Selwyn, E. D. Miller.

1895. E. D. Miller's team : Walter Jones, L. de Errazu, H. Scott Robson, E. D. Miller.

1896. Rugby : Walter Jones, Lord Shrewsbury, G. A. Miller, E. D. Miller.

1897. Winwick : Lord Shrewsbury, F. M. Freake, C. D. Miller, A. Rawlinson.

1898. Winwick : G. Ansell, A. Rawlinson, Neil Haig, Capt. MacLaren.

1899. Old Cantabs : W. McCreery, F. M. Freake, W. S. Buckmaster, G. Heseltine.

1900. W. S. Buckmaster's team : F. J. Mackey, F. M. Freake, W. S. Buckmaster, M. R. Duval.

1901. Old Cantabs : G. Heseltine, F. M. Freake, W. S. Buckmaster (and C. D. Miller), F. Hargreaves.

ST. NEOTS POLO CLUB.

ANNUAL TOURNAMENT HELD IN JULY.

Conditions :—A Challenge Cup presented by MAJOR SHUTTLEWORTH will be competed for, to be held by the winning team for the year, but which will become the property of the team winning it the second time.

The team must contain at least two of the original players.   Open to any Polo Team, Club, or Regiment, with the exception that not more than one man, who has played in the winning team of the Champion Cup at Hurlingham, Open Cup at Ranelagh, Open Cup in Dublin, during the last five years, may play in the same team.

1900. Handley Cross : H. Rich, F. J. Mackey, L. Bucknell, F. O. Ellison.
1901. Handley Cross : H. Rich, G. Lousada, F. J. Mackey, F. O. Ellison.

STRATFORD-ON-AVON POLO CLUB.

ANNUAL TOURNAMENT HELD IN JULY.

For a Challenge Cup presented by MISS MARIE CORELLI.

Open to any Polo Team, Club, or Regiment, with the exception that not more than one man, who has played in the winning team of the Champion Cup at Hurlingham, Open Cup at Ranelagh, Open Cup in Dublin, during the last five years, may play in the same team.

1901. Handley Cross : H. Rich, F. J. Mackey, F. O. Ellison, L. Bucknall.

CIRENCESTER POLO TOURNAMENT.

Conditions :—Open to any Polo Team, Club, or Regiment, with the exception that not more than one man who has played in the winning team of the Champion Cup at Hurlingham, Open Cup at Ranelagh, Open Cup in Dublin, or the Military Tournament at Hurlingham, during the last five years, may play in the same team. Played in August.

1895. Scots Greys: Capt. Maxwell, Capt. Pringle, Capt. Harrison, Capt. Richards.
1896. Siddington Wanderers : C. Beatty, Comte J. de Madre, J. Adamthwaite, G. B. Milne.
1897. W. J. Drybrough's team : Capt. Pedder, C. Beatty, Capt. Egerton Green, W. J. Drybrough.
1898. Kemble Scorchers: J. D. Gouldsmith, F. J. Mackey, F. M. Freake, C. Beatty.
1899. Cirencester : J. Adamthwaite, H. Rich, D. C. Master, G. B. Milne.
1900. Cirencester A : B. C. Burdon, H. Rich, R. R. Barker, J. Adamthwaite.
1901. Wanderers : P. C. Puckle, F. M. Freake, G. Heseltine, F. O. Ellison.

PARIS INTERNATIONAL OPEN CUP.

1893. 17th Lancers : W. A. Tilney, Capt. Renton, B. P. Portal, N. T. Nickalls.
1894. Hurlingham : Gerald Hardy, J. Reid Walker, Capt. Le Gallais, E. D. Miller.
1895. Ranelagh : E. Hohler, A. Rawlinson, E. B. Sheppard, W. S. Buckmaster.
1896. Staffordshire : Lord Shrewsbury, F. J. Mackey, W. Hall Walker, A. Rawlinson.
1897. Rugby : Comte J. de Madre, Capt. Renton, W. S. Buckmaster, W. J. Drybrough.
1898. Paris : J. H. Wright, E. de Escandon, Marquis de Villaviega, M. Raoul Duval.
1899. Paris : J. H. Wright, E. de Escandon, M. Raoul Duval, Marquis de Villaviega.
1900. Foxhunters : A. Rawlinson, F. J. Mackey, Foxhall Keene, Capt. Daly.
1901. The Tournament did not take place.

DEAUVILLE INTERNATIONAL TOURNAMENT.

1895. Ranelagh : G. Heseltine, W. C. Harrild, F. G. Menzies, E. Hohler.
1896. Buccaneers : L. Whitburn, Hon. R. Ward, F. G. Menzies, F. Furber.
1897. Buccaneers : E. H. Bald, Hon. R. Ward, R. McCreery, F. G. Menzies.
1898. Buccaneers : — Davidson, Hon. R. Ward, F. G. Menzies, Hon. D. Marjoribanks.
1899. Foxhunters : W. McCreery, F. J. Mackey, F. M. Freake, A. Rawlinson.
1900. }
1901. } Tournament did not take place.

CHAMPIONSHIP OF AMERICA.

1895. Myopia Hunt Club Team, Hamilton, Mass. : A. P. Gardner, R. L. Agassiz, R. G. Shaw, F. Blackwood-Fay.

1896. Rockaway Club, Cedarhurst, L.I. : J. S. Stevens, Foxhall P. Keene, J. E. Cowdin, G. P. Eustis.

1897. Meadow Brook Club, Westbury, L.I. : W. C. Eustis, Thos. Hitchcock, jun., H. P. Whitney, B. Nicoll.

1898. Meadow Brook Club, Westbury, L.I. : W. C. Eustis, Thos. Hitchcock, jun., C. C. Baldwin, H. P. Whitney.

1899. Westchester Polo Club, Newport, R.I., By default : J. M. Waterbury, jun., Foxhall P. Keene, J. E. Cowdin, L. Waterbury.

1900. Dedham Polo Club, Dedham, Mass. : Allan Forbes, E. M. Weld, W. H. Goodwin, Joshua Crane, jun.

1901. Lakewood : C. R. Snowden, J. M. Waterbury, jun., Foxhall P. Keene, L. Waterbury.

JUNIOR CHAMPIONSHIP OF AMERICA.

1900. C.C. Philadelphia, Bala, Pa. : J. P. Lippincott, M. G. Rosengarten, jun., A. E. Kennedy, J. F. McFadden.

1901. Rockaway : W. A. Hazard, R. La Montague, jun., R. J. Collier, P. F. Collier.

INTERNATIONAL MATCH, AMERICA *v.* ENGLAND.

1886. Played in America, at Newport, for Challenge Cup, won by Hurlingham by Malcolm Little, T. Hone, Hon. R. T. Lawley, John Watson.

1900. Played at Hurlingham for Challenge Cup, won by Hurlingham by Capt. Hon. J. Beresford, F. M. Freake, W. S. Buckmaster, John Watson.

INDIAN CHAMPIONSHIP.

1898. 2nd Durham L.I. : L. F. Ashburner, H. B. Wilkinson, Capt. H. de B. De Lisle, Capt. C. C. Luard.

1899. Patiala : General Pretam Singh, Maharajah of Patiala, Chandu Singh, Goorchit Singh.

1900. Freebooters : A. Hewlett, Ibrahim, Capt. Watson, Capt. Cotgrave.

1901. Ulwar State : Moti Lal, H.H. the Maharajah of Ulwar, Capt. Ricketts, Amar Singh.

INDIAN REGIMENTAL TOURNAMENT.

1877. 9th Lancers : Adams, B. Gough, S. Chisholm, Capt. Beatson.

1878. 9th Lancers : J. Trower, G. A. P. Evans, B. Gough, S. Chisholm.

1879. ⎫
1880. ⎭ No Tournament on account of Afghan War.

1881. 10th Hussars : Lord Airlie, C. S. Greenwood, R. B. Fisher, H. T. Allsop.
1882. 10th Hussars : Lord A. Compton, C. S. Greenwood, R. B. Fisher, H. T. Allsop.
1883. 9th Lancers : C. Bishop, W. Jenner, Major B. Gough, C. Cameron.
1884. 9th Lancers : W. K. Jenner, F. F. Colvin, Major B. Gough, Capt. Cameron.
1885. 9th Lancers : W. K. Jenner, M. Little, J. Lamont, Major Chisholm.
1886. 8th Hussars : P. W. Le Gallais, Capt. C. N. Vesey, Major Fell, Capt. C. E. Duff.
1887. 8th Hussars : P. W. Le Gallais, Capt. C. N. Vesey, J. F. Henderson, Capt. C. E. Duff.
1888. 17th Lancers : E. D. Miller, A. Rawlinson, B. Portal, W. G. Renton.
1889. 17th Lancers : Lord Ava, G. Milner, E. D. Miller, Hon. H. A. Lawrence.
1890. 5th Lancers : W. E. Collis, A. Daniell, H. V. Bailey, Capt. Beddy.
1891. 7th Hussars : E. W. Sutton, Capt. D. Haig, Capt. Carew, R. M. Poore.
1892. Queen's Bays : W. H. Persse, V. G. Whitla, Capt. Kirk, C. K. Bushe.
1893. Queen's Bays : ⎰ W. H. Persse, H. W. Wilberforce, Capt. Kirk, C. K.
1894. Queen's Bays : ⎱   Bushe.
1895. 7th Hussars : R. G. Brooke, Hon. J. Beresford, Capt. Carew, R. M. Poore.
1896. Durham L.I. : ⎰ W. J. Ainsworth, Capt. H. B. Wilkinson, Capt. H. de B.
1897. Durham L.I. : ⎱   De Lisle, Capt. C. C. Luard.
1898. Durham L.I. : L. F. Ashburner, Capt. H. B. Wilkinson, Capt. H. de B. De Lisle, Capt. C. C. Luard.
1899. 4th Hussars : Winston Churchill, A. Savory, Capt. R. Hoare, R. W. Barnes.
1900. 3rd Rifle Brigade : E. W. Bell, Capt. C. B. Gosling, Capt. Hon. J. H. Morris, P. R. Creed.
1901. 20th Hussars : J. S. Cawley, Capt. Dunbar, Capt. Bayley, Capt. Lee.

BENGAL CAVALRY TOURNAMENT.

1883. 12th B.C. :
1884. 11th B.L. :
1885. 18th B.C. :
1886. 18th B.L. :
1887. 9th B.L. :
1888. 18th B.L. :
1889. No Tournament.
1890. 9th B.L. :
1891. 9th B.L. :
1892. 14th B.L. :
1893. 9th B.L. : Capt. A. G. Peyton, S. F. Crocker, F. W. Angelo, H. L. Dawson.
1894. 9th B.L. : Capt. Crocker, Capt. Peyton, Capt. Angelo, Brasier Creagh.
1895. 18th B.L. : Capt. Swanston, Capt. Chesney, Capt. Pirie, Capt. Grimston.

1896. 18th B.L. : F. A. Maxwell, Capt. Grimston, Capt. K. Chesney, Colonel Richardson.

1897. 2nd C.I.H. : A. S. Capper, Ibrahim, Major Campbell, Capt. Cotgrave.

1898. 8th B.C. : J. R. Gaussen, Capt. Winterley, R. Chaplin, Major Rivett Carnac.

1899. 18th B.L. : F. A. Maxwell, Capt. K. Chesney, A. G. FitzGerald, Jemadar Gul G. G. Mowaz Khan.

1900. 18th B.L. : Capt. K. Chesney, Capt. H. W. Campbell, Lt.-Col. A. Money, Jemadar Gul G. G. Mowaz Khan.

1901.

INDIAN INFANTRY TOURNAMENT.

1884. 1st King's O.B. : R. H. B. Taylor, G. N. Mayne, J. H. E. Reid, L. Gordon.

1885. 1st King's O.B. : R. H. B. Taylor, G. N. Mayne, Capt. A. E. Headwell, J. H. E. Reid.

1886. 1st Duke of W.R. : Capt. A. J. Wrench, C. D. Bruce, W. J. Anderson, Capt. H. Saunders.

1887. 1st Duke of W.R. : C. D. Bruce, W. J. Anderson, S. Gordfrey, E. G. Harrison.

1888. 1st Duke of W.R. : C. D. Bruce, W. J. Anderson, A. J. Godfrey, W. M. Watson.

1889. 1st King's O.S.B. : Capt. J. H. Reid, Capt. G. N. Mayne, A. S. Koe, H. T. Pritchard.

1890. 2nd Royal I.R. : C. W. Garraway, R. O'Kellett, Capt. X. Apthorp, J. E. Cullinan.

1891. 2nd West Y.R. : Capt. H. Vialls, Capt. J. C. Yale, A. J. Stephen, G. G. Lang.

1892. 2nd Gloucester R. : Capt. Capel Cure, Capt. C. F. Baxter, C. J. Venables, H. E. Platt.

1893. 2nd Gloucester R. : Capt. C. Moss, Capt. C. Baxter, Capt. Capel Cure, Capt. H. Tufnell.

1894. 2nd Durham L.I. : H. B. Wilkinson, Capt. H. de B. De Lisle, C. C. Luard, Capt. F. Sitwell.

1895. 2nd Durham L.I. : W. J. Ainsworth, H. B. Wilkinson, Capt. H. de B. De Lisle, Capt. C. C. Luard.

1896. 2nd Durham L.I. : D. A. Mander, H. B. Wilkinson, Capt. H. de B. De Lisle, C. C. Luard.

1897. 2nd Durham L.I. : L. Ashburner, H. B. Wilkinson, W. J. Ainsworth, D. A. Mander.

1898. No Tournament.

1899. 2nd South W.B. : Capt. Cooke, Capt. Smith, A. J. Reddie, F. W. Gray.

1900. 3rd Rifle Brigade : E. W. Bell, Capt. G. B. Gosling, Capt. Hon. G. H. Morris, P. R. Creed.

1901. 3rd Rifle Brigade : H. R. Sturgis, E. W. Bell, C. Shawe, A. T. Paley.

RIVER PLATE CHAMPIONSHIP.

October, 1893, at Cañada de Gomez. Hurlingham : F. J. Balfour, F. Furber, C. J. Tetley, H. Scott Robson.

March, 1894, at Hurlingham. The Casuals : R. MacSmyth, P. Talbot, F. Robinson, Follett Holt.

October, 1894, at Hurlingham. Flores A. : J. Bennett, F. J. Bennett, T. Scott Robson, H. Scott Robson.

April, 1895, at Cañada de Gomez. Las Petacas : F. Benitez, F. E. Kinchant, José Martinez, Sixto Martinez.

October, 1895, at Hurlingham. The Casuals : C. J. Tetley, R. S. Moncrieff, P. Talbot, Follett Holt.

———

After 1895 only one championship meeting was held each year.

1896. Las Petacas : F. Benitez, F. E. Kinchant, José Martinez, Sixto Martinez.

1897. Hurlingham : H. Scott Robson, Follett Holt, F. Furber, M. Finlayson.

1898. The Casuals : F. Hinchcliffe, E. Traill, R. W. Traill, F. S. Robinson.

1899. Hurlingham A. : F. J. Balfour, F. J. Bennett, T. Scott Robson, H. Scott Robson.

1900. La Victoria : W. Hinchcliffe, J. L. Bury, Magnus Fea, F. E. Kinchant.

1901. San Carlos : Baron Peers, P. Talbot, J. Carriso, Roque Fredes.

LIST OF POLO CLUBS,

WITH ADDRESSES OF SECRETARIES.

ENGLAND.

LONDON.

HURLINGHAM CLUB, Fulham, S.W.—Polo Manager, G. L. St. Quintin, Esq.
RANELAGH CLUB, Barnes, S.W.—Polo Manager, F. A. Gill, Esq.
ROEHAMPTON CLUB, Barnes, S.W.—Manager, C. D. Miller, Esq.
LONDON POLO CLUB, Crystal Palace, S.E.—Manager, Eustace Blake, Esq.
GUARDS' CLUB, Wimbledon.
EDEN PARK, Beckenham.—Polo Manager, Hubert Marsham, Esq., Barton Seagrave Rectory and Eden Park, Beckenham.

LIST OF POLO CLUBS AFFILIATED TO THE COUNTY POLO ASSOCIATION.

BLACKMORE VALE.—Hon. Sec., H. E. Lambe, Esq., Grove House, Stalbridge, Dorset.
CATTERICK BRIDGE.—R. Hague Cook, Esq., Moulton Hall, Middleton Tyas, S.O., Yorkshire.
CIRENCESTER.—Hon. Sec., C. C. Gouldsmith, Esq., The Cranhams, Cirencester.
CLEVELAND.—
CRICKLEWOOD.—Hon. Sec., C. H. Biddle, Esq., Upover, Mapesbury Road, Brondesbury.
EDEN PARK.—Polo Manager, Hubert Marsham, Esq., Barton Seagrave Rectory, Kettering, and Eden Park Polo Club, Beckenham.
EDINBURGH.—Hon. Sec., J. H. Rutherford, Esq., 14, Great Stuart Street, Edinburgh.
HOLDERNESS (Hull).—Hon. Sec., N. P. Dobree, Esq., Beverley, E. Yorks.
HUTTON.—Hon. Sec., Alexander Ward, Esq., Lockers, Billericay, Essex.
KINGSBURY.—Hon. Sec., Paul Sechiari, Esq., Newlands Grange, Edgware, Middlesex.
LIVERPOOL.—Hon. Sec., G. H. Pilkington, Esq., Wheathill, Huyton, Liverpool.
MIDDLEWOOD.—Hon. Sec., F. W. Taylor, Esq., Danfield, near Barnsley.
OXFORD UNIVERSITY, Oxford.
RUGBY.—Sec., Mr. W. Bryant, 8, Barby Road, Rugby.

STANSTED.—Hon. Sec., Treslam Gilbey, Esq., 9, New Bridge Street, E.C.
STRATFORD.—Hon. Sec., F. W. Evans, Esq., The Hill, Stratford-on-Avon.
TIVERTON.—Hon. Sec., A. de Las Casas, Esq., Worth House, Tiverton.
WARWICKSHIRE.—Sec., Mr. J. Stanley, Sydenham Farm, Leamington.
WIRRAL.—Hon. Sec., G. Gordon Lockett, Esq., 6, Commercial chambers, 15, Lord Street, Liverpool.

LIST OF POLO CLUBS NOT AFFILIATED TO THE COUNTY POLO ASSOCIATION.

BOWDON.—Hon. Sec., W. Dunkerley, Esq., Bowdon, Cheshire.
BEDFORD.—Hon. Sec., T. H. Woodcock, Esq., Felmersham, Sharnbrook, Beds.
BURGHLEY PARK.—Hon. Sec., Blundell Williams, Esq., Stamford, Lincolnshire.
CAMBRIDGE UNIVERSITY, Cambridge.
DERBYSHIRE.—Hon. Sec., Revd. C. Prodgers, Thurlaston Grange, near Derby.
DULVERTON.—Hon. Sec., J. C. de Las Casas, Esq., Worth House, Tiverton.
EASTBOURNE.—Hon. Sec., Col. W. A. Cardwell, The Moat, Croft, Eastbourne.
FOUR SHIRE.—Hon. Sec., Allan Gott, Esq., Stow-on-the-Wold, Gloucester.
HERTFORDSHIRE.—Hon. Sec., M. de C. Elmsdale, Ludwick, Hatfield, Herts.
MANCHESTER.—Hon. Sec., W. King, Esq., Trafford Park, Manchester.
NORTH WILTSHIRE.—Hon. Sec., H. B. Harrison, Esq., Sutton Benger, Chippenham, Wilts.
PLYMOUTH.—Hon. Sec., Hon. L. Lawbart, R.N., Admiralty House, Devonport.
SOUTH HANTS.—Hon. Sec., Michael Gambier, Esq., Basketts Lawn, Totton, Hants.
ST. NEOTS.—Hon. Sec., Mr. A. Jordan, St. Neots, Huntingdonshire.
WELLINGTON.—Hon. Sec., Major Vaughan, Staff College, Camberley.
WILTSHIRE, SOUTH.—Hon. Sec., P. Case, Heytesbury.
YORKSHIRE.—

Polo clubs have also existed lately, but play did not take place in 1900, at Brentwood, Chislehurst, Fetcham Park, Ledbury, Ludlow, Abergavenny, Harrow-Weald, Woldingham, and Worcester.

LIST OF CLUBS BELONGING TO THE IRISH COUNTY POLO CLUB UNION, 1901.

Co. ANTRIM.—Hon. Sec., E. M. Stewart, 14, Donegall Street, Belfast.
Co. CARLOW.—Hon. Sec., Steuart Duckett, Russellstown Park, Carlow.
Co. DERRY.—Hon. Sec., F. Cooke, Esq., St. Columb's Ct., Londonderry.
Co. DUBLIN.—Hon. Sec., F. Perry, Deer Park, Castleknock.
Co. FERMANAGH.—Hon. Sec., C. D'Arcy Irvine, Castle Irvine, Irvinestown, Co. Fermanagh.
Co. KILDARE.—Hon. Sec., Captain Hall, Prospect, Sallins, Co. Kildare ; Manager, Walter Lindsay, Celbridge.
Co. KILKENNY.—Hon. Sec., G. Swifte, Swifte's Heath, Kilkenny.

KING'S COUNTY.—Hon. Sec., H. Gairdner, Birr, King's County.
Co. SLIGO.—Hon. Sec., K. Campbell, Cranmore, Sligo.
Co. WESTMEATH.—Hon. Sec., J. Malone, Bryanstown, Mullingar.
NORTH WESTMEATH.—Hon. Sec., E. F. Dease, Gaulstown, Coole, Co. Westmeath.
Co. WEXFORD.—Hon. Sec., J. E. Barry, Esq., Summerhill, Wexford.

NORTH AMERICA.

CANADA.

ALBERTA.

BEAVER CREEK.—A. G. W. George, Esq., Highfield, Macleod.
CALGARY.—T. S. C. Lee, Esq., Calgary.
HIGH RIVER.—T. W. Robertson, Esq., High River, Calgary.
MACLEOD.—Duncan J. Campbell, Esq., Macleod.
NORTH FORK.—A. Kennington, Esq., Livingston.
PINCHER CREEK.—F. Rimmington Mead, Esq., Pincher Creek.
PINE CREEK.—W. G. Hooley, Esq., Pine Creek.
SHEEP CREEK.—
SOUTH FORK.—R. B. Clarkson, Esq., Pincher Creek.

ASSINBOIA.

GRENFELL.—
REGINA.—Lawson, Esq.

MANITOBA.

MOO SOMIN.—

ONTARIO.

HAMILTON.—
OTTAWA.—

UNITED STATES.

THE POLO ASSOCIATION.—H. L. Herbert, Esq., Chairman, 15, Church Street, New York ; W. A. Hazard, Esq., Secretary and Treasurer, 36, Wal Street, New York.
BROOKLINE, COUNTY CLUB OF.—*White, Cherry Hoop and Cap.*—F. Blackwood Fay, Esq., Brookline, Mass.
BUFFALO COUNTRY CLUB.—*White, Red Cap and Sash.*—R. K. Root, Esq., 24, Wells Street, Buffalo, New York.
DEDHAM.—*White, Yellow Sash and Cap.*—Samuel D. Warren, Esq., Dedham, Mass.
DEVON (PA.).—*White, Red Sash.*—C. R. Snowden, Esq.
ESSEX COUNTY.—*White Shirt, Orange Cap.*—C. A. Munn, Esq., Orange, New Jersey.
EVANSTON COUNTRY CLUB.—W. Bruce Kirkman, Esq., Evanston, Ill.
MEADOW BROOK.—*Sky Blue.*—Oliver W. Bird, Esq., Westbury, Long Island, New York.

MORRIS COUNTY COUNTRY CLUB.—*Green Body, White Cap.*—Benjamin Nicoll, Esq., Morristown, New Jersey.

MYOPIA.—*Light Blue, White Sash and Cap.*—R. L. Agassiz, Esq., Hamilton, Mass.

ONWENTSIA.—W. W. Keith, Esq., Lake Forest, Ill.

PHILADELPHIA COUNTRY CLUB.—*Black Blouse, White Cap.*—J. C. Groome, Esq., Bala.

POINT JUDITH COUNTRY CLUB. — *White, Green Sash and Cap.* — W A. Hazard, Esq., Narraganset Pier, Rhode Island.

RIDING AND DRIVING CLUB.—R. Wooward, Esq., Brooklyn, New York.

ROCKAWAY CLUB. — *Dark Blue.*—Foxhall Keene, Esq., Cedarhurst, Long Island, New York.

ST. LOUIS, COUNTRY CLUB OF.—*Lilac Shirt, White Cap.*—Chas. Hodgman, Esq., St. Louis, Mo.

SOUTHAMPTON.—*White.*—R. J. Collier, Esq., Hollywood, N.J.

STATEN ISLAND.—M. W. Smith, Esq., West Brighton, New York.

WASHINGTON.—J. Van Ness Philip, Esq., Washington, D.C.

WESTCHESTER.— *Yellow.*—Thomas Hitchcock, jun., Esq., Newport, Rhode Island.

WESTCHESTER, COUNTRY CLUB OF.—*Scarlet and White Cap.*—E. C. Potter, Esq., 36, Wall Street, New York.

CALIFORNIA.

BURLINGAME.—San Francisco.

RIVERSIDE.—*Red, Black Sash.*—C. E. Maud, Esq., Riverside.

SOUTHERN CALIFORNIAN.—*Black and Orange.*—G. L. Waring, Esq., Santa Monica.

SANTA BARBARA.—

SANTA MONICA.—

WALLA WALLA.—Washington.

ARGENTINA.

ASSOCIATION OF THE RIVER PLATE.—A. L. Williamson, Esq., 559, Piedad, Buenos Aires.

BAHIA BLANCA.—J. Hampson, Esq., Loma Amarilla, Bajo Hondo, Bahia Blanca, F.C.S.

BELGRANO.—*Black and White.*—F. M. Still, Esq., Piedad, 370.

BELLACO.—*Red and Blue.*—T. Murray Lees, Esq., Banco de Londres, Paysandu, B.O.

BELLVILLE.—J. C. M. Pinnell, Esq.

CAMP OF URUGUAY.—*Pale Blue.*—L. Edwards, Esq., Barrancas, Coloradas Colonia.

CANADA DE GOMEZ.—*Red and Yellow.*—The Hon. F. White, C. de Gomez, F.C.C.A

CASUALS.—*Crimson and White.*—C. J. Tetley, Esq., La Chacra Estacion, Halsey, F.C.O., Buenos Aires.

CORDOBA.—Buttrie, Esq., Las Perdices, F.C.N.A.

GUALEGUAY. — *Crimson and French Grey.*—H Jewsbury, Esq., Gualeguay, Entre Rios.

HURLINGHAM.—*Blue, Red and Yellow.*—F. W. Clunie, Esq., 559, Piedad Buenos Aires.

JUJUY.—*Black.*—Norman Leach, Esq., Salta.

LA COLINA.—*Dark Green and White.*—Glynne Williams, Esq., Estancia San Anselmo, La Colina, F.C.S.

LA CARLOTA.—J. C. Todd, Esq., Estacion Villa, Nueva, F.C.V.M.R.

LA VICTORIA.—*Brown and Yellow.*—Magnus Fea, Esq., Estacion El Trebol, F.C., Central Argentino.

LABOULAYE.—*Green and White.*—W. J. Grant, Esq., Laboulaye, F.C.P.

LAS PETACAS.—Frank E. Kinchant, Esq., Las Petacas, San Jorge, F.C.C.A.

LOCUSTS.—C. A. Hay, Esq.

MEDIA LUNA.—*Pale Blue with Crescent.*—J. Weinberg, Esq.

RANGERS.—J. M. Mullaly, Esq.

RIO NEGRO.—*Gold and Black.*—F. A. Smeaton, Esq., Estacion Francia, F.C.M.U.

SAN JORGE.—C. H. Hall, Esq., San Jorge, Estacion Molles, F.C.C., de Uruguay, Montevideo.

SANTA FE.—*Red and Blue.*—A. J. Dickinson, Esq., Las Castanas Las Rosas, F.C.C.A.

SANTA FE (NORTH).—L. T. Wasey, Esq., Las Limpias, Estacion Carlos, Pellegrini, F.C.C.A.

SANTIAGO DEL ESTERO.—*Green.*—F. Holt, Esq., La Banda, Santiago de Estero.

TUYU.—H. Gibson, Esq., Los Ingleses, Ajó, F.C.S.

VENADO TUERTO.—*Chocolate and Gold.*—H. Miles, Esq., Venado Tuerto F.C.O. Santa Fé y Cordoba.

WESTERN.—N. C. Slack, Esq., San Tomas, Carlo Casares, F.C.S.

WEST INDIES.

BARBADOS.

GARRISON POLO CLUB.—

BRITISH HONDURAS.

BELIZE.—T. J. McSweaney, Esq., Gabouriel Street, Belize.

JAMAICA.

GARRISON.—

KINGSTON.—Frank E. Jackson, Esq., Kingston.

ST. ANN'S.—S. C. Burke, jun., Esq., Friendleys Pen, St. Ann's.

AUSTRALASIA.

AUSTRALIA.

VICTORIA.

VICTORIA POLO ASSOCIATION.—J. C. Manifold, Esq., Camperdown.
CAMPERDOWN.—L. G. McArthur, Esq., Camperdown.
CARAMUT.—E. R. De Little, Esq., Caramut.
COLAC.—W. St. L. Robertson, Esq., The Hill, Colac.
GEELONG.—
MELBOURNE.—G. H. Whittingham, Esq.

NEW SOUTH WALES.

POLO ASSOCIATON.—A. J. Dodds, Esq., Hunter Street, Sydney.
ARGYLE.—F. J. Curtis, Esq., Goulburn.
BLAND.—
BROKEN HILL.—F. W. Pell, Esq., Broken Hill.
CAMDEN.—Dr. Bell, Camden.
COOLAH.—J. McMaster, Esq., Weetalabah.
COOMA.—Charles Hudson, Esq., Cooma.
DUBBO.—
MUSWELLBROOK.—E. Price, Esq., Muswellbrook.
NARANDERA.—H. L. Cully, Esq., Narandera.
QUIRINDI.—P. D. Cox, Esq., Quirindi.
ROCK.—
SCONE.—F. A. Parbury, Esq., Scone.
SINGLETON.—
SYDNEY.—E. Beadell, Esq., Hunter Street
TAMARANG.—T. J. Finlay, Esq., Bundello, Willow Tree.
WAGGA WAGGA.—C. K. Horwood, Esq., Wagga Wagga.
WARDRY.—

QUEENSLAND.

QUEENSLAND POLO ASSOCIATION.—Claude Musson, Esq., 139, Elizabeth
    Street, Brisbane.
BRISBANE.—Claude Musson, Esq.
GATTON.—W. Mc.Leod, Esq., Gatton.
HALF HOLIDAY.—Thos. Price, Esq., Toowoomba.
IPSWICH.—W. T. Deacon, Esq., Ipswich.   •
TOOWOOMBA.—A. McPhie, Esq., Downs Club, Toowoomba.

SOUTH AUSTRALIA.

ADELAIDE.—Frank H. Downer, Esq., King Urn Street, Adelaide.
BURRA.—C. W. Bowman, Esq., The Burra, Adelaide.
MOUNT CRAWFORD.—H. E. Barritt, Esq., Gawter, Adelaide.

NEW ZEALAND.

NEW ZEALAND POLO ASSOCIATION.—Arthur E. G. Rhodes, Esq., Christchurch.

AUCKLAND.—W. R. Bloomer, Esq., Auckland.

CHRISTCHURCH.—George Gould, Esq., Christchurch.

HAWKES BAY.—Thomas Crosse, Esq., Woodland, Hastings.

HAWERA.—

HOROWHENUA.—

MANAWATU.—F. W. Sewell, Esq., Box 25 P.O., Palmerston North.

MANGAHEIA.—Tokomaru Bay.

NOMADS.—

OROUA.—J. R. McLennan, Esq., Oroua Downs, Manawatu.

POVERTY BAY.—C. G. Grant, Esq., Gisborne.

RANGITIKEI.—E. F. Blundell, Esq., Bulls.

RUATANIWHA.—D. D. Evans, Ashcott, Onga-Onga.

TE ARAI.—Gisborne.

WAINGARO.—Waikato.

WELLINGTON.—A. D. Crawford, Esq., Kilbirnie, Wellington.

WANGANUI.—R. Burton Pynsett, Esq., Wanganui.

WHARERANGI.—C. H. Cato, Esq., Napier.

TASMANIA.

HOBART TOWN.—Claud Clark, Esq., Cathedral Chambers, Hobart Town.

SAMOA.

BRITISH CONSULATE CLUB.—W. C. Dean, Esq., Samoa.

HURLINGHAM RULES OF POLO.

HEIGHT.

1.—The height of ponies shall not exceed 14 hands 2 inches, and no pony shall be played either in practice games or matches unless it has been registered in accordance with the Bye-laws.

No pony showing vice shall be allowed in the game.

GROUND.

2.—The goals to be not less than 250 yards apart, and each goal to be 8 yards wide.

A full sized ground should be 300 yards long by 200 yards wide.

SIZE OF BALLS.

3.—The size of the balls to be 3 inches in diameter.

UMPIRE AND REFEREE.

4.—Each side shall nominate an Umpire, unless it be mutually agreed to play with one instead of two ; and his or their decisions shall be final. In important matches, in addition to the Umpires a Referee may be appointed, whose decisions shall be final.

NUMBER OF PLAYERS.

5.—In all matches for cups or prizes the number of players contending to be limited to four a side.

HOW THE GAME COMMENCES.

6.—The game commences by both sides taking up their position in the middle of the ground, and the Manager throwing the ball in the centre of the ground.

DURATION OF PLAY.

7.—The duration of play in a match shall be one hour, divided into three periods of twenty minutes, with an interval of five minutes between each period.

The two first periods of play shall terminate as soon as the ball goes out of play after the expiration of the prescribed time ; any excess of time in either of the first two periods, due to the ball remaining in play, being deducted from the succeeding periods. The last period shall terminate immediately on the expiration of the hour's play, although the ball is still in play.

EXCEPTION.

In case of a tie the last period shall be prolonged till the ball goes out of play, and, if still a tie, after an interval of five minutes, the ball shall be started from where it went out of play, and the game continued as before until one side obtain a goal, which shall determine the match.

CHANGING PONIES.

8.—As soon as the ball goes out of play, after the expiration of the first ten minutes of each period of play, the game shall be suspended for sufficient time, not exceeding two minutes, to enable players to change ponies. With the above exception the play shall be continuous, and it shall be the duty of the Umpire to throw in the ball punctually, and in the event of unnecessary delay in hitting out the ball, to call upon the offending side to proceed at once. Any change of ponies, except according to the above provision, shall be at the risk of the player.

BELL.

9.—The bell shall be rung to signify to the players that the ten minutes has expired, and it shall be rung again when the ball next goes out of play, to show the time for changing ponies.

10.—An official Time-keeper shall be employed in all important matches.

GOAL.

11.—A goal is gained when a ball is driven between the goal posts, and clear of the goal line, by any of the players or their ponies.

OVER TOP OF GOAL POSTS.

12.—If a ball is hit above the top of the goal posts, but, in the opinion of the Umpire, through, it shall be deemed a goal.

TO WIN GAME.

13.—The side that makes most goals wins the game.

WHERE BALL TO BE HIT FROM ; POSITION OF PLAYERS.

14.—If the ball be hit behind the back line by one of the opposite side it shall be hit off by one of the side whose line it is, from a spot as near as possible to where it crossed the line. None of the attacking side shall be within thirty yards of the back line until the ball is hit off. If, however, the ball be hit behind the back line by one of the players whose line it is, they shall hit it off from behind the goal line between the posts, and all the defending side shall, until the ball is hit off, remain behind their back line and between two lines which shall be drawn at right angles to the goal line produced, from points ten yards distant from the centre of the goal on either side, the attacking side being free to place themselves where they choose, but not within twenty-five yards of the centre of the goal posts. The penalty shall not be exacted should the ball glance off a player or pony.

BALL THROWN IN BY UMPIRE.

15.—When the ball is hit out of bounds, it must be thrown into the ground by the Umpire from the exact spot where it went out of play, in a direction parallel to the two goal lines, and between the opposing ranks of players.

NO DELAY ALLOWED.

There must be no delay whatsoever, or any consideration for absent players.

RIDING OUT AN ANTAGONIST AND CROSSING.

16.—A player may ride out an antagonist, or interpose his pony before his antagonist, so as to prevent the latter reaching the ball, but he may not cross another player in possession of the ball, except at such a distance that the said player shall not be compelled to check his pony to avoid a collision.

POSSESSION OF THE BALL.

(I). Any player who follows the exact line of the ball *from* the direction from which it has been last hit, is in possession of the ball rather than any player coming from any other direction.

The last striker is in possession provided that no other player can, without causing the striker to check his pony to avoid a collision, get on the line of the ball in front of him.

No player shall be deemed to be in possession of the ball by reason of his being the last striker if he shall have deviated from pursuing the exact course of the ball.

(II). Any player who rides to meet the ball on the exact line of its course is in possession rather than any other player riding at an angle from any other direction.

(III). Any player riding *from* the direction from which the ball has been hit, at an angle to its course, has possession rather than any player riding at an angle in the opposite direction—always excepting any player riding as described in No. 2.

(IV). If two players are riding from the same direction, that player is in possession whose course is at the smallest angle to the line of the ball.

N. B.—The line of the ball is the line of its course, or that line produced at the moment any question arises.

CROOKING STICK.

17.—No player shall crook his adversary's stick unless he is on the same side of the adversary's pony as the ball, or in a direct line behind, and his stick is neither over nor under the adversary's pony.

OFF-SIDE.

18.—No player who is off-side shall hit the ball, or shall in any way prevent the opposite side from reaching or hitting the ball.

DEFINITION OF OFF-SIDE.

A player is off-side when at the time of the ball being hit he has no one of the opposite side nearer the adversaries' goal line, or that line produced, or behind that line, and he is neither in possession of the ball nor behind one of his own side who is in possession of the ball. The goal line means the eight-yard line between the goal posts. A player, if off-side, remains off-side until the ball is hit or hit at again.

ROUGH PLAY.

19.—No player shall seize with the hand, strike, or push with the head, hand, arm, or elbow, but a player may push with his arm, above the elbow, provided the elbow be kept close to his side.

CARRYING BALL.

20.—A player may not carry the ball. In the event of the ball lodging upon or against a player or pony, it must be immediately dropped on the ground by the player or the rider of the pony.

21.—No player shall intentionally strike his pony with the head of his polo stick.

PENALTY FOR FOUL.

22.—Any infringement of the rules constitutes a foul. In case of an infringement of Rules 16, 17, 19, 20, and 21, the Umpire shall stop the game : and in case of an infringement of Rule 18, the Umpire shall stop the game on an appeal by any one on the side which has been fouled. On the game being stopped as above, the side which has been fouled may claim either of the following penalties.

(*a*) A free hit from where the ball was when the foul took place, none of the opposing side to be within 10 yards of the ball. The ball must be struck to constitute a free hit.

(*b*) That the side which caused the foul take the ball back and hit it off from behind their own goal line.

PENALTY FOR DISABLING A PLAYER.

23.—In the case of a player being disabled by a foul, the side who have been fouled shall have a right to designate any one of the players on the opposite side who shall retire from the game. The game shall be continued with three players a-side, and if the side that causes the foul refuse to continue the game, it shall thereby lose the match. This penalty shall be in addition to that provided by Rule 22.

CHANGING ENDS.

24.—Ends shall be changed after every goal, or if no goal has been obtained, after half-time.

BALL OUT.

25.—The ball must go over and clear of the line to be out.

THROWING IN BALL.

26.—If the ball be damaged, the Umpire shall, at his discretion, stop the game, and throw in a new ball at the place where it was broken, towards the nearest side of the ground, in a direction parallel to the two goal lines and between the opposing ranks of players.

N.B.—It is desirable that the game shall be stopped and the ball changed when the damaged ball is in such a position that neither side is favoured thereby.

BROKEN STICKS.

27.—Should a player's stick be broken, he must ride to the place where sticks are kept and take one. On no account is a stick to be brought to him.

DROPPED STICK.

28.—In the event of a stick being dropped, the player must pick it up himself. No dismounted player is allowed to hit the ball.

GROUND KEPT CLEAR.

29.—No person allowed within the arena—players, umpires, and Manager excepted.

ACCIDENTS.

30.—If any player or pony fall or be injured by an accident the Umpire may stop the game, and may allow time for the injured man or pony to be replaced, but the game need not be stopped should the player fall through his own fault.

WHERE BALL THROWN IN.

31.—On play being resumed, the ball shall be thrown in where it was when the game was stopped, and in the manner provided for in Rule 26.

LEFT-HANDED PLAYERS.

32.—If two players are riding from opposite directions to hit the ball, one of these being a left-handed player, the latter must give way.

DISREGARDING UMPIRE'S DECISION.

33.—Any deliberate disregard of the injunctions of the Umpire shall involve the disqualification of the team so offending.

UMPIRE'S POWER TO DECIDE ALL DISPUTES.

34.—Should any incident, such as the repeated dangerous use of the stick or any other question not provided for in the Rules arise, such incident or question to be decided by the Umpire.

BYE-LAWS.

OFFICERS ELECTED TO SERVE ON POLO COMMITTEE.

1.—Every Regiment and every registered Polo Club which is not already represented shall have the right to send one officer or member to represent the Regiment or Club on the Polo Committee at all meetings where any alteration in the Rules or where any questions affecting such Regiments or Clubs are to be considered, on which occasion due notice of the Agenda shall be sent to them. All such representatives must be members of Hurlingham.

REGISTRATION OF PONIES.

2.—A book shall be kept by the Manager in which all ponies shall be registered with sufficient particulars for the purpose of identification.

PONIES TO BE MEASURED.

3.—All ponies may be registered if adjudged not to exceed the prescribed height when measured according to the rules of Measurement.

TIME SHORTENED.

4.—In order that all members may play during the afternoon, the Manager shall have power to shorten the time, and stop the match or game at the appointed hour. If a match is timed to commence at 4, 5.20 shall be the time at which it may be stopped.

TIME.

5.—On ordinary days, in case of a match taking place before the members game, such match must finish at 5, unless by special leave from the Committee. This does not apply to the tie games in Cup Competitions.

REGISTRATION.

6.—All Polo Clubs must be registered with the Manager on May 15 in each year. A Book of Rules and Members of such Club to be forwarded at time of Registration.

PONIES PROPERTY OF CLUB, &c.

7.—In matches for cups or prizes the ponies must be *bonâ fide* the property of the Club or Regiment contending.

HURLINGHAM RULES. 345

SPURS AND BLINKERS.

8.—No blinkers, or spurs with rowels, allowed except on special occasions when sanctioned by the Committee.

FOUR PLAYERS.

9.—Not more than four players on each side are allowed to play ; the members arriving first at the pavilion to be allowed precedence.

WHISTLE.

10.—The Umpire shall be required to carry a whistle, which he shall use as required.

TIME OF GROUND BEING OPENED AND SHUT.

11.—If, in the opinion of the Manager, the ground is in a fit state for play, it shall be opened, for not less than six players, at 3 o'clock each day, Fridays excepted, when the ground is closed. Each set of players shall be allowed the use of the ground for 20 minutes. All play shall cease and the ground shall be cleared by 7.15 p.m.

COLOURS.

12.—The colours of the Hurlingham Club shall be light blue shirts. The second colours white and red. In members' matches every player shall wear a white shirt or jersey, the sides being distinguished by red and blue waistcoats, supplied by the Manager.

RULES OF MEASUREMENT.

OFFICIAL MEASURER.

1.—The measurement shall be made by an Official Measurer under the supervision of the Polo Committee. Such Official Measurer shall be appointed by the Committee, and shall be a duly qualified Veterinary Surgeon.

TIME OF MEASUREMENT.

2.—The Official Measurer shall attend for the purpose of measuring ponies on the first day in the season on which the ground is open for play, and on certain subsequent days which shall be advertised in due course.

DESCRIPTION OF PONY TO BE SIGNED AND FEE PAID.

3.—The person presenting a pony for measurement shall fill up and sign a form, supplied by the Club, containing particulars and a description of the pony, and shall pay to the Manager at Hurlingham or the Official Measurer at other places a fee of 10/- before the pony can be measured.

AGE OF PONY.

4.—Ponies aged five years and upwards may be measured and registered for life ; ponies under five years can be registered for the current season only. The Official Measurer shall determine the age of the pony.

5.—A pony shall not be measured if he appears to have been subjected to any improper treatment with a view to reduce his height, or if he is in an unfit state to be measured. If a pony is rejected under this Rule he shall not be presented again for measurement until the following season.

STANDARD AND PLACE OF MEASUREMENT.

6.—The measurement shall be made with a standard approved by the Club, and in a box with a level floor specially erected for the purpose.

ACCESS TO MEASURING.

7.—Neither the owner of the pony nor his servant shall on any account enter the box during the measurement, nor shall any other person be admitted unless specially authorised by the Official Measurer, but members of the Polo Committee shall have a right to attend the measurement when their own ponies are not being measured.

POSITION OF PONY AND STANDARD.

8.—The pony shall stand stripped on the level floor and the measurement shall be made at the highest point of the withers.

HURLINGHAM CLUB.

FORM FOR DESCRIPTION OF PONY PRESENTED FOR MEASUREMENT.

Owner's Name.	Pony's Name.	Colour.	Sex.	Age.	Distinctive Marks.

Date   Signature of Owner

HOLDING PONY.

9.—The pony shall be held by a person deputed by the Official Measurer.

POSITION OF THE HEAD.

10.—The head shall be so held that a line from the poll to the withers would be parallel to the floor.

LEGS.

11.—The forelegs from the point of the shoulder and the hind legs from the back downwards, shall be as perpendicular to the floor and as parallel to each as the conformation of the horse allows.

HAIR AND SKIN.

12.—The wither may be shaved, but the mane must not be pulled down, or the skin of the neck or wither in any way interfered with.

SHOES.

13.—Ponies may be measured with or without shoes, but no allowance shall be made.

APPEAL.

14.—Any person who is dissatisfied with the determination arrived at may, by a written application, presented to the Manager within seven days from the time of measurement, apply for a re-measurement. Such re-measurement shall take place in the presence of one member of the Polo Committee, and on the first convenient day which may be appointed, and their decision shall be final.

COUNTY POLO ASSOCIATION, 1901.

PRESIDENT.

Sir H. F. De Trafford, Bart.

COMMITTEE OF MANAGEMENT.

C. Adamthwaite, Rugby.

W. A. Ball, Wirral.

Col. S. Darley, Eden Park.

Tresham Gilbey, Stansted.

C. C. Gouldsmith, Cirencester.

A. M. Tree, Warwickshire.

Harry Whitworth, Middlewood.

SECRETARY & TREASURER.

A. B. Charlton, 12 Hanover Square, London, W.

THE DIVISIONAL HONORARY SECRETARIES.—1901.

Northern.—W. A. Ball, 16 Tithebarn Street, Liverpool.

Midland.—C. Adamthwaite, Rugby Polo Club, Rugby.

South-Eastern.—Col. Sanders Darley, 155 Ashley Gardens, London S.W.

South-Western.—C. C. Gouldsmith, The Cranhams, Cirencester.

RULES OF THE COUNTY POLO ASSOCIATION.

NAME.

1.—That the Association be called the County Polo Association.

SCOPE.

2.—The Association shall be open to all County Polo Clubs, and the Universities of Oxford and Cambridge.

DELEGATES.

3.—Each Club shall be represented by one Delegate.

MANAGEMENT.

4.—There shall be an Annual General Meeting of the Delegates, to be called the Council, of whom five shall form a quorum, who shall elect a Committee of Management, to consist of not less than five in number, of whom three shall form a quorum.

SUBSCRIPTION.

5.—Each Club of the Association shall pay an Annual Subscription of Two Guineas.

MEMBERSHIP.

6.—Any Club desiring to join the Association shall send in an application to the Secretary, who shall bring it before the Committee at their next Meeting for consideration.

RULES.

7.—Polo Clubs joining the Association shall play under Hurlingham Rules.

TOURNAMENT.

8.—A County Cup Tournament shall be held annually, to compete for a Challenge Cup, which shall be held by the winning team for the year. The Tournament shall consist of Preliminary ties—Semi-finals—and a Final to be played as follows :—

DIVISIONS.

9.—For the purposes of the Tournament, the County shall be divided into four divisions :—Northern, Midland, South-Eastern, South-Western, and a map with the divisions marked thereon shall be forwarded to each Honorary Divisional Secretary.

DIVISIONAL SECRETARIES.

10.—Honorary Divisional Secretaries shall be appointed to arrange for ties to be played in their respective divisions by the 30th June in each year between all the clubs desiring to compete. The semi-finals and final matches to be played at Hurlingham in July.

CLUBS OPEN TO PLAY IN TOURNAMENT.

11.—The County Cup Tournament shall only be open to Clubs that have joined the Association.

QUALIFICATION OF PLAYERS.

12.—No one shall be eligible to play for his Club for the County Cup unless he has played regularly in games or matches during the current season on his Club Ground. The word " regularly " shall mean not less than eight times, or has played more frequently on his Club ground than elsewhere, and such attendance shall nullify Rule 16. Ponies played in the ties of the County Cup Tournament shall belong to a member of the competing Club.

13.—No one shall be eligible to play who, during the current or previous two years, has played in the finals of the following Tournaments :—

> The Champion Cup at Hurlingham.
> The Ranelagh Open Cup.
> The Open Cup in Dublin.
> The Inter-Regimental Tournament, Hurlingham.

14.—An Officer belonging to a Regiment which has no Polo Team in the United Kingdom, but otherwise qualified, may play.

15.—The fact of an officer being quartered in the neighbourhood does not constitute a residential qualification, with the exception that an Officer with a Militia, Volunteer, Yeomanry or Staff appointment for not less than three years, and who has not played for his Regiment in the Regimental Tournament of the same year, is eligible to play for his Club.

16.—That each player must be a resident in the County, or reside within twenty-five miles of his Club Ground.

17.—The Hon. Sec. of each Club shall be held responsible for the qualifications of each member of the team entered from his Club.

SUBSTITUTES.
18.—Should any team fall short after the names are once sent in, at time of play another Member, properly qualified, may, with the consent of the Divisional Secretary, be substituted. All matters connected with the final shall be decided by the Committee of Management.

ENTRANCE FEE.
19.—There will be an Entrance Fee of £2 2s. for each team entered.

SEVERAL TEAMS MAY ENTER.
20.—More than one team may be entered from the same Club.

SEMI-FINALS.
21.—The names of the teams left in for the semi-finals must be forwarded to the Secretary of the County Polo Association by the 1st of July.

PRELIMINARY TIES.
22.—The Divisional Secretaries must advise the Committee of the dates of all matches and the ground where play will take place at least three days before they are played, with the names of the players and the Club colours, and also of the result immediately afterwards, with names of Umpire and Timekeeper.

NOT ELIGIBLE.
23.—The following are not considered as County Clubs for the purposes of this Association :—Hurlingham, Ranelagh, Wimbledon, Crystal Palace.

RULES AND REGULATIONS.
The Committee do not propose any alteration in the conditions or arrangements for the 1901 Tournament. To encourage competition in the Preliminary Ties, the Committee will award to the winners in each division a bronze replica of the Pony on the Challenge Cup, mounted on ebonised plinth. They will be suitable mementos of the Clubs' entry into the semi-finals. The Club declared by the Divisional Hon. Secretary as the winner must have played and won at least one game against another Club in the division. A "walk-over" will not qualify such Club for this divisional Trophy.

The Hurlingham Club will again present Cups to the Members of the winning Team, and will also reserve two dates in July for the Semi-Finals and the Final Tie.

By order of the Committee of Management,

A. B. CHARLTON, *Secretary.*

March, 1901.

RULES OF THE IRISH COUNTY POLO CLUB UNION, 1901.

PRESIDENT :—STEUART DUCKETT.

COMMITTEE.—One Representative Member of every County Polo Club in Ireland.

HON. SEC. AND TREASURER :—STEUART DUCKETT. Russellstown Park, Carlow.

1.—The Association be called "THE IRISH COUNTY POLO CLUB UNION," having for its object the promotion of County Polo.

2.—That it shall consist of *bona fide* County Polo Clubs in Ireland.

3.—That each County Polo Club shall pay an Annual Subscription of £2.

4.—That the Committee, consisting of one representative of each County Polo Club, be empowered to transact the business.

5.—That three Members of such representatives form a quorum.

6.—That each County Polo Club joining the Irish County Polo Club Union shall subscribe £5 towards purchasing the County Polo Club Challenge Cup.

7.—That the Annual Meeting be held in Dublin during Punchestown Week.

RULES AND CONDITIONS OF THE COUNTY POLO CHALLENGE CUP.

The County Polo Challenge Cup, value £50, is open to all *bona fide* County Polo Clubs in Ireland that have joined the Irish County Polo Club Union. The holders of the Cup each year to have the names of the winning team engraved on the Cup at their own expense. Entrance for the Cup free.

The Cup to be played for under the Hurlingham Club Rules of the game.

To be a *bona fide* County Polo Club, a Club must have a Club Ground, and regular fixed days for play on their ground.

The Hon. Sec. of each Club must certify, at the time of entry, that each member of the Team is properly qualified.

No player can play for two Counties.

Each County may enter one or more Teams.

In all Matches for County Challenge Cup the ponies must be *bona fide* the property of the Members of the Club contending.

QUALIFICATION OF PLAYERS IN A COUNTY TEAM FOR CHALLENGE CUP.

    (*a*) That he be a resident in the County, or

    (*b*) That he owns or holds land in the County, or

    (*c*) That he resides within 20 miles of the County Polo Ground.

    (*d*) Officers of Army quartered in a County not to be counted as resident.

    (*e*) *Adjutants of Militia Regiments*, Resident Magistrates and officers of R.I.C. are counted as residents.

Members of Clubs not qualified as above, but who are living outside the boundary of the County whose Club they support, are members of, and on whose ground they play regularly, *may play for that County*, provided they send their names before the Committee of the Irish County Polo Club Union and obtain their sanction.

Each Member of a Team competing for the Challenge Cup must have played on the County Club Ground at least six times during the season. A Member of a Club playing in a Match for his County Club, previous to the Competition for the Challenge Cup, may count it as playing once on his County Ground, though the Match was not played on the County Ground.

Officers of the Army and Navy may play for their native County, provided they have played in 12 Games during the Season on the County Club Ground.

RULES AND CONDITIONS OF IRISH COUNTY POLO CLUB UNION.
NOVICES' TOURNAMENT, 1901.

I.—A Novices' Tournament will be held each year, open to Counties belonging to the Irish County Polo Club Union. Entrance, £2.

II.—Each member of the winning team will receive a cup, to become his property.

III.—Not more than one player is eligible in each team who has played in any of the following Tournaments :—Hurlingham—Champion, Regimental or Social Cups ; Ranelagh—Open, Subalterns', or Hunt Cups ; Dublin—Open, County, Regimental, or Subalterns' Cups ; Paris—International Tournament ; Rugby—Rugby Tournament ; India—Regimental Tournament.

IV.—Same rules and qualifications as laid down for players in a County Cup team.

V.—The Ties to be played on County Club grounds.

VI.—The following counties to form the Northern Division :—Antrim, Derry Fermanagh, Sligo, Westmeath. Manager for Northern Division, C. K. O'Hara, Annaghmore, Collooney, Sligo. The following counties to form the Southern Division : — Carlow, Dublin, Kildare, Kilkenny, King's County, Wexford. Manager for Southern Division, W. Lindsay, Kildraught House, Celbridge.

VII.—Entries to close with the Managers on June 1st.

VIII.—The two Divisions to play the ties separately, as directed by the Managers.

IX.—The final to be played between the winners of the Northern Division and winners of Southern Division by the second week in July.

X.—The grounds on which the ties will be played off will be left to the choice of the contending clubs, but should they be unable to decide on what ground the matches are to be played, they must notify the same to the manager of the Division, who will toss up and thereby decide on which of the two grounds the match is to be played.

XI.—Any Club refusing to abide by this decision will be counted as beaten.

XII.—Dates to be fixed by the Managers by which ties are to be played off. Should contending teams fail to agree as to day on which a tie is to be played off, two dates may be sent to the Manager, who will toss up and thereby decide on which day the tie is to be played.   Any team failing to play on day notified will be counted as beaten.

XIII.—A team having once entered shall forfeit the entrance fee if it fails to compete.

STEUART DUCKETT. *Hon. Sec. I. Co. P.C.U.*

INDIA.

RULES FOR THE REGULATION OF TOURNAMENTS.

STEWARDS.

1.—All Tournaments played under the Rules of the Indian Polo Association shall be under the management of three Stewards, who shall be elected locally.

RIGHT OF APPEAL TO STEWARDS.

2.—There shall be a right of appeal to the Stewards upon all questions which are not by these Rules declared to be subject to the final decision of some other authority, such as umpires, etc., and the decision of the Stewards in all such appeals shall be final.

QUESTIONS TO BE REFERRED TO STEWARDS.

3.—Any question which may arise in the course of a Tournament, and which is not provided for by these Rules, shall be referred for decision to the Stewards, who may, if they think fit, refer the matter to the Committee of the Indian Polo Association, whose decision shall be final.

LIMIT OF TIME AND NUMBER OF PONIES.

4.—The duration of play, and the number of ponies allowed to be played by teams in a Tournament, shall be decided locally: provided that the maximum duration of play in any match does not exceed forty minutes, exclusive of stoppages. Each team to consist of not more than four players.

DRAWING OF TIES.

5.—In case of the number of competing teams for a Tournament not being a power of 2, as 4, 8, 16, etc., all byes to be in the first round. For instance, 13 teams competing, three are drawn as byes; the remainder play off, leaving 8 to play in the second round.

6.—The Honorary Secretary of a Tournament will obtain from the Captain of each team, before play is commenced, a correct list of the ponies proposed to be played in the Tournament by his team. Printed forms will be supplied by the Honorary Secretary Indian Polo Association for this purpose. The lists, together with a short description of the Tournament for record in the calendar, will be forwarded to the Honorary Secretary Indian Polo Association, as soon as possible after the conclusion of the Tournament.

7.—No pony without an Indian Polo Association certificate or certificate of measurement fourteen hands one inch, or under, from an authorised measurer of the Association, or from an official measurer of the Calcutta or Western India Turf Club granted since 1st April, 1899, shall be allowed to play in a Tournament, except when a local measuring is sanctioned.

8.—The Honorary Secretary of a Tournament will be responsible that a fee of Rs. 2 is collected for each pony, with a racing certificate, that has not been previously registered as a polo pony, before such pony is allowed to play.

9.—A measuring of ponies for Indian Polo Association certificates by a selected measurer, will be arranged and sanctioned, when possible, on any date, or at any place it may be desired. Applications for such measurings should be made to the Honorary Secretary, Indian Polo Association, if possible, one month before the measuring is required. In the application, the number of ponies for which the measuring is requisitioned, should be stated.

10.—In the case of a tournament where an Indian Polo Association measuring cannot be arranged, a local measurer will be appointed, whose measurements will be accepted for that Tournament only.

11.—Any team knowingly playing a pony in a Tournament that has not been measured and passed in accordance with these rules, shall be disqualified for that Tournament.

RULES OF THE GAME OF POLO.

GROUND, ETC.

SIZE OF THE GROUND.

1.—The size of the ground shall be as nearly as possible 300 yards long and 200 yards broad.

BOUNDARY LINES.

2.—The four corners shall be marked by flags. The boundary lines joining the corner flags shall be spitlocked, except between the goal posts, and inside the subsidiary goal marks ; those marking the length of the ground shall be called the side lines, those marking the breadth of the ground shall be called the back lines.

MARKING OF SIDE LINES.

3.—Small flags shall be placed on each side line to mark points, which shall be, 30 yards from each back line, 50 yards from each back line, and the centre of each side line (centre flags).

MARKING OF BACK LINES.

4.—In the centre of each back line there shall be a goal, marked by goal posts, which shall be at least ten feet high and twenty-two feet apart. Eleven feet from the outside of each goal post, subsidiary goal marks will be shown on the ground by a small white line perpendicular to the back line.

GOAL LINE AND SUBSIDIARY GOAL LINE.

5.—The line between the goal posts shall be called the goal line. The line between the subsidiary goal mark and the goal post nearest to it, shall be called

23*

the subsidiary goal line. For matches, the goal line and the subsidiary goal line shall be marked by a narrow line of whitewash.

PLAYERS AND UMPIRES ONLY ALLOWED ON THE GROUND.

6.—Each team shall consist of not more than four players. No person, other than players and umpires, shall come on the ground while the ball is in play.

THE BALL.

7.—The ball shall be about four ounces in weight and ten and a half inches in circumference.

DURATION OF PLAY AND GOALS.

DURATION OF PLAY.

8.—Each match shall last for not more than forty minutes' actual play, divided into periods of five minutes. Time must be called, irrespective of the ball being in play, when the game shall have lasted its specified maximum time.

PERIODS.

9.—A period will end the first time the ball goes out, after five minutes' actual play, except that the penalty mentioned in rule 17 (f), or the penalty for any foul, must be enacted in the same period in which the breach of rules occurred. Any excess of time over five minutes, in each period, will be deducted from the last period, and if the aggregate of such overtime exceeds five, or ten minutes, from the last period but one, or the last period but two, as may be found necessary.

INTERVALS.

10.—There shall an interval of not more than three minutes between each period. and of one minute after each goal. At the conclusion of each interval, and. otherwise, whenever the ball goes out of play. the game must be re-started as laid down in rule 17.

A MATCH HOW DECIDED.

11.—A match is won by the team that scores the greatest number of goals, or, in the event of a tie, by the team that scores the greatest number of subsidiary goals. No number of subsidiary goals will ever equal a true goal. If at the expiration of time, each team has scored the same number of goals and subsidiary goals, the goals shall be widened up to the subsidiary goal marks, and fresh subsidiary goal marks drawn at the usual distance outside them. The game shall then be re-started from the centre of the ground (*vide* rule 17 *a*), and play shall be continued for five minutes. If, at the expiration of this additional five minutes, the game is no longer a tie, time shall be called, and the match shall end. But if the game is still a tie, time shall not be called until the ball goes out of play. The game shall then be continued, with the usual periods and intervals, until one side scores, when it shall end, or otherwise, until play is no longer possible. In the latter case the local tournament committee will settle whether the match is to be played over again, or the most equitable way in which a decision shall be arrived at.

GOAL HOW OBTAINED.

12.—A goal is obtained if the ball *cross over* the back line between the goal posts, or, if higher than the goal posts, between the goal posts produced perpendicularly, or, if one or both goal posts have been displaced, between the points where the goal posts should stand.

SUBSIDIARY GOAL HOW OBTAINED.

13.—A subsidiary goal post is obtained in the same way as a goal, except that to score a subsidiary goal the ball must pass between the subsidiary goal mark and the goal post which is nearest to it. After a subsidiary goal the ball shall be hit off in accordance with rule 17·(*e*) or (*f*).

GOALS OBTAINED BY UNFAIR PLAY.

14. —No goals or subsidiary goals shall be counted which have been obtained by unfair play. Any infringement of the rules constitutes unfair play.

CHOICE AND CHANGE OF GOALS.

15.—Sides shall toss for choice of goals. If neither side has scored a goal, goals shall be changed at half-time : but after the first goal, goals shall only be changed after each goal obtained.

16.—If a game has to be stopped from any cause, for any length of time, before the full time of play has been completed, the local committee shall decide when the game shall be resumed.

BRINGING THE BALL INTO PLAY.
STARTING AND RE-STARTING GAME.

17.—The umpires shall have the power of ordering play to begin, after the time fixed, notwithstanding the absence of any player.

(*a*) To start the game, and after each change of goals, the ball shall be brought into play between the centre flags, by one of the umpires (who will remain mounted) bowling the ball underhand along the ground, close to his pony, as hard as possible, at right angles to the side line towards the centre of the ground, between the two sides, who will range themselves opposite to each other : no player to be closer to the umpire than ten yards. The umpire will bring the ball into play, from a point about eighty yards from the side line, and always from the same side of the ground.

(*b*) The same procedure will be adopted in the case of a broken ball or an accident, but in these cases the ball will be brought into play, *outwards from the centre*, at the spot where the ball was broken, or the accident occurred.

(*c*) When the ball goes out at the side, the ball shall be thrown in at once at the spot where it went out, either by the umpire in the manner detailed above, or by any one on foot deputed by him to do so, who will bowl it in underhand : no player to be within ten yards of the line. The umpire will not wait for both sides to form up.

(*d*) To re-start the game after a foul has been given, the penalty for that foul will be carried out.

(*e*) When the ball is hit behind the adversary's back line by one of the attacking side, the goal referee will place the ball on a spot as near as possible to that at which it crossed the line, but behind it. The umpires will see that the ball is hit off by one of the defending side without delay, and that none of the attacking side approach within thirty yards of the back line up to the moment it is hit off. At the commencement of a new period, should none of the defending side be at the spot, where the ball went behind, ready to hit off, it is the duty of the goal referee to at once bowl in the ball underhand, at the spot, at right angles, to the back line, as hard as possible. And in this case the penalty for an off side shall not be claimed against the attacking side, should no one of the defending side be between them and the back line.

(*f*) When the ball is hit, with a stick, behind the back line by one of the defending side, one of that side shall hit it off from behind the goal line, between the goal posts. All the players of the defending side shall stand behind the back line, not outside the subsidiary goal marks on each side ; none of the attacking side to be within thirty yards of the back line, in each case, until the ball is hit off across the back line. The penalty will not be exacted should the ball go behind by reason of a glance off a pony or a player.

BALL IN, AND OUT OF, PLAY.

18.—The ball shall be considered to be in play whenever it has been hit off across the back line ; or, in the case of a penalty other than a hit off from behind, whenever it has been struck, or struck at, with the intention of hitting off ; or whenever it has been thrown in, unless immediately recalled by the umpire. The ball is out of play if it goes over and clear of the side or back line (*vide* rule 34), or, if these lines are marked by a trench, into that trench.

ORDINARY FOULS.

DISMOUNTED PLAYER.

19.—No dismounted player shall be allowed in any way to take part in the game while dismounted.

LEFT-HANDED PLAY AND CATCHING THE BALL.

20.—A player must not play left-handed. If any player catch the ball in any way during the game, it must be dropped on the ground at once.

REVIVING THE BALL.

21.—The ball must be revived, whenever the ball goes out of play, with the least possible delay. If unnecessary delay occurs the umpire will either revive the ball himself in the necessary direction, or give a foul against the offending side (*vide* rule 36 *a.*)

CROOKING OR STOPPING STICKS.

22.—No player shall crook or stop an adversary's stick except when the latter is about to strike the ball, and unless he is on the same side of the adversary's pony as the ball, or immediately behind.

ROUGH PLAY.

23.—No player shall seize with the hand, strike, or push with the head, elbow, hand, stick or whip, another player or pony ; but a player may push with his arm above the elbow, *provided the elbow be kept close to his side.* A player who after being once warned by the umpire continues to play roughly, renders himself liable to be ordered off the ground for " unfair play " under rule 37 (*a*).

24.—No player shall intentionally strike his pony with the head of his polo stick.

NO PLAYER TO INTERFERE WHEN OFF SIDE.

25.—No player, when " off side," shall be allowed to hit the ball, or shall in any way prevent the opposite side from reaching or hitting the ball, or in any way interfere in the game, intentionally or otherwise.

DEFINITION OF OFF SIDE.

26.—A player is " off-side " when at the time of the ball being hit, he has no adversary nearer than he is to such adversary's back line or behind that line, and he is neither in possession of the ball, nor behind one of his own side, who is in possession of the ball. He shall be deemed to remain " off side " until the ball is hit, or hit at, again.

DANGEROUS FOULS.

DEFINITION OF POSSESSION OF THE BALL.

27.—The player who last hit the ball, *if still following the line of the ball,* remains in possession of the ball, so long as he can, *at the pace at which he is moving,* reach the ball again before any other player : and the possession of the ball only passes to another player, when that other player,

    (*a*) Is riding *on a line closer and more nearly parallel to the line on which the ball is travelling* than the original striker (example 2) ;

    (*b*) Can unquestionably reach the ball first *without causing the original striker to check to avoid a collision* (example 3) ;

    (*c*) Can fairly " ride off " (rule 29) the original striker (example 4).

28.—One player crosses another player,

CROSSING.

    (*a*) Who, *when not entitled to possession* of the ball (as defined in rule 27), crosses the line on which the ball is travelling, or that line produced, and thereby collides with the player in possession of the ball, or causes the latter to check to avoid collision (examples 5 and 6) :

    (*b*) Who, *when in possession* of the ball, turns on the ball, except at such a distance as to obviate any chance of collision with another player riding on the line, produced either way, on which the ball is, or has been, travelling ;

(*c*) Who, when two players (*neither entitled to possession*) start from different directions to try and obtain possession of the ball, does not give way to the other player of the two who is moving on a line more nearly parallel to that on which the ball is, or has been, travelling (example 7).

N.B.—In no case can a player be made to pay the penalty for a cross, who is so ridden off as to be forced across the line of a player who is in possession of the ball. In this case the player who caused the danger is to blame (example 8).

FAIR RIDING.

29.—A player shall be considered to ride off fairly, when, having placed himself abreast of an adversary (after following a line of direction as nearly as possible parallel to that in which his adversary is moving), he gradually forces him from, or prevents his continuing in, the direction in which he is riding.

DANGEROUS RIDING.

30.—Riding into an adversary in any other way than as defined in rule 27, or placing a stick, in a dangerous manner, over or under the body, or across the legs, of an adversary's pony, constitutes dangerous riding. A player, however, who deliberately rides his pony up to an adversary who is in possession of, *and striking at*, the ball ; or who deliberately rides his pony over the ball to prevent an adversary striking at it, does so at his own risk.   .

PENALTIES.
PENALTY FOR AN "ORDINARY FOUL."

31.—The penalty for an "ordinary foul," *i.e.*, for any infringement of rules 19-26, is either :—

(i) A free hit from where the ball was when the foul occurred, none of the side causing the foul to be within ten yards of the ball.

(ii) The side causing the foul to take the ball and hit it off from behind their own back line, as in rule 17 (*f*).

The side which is not the offending one, has the choice of penalties.

PENALTY FOR A "DANGEROUS FOUL."

32.—The penalty for a "dangerous foul," *i.e.*, for crossing or dangerous riding, is as follows :—

A free hit from a spot fifty yards from the back line of the side causing the foul, *opposite the centre of the goal*, or, if preferred, from where the foul occurred : all the side causing the foul to be behind the back line until the ball is in play, but not between the goal posts, nor when the ball is brought into play may any of that side ride out from between the goal posts ; none of the other side to be nearer the back line than the ball is, at the moment the ball is brought into play.

UMPIRES, &c.
UMPIRE STAFF.

33.—Two umpires, four goal-referees, a time-keeper and a scorer shall be nominated for each match. The umpires and goal-referees shall each be provided with a whistle. Each pair of goal-referees shall in addition be provided with a coloured flag for signalling goals, and a white flag for signalling subsidiary goals. The time-keeper shall be provided with a stop-watch.

THE WHISTLE.

34.—Umpires and goal-referees will blow a whistle whenever the ball is out of play, as a signal that the game must be stopped. The whistle must never be blown to show that the ball is brought into play.

QUALIFICATIONS OF UMPIRES.

35.—Umpires must be regular polo players, and must possess a thorough knowledge of the rules of the game. They must be mounted on well-trained and fast ponies, so as to be able to ride near enough to the ball to give a decision at any moment, and yet not to interfere with the players. Their decision is final on all questions arising out of the actual play of the game, as well as on questions declared by these rules to be subject to their final decision.

DUTIES OF UMPIRES AS TO STOPPING THE GAME.

36.—It shall be the duty of umpires to stop the game, when :—

    (*a*) The ball is sufficiently damaged to interfere with the game ;
    (*b*) The ball is not brought properly into play ;
    (*c*) The ball crosses the side line ;
    (*d*) They see, whether appealed to or not, any infringement of these rules constituting an " ordinary foul " or a " dangerous foul."
    (*e*) Any fall or accident involving danger occurs.

DUTIES OF UMPIRES AS TO DANGEROUS PLAYERS AND PONIES.

37.—It shall be the duty of the umpires to order off the ground :—

    (*a*) Any player who deliberately plays unfairly or rides dangerously, and he shall not be replaced ;
    (*b*) Any pony, which they may consider dangerous or improperly bitted, or which the rider has not under thorough control.

DUTIES OF UMPIRES AS TO REVIVING THE BALL, &C.

38.—It is the duty of umpires—

    (*a*) To see that no delay occurs in reviving the ball under rule 17 (*d*), (*e*), and (*f*), (*vide* rule 21.)
    (*b*) To order any player to take off his spurs, or to use spurs without rowels, who, in his opinion, is ill-treating his pony.

DUTIES OF THE GOAL-REFEREES.

39.—Goal-referees shall blow the whistle the moment the ball crosses the back line at any point. They are the judges of the goals and subsidiaries : but if at any time they are in doubt, the umpires must be consulted. In the case of a goal or a subsidiary goal, they will at once signal to the scorer, and see that the signal is answered. Their duties as to re-starting the game are explained in rule 17 (*e*).

DUTIES OF TIME-KEEPER.

40.—The time-keeper is responsible that a bell is rung, or a bugle sounded, at the conclusion of each period and interval. He will stop his watch whenever the whistle is blown. No time shall be counted while the ball is out of play.

HINTS TO UMPIRES.

1. Umpires should endeavour to place themselves in the most advantageous place for seeing the game, and apportioning the work. One on each side of the play, level generally with the back, will be found the best place as a rule for attaining this end.

2. By dividing the ground in two, both lengthways and breadthways, each umpire can take one back line and one side line.

3. There is a tendency on the part of umpires, from natural causes, to watch only the play in the immediate vicinity of the ball. For this reason much unfair riding by No. 1's, when in reality off-side, escapes their attention. This may be obviated, by each umpire keeping under special observation the four players who happen to be, at any given time, nearer to his own back line.

4. Umpires should have new balls in their pockets, with which to re-start the game at once, if the ball goes out of play. An umpire will find it easy to bowl in correctly, if he puts his horse in motion in the direction he wishes to bowl the ball.

5. They, and goal-referees, should blow their whistles loud enough for the time-keeper to hear. This point is sometimes forgotten.

6. They should make up their minds, and give their decisions clearly and firmly, refusing to enter into any discussion as to the why, or wherefore, of their decisions.

7. Either umpire should, whether appealed to or not, stop the game if he sees a foul, and award a penalty, although it may have happened on the side of the game away from him. But he should use his discretion in not adjudging a foul, if the other umpire, nearest to the incident and in full view, has evidently taken no objection. .

8. They must bear in mind that if they do not order off the ground any dangerous or unmanageable pony, they more or less make themselves responsible for any accident that may occur through that pony. The same applies in the case of a player riding dangerously, and repeating the offence after being warned. It is their first and most imperative duty to stop dangerous and unfair play of any sort or kind.

9. The special attention of umpires is drawn to the following :—

    (a) As crosses frequently occur in the meeting of the ball, when hit out from the back line, the nearest umpire should place himself on the line of the ball, produced in either direction (*vide* example 5).

    (b) When a player is pursuing an adversary with the intent to hook his stick, the umpire should see, that when he does so, he is on the same side as the ball, or immediately behind. This particular breach of rules often occurs in a scrimmage in the vicinity of goal.

(*c*) When a player, with the intention of hitting a backhander, comes in at an angle, on the line of the ball, the umpire should see that he is entitled to possession under rule 27 ; as if he is not entitled to possession of the ball, and the player in possession of the ball has to check to avoid a collision, it is a "cross" (*vide* example 6).

(*d*) In all doubtful cases of crossing, *the pace at which both players are moving must be carefully considered*, as on this depends the question whether the player entitled to possession has to check to avoid collision.

(*e*) The umpire should see that none of the attacking side are within 30 yards of the back line, when the ball is hit off from behind.

(*f*) The umpire should see that none of the players, who have been sent behind their back line under rules 17 (*f*), 31 (*ii*), or 32, when the ball is hit out, cross that line before the ball.

(*g*) Each umpire should watch the position of the back and No. 1, under his immediate observation, at the moment the ball is hit, or hit at, either in front of or behind these two players, as this moment determines the question of "off-side."

STATION POLO.

1. In every station where polo is regularly played, the players shall elect a Committee from amongst the most experienced polo players, to be called the "Station Polo Committee."

2. It is the duty of this Committee to regulate all matters, in the station, connected with polo, and to see that the station games are played in accordance with the rules. Ignorance of the rules by young players tends to a great deal of the unfair and dangerous riding often seen in station games, which it is the duty of the Committee to stop.

3. The Committee will arrange for occasional "slow periods" for unbroken ponies and beginners. No pony which is not thoroughly broken, and no player who is a bad horseman, or who does not know the rules of the game, should be allowed to play in a "fast period."

4. An umpire must be appointed for matches of any sort. But for ordinary station games, as it is generally impracticable to provide an umpire, any two members of the polo Committee must interpret the rules, and settle any disputes that may occur.

5. The Committee will see that no player plays any portion of a game without a polo helmet or lungi. But even this precaution is useless, unless players themselves see that their helmets are firmly secured under their chins with a strong strap, which will not break or come off in a fall.

RULES FOR HEIGHT AND MEASUREMENT OF POLO PONIES.

1.—The maximum height of Polo Ponies shall be fourteen hands and one inch.

2.—All ponies must be measured according to these rules before they can be played in a tournament, with the exceptions :—

(*a*) Those holding Indian Polo Association Life Certificates.

(*b*) Those holding Season Indian Polo Association Certificates which are in force on the day of playing.

(*c*) Those holding Life Certificates from the Calcutta or Western India Turf Clubs of 13-2¾ (or under) up to 31st March, 1899, or 14.1 (or under) since that date.

(*d*) Those holding Season Certificates from the Calcutta or Western India Turf Clubs of 14.1 (or under) which are still in force.

3.—At tournaments in which teams wish to play ponies they have had no opportunity of bringing before an authorised measurer, a local measurer will be appointed, with the sanction of the Indian Polo Association Committee, to measure ponies, their measurements being in force for that tournament only. Such measurements will be carried out strictly in accordance with these rules, and a fee of Rs. 2, payable in advance, will be levied on each pony brought up for measurement, and forwarded with the lists of ponies played in the tournament to the Honorary Secretary Indian Polo Association.

4 —A measuring for Indian Polo Association certificates will be sanctioned by the Indian Polo Association Committee, at any place and on any date it may be required, provided the services of a measurer selected by the Committee can be obtained.

5.—Applications for such a measuring should be made to the Honorary Secretary. Indian Polo Association, if possible 30 days before it is required. The probable number of ponies which will be brought up for measurement should be stated in the application.

6.—All expenses incurred by the measurer in proceeding to a place to measure ponies, veterinary fees and other charges in connection with the measuring will be passed and paid by the Honorary Secretary Indian Polo Association.

7.—When a " measuring " has been arranged and sanctioned, a measuring standard and printed forms will be supplied to the measurer by the Honorary Secretary Indian Polo Association.

8.—No person dissatisfied with a measurement can demand, as a right, a fresh measurement ; but the official measurer may, on application, re-measure a pony which has been measured by him, if the application is made at once, and if he considers that the measurement, from the fretfulness of the pony or other cause, was not satisfactory.

When a re-measurement is allowed, the pony, if presented at the time and place directed by the measurer, shall be again measured on payment of the prescribed fee ; otherwise the original measurement shall stand.

9.—A measurer shall refuse to measure any pony that is known to have previously been measured and declared over 14.1 by a measurer authorised to measure by the Indian Polo Association Committee, or by an official measurer of the Calcutta or Western India Turf Clubs.

A certificate granted to a pony which has been previously measured will be cancelled.

10.—A pony shall not be measured if he appears to have been subjected to any improper treatment with a view to reduce his height, or if he is in an unfit state to be measured, and he shall not be aged or measured, if he is unnamed or if all the particulars required by the measurer for filling in the forms are not furnished.

If a pony is rejected on the ground that he has been subjected to improper treatment, the measurer may order that he shall not be again presented within a period of six months.

11.—The following fees shall be paid in advance, and shall be remitted by the measurer to the Honorary Secretary Indian Polo Association :—

For every pony presented for measurement Rs. 10.

For the re-measurement of a pony . . ,, 5.

12.—A measurer, after entering up the description and ages of the ponies before him on the form and in the columns prescribed, shall measure them and pass them as polo ponies, provided they are 14.1 (or under), certifying to the correctness of the measurements by signing the form referred to.

13.—No person shall take any part in ageing or measuring his own pony, or a pony in which he has an interest.

14.—The following rules shall be strictly observed in measuring ponies :—

(a) The pony shall stand stripped on a perfectly level platform.

(b) The head shall be so held that a line from the poll to the wither would be parallel to the platform. The forelegs from the point of the shoulder, and the hind legs from the back downwards, shall be as perpendicular to the platform, and as parallel to each other as the conformation of the pony allows.

(c) The withers may be shaved, but the mane must not be pulled down, or the skin of the neck or wither in any way interfered with.

(a) The pony shall be held by a person deputed by the measurer, and shall not be touched by any one else without his permission.

(e) The measurement shall be made at the highest point of the wither with a measuring rod of a pattern approved of by the Indian Polo Association Committee.

(f) No allowance shall be made for shoes.

17.—The measurer may direct that any pony, which cannot be properly measured within such time as he considers reasonable; within a limit of five minutes, shall be brought up again. In such case no additional fee shall be charged.

18.—In ageing ponies a Veterinary Surgeon shall be consulted. He shall be entitled to fees on the following scale :—

Rs.	16	for	12	ponies	or	less
,,	32	,,	13	,,	to	24
,,	48	,,	25	or		more.

19.—Ponies thus measured 14.1 or under, by a selected measurer, shall be entitled to certificates. Certificates so granted shall be life certificates, except in the case of ponies under six years old, when the certificates will be available for the current season only.

20.—Any person may, on payment of a fee of Re. 1, obtain from the Honorary Secretary Indian Polo Association a certified extract of any entry in the register of ponies.

THE INDIAN POLO ASSOCIATION ANNUAL CHAMPIONSHIP TOURNAMENT.

A Challenge Cup, presented by the Indian Polo Association, will be played for each year, as soon as possible after the Inter-Regimental Tournament.

This Cup, which will remain in the possession of the winning team till the next year, cannot be won outright. It will be competed for under the Indian Polo Association rules of Polo, with the following conditions :—

CONDITIONS.

1. Open to any team.

2. Number of ponies limited to 24 per team.

3 Place and date to be decided by the Executive Committee I. P. A. after the date of closing of the first entries.

4. First entries, closed, on 1st December, Rs. 100.

    Second entries, closed, on 1st January, Rs. 150.

    Third entries, closed, on 1st February, Rs. 200.

5. After deducting the expenses of the Tournament, the balance of money received from entries fees, will be paid to the winning team.

The right is reserved to the Executive Committee of modifying or altering the conditions of the Championship Tournament.

INTER-REGIMENTAL POLO TOURNAMENT.

RULES FOR THE REGULATION OF THE TOURNAMENT,
1899-1900.

1. Open to any regiment of British Cavalry, Battalion of Infantry, Royal Engineers, or Royal Artillery of any one Presidency ; or any two regiments of Native Cavalry or Native Infantry of one district may combine to form one team. No native shall play in a Tournament.

2. The entrance fee shall be Rs. 120-0-0.

First entries to close on 15th June in each year. Those regiments entering by that date to vote as to date and place where the Tournament shall be held, when an Honorary Secretary shall be elected by the British Cavalry Regiments stationed at the place appointed.

Second entries may be made up to within one month of the date fixed for the commencement of the Tournament.

3. A regiment entering for the Inter-Regimental Polo Tournament which has not previously subscribed towards the challenge cup, shall pay a subscription of £10 in addition to the entrance fee.

4. The Tournament to be played under the Rules of the Indian Polo Association.

5. The Tournament shall be under the management of three Stewards who shall be elected by the Honorary Secretary.

6. There shall be a right of appeal to the Stewards upon all questions which are not by these rules declared to be subject to the final decision of some other authority, such as Umpires, etc., and the decision of the Stewards in all such appeals shall be final.

7. Any question which may arise in the course of the Tournament, which is not provided for by these rules, shall be referred for decision to the Stewards, who may if they think fit refer the matter to a Committee of five Members of the Indian Polo Association, whose decision shall be final.

8. This Committee of I. P. A. to consist of a representative of the British Cavalry, British Infantry and Native Cavalry nominated by their respective branches. The remaining two Members to be chosen by these three.

9. Any two Stewards and the Polo Secretary shall form a quorum for the transaction of all matters contemplated by these rules.

10. Each team shall be composed of four players who shall not be changed during the meeting, unless through any accident, sickness or unavoidable absence, any of them are not able to play, when the Stewards shall have the power of allowing the team to be made up by other players of the same regiment.

11. The number of ponies to be limited to twenty-four. No pony shall play for two different regiments during one Tournament. The duration of play shall be forty minutes, *viz.*, 8 periods of 5 minutes.

12. Ponies shall be *bonâ fide* and unconditionally the property of the Officers, Non-Commissioned Officers, or men of the Regiment or Batteries which the team represents.

13. Captains of teams to certify as to ownership of ponies (if required to do so) before play begins.

14. The order in which the several matches of a Tournament shall be played shall be decided in the first instance by drawing lots. The lots shall be drawn at such time and in such manner as may be directed by the Stewards. If however, by reason of any team being unable to arrive in time for the commencement of any Tournament or for any other reason, the order of play decided by the drawing of lots cannot be observed, the order of play shall in such case be decided by the Stewards, who shall be guided in their decision by what they consider to be fair, having regard to the interest of all the teams.

15. The duration of play and the number of ponies allowed to be played by teams in a Tournament shall be decided by the local Stewards of each Tournament, provided that the maximum duration of play in any match does not exceed forty minutes exclusive of stoppages.

INFANTRY POLO TOURNAMENT.

BYE-LAWS.

[As amended by Meetings of 10th February, 1895 and 8th February, 1896.]

Lucknow, 8th February, 1896.

1. The Infantry Polo Tournament will be held under the rules of the Indian Polo Association.

2. An annual meeting will be held during the week of the Tournament ; no alteration shall be made in these Bye-Laws except at that meeting.

Any proposition or alteration in Bye-Laws that it is intended to bring forward should be sent to the Honorary Secretary twenty-four hours before the Meeting. A representative from any Regiment subscribing to the current Tournament shall have a vote ; no others entitled to vote.

3. The Infantry Polo Tournament shall be open to a team from any Battalion of British Infantry or any Regiment of Native Infantry.

4. Each team shall be composed of four Officers belonging to the Battalion or Regiment, who shall not be changed during the Meeting unless through any accident, sickness, or unavoidable absence any of them are not able to play, in which case the local Stewards shall have the power of allowing the team to be made up by other Officers of the same Battalion or Regiment. Seconded Officers shall not be allowed to play.

5. The entrance fees shall be Rs. 120 per team, of which Rs. 100 shall be paid to the winning team and Rs. 20 to a current account for defraying the incidental expenses of the Tournament from year to year. Donations from teams not competing shall be paid to the winning team.

6. The first entries will close on the 30th October in each year. These entries and the votes as to date and place of playing the Tournament to be sent, registered, together with the full entrance fee to the Honorary Secretary, Infantry Polo Tournament, at the station where the Tournament was played the previous year. Second entries can be made up to within a week of the date fixed for the commencement of the Tournament.

7. Only those Battalions or Regiments who enter, pay their full entrance fee by 30th October, have a right to vote in deciding the date and the place where the Tournament is to be held. This decision will be taken on the votes given with the first entries, and an Honorary Secretary in the Station where the Tournament is to be held shall at once be asked to act by the Honorary Secretary of the Infantry Polo Tournament of the previous year.

In the event of there being a tie between two stations voted for, the Tournament shall be held at that station at which it was not held the previous year.

8. The Honorary Secretary for the year will as soon as possible assemble a Committee of three who will decide the date on which the Tournament is to be held, in accordance with Bye-Law 7.

9. No pony shall play for two different teams during one Tournament ; they must be *bonâ fide* and unconditional property of the Officers, Non-Commissioned Officers or men of the Battalion or Regiment which the team represents.

Number of ponies for each team is limited to 18.

10. Each match shall consist of 6 periods of 5 minutes each.

11. The Tournament shall not be held under any circumstances at the same time as the Inter-Regimental Tournament.

12. No number of wins entitle any Regiment to obtain possession of the Cup.

NATIVE CAVALRY POLO TOURNAMENT.

A Challenge Cup to be competed for annually, by all Regiments of Bengal and Punjab Cavalry and Central India Horse.

This Cup can never become the permanent property of any Regiment.

The place for the Native Cavalry Polo Tournament for the following year will be fixed at the general meeting held during the Polo Tournament Week.

The date of Native Cavalry Polo Tournament will be fixed by the majority of votes of the first entries, closing on the 15th November in the season in which it is played. The votes of competing teams only will be considered, and should be addressed to the Honorary Secretary as early as possible.

Competing Teams must play at least three British Officers. The fourth player may be a Native Officer or Duffadar.

Teams are limited to sixteen ponies per team, which must be unconditionally and *bonâ fide* the property of Officers, Non-Commissioned Officers or men of the Regiment which the team represents.

During the Tournament, games will be played morning and evening as decided by the drawing, in order to enable all, both players and spectators alike, to watch the Tournament throughout, and to avoid the difficulty experienced, when two games are being played simultaneously, of finding the Umpires, etc.

The games shall consist of 6 periods, of 5 minutes each, *actual play*.

Seconded Officers may play for their Regiments. With the above exception, no Officer will be permitted to represent his Regiment unless he is actually entitled to a portion of the Regimental pay, for the date the match is played.

In the instance of an Officer being permanent with one Regiment, but officiating in another, he is eligible to play only in the team of the Regiment with which he is officiating.

Any Regiment prepared to compete for the Cup at a fixed time and place, *vide* condition (II), can claim to be the winners of the same for that year.

Indian Polo Association Rules to be in force except where otherwise stated.

AMERICA,

UNITED STATES OF.

THE POLO ASSOCIATION, NEW YORK.

COMMITTEE.

H. L. HERBERT *(Chairman).*
R. L. AGASSIZ.
GEO. J. GOULD.

JOHN C. GROOME.
W. A. HAZARD.
THOMAS HITCHCOCK, JUN.

SECRETARY AND TREASURER.

W. A. HAZARD, 29, Broadway, New York.

LIST OF AFFILIATED CLUBS.

Aiken.
Buffalo.
Bryn Mawr.
Camden Country Club.
Country Club of West-
chester (of Westches-
ter, N.Y.).
Dedham.
Devon.
Great Neck Polo Club.
Jacksonville.

Lakewood.
Meadowbrook.
Morris County.
Myopia Hunt Club.
Onwentsia.
Philadelphia.
Point Judith.
Rockaway.
Romsen.
Saratoga Polo Club.
Somerset.

Southampton.
Squadron " A " Polo
Club.
Staten Island.
St. Louis.
The Country Club, Brook-
line.
Washington.
Westchester Polo Club
(of Newport, R.I.).

THE POLO ASSOCIATION.

CONSTITUTION.

1.—The Polo Association shall consist of an Association of Polo Clubs, each to be represented by one delegate, who shall out of their number elect at the Annual Meeting a Committee of five for the term of one year.

THE COMMITTEE.

2.—To have the entire control of all matters relating to the Polo Association, and shall be the Authority for enforcing the rules and deciding all questions relating thereto. They shall have the power to appoint all officials for a term not exceeding their own, and to make such changes in the rules and by-laws as they may consider necessary. The Chairman of the Association shall be a member of the Committee *ex-officio.*

ELECTION TO MEMBERSHIP.

3.—Every Club and its delegate up for election shall be proposed and seconded in writing by two delegates, and the election may take place at any meeting of the Committee. The election to be determined by ballot. One black ball in five to exclude. When any Club shall withdraw its delegate his successor shall be proposed, seconded and voted for in like manner.

SUBSCRIPTION.

4.—Each Club a member of the Association shall pay an annual subscription of $75.00. All subscriptions shall become due and payable in advance on May 1st of each year. The subscription remaining unpaid after the 1st of June is to be considered as in arrear, and no Club whose subscription is in arrear shall enjoy any privileges of the Association nor take part in any games with members in good standing.

MEETINGS.

5.—The Annual Meeting of the Association shall be held on the third Tuesday in April, at such place in New York City *as the Committee* may designate. The Committee shall meet once a month or oftener, from April to September inclusive. Three members to constitute a quorum at the Committee meetings.

PROXIES.

6.—In the absence of a Club delegate the President or Secretary of such Club may furnish a written proxy to be used at the meeting for which it is named.

MINUTES.

7.—Minutes of the proceedings of every meeting shall be taken during their progress by the Secretary, or in case of his absence, as the Chairman shall direct, and be afterwards copied into a Minute Book, to be kept for that purpose, and after being read at the next meeting, shall be signed by the Chairman of that meeting.

8.—The order of business at the Annual Meetings shall be as follows :—

1. The noting of the members present.
2. Reading of minutes of last Annual Meeting, and subsequent special meetings.
3. Reports of Treasurer and other officers.
4. Reports of Special Committees, and consideration of any resolutions attached thereto.
5. Elections of officers.
6. Deferred business.
7. New business.

The order of business may be suspended, on motion, by vote of two-thirds of the members present.

CONDUCT OF MEMBERS.

9.—In case the conduct of a delegate be considered injurious to the character or interests of the Association, in the opinion of any five members, who shall certify the same in writing to the Committee, a meeting of the Committee shall be held to consider the case.

If the member whose conduct is in question shall not explain the same to the satisfaction of the Committee, or if the Committee, acting as Judges, shall be of the opinion that the member has committed a breach of the Rules of

24*

Polo, or of the By-Laws, or been guilty of conduct injurious to the interests of the Association, which ought not to be condoned, they may call upon such member to resign ; or shall request the Club whose representative he is to withdraw him and nominate his successor for election, and in event of their neglecting to do so, the Committee shall have power to expel him, and his Club shall be erased from the list of members ; provided always that such expulsion shall only be by a majority of two-thirds, at a Committee Meeting consisting of not less than five members.

In any case where the expulsion of a delegate is deemed necessary, the decision of the Committee shall be without appeal, and the Club so expelled shall have no remedy against the Committee.

10.—A delegate may issue free tickets of admission to members of the Club he represents, good for one week at any Club Ground during Association week there.

RULES OF THE POLO ASSOCIATION.
Revised May 24, 1901.

GENERAL RULES.
GROUND.

1.—The ground should be about 900 feet long by 450 feet wide, with a ten-inch guard from end to end on the sides only.

GOAL POSTS.

2.—The goal posts shall be 24 feet apart, at least 10 feet high, and light enough to break if collided with.

BALLS AND MALLETS.

3.—The ball shall be of wood, with no other covering than white paint, $3\frac{1}{8}$ inches in diameter, and not exceeding 5 oz. in weight.

Mallets shall be such as are approved by the Committee.

PONIES.

4.—The height of ponies shall not exceed 14.2.

Ponies aged five (5) years and upwards may be measured and registered for life ; ponies under five (5) years may be registered for the current season only. Any member of the Committee may measure ponies not his own and issue certificates of registry. He shall determine the age of the pony. The Committee may by vote appoint one or more official measurers, who shall have all the powers hereby given the Committee in respect to the measurement of ponies and the issue of certificates.

PERIODS.

5.—*A.* In match games between pairs there shall be two periods of fifteen (15) minutes each actual play.

B. In match games between teams of three (3) there shall be three (3) periods of fifteen (15) minutes each actual play.

Under A, and B, two (2) minutes shall be allowed after each goal, and intervals of five (5) minutes between periods, unless otherwise agreed.

C. In match games between teams of four (4), there shall be four (4) periods of fifteen (15) minutes each actual play. Two (2) minutes shall be allowed after each goal, and intervals of seven (7) minutes between periods, unless otherwise agreed.

Under A, B and C, time between goals and delays shall not be counted as actual play.

ELIGIBILITY.

6.—A member of a club which is a member of the Polo Association shall not play any match games with or against any club which is not a member of the Association, nor shall any player play on the team of any club of which he is not a member, except on written consent of the Committee, and the approval of the captains of the teams entered.

7.—A player shall be handicapped with but one club at a time.

8.—A player shall not play for the same prize on more than one team or pair.

Any player in his first tournament events shall be handicapped at not less than two goals and shall so continue until changed by the Committee.

ENTRIES.

9.—Entries for tournament events shall be made in writing, naming the probable players and substitutes, and be accompanied by an entrance fee of ten (10) dollars for each player, which is to be returned if the team plays, otherwise it is forfeited to the Association. Entries absolutely close on the day announced. No conditional entries shall be received.

The entrance fee for Championship events shall be one hundred (100) dollars for each team.

DRAWINGS.

10.—The drawings for all tournaments shall be made under the Bagnall-Wilde system. (This consists of playing a preliminary round to reduce the number of contesting teams to two, four, eight or sixteen, thus eliminating the bye at once, and putting all contestants on the same footing.)

UNIFORM.

11.—Captains shall not allow members of their team to appear in the game otherwise than in Club uniform.

COLORS.

12.—The Polo Association colors are white and dark blue.

CHAMPIONSHIP.

13.—*A.* There shall be a Senior and a Junior Championship tournament, the latter immediately preceding the former. The Senior Championship shall be open to teams without limit of handicap. The Junior Championship shall be open to teams whose aggregate handicap does not exceed twenty (20) goals, but this limit is simply to define the class, and all games in both classes shall be played without handicap.

No player with a higher handicap than five (5) goals on May 15th shall compete in the Junior Championship.

The handicap governing eligibility to Junior Championship teams shall be that in force May 15th of the year in which the championship events take place.

B. The winner of the Junior Championship events shall have the privilege of making a post-entry for the Senior Championship events.

C. Except as provided in Section B paragraph, a player shall not be allowed to play in both classes.

D. In both classes, the Championship may be won by default, but in such case no individual trophies shall be added. ·

E. In all Championship events, a player shall not represent a club with which he is not handicapped, and a player shall not be handicapped with more than one club at a time. Every player in the Association shall elect with what club he will be handicapped and the Committee shall be notified in writing prior to the fifteenth day of May in each season.

F. No player shall be eligible to play for his club in Championship events, unless he has played on at least six (6) different days during the current year on the club ground in practice games or in matches.

FIELD RULES.

FIELD CAPTAIN.

1.—There shall be a field captain for each team who shall have the direction of positions and plays of his men. He shall have the sole right to discuss with the Referee questions arising during the game, and to enter protests with the Referee, provided that a player fouled may claim the foul. Other players shall testify only when requested by the Referee.

REFEREE.

2.—The two captains shall agree upon a Referee, whose decision shall be final in regard to all questions of actual play, but as regards eligibility of players, handicaps, and interpretation of the General Rules, an appeal may be made by either captain to the Committee, whose decision shall be final.

DISQUALIFICATION OF PONIES.

3.—Any pony may be protested on the field under General Rule 4 (if possible, before play begins), by the field captain of the side against which the pony is offered to be played. Unless a certificate of registry under said Rule 4 is then· produced, the Referee shall forthwith measure the pony and decide the protest. If sustained, the pony shall be ruled off the field for the match.

The Referee shall exclude from the game any dangerous or vicious pony.

TIMER AND SCORER.

4.—The two captains shall agree upon a timer and a scorer who shall perform their duties under the direction of the Referee.

GOAL JUDGES.

5.—The home captain shall appoint two goal judges, acceptable to the visiting captain, each of whom shall give testimony to the Referee, at the latter's request, in respect to goals and other plays near his goal, but the Referee shall make all decisions.

SUBSTITUTE.

6.—Each team should have a substitute in readiness to play in case of accident or disqualification.

CLEAR FIELD.

7.—Only players and Referee shall be allowed upon the ground during the progress of the game.

CHOICE OF ENDS.

8.—The choice of ends shall be determined by the toss of a coin between the field captains.

CHANGE OF ENDS.

9.—Ends shall be changed after every goal.

THROW-IN.

10.—The game begins when the ball is thrown in by the Referee between the contestants who shall each be on his own side of the middle line

11.—After an interval, the Referee shall throw in the ball when the proper signal is given by the timer, whether all the players are lined up or not.

GOAL.

12.—A goal is made when the ball goes over and clear of the line between the goal posts, or above the top of the goal posts between centre lines.

SAFETY.

13.—Whenever a player, either accidentally or intentionally, gives the ball an impetus with his mallet which carries the ball over the goal line he is defending, and it touches nothing except the goal post or the ground after leaving his mallet, it shall be deemed a safety.

SCORE.

14.—(a) A goal counts one.

(b) A safety counts minus one-quarter.

(c) A foul counts minus one-half.

The side wins which is credited with the largest score at the end of the match.

TIME LIMIT.

15.—When the time limit of any period (except the last) expires, the signal shall be given, but the game shall continue until the ball goes out of bounds or a goal is made. Such overtime in any period shall be deducted from the playing time of the succeeding period. When the time limit of the last period is reached, the signal shall be given and the game shall then cease with the ball in its position at the moment of the signal.

16.—If a goal is made when any fraction of time remains to be played the game shall continue.

17.—When the ball is out of bounds, and the limit of time expires before it is put in play, the period ends.

TIE.

18.—In event of a tie at the end of the last period, the game shall continue (after the usual interval between periods) until a goal or safety is made, or a foul is penalised.

OUT OF BOUNDS.

19.—When the ball crosses a side line, it is out of bounds, and shall be put in play by the Referee throwing it up between the contestant (lined up as at the beginning of the game) toward the middle of the field, and parallel to the goal lines, at the point where it went over the boards. He shall throw from outside the side boards.

KNOCK-IN.

20.—When the ball crosses an end line it is out of bounds, and the side defending the goal at that end is entitled to a knock-in, the ball being placed on the line at the point which it crossed, but in no case nearer than ten (10) feet to the goal posts or to the side boards.

21.—A ball must be over and clear of the line to be out.

22.—When a player having the knock-in causes delay, the Referee may throw a ball on the field and call play. No opponent shall come within fifty (50) feet of the ball, when placed for a knock-in, until the same has been hit by a mallet. As soon as the ball is touched by a mallet after being placed for a knock-in, it is in play, and subject to the rules of play.

PLAYER SUBSTITUTED.

23.—When a player is replaced by a substitute, he cannot return to the team the same day, except to take the place of a player who is disabled or disqualified.

HANDICAP.

24.—When a change of players takes place after the game has begun, the handicap of the man having the highest number of goals shall be counted.

FOULS.

25.—The Referee shall declare any violation of Rules 27, 28, 29 and 30 a foul, when seen by him, without waiting to have it claimed ; or, when not seen, upon evidence satisfactory to him. He may suspend the player committing the foul for the match, but he shall also allow the usual penalty of one-half goal.

26.—In case of repeated or wilful violation of said rules, especially by conduct dangerous to the safety of other players, the Referee shall suspend the player guilty thereof for the match.

27.—In ease of a player being disabled by a foul so that he is unable to continue, the side which has been fouled shall have the option, instead of providing a substitute, to designate the player on the opposite side whose handicap is nearest above that of the disabled player, and the former shall thereupon retire from the game. This penalty shall be in addition to those hereinbefore provided, and the game shall continue with each side reduced by the above withdrawals.

DANGEROUS RIDING.

28.—Careless or dangerous horsemanship or a lack of consideration for the safety of others is forbidden.

The following are examples of riding prohibited under this rule :—

(a) Bumping at an angle dangerous to a player or to his pony.

(b) Zigzagging in front of another player riding at a gallop.

(c) Pulling across or over a pony's forelegs in such a manner as to risk tripping the pony.

RIGHT OF WAY.

29.—A. The right of way is given to the player who has last hit the ball or to the player who has entered safely on the line of the ball between it and the last hitter, or (as against players not in possession of the ball) to the player who is following nearer than any other player the line of direction of the ball.

CROSSING.

B. A player shall not cross the player having the right of way, except at an unquestionably safe distance ; nor shall he pull up in front of the latter unless he is far enough ahead to give the latter unquestionably enough time to pull up also ; nor shall he pull up *across* the latter on any consideration whatsoever.

MEETING.

30.—Whenever two players are riding in opposite directions for the ball, each shall leave the ball on his off side.

OTHER PROHIBITIONS.

31.—*A.* A player shall not strike an adversary or his pony, with the hands or mallet, or strike the ball when dismounted.

B. A player shall not interpose his mallet to interfere with an opponent's stroke.

C. A player shall not put his mallet over his adversary's pony either in front or behind.

D. A player shall not seize with the hand, strike or push with the head, hand, arm, or elbow, but a player may push with his shoulder, provided the elbow be kept close to his side.

E. A player requiring a mallet, pony or assistance from an outside person, during the game, shall ride to the end or side lines to procure it. No person shall come on the field to assist him.

F. A player shall not hold the ball in his hand, arm, or lap, nor shall he kick or hit the ball with any part of his person. He may, however, block the ball with any part of his person or with his pony.

FINES.

32.—The Referee shall also have the power to impose a fine (the amount to be determined by the Committee) on any team or member of a team failing to appear within reasonable time of the hour named for the events for which they have entered, or for any misconduct or violation of the rules during the progress of the game, and shall report the same in writing to the Committee for enforcement.

PENALTY.

33.—The Referee may at his discretion award a penalty of half a goal for any violation of Field Rules not covered by Rule 24.

SUSPENSION OF PLAY.

34.—*A.* When a foul is allowed by the Referee, he may or may not stop the game, according to his judgment as to the advantage gained or lost by the foul.

ACCIDENT.

B. In case of an accident to a player or to a pony, or to a pony's gear which in the opinion of the Referee involves danger to a player, he shall stop the game. It shall not be stopped for a broken or lost mallet, stirrup leather, curb chain, or martingale (unless liable to trip a pony).

BROKEN BALL.

C. When a ball is broken or trodden into the ground in a manner to be unserviceable, in the opinion of the Referee, or when it strikes the Referee or his pony so as in his opinion to affect the game seriously, he shall stop the game, and may substitute another ball by throwing it toward the middle of the field between the players at the point where the event occurred.

CHANGE OF PONIES.

D. In the case of ten (10) minutes continuous play, the Referee shall stop the game for a change of ponies as soon thereafter as the ball goes out of bounds. Not exceeding two (2) minutes shall be allowed for this purpose.

OTHER CAUSE.

E. The Referee may suspend the game for any other reasonable cause.

TIME LOST.

F. Time lost under paragraphs A, B, C, D and E shall not be counted as actual play.

REFEREE'S WHISTLE.

35.—In all the above cases the play is not suspended until the Referee's whistle blows, but the game shall be considered stopped at the time the event occurred. The ball, when placed again in play, shall be thrown by the Referee toward the middle of the field at the point at which the ball was when the event occasioning the suspension of the game occurred.

FAILURE TO FINISH.

36.—In the event of a game being stopped by darkness, or for any cause which prevents a finish the same day, it shall be resumed at the point at which it stopped, as to score and position of the ball, at the earliest convenient time, unless settled otherwise by agreement between the captains.

LIST OF EXISTING POLO PONIES.

ABBOTT (Mr. N. W. Curzon, 10th Hussars), ch g ; Inter-Regimental, Hurlingham, 1896 (88).

ACE OF HEARTS (Mr. W. J. Drybrough), skew g, a ; Paris, 1896 (286).

ALLY SLOPER (Major W. H. Walker), b g, a; County Cup, Hurlingham, 1895 (108).

ALUMINIUM (Mr. R. Court), b g, a ; County Cup, Hurlingham, 1895 (202).

AMAZON (Mr. W. J. Drybrough), b m, a ; County Cup, Hurlingham, 1895 (287).

ARAB CHIEF (Capt. Dundas), b h, a ; Inter-Regimental, Hurlingham, 1896 (223).

ARABI (Mr. J. Porter-Porter), wh g, a ; All Ireland Cup, 1895 (266).

ARCHEDUC (Baron Lejeune), blk g, a ; International Tournament, Paris (365).

ARTEE (Mr. W. D. Watson), b g, a ; Subalterns' Tournament, Ranelagh (120).

AURUM (Capt. the Earl of Longford, 2nd Life Guards), ch m ; Irish County Cup, 1894 (74).

AZUN (Mr. P. E. Bucknell), gr g, a ; Novices' Cup, Ranelagh (339).

BACCHIA (Mr. G. H. Hardy), b m, a ; Open Cup, Hurlingham, 1894-95-96 (167).

BALLET GIRL (Capt. G. FitzGerald), br m, a ; Inter-Regimental, Hurlingham, 1896 (10).

BAMBOO (Baron Lejeune), br g, a ; International Tournament, Paris, (367).

BANTAM (Major C. Peters), b m, a ; Open Cup, Hurlingham, 1896 (280).

BARD, THE (Mons. R. Raoul Duval), gr h, a; Paris, 1896 (306).

BARON (Messrs. E. D. and G. A. Miller), b g; Open Tournament, Ranelagh, 1896 (29).

BARONET (Capt. Gordon Mackenzie), b g, 5; Inter-Regimental, Hurlingham, 1896 (5).

BAY RHUM (Capt. Meyrick, 15th Hussars), b g, a; Irish Military Tournament, 1895 (150).

BEAR, THE (Mr. A. Rawlinson), b g, a; Champion Cup, Hurlingham, 1896 (127).

BEDOUIN (Major W. H. Walker), ch g, a; County Cup, Hurlingham, 1894 (109).

BEESWING (Mr. P. Sechiari), dun m; Novices' Cup, Ranelagh, 1896 (98).

BEL HASSIM (Mr. Herbert Wilson), gr h, 6; Novices' Cup, Ranelagh (209).

BELL (Capt. R. A. Christie), b m, a; Ranelagh, 1893 (358).

BELLE (The Marques de Villavieja), b m, a; Paris, 1896 (295)

BENBOW (Mons. R. Raoul Duval), b g, a; Paris International, 1896 (210).

BENEDICT (Mr. N. W. Curzon, 10th Hussars), b g; Inter-Regimental, Hurlingham, 1896 (89).

BIG BEN (Mr. J. G. Fort), wh m, a; Novices' Tournament, Ranelagh, 1895 (153).

BILLY (Mr. W. J. H. Jones), ch g, 6; Champion Cup, Hurlingham, 1896 (53).

BISMARCK (Mr. H. Scott-Robson), b g, a; Open Tournament, Ranelagh, 1896 (30).

BLACK BELLA (Messrs. E. D. and G. A. Miller), blk m, a; Open Cup, Hurlingham, 1896 (24).

BLACK PRINCE (Mr. F. Menzies), br h; Novices' Cup, 1896 (352).

BLACKMAN (Mr. Gerald Gold), blk g; Champion Cup, Hurlingham, 1894 (79).

BLARNEY (Mons. L. de Errazu), blk g, a; Paris, 1896 (304).

BLAZES (Capt. the Earl of Longford, 2nd Life Guards), br m; Inter-Regimental, Hurlingham (71).

BLUE BEARD (Mr. R. Court), blue roan g, a; County Cup, Hurlingham, 1895 (201).

BLUE BLOOD (Mr. G. F. Buchan), gr h, a; Subalterns' Tournament, 1896 (351).

BOMBASTE (Mr. T. B. Drybrough), gr h, a; County Cup, Hurlingham, 1893-94 (165).

BOS, THE (Mr. W. B. Longdon), blk g; Novices' Cup, Ranelagh, 1896 (111).

BOY, THE (Mr. J. C. Harrison, Scots Greys), b h, ᴄ; Inter-Regimental, Hurlingham, 1895-96 (157).

BRIEF (Messrs. E. D. and G. A. Miller), br m, a; Open Cup, Hurlingham, 1896 (23).

BROWN STOUT (Capt. P. Langdale), dark br m, ᴄ; Inter-Regimental, Hurlingham, 1896 (232).

BRUNETTE (Mr. C. K. O'Hara), br m, a; Irish C.P.U. Cup, 1894-95-96 (316).

CAFE AU LAIT (Mr. Neil Haig), dun g, a; Inter-Regimental, Hurlingham (197).

CARLO (Capt. Carden, 1st Life Guards), dun g; Inter-Regimental, Hurlingham, 1896 (67).

CARLOW (Mr. C. S. Schreiber), b m, a; Subalterns' Cup, Ranelagh, 1896 (11).

CARLOW (Capt. H. A. L. Tagart, 15th Hussars), b g, a; Irish Military and Open Tournaments, 1895 (35).

CATARINA (Mr. H. J. Selwyn), ch m, a; County Cup, Hurlingham, 1894 (277).

CATCH-'EM-ALIVE (Mr. W. Harrild), br m, a; County Cup, Hurlingham, 1893 (235).

CHANCE (Capt. Dalgety), br g, a; Novices' Cup, Ranelagh (268).

CHARLTON (Mr. Wm. Younger), ch m; County Cup, Hurlingham, 1893-94 (75).

CHATTER BOX (Mr. F. J. Mackey), b m, 6; Novices' Cup, Ranelagh (323).

CHEEKY BOY (Capt. D. Daly), ch h, a; All Ireland Cup, 1895 (332).

CHIEF OF ORAN (12th Lancers Polo Club), ch g, a; Inter-Regimental, Hurlingham, 1891-95 (212).

CID, THE (Mr. A. R. Wyndham), gr h; Inter-Regimental, Hurlingham, 1894-95 (69).

CICELY (Major W. H. Walker), b m, a; County Cup, Hurlingham, 1895 (103).

CLINKER (Col. Campbell), b g, a; Irish C.O. Cup, 1895 (240).

COFFEE (Mr. W. F. Robinson), br m; Novices' Cup, Ranelagh, 1896 (93).

COFFEE (Mr. R. B. Sheridan), b g, a; Novices' Tournament, Ranelagh, 1896 (149).

COMET (Mr. E. Holland), gr g, a; Inter-Regimental, Hurlingham, (258).

COMMON (Capt. Gordon Mackenzie), gr g, 6; Open Cup, Hurlingham 1895 (8).

CORELIA (Hon. T. W. Brand, 10th Hussars), ch m ; Inter-Regimental, Hurlingham, 1896 (83).

COUNT, THE (Capt. Loder), gr g, a; Inter-Regimental, Hurlingham, 1894 (227).

CUENCA (Mr. Donaldson Hudson), gr g, a ; Inter-Regimental, Hurlingham, 1893 (181).

CURACOA (Mr. A. Rawlinson), br m, a ; Paris International Tournament (191).

CYCLONE (Mr. W. S. Buckmaster), b m, a ; Champion Cup, Hurlingham, 1896 (123).

CYDER CUP (Capt. G. Milner), br m, a ; Inter-Regimental, Hurlingham, 1896 (7).

DAINTY (Sir H. F. de Trafford), br m, a ; County Cup, Hurlingham, 1895 (114).

DAIRY MAID (Mr. E. Rose), ch m, a ; Open Cup, Ranelagh (249).

DANCING GIRL, THE (Mr. Tresham Gilbey), ch m ; Inter-Regimental, Hurlingham, 1896 (62).

DANDY (Capt. C. A. S. Warner, 17th Lancers), ch g ; Inter-Regimental, Hurlingham, 1896 (55).

DAPHNE (Mr. A. Rawlinson), br m, 6 ; Open Cup, Ranelagh, 1896 (15).

DAYLIGHT (Duc de Besacia), b m, a ; International Tournament, Paris, 1896 (362).

DAYSTAR (Mr. W. J. H. Jones), b g, 6 ; Novices' and Open Cups, Ranelagh, 1896 (48).

DAWN (Hon. Dudley Marjoribanks), gr m, a ; Novices' Cup, Ranelagh (254).

DEAN, THE (Mr. A. Rawlinson), b g, a ; Champion Cup, Hurlingham, 1896 (334).

DEAREST (Capt. Dalgety), br m, a; Inter-Regimental, Hurlingham, 1895 (243).

DENIS (Capt. E. W. Pedder), gr g ; Inter-Regimental, Hurlingham, 1896 (133).

DOCTOR (Mr. Gerald W. Hobson), ch g, 5 ; Novices' Cup, Ranelagh, 1896 (58).

DOCTOR, THE (Mr. C. P. Foster), rn g, a ; Inter-Regimental, Hurlingham, 1896 (220).

DR. JIM (Mr. R. Lambert), ch h, a ; Inter-Regimental, Hurlingham, 1896 (147).

DOLLAR (Mr. H. J. Selwyn), b g ; Ranelagh Open Tournament (31).

DOLLY (Hon. T. W. Brand, 10th Hussars), ch m ; Inter-Regimental, Hurlingham, 1896 (84).

DOROTHY (Major C. Peters), b m, a ; Open Cup, Hurlingham, 1896 (278).

DOROTHY (Mr. F. Wormald), ch m, a ; Inter-Regimental, Hurlingham, 1895 (217).

DRAHAM (Mr. J. D. Watson), ch g, a ; Novices' Cup, 1896 (313).

DUBLIN (Mr. W. J. H. Jones), gr g, a ; Novices' and Open Cup, Ranelagh, 1896 (49).

DUMPS (Capt. Dalgety), br m, a ; Inter-Regimental, Hurlingham, 1896 (241).

DWARF (Mr. C. F. Dixon Johnson, Inniskilling Dragoons), ch g ; Inter-Regimental, Hurlingham, 1896 (66).

DYNAMITE (Major W. H. Walker), b m, a ; County Cup, Hurlingham, 1895 (104).

EARLY DAWN (Mr. W. S. Buckmaster), ch m, a ; Open Tournament, Hurlingham, 1895 (121).

EILEEN (Capt. M. F. Rimington), b m, a ; Inter-Regimental, Hurlingham, 1896 (46).

ELASTIC (Mr. G. H. Hardy), br m, a ; Open Cup, Hurlingham, 1896 (170).

ELDUO (Mr. F. J. Mackey), ch g, a ; Novices' Cup, Ranelagh, (322).

EL HELM (Mr. F. A. B. Fryer), ch h, 5 ; Novices' Cup, Ranelagh, 1896 (102).

ELISHA (Capt. Gordon Mackenzie), gr g, a ; Inter-Regimental, Hurlingham, 1894 (3).

ELSTOW (Earl of Shrewsbury), br m, a ; County Cup, Hurlingham, 1895 (177).

ERCELIA (Capt. E. Green), ch m, a ; Inter-Regimental, Hurlingham, 1895 (193).

EVY (Mr. D. Hudson), gr m, a ; County Cup, Hurlingham, 1894 (270).

EXCHANGE (Capt. G. Milner), ch g, a ; Inter-Regimental, Hurlingham, 1894 (6).

FAIR HELEN (Capt. M. F. Rimington), br m, a ; Inter-Regimental, Hurlingham, 1896 (47).

FANCY (Capt. Vaughan Lee), br m, a ; Inter-Regimental, Hurlingham, 1895 (182).

FAWN (Mr. H. W. H. Lambton), ch m, a ; County Cup, Hurlingham, 1895 (45).

FIDDLES (17th Lancers Club), ch g, a ; Inter-Regimental, Hurlingham, 1896 (137).

FIDDLESTRING (Capt. Eley), b m, a ; Inter-Regimental, Hurlingham, 1895 (207).

FIDGET (Mr. H. Spender Clay), b m, a ; Novices' Cup, Ranelagh, (267).

FIDGET (Capt. Renton), ch m, 6 ; Open Cup, Hurlingham, 1894 (173).

FIZZ (Mr. W. Walton), b g ; Novices' Cup, Ranelagh, 1896 (99).

FIZZER (Lord Kensington), b g, a ; (382).

FLEXIBLE (Mr. N. W. Curzon, 10th Hussars), dun m ; Inter-Regimental, Hurlingham, 1896 (87).

FLIRT (Sir E. Stracey), ch m, a ; Novices' Cup, Ranelagh (187).

FLIRT (Sir H. F. de Trafford), b m, a ; County Cup, Hurlingham, 1895 (113).

FLO (Hon. T. W. Brand, 10th Hussars), b m ; Open Cup, Ranelagh, 1896 (85).

FOAM (12th Lancers Polo Club), b m, a ; Inter-Regimental, Hurlingham, 1891-95 (214).

FRILLS (Capt. Vaughan Lee), drk b m, a ; Inter-Regimental, Hurlingham, 1895 (185).

FUSILIER (Mr. W. J. Drybrough), gr g, a ; County Cup, Hurlingham (261).

FUSSER (Major W. H. Walker), ch m, a ; County Cup, Hurlingham, 1895 (107).

GAMECOCK (Mr. G. H. Hardy), b g, a ; Open Cup, Hurlingham, 1896 (168).

GAYLAD (Mr. Frank Siltzer), b g, a ; Open Cup, Hurlingham, 1894 (158).

GAZELLE (12th Lancers Polo Club), ch m, a ; Inter-Regimental, Hurlingham, 1891-95 (211).

GHOST (Capt. N. T. Nickalls, 17th Lancers), b h, a ; Inter-Regimental, Hurlingham, 1893-96 ; Paris, 1896 (39).

GIFT, THE (Major J. G. Morris), wh g, a ; Novices' Cup, 1896 (373).

GINGER (Mr. P. E. Bucknell), ch m, a ; Novices' Cup, Ranelagh (338).

GIPSEY QUEEN (Mr. W. Harrild), b m, a ; County Cup, Hurlingham, 1893 (234)

GIRL, THE (Mr. P. Hambro, 15th Hussars), ch m ; Inter-Regimental, Hurlingham, 1896 (65).

GLUTTON (Capt. Dalgety), ch g, a ; Novices' Cup, Ranelagh (245).

GOLDEN HACKLE (Mr. P. E. Bucknell), ch g, a ; Novices' Cup, Ranelagh (336).

GOLIGHTLY (Mr. C. Adamthwaite) ; Novices' Cup, Ranelagh (342).

GRASSHOPPER (Mr. C. A. D'Estrange), dun m, a ; Irish C.P.U. Cup, 1894-95-96 (319).

GREY FRIAR (Mr. W. Burdon), gr h, 7 ; Inter-Regimental, Hurlingham, 1896 (269).

GREYFRIARS (Sir. E. Stracey), gr Arab g, 7 ; Novices' Cup, Ranelagh (186).

GREY LEGS (Sir H. F. de Trafford), ro g, a ; County Cup, Hurlingham, 1896 (116).

HAPPY LAD (Mr. F. Freake), g h, a ; Novices' Cup, Ranelagh (345).

HATFIELD (Mr. J. G. Fort), b g, 7 ; Novices' Tournament, Ranelagh, 1895 (155).

HAWTHORN (Mr. A. A. Longdon), b m, a ; Novices' Cup, Ranelagh (112).

HIPCAT (Capt. Renton), br m, a ; Open Cup, Hurlingham, 1894-95-96 (171).

HITTITE (Mr. A. Stuart), ch g, 7 ; Novices' Cup (272).

HOUSEMAID (Mr. W. J. H. Jones), b m, 5 ; Novices' Cup, Ranelagh, 1896 (51).

HURRICANE (Capt. Vaughan Lee), ch g, a ; Inter-Regimental, Hurlingham, 1895 (183).

HUSMAM (Mr. M. Ephrusi), gr h, a ; Paris, 1896 (292).

HUSSAR (Mr. C. S. Schreiber), b g, 6 (349).

INDIAN (Baron Lejeune), b g, a ; International Tournament, Paris (366).

IRISH, GIRL late Alphosine (Messrs. F. D. and G. A. Miller), ch m, a ; Inter-Regimental, Hurlingham, 1896 (36).

JACK (Mr. P. E. Bucknell), ch g, a ; Novices' Cup, Ranelagh (337).

JACK (Mr. Herbert Wilson), br g, 7 ; Novices' Cup, Ranelagh (208).

JACK IN THE BOX (Mr. Percy Bullivant), b g, a ; Novices' Cup, Ranelagh (189).

JACK TAR (Mr. J. Belleville), b g, a ; Novices' Cup (379).

JANE (Mr. N. W. Curzon, 10th Hussars), br m ; Inter-Regimental, Hurlingham, 1866 (86).

JANE (Major J. G. Morris), b m, 6 ; Novices' Cup, 1896 (371).

JENNY (Capt. Loder), b m, a ; County Cup, Hurlingham, 1894 (224).

JIM CROW (Mr. Percy Bullivant), roan g, a ; Novices' Cup, Ranelagh (190).

JOCK SCOTT (17th Lancers Polo Club), dark ch g, 6 ; Open Tournament, Ranelagh (238).

JOE (Viscount Villiers), gr g ; Novices' Cup, Ranelagh, 1896 (126),

JOHNNY (Capt. Loder), ch h, a ; Inter-Regimental, Hurlingham, 1894 (226).

JOHNNY LONGTAIL (Mr. H. Montgomery), gr g, a ; Inter-Regimental, Hurlingham, 1896 (136).

JOKER, THE (Mr. J. Watson), br g, 6 ; Open Cup, Ranelagh, 1896 (359).

KETTLE (The Marques de Villavieja), b m, a ; Paris, 1896 (297).

KHALIFA (Mr. T. B. Drybrough), b m, a ; County Cup, Hurlingham, 1892, 1893-94 (164).

KHEDIVE (Mr. W. J. Drybrough), blk h, a ; County Cup, Hurlingham, 1892 (285).

KISMET (Mr. J. B. Aldridge, R.H.A.), gr g, a ; Inter-Regimental, Hurlingham, 1896 (143).

KITTEN (Capt. Lord W. Bentinck, 10th Hussars), b m ; Inter-Regimental, Hurlingham, 1896 (80).

LADY (Mr. C. Adamthwaite), b m, 7 ; Novices' Cup, Ranelagh (341).

LADY BIRD (17th Lancers Polo Club), b m, 10 ; Inter-Regimental, Hurlingham, 1895 (237).

LADY DIAMOND (Mr. F. J. Mackey), ch m, 6, Novices' Cup, Ranelagh (325).

LADY FULLARTON (Mr. Wm. Younger), ch m ; County Cup, Hurlingham, 1893-94 (77).

LADY GREY (Mr. R. Court), wh m, a ; County Cup, Hurlingham, 1895 (200).

LADY ILEEN (Mr. W. J. Drybrough), b m, a ; County Cup, Hurlingham, 1894 (284).

LADY JANE (Major W. H. Walker), b m, a ; County Cup, Hurlingham, 1895 (106).

LADY'S MAID (Baron Lejeune), b m, a ; International Tournament, Paris (368).

LADY'S MAID (Mr. F. J. Mackey), br m, 6 ; Novices' Cup, Ranelagh (324).

LADY'S MAID (Earl of Shrewsbury), b m, a ; County Cup, Hurlingham, 1895 (179).

LADY SUPERIOR, THE (Mr. W. J. Drybrough), b m, a; County Cup, Hurlingham, 1894 (283).

LAM LASS (Mr. F. Menzies), ch m, a; Novices' Cup, 1896 (354).

LANCET (Capt. G. FitzGerald), br g, a; Inter-Regimental, Hurlingham, 1896 (9).

LANGOSTA (Messrs. E. D. & G. A. Miller), br g; Open Tournament, Ranelagh, 1896 (26).

LANGOSTA (Capt. Renton), blk g, 6; Open Cup, Hurlingham, 1894 (175).

LARIOS (Mons. R. Raoul Duval), gr h, 11; Paris, 1896 (307).

LIGHTNING (Mr. W. A. Tilney, 17th, Lancers), b m, 6; Inter-Regimental, Hurlingham, 1896 (20).

LILLY (Mr. John Watson), gr m, a; Ranelagh (205).

LITTLE FAIRY (Mr. A. Stuart), ch m, a; Novices' Cup (271).

LIZZIE (Hon. Dudley Marjoribanks), br m, a; County Cup Tournament, Hurlingham (255).

LOCUST (Mr. C. A. D'Estrange), b m, a; Irish C.P.U. Cup, 1894-95-96 (318).

LORD DALMAHOY (Mr. W. J. Drybrough), gr g, 6; County Cup, Paris (263).

LOTTIE (Duc de Besacia), b m, a; International Tournament, Paris, 1896 (363).

LUCKY PENNY (Mr. C. S. Schreiber), b m, 6; Subalterns' Tournament, 1896 (346).

LUNA (Mr. W. J. H. Jones), b m, a; Novices' and Open Cups, Ranelagh, 1896 (52).

LYRA (Capt. Sir Henry Rawlinson, Coldstream Guards), gr m, a; Champion Cup, Hurlingham, 1895 (18).

MADAM CLARK (Mr. Wm. Younger), b m; County Cup, Hurlingham, 1893-94 (76).

MAGIC (Major W. H. Walker), ch h, a; County Cup, Hurlingham, 1894 (110).

MAGIC SPELL (Mr. W. J. Drybrough) b h, 7; County Cup, Paris (264).

MAGNET (Capt. Renton) br g, a; Open Cup, Hurlingham, 1894 (174).

MAHOMET (Hon. Dudley Marjoribanks), dark gr g, a; Novices' Cup, Ranelagh (253).

MAINSPRING (Mr. F. J. Mackey), br m, 7; Novices' Cup, Ranelagh (321).

MARGOT (Major J. G. Morris), br m, 6; Novices Cup, 1896 (372).

25*

MARY ANNE (Mr. F. H. Wise, 13th Hussars), b m, a ; Inter-Regimental, Hurlingham, 1896 (138).

MATCHBOX (Capt. Renton), ch m, 7 ; Open Cup, Hurlingham, 1894 (172).

MAY BLOSSOM (Mr. P. Hambro, 15th Hussars), ch m ; Military Tournament, Dublin, 1895 (63).

MAYFLY (Capt. B. Johnson, Scots Greys), br m, 7 ; Inter-Regimental, Hurlingham, 1896 (141).

MICKEY (Capt. E. W. Pedder), dun g, a ; Inter-Regimental, Hurlingham, 1892-96 (132).

MICKEY FREE (Capt. T. G. Collins, 17th Lancers), b h, a ; Inter-Regimental, Hurlingham, 1896 (56).

MIDGET (12th Lancers Polo Club), b m, a ; Inter-Regimental, Hurlingham, 1891-95 (213).

MIDNIGHT (Capt. Sydney Mills, Rifle Brigade),br m ; Open Cup, Hurlingham, 1894-95-96 (176).

MISS BUSYBODY (Mr. Gerald W. Hobson), ch m, a ; Novices' Cup, Ranelagh, 1896 (59).

MISS EDGE (Sir H. F. de Trafford), b m, a ; County Cup, Hurlingham, 1896 (117).

MISS McKEEVER (Capt. Dalgety), b m, 8 ; Inter-Regimental, Hurlingham, 1895 (242).

MOLLY (Mr. W. Burdon), bl m, 7 ; Inter-Regimental, Hurlingham, 1896 (230).

MOLOCK (Messrs. E. D. and G. A. Miller), blk g ; Open Tournament, Ranelagh, 1896 (27).

MONK (Mr. E. B Sheppard), blk g, a ; Open Cup, Ranelagh, 1896 (160).

MONTE CHRISTO (Mons. E. de Escandon), b g, a ; Paris, 1896 (300).

MOONSHINE (Mr. Conolly), gr h, 6 ; Inter-Regimental, Hurlingham, 1896 (239).

MORLEY (Mr. W. J. Drybrough), blk m, 8 ; Inter-Regimental, Hurlingham, 1894 (265).

MOROCCO BOUND (Mr. L C. D. Jenner), b h, a ; Novices' Cup, Ranelagh, 1896 (37).

MOSS MARY (Mr. P. Hambro, 15th Hussars), ch m ; Military Tournament, Dublin, 1895 (64).

MUSTAPHA (Mr. J. D. Watson), ch g, 7 ; Novices' Cup, 1896 (312).

MYALL (Hon. Dudley Marjoribanks), br g, a ; Novices' Cup, Ranelagh (251).

MYSTERY (Mr. L. S. Cobham), br m, a ; Novices' Cup, Ranelagh, 1896 (1).

NAUGHTY (Hon. Du dley Marjoribanks), b m, a ; Novices' Cup, Ranelagh (252).

NELLIE (Mons. E. de Escandon), b m, a; Paris 1896 (299).

NELLIE (Mr. John Watson), ch m, 6; Ranelagh (204).

NELLIE (Earl of Shrewsbury), b m, a ; County Cup, Hurlingham, 1895 (180).

NIGHT (Mr. Donaldson Hudson), b m, a ; Inter-Regimental, Hurlingham, 1894-95 (228).

NIGGER (Mr. W. D. Watson), blk g, a ; Subalterns' Tournament, Ranelagh (119).

NIMBLE (Mr. C. A. D'Estrange), gr m, a; Irish C.P.U. Cup, 1894-95-96 (320).

NIMBLE (Major W. H. Walker), b m, a ; County Cup, Hurlingham, 1895 (105).

NINEPINS (Mr. H. Montgomery), dun m, a ; Inter-Regimental, Hurlingham, 1896 (135).

NUTMEG (Mr. L. C. Brunton), b g, a ; Novices' Cup 1896 (356).

OCHRE (Mons. E. de Escandon), b g, a ; Paris, 1896 (298).

OONAH (Mr. F. Freake) ch m, 6; Inter-Regimental, Hurlingham, 1896 (360).

ORPHAN, THE (Mr. W. J. Drybrough), b g, a ; Open Cup, Ranelagh, 1896 (282).

ORPHAN MAID (Mr. C. K. O'Hara), br m, a ; Irish C.P.U. Cup, 1894-95-96 (315).

OTTER (Mr. A. S. Dyas), b h, 5 ; Inter-Regimental, Hurlingham, 1896 (146).

PADDY (Mons. R Raoul Duval), blk h, a ; Paris, 1896 (308).

PARSON (Mr. E. B. Sheppard), br g, a ; Open Cup, Ranelagh, 1896 (159).

PASHA (Capt. Lord W. Bentinck, 10th Hussars), b g ; Inter-Regimental, Hurlingham 1896 (82).

PAUL (Capt. Eley), gr g, a ; Paris Tournament, 189_ (206).

PENNY-A-SHOT (Mr. J. Belleville), b m, a ; Novices' Cup (381).

PEPPER (Mr. D. Jay), gr m ; Novices' Cup, Ranelagh, 1896 (96).

PERIWINKLE (Mr. D. Jay), b m ; Novices' Cup, Ranelagh, 1896 (94).

PETER (Mr. L. S. Cobham), ch h, a; Novices' Cup, Ranelagh, 1894 (2).

PETER (Capt. Vaughan Lee), bl g, a ; Inter-Regimental, Hurlingham, 1895 (184).

PETER'S WIFE (Mr. A. Suart), drk ch m, a; Novices' Cup, (274).

PHARAOH (Mr. F. Menzies), b h, a; Inter-Regimental, Hurlingham, 1896 (355).

PIGGY (Mr. J. F. Church, 13th Hussars), b g, a; Inter-Regimental, Hurlingham, 1896 (144).

PIPER (Sir H. F. de Trafford), ch g, a; County Cup, Hurlingham, 1896 (118).

PIQUET (Capt. The Earl of Longford, 2nd Life Guards), b m; Novices' Cup, Ranelagh, 1896 (73).

PLUS (Mr. G. A. Miller), b g, 6; Novices' Tournament, Ranelagh, 1895 (151).

PRETTY GIRL (Mr. W. J. Drybrough), b m, 6; County Cup, Hurlingham (262).

PRIDE, THE (Capt. Collins), br g, 6; Subalterns' Tournament, Ranelagh, 1896 (198).

PRINCE (Mr. J. Belleville), ch g, a; Novices' Cup (370).

PRINCESS (Mr. E. B. Sheppard), b m, a; Open Cup, Ranelagh, 1896 (161).

PROFESSOR (Mr. W. Harrild), b g, a; County Cup, Hurlingham, 1893 (233).

PSYCHE (Mr. A. Suart), br m, 7; Novices' Cup (273).

QUEEN OF THE MAY (Mr. Tresham Gilbey), b m; Inter-Regimental, Hurlingham, 1896 (61).

RAKE, THE (Mr. T. B. Drybrough), b h, a; County Cup, Hurlingham, 1893-94 (166).

RASPBERRY (Lord Southampton), ro m, a; Open Cup, Hurlingham, 1896 (129).

RASCAL (Capt. Garden), br g, a; Open Tournament, Dublin, 1893 (57).

RAZZLE (Mr. Gerald W. Hobson), gr g, a; Novices' Cup, Ranelagh, 1896 (60).

RECOVERY (Messrs. E. D. & G. A. Miller), br g; Open Tournament, Ranelagh, (28).

RED KING (Capt. Hon. E. Baring, 10th Hussars), ch h; Inter-Regimental, Hurlingham, 1896 (90)

REDOUTE (Mons. L. de Errazu), ch m, a; Paris, 1896 (302).

RED TICKET (Mr. C. K. O'Hara), b g, a; Irish C.P.U. Cup, 1894-95-96 (314).

REGINA (Capt. the Earl of Longford, 2nd Life Guards), br m; Novices' Cup, Ranelagh, 1896 (72).

REGULATION (Mons. L. de Errazu), b h, a; Paris, 1896 (301).

REGULUS (Mr. W. Burdon), b g, 7 ; Inter-Regimental, Hurlingham, 1896 (229).

ROSE BUD (Mr. C. K. O'Hara), b m, a ; Irish C.P.U. Cup, 1894-95-96 (317).

ROYAL (Mr. W. A. Tilney, 17th Lancers), b h, a ; Inter-Regimental, Hurlingham, 1896 (19).

RUBY (Mr. H. Spender Clay), ch m, a ; Open Cup, Hurlingham, 1895 (134).

RUGBY (Sir H. F. de Trafford), ch g, a ; County Cup, Hurlingham, 1896 (115).

RYE (Mr. F. Wormald j, ch m, 8 ; Inter-Regimental, Hurlingham, 1895 (216).

SABIN (Capt. E. Green), blk m, 8 ; Inter-Regimental, Hurlingham, 1894 (192).

SAILOR (Mr. G. H. Hardy), br g, a ; Open Cup, Hurlingham, 1896 (169).

SALYCO (Major Butler), gr g, a ; Inter-Regimental, Hurlingham, 1896 (148).

SANFOIN (Mr. Niel Haig, Inniskilling Dragoons), b g, a ; Open Cup, Hurlingham (40).

SATANITA (Mons. M. Raoul Duval), gr m, a ; Paris, 1896 (294).

SAUCY MARY (Mr. Neil Haig, Inniskilling Dragoons), blk m, a, Inter-Regimental, Hurlingham, 1896 (42).

SCOTS GREYS (Mr Niel Haig, Inniskilling Dragoons), wh g, a ; Inter-Regimental, Hurlingham (39).

SEAFIELD (Mons. de Errazu), ch m, 8 ; Paris, 1896 (288).

SEAGULL (Capt. Lord W. Bentinck, 10th Hussars), gr g ; Inter-Regimental, Hurlingham, 1896 (81).

SEAGULL (Mr. F. H. Wise, 13th Hussars), gr g, a ; Inter-Regimental, Hurlingham, 1896 (140).

SEMINADA (Mons. L. de Errazu), br m, a ; Paris, 1896 (303).

SERF BEAUTY (Mr. A. Rawlinson), b m, 5 ; Open Cup, Ranelagh, 1896 (14).

SHABA (Mr. C. Adamthwaite), gr g, a ; Novices' Cup, Ranelagh (344).

SHADAZA (Mr. T. Greenway), gr h ; Novices' Cup, Ranelagh, 1896 (101).

SHADOW (The Marques de Villavieja), blk m, a ; Paris, 1896 (290).

SHORT TAIL (Capt. Loder), b m, a ; Inter-Regimental, Hurlingham, 1895 (225).

SILENCE (Mr. M. Ephrusi), b m, a ; Paris, 1896 (291).

SILURIAN GREY (Mr. R. Hudson), br m, a ; Open Tournament, Ireland (130).

SILVERTAIL (Mr. Niel Haig, Inniskilling Dragoons), dun g, 5 ; Inter-Regimental, Hurlingham, 1896 (42).

SINKAT (Mr. F. Mussenden), gr g, a ; Inter-Regimental, Hurlingham, 1896 (195).

SIR PERTAB (Mr. G F. Buchan), br h, a ; Inter-Regimental Tournament, 1894-96 (350).

SISTER SUE (Mr. E. Holland), b m, a ; Inter-Regimental, Hurlingham (257).

SISTER SUE (Mr. C. S. Schreiber), ch m, a ; Inter-Regimental, Hurlingham, 1896 (12).

SKIPPING JENNY (Sir E. Stracey), br m, 8 ; Novices' Cup, Ranelagh (188).

SKITTLES (Mr. G. F. Buchan), rn g, a ; Subalterns' Tournament, 1896 (347).

SKITTLES (Capt. D. Daly), b m, a ; Open Cup, Hurlingham, 1894-95 (331).

SLY FOX (Mr. J. Belleville), b g, a ; Novices' Cup (380).

SNAP SHOT (Mr. M. Ephrusi), b g, a ; Paris, 1896 (293).

SNOWBALL (Mr. P. E. Bucknell), gr g, 7 ; Novices' Cup, Ranelagh (340).

SNOWBALL (Major E. B. Herbert, 17th Lancers`, gr h, a ; Inter-Regimental, Hurlingham, 1896 (21).

SOLOMON (Mr. F. Menzies), b g, a ; Novices' Cup, 1896 (353).

SORCERESS (Mr. J. Hargreaves), b m, a ; Champion Cup, Hurlingham, 1896 (17).

SPEED OF THOUGHT (Capt. Yardley), gr ; Inter-Regimental, Hurlingham, 1896 (231).

SPIDER (Major C. Peters), br m. a ; Open Cup, Hurlingham, 1896 (279).

SPINSTER (Capt. H. Farrar), b m, a ; Inter-Regimental, Hurlingham, 1896 (219).

SPINSTER (Earl of Harrington), br m, a ; International Tournament, Paris, 1895 (374).

SPRINGHILL (Mr. J. Hargreaves), br g, a ; Champion Cup, Hurlingham, 1896 (16).

STAR (Mr. J. G. Fort), b h, a ; Novices' Tournament, Ranelagh, 1895 (154).

STAR OF INDIA (Major Duff), b h, 9 ; Inter-Regimental, Hurlingham, 1895 (250).

STARLIGHT (The Marques de Villavieja), blk m, a ; Paris, 1896 (296).

SUCCESS (The Marques de Villavieja), blk g, a; Champion Cup, Hurlingham, 1896 (289).

SULTAN (12th Lancers Polo Club), gr g, a; Inter-Regimental, Hurlingham, 1891-95 (215).

SUNLIGHT (Sir P. Nickalls), ch m, a; Champion Cup, Hurlingham, 1895 (335).

SUNRAY (Mr. C. Adamthwaite), ch h, a; Novices' Cup, Ranelagh, (343).

SURPRISE (Mr. E. Rose), b m. a; Inter-Regimental, Hurlingham, 1896 (246).

SUSAN (Capt. Dundas), br m, a; Inter-Regimental, Hurlingham, 1896 (222).

SUSIE (Capt. E. W. Pedder), b m, a; Inter-Regimental, Hurlingham, 1891-96 (131).

SWALLOW (Mr. J. Hetherington), br m; Novices' Cup, Ranelagh, 1896 (100).

SYLVIA (Capt. Hon. E. Baring, 10th Hussars), br m; Inter-Regimental, Hurlingham, 1896 (91).

TAMARA (Capt. Dalgety), br m, 6; Novices' Cup, Ranelagh, (244).

TARGET (Earl of Shrewsbury), b m, a; County Cup, Hurlingham, 1895 (178).

TEMPEST (Mr. F. A. Belleville), ch g, a; (256).

TESS (Mr. C. S. Schreiber), b m, a; Inter-Regimental, Hurlingham, 1896 (13).

THRIFT (Mr. Niel Haig, Inniskilling Dragoons), b m, 6; Inter-Regimental, Hurlingham, 1896 (43).

TIT-BITS (Mr. D. Jay), ch m; Novices' Cup, Ranelagh, 1896 (95).

TOFFY (Mr. P. Sechiari), b m; Novices' Cup, Ranelagh, 1896 (97).

TOM-TIT (Capt. C. A. S. Warner, 17th Lancers), ch g, a; Inter-Regimental, Hurlingham, 1896 (54).

TOMMY (Mr. J. B. Aldridge, R.H.A.), gr g, 6; Inter-Regimental, Hurlingham, 1896 (142).

TORNADO, late Fortham (Messrs. E. D. and G. A. Miller), br g; Open Tournament, Ranelagh, 1896 (25).

TOSS UP (Capt. H. Ferrar), ch g, a; Inter-Regimental, Hurlingham, 1896 (218).

TRAPPIST (Baron Lejeune), gr h, a; International Tournament, Paris, 1896 (364).

UMPIRE (Mr. Niel Haig, Inniskilling Dragoons), ch h, a ; Inter-Regimental, Hurlingham, 1896 (41).

VALENTINE (Capt. Jeffcock), b g ; Inter-Regimental, Hurlingham, 1896 (78).

VANITY (Mr. E. Rose), b m, a ; Inter-Regimental, Hurlingham, 1896 (248).

VARMINT (Mr. W. J. H. Jones), br m. 6 ; Novices' and Open Cups, Ranelagh, 1896 (50).

VENDETTA (Mr. J. C. Harrison, Scots Greys), br m, a ; Inter-Regimental, Hurlingham, 1895-96 (156).

VENUS (Capt. Paynter), br m, a ; Inter-Regimental, Hurlingham, 1893 (236).

VIC (Mr. F. H. Wise, 13th Hussars), b m, a : Inter-Regimental, Hurlingham, 1896 (139).

VICTOR (Mr. L. C. D. Jenner), gr h, a ; Novices' Cup, Ranelagh, 1896 (38).

VORO (Capt. Gordon Mackenzie), ch g, a ; Inter-Regimental, Hurlingham, 1896 (4).

WARDIE (Mr. W. S. Buckmaster), br g, a ; Champion Cup, Hurlingham, 1896 (122).

WATCH SPRING (Mr. H. C. Fraser, 1st Life Guards), b m, a ; Subalterns' Tournament, Ranelagh, 1896 (162).

WATER LILY (Mr. A. Suart), br m, a ; Inter-Regimental, Hurlingham, (275).

WHIMS (Mr. D. A. Teaast), ch g ; Inter-Regimental, Hurlingham, 1894-95 (70).

WHITEFOOT (Mr. A. Jones), b g, a ; Novices' Cup, Ranelagh, 1896 (128).

WHITE ROSE (Mr. R. Court), w h, a ; County Cup, Hurlingham 1895 (199).

WHITEWINGS (Mr. G. Heseltine), b m. a ; County Cup, Hurlingham, 1896 (163).

WILD DUCK (Mr. A. Joyce), b m, 7 ; Irish County Cup, 1895 (328).

WITCH, THE (Capt. D. Daly), b m, a ; All Ireland Cup, 1895 (333).

YANKEE (Lord William Bentinck), b g, a ; Open Tournament, Ranelagh (32).

YELLOWHAMMER (Mr. J. F. Church, 13th Hussars), dun m, a ; Inter-Regimental, Hurlingham, 1896 (145).

YELLOWHAMMER (Mr. John Watson), dun g. 6; Ranelagh (203).

YELLOWMAN (Mr. E. Rose), dun g, a; Inter-Regimental, Hurlingham, 1896 (247).

YELLOWSTONE (Mr. W. J. Drybrough), ch g, a; Open Cup, Ranelagh, 1896 (281).

ZAZEL (Capt. Hon. E. Baring, 10th Hussars), br m; Inter-Regimental, Hurlingham, 1896 (92).

ZINGIT (Major E. B. Herbert, 17th Lancers), br m, a; Inter-Regimental, Hurlingham, 1896 (22).

UNNAMED PONIES.

Mr. A. Joyce, br m; I.C. Cup (310).

Capt. N. T. Nickalls, 17th Lancers, b h, a; Inter-Regimental, Hurlingham, 1893-96, Paris, 1896 (33).

Mr. W. A. Tilney, 17th Lancers; Inter-Regimental, Hurlingham, 1896 (68).

POLO PONIES MEASURED & REGISTERED AT HURLINGHAM, 1897.

A (Mr. C. S. Schreiber), br g ; star, snip, near fore and both hind fetlocks white, brand near hind quarter (239).

ABDOOL (Capt. Whitla), ch h ; star, blaze, snip, white lower lip, white off hind leg, near hind fetlock and near fore pastern, girth marks (303).

ACCIDENT (Lord Harrington), b g ; white star, white strip on nose, white near hind pastern (92).

AEROLITE (Mr. Miller), br m ; star, two white hind heels, saddle marks, tan muzzle (34).

AGAY (Mr. Ashmore), ch m ; star, scar outside off hock (644).

AIBLENS (Capt. F. H. Milsom), b m ; star on forehead, small snip on nose, saddle marks (26).

ALI HASSAN (Mr. W. D. P. Watson), b h ; star, very narrow blaze, near fore and both hind fetlocks white (238).

AMBASSADRESS (Lord Harrington), br m ; white star, white hips, saddle marks (90).

AMELIA (Sir H. Rawlinson), b m ; black points, saddle marks, small white spot near fore shin and near hind shin (446).

AMERICA (Mr. Neil W. Haig), blk g ; scar near hind quarter, brand off hind quarter (337).

AMY (Mr. F. J. Siltzer), b m ; white hairs tail and mane, near fore and near hind pastern white, star and snip (71).

ANTELOPE II. (Major Robertson Aikman), gr m ; narrow blaze, snip, brown patch on face, white off hind fetlock, white mark front off hind shin and both fore shins (318).

ANTIC (Lord Harrington), br m ; white star, saddle marks, white spot outside off fore arm (91).

ARAB CHIEF (Capt. Dundas), b h ; four white legs, white marks above near hock, small star, snip, saddle marks (125).

ARAB, THE (Mr. R. F. Glynn), br h ; small star, white off hind fetlock, scar inside both hind legs (454).

ARABELLA (Marquis of Waterford), ch m ; white near hind leg and off foot, star, blaze, snip, girth marks (291).

ARGENTINA (Mr. F. Pilkington), br g ; small snip, white off hind coronet, grey near hind leg, brand near hind quarter (403).

ARTFUL (Lord Kensington), br m ; white spot on off ribs (156).

AZUL (Mr. Talbot Rice), gr g ; small snip on nose, both ears nicked (51).

B (Mr C. S. Schreiber), ch g ; star, blaze, grey hairs in flank and over back (240).

BABY (Capt. J. F. Dalgety), br m ; star, white near hind fetlock, white near fore heel (134).

BABY (Mr. H. J. Smith), b m, 4 ; star, saddle marks, white off hind pastern, white mark off side off leg ; this year (469).

BANG (Lord Harrington), b m, 4 ; large star, narrow blaze, snip, lower lip white, saddle marks ; for the season (275).

BANJO (Mr. W. B. Longsdon), ch g, large snip, white off fore pastern, and white near hind leg (504).

BANSHEE (Mr. W. Buckmaster), ch m ; small white star, little white off hind coronet, (76).

BANSHEE (Mr. G. A. Lockett), gr m ; dappled, small white circle under girth near side ; two small scars inside both fore legs (82).

BARB, THE (Capt. R. A. Christie), ch h (441).

BARBARA (Mr. C. Wheeler), blk br m ; slit off ear, white spots on chest and off side of neck (216).

BARON (Major Peters), not passed (352).

BARONESS (Mr. J. M. Walker), br m ; black points, white mark back and front of near fore leg (411).

BARTER (Mr. F. Hargreave), br m ; small star, white spot off hind heel, saddle marks (33).

BAY LEAF (Capt. F. Herbert), b m ; near hind stocking white, very narrow blaze, small snip, white patch under lip (130).

BAY QUEEN (Capt. J. F. Dalgery), b m ; black points, scars on shoulders (133).

B. B. (Mr. Stuart Duckett), blk m ; star, very narrow blaze white ticks, girth marks (545).

BEAUTY (Mr. Jameson), b m, 4 ; star, blaze, snip, white inside near fore pastern (590).

BECKETT (Capt. B. Johnson), b g ; white star, black points (209).

BECKY SHARP (Mr. R. Hudson), br m ; star, blaze, snip, black points, girth marks, white patch near side ribs (580).

BELINDA (Mr. E. A. Herbert), b m, 4 ; star, faint snip, white hind fetlocks, star both sides of back (336).

BELL (Capt. R. A. Christie), b m ; existing pony (440).

BELLE (Mr. E. A. R. Shearman), b m ; star, white near hind fet-lock, scar off hind fetlock (466).

BELLINDA (Mr. F. Wormald), ch m ; star, blaze, snip, little white lower lip, white hind leg (362).

BEN BOLT (Mr. J. D. Gouldsmith), ch m ; white near fore leg, star, blaze, snip (359).

BENITO (Mr. C. Wheeler), br g ; white off hind fetlock, few white hairs off side neck (217).

BERKSHIRE (Mr. A. Rawlinson), br m ; star, white hind heels, white mark near side neck (150).

BIDDY (Mr. Burgess), b br m ; black points, small scar off side wither, saddle marks, white hairs in tail (191).

BIDDY FLANAGAN (Major Rimington), b m ; star, white spot near side ribs, girth marks (604).

BILLY (Lord Crichton), ch g ; star, blaze, snip, brand on near shoulder, scar on nose, white near pastern (290).

BILLY (14th Hussars), b g ; star, white near hind pastern (628).

BIMETALLIST (Mr. G. Heseltine), gr m ; white spot both sides neck (161).

BIRD OF PARADISE (Mr. C. M. Grenfell), br m ; star, snip, black points, small saddle marks ; not passed (499).

BIRD, THE (Mr. Neil Haig), b m ; black points, very faint star and snip, branded near fore and near hind quarters (339).

BIRTHDAY (Mr. Freake), ch m ; white off hind pastern, white star, white snip centre of nose (45).

BISCUIT (Mr. J. Scott-Robson), rn g ; star, blaze, snip, white hind legs, and off fore leg and near fore fetlock, brand near hind quarter (424).

BISCUIT (Mr. P. J. Bailey), ch g ; star, blaze, snip, white lower lip and hind legs and off fore coronet, white spots over body (472).

BISMARCK (Mr. J. Scott-Robson), b g ; white legs, star, blaze, snip, white lower lip, white spots on hind quarters, brand near shoulder ; not passed (423).

BLACK BASS (Capt. Bidgood), blk g, 4 ; white off hind coronet, small saddle mark off side ; this season only (507).

BLACK PEARL (Hon. A. Hamilton Russell), blk m ; large star, small snip, white spot near fore fetlock, white off hind coronet (453).

BLACK PEARL (Capt. Renton), blk m ; faint star, white off hind fetlock, white spots over body, brand off hind quarter and off side of neck (483).

BLACK SKIN (Mr. J. H. Locke), br m ; faint star, snip, white hind legs, off fore fetlock, and near fore coronet (566).

BLAZE (Mr. F. J. Siltzer), ch h ; star, narrow blaze, snip, white near hind stocking, saddle marks (70).

BLAZER (Mr. S. M. Dennis), b g ; small star, white near hind fetlock, large scar near hind quarter (393).

BLAZER (Mr. C. Adamthwaite), b g ; black points, white ticks (674).

BLEEDAH (Mr. J. W. Archdale), br g ; white near hind pastern, white mark back of both fore legs (543).

BLUE JAY (Mr. T. B. Drybrough), gr g ; brand W near hind quarter, scars near shoulder (118).

BLUE PETER (Sir P. Nickalls), gr h ; white snip, short tail, scar on withers, white hind legs (141).

BLUE SLEEVE (Sir P. Nickalls), gr m ; snip, white lower lip, white hind fetlocks, white spots on hocks (143).

BLUE STAR (Sir P. Nickalls), b m ; star, scar on off hind fetlock (142).

BOADICEA (Capt. Schofield), b m ; white off fore and near hind pasterns, star, narrow blaze, snip (233).

BOBBY (Mr. J. M. Walker), b h ; white near fore leg and both off fetlocks, white mark front hind shins, scar off hind quarter and near shoulder (412).

BOOMERANG (Mr. Aubrey Price), b m ; small snip, black points, white mark on off ribs (489).

BORAS (Mr. G. K. Ansell), ch g ; star, blaze, snip, white near hind leg and near fore fetlock, and above near hock (341).

BOULAK (Mr. G. H. Pilkington),b g ; star, blaze, snip, black points, white marks on neck and near shoulder (387).

BRANDY BALL (Mr. G. A. Miller), blk g ; star, white off fore fetlock, brand on off hind quarter (152).

BRAVE (Mr. J. M. Walker), br g ; ticked with white, star, white near fore pastern and off hind fetlock (410).

BRIDE (Mr. Rourke), gr m ; small scars on forehead, scar off knee (549).

BRIDEGROOM (Mr. Grogan), gr g ; star, narrow blaze, white near hind pastern ; this season (532).

BRIDESMAID (Mr. C. Adamthwaite), gr m ; snip, and white mark off side neck (675).

BRIDGET (Mr. F. C. Pilkington), gr m ; little white both hind heels (127).

BRISTON (Mr. Peel), br g ; white spots all over body, brand mark off hind quarter, little white near hind coronet (201).

BROAD ARROW (Mr. Neil W. Haig), b m ; star, white near hind pastern, collar marks (338).

BROOMSTICK (Earl of Harrington), b m ; large star, narrow blaze, snip, scar near side face, black points (276).

BROWNIE (Mr. W. H. Lambton), br m ; black points, very small star, fired fore egs (225).

BROWN STOUT (Mr. D. Rawson), b or br g ; narrow blaze, white near hind and off fore pasterns and off hind fetlock, white mark top off shoulder (539).

BRUNETTE (Capt. Minchin), br m ; small star, white on upper lip, scar near side of neck, girth mark off side, saddle marks (175).

BRUNETTE (Mr. A. M. Knowles), br m ; large star, blaze, small snip, black points (214).

BUMPTIOUS (Mr. J. Belleville), b m ; white off hind fetlock, star, scar on withers (140).

BUSTLE (Mr. G. H. Pilkington), ch m ; star, blaze, snip, white marks near shoulder and front of near hind shin (386).

BUTTONS (Capt. E. W. Clowes), br g ; both hind pasterns white, brand near side shoulder (113).

CÆSAR (Mr. E. D. Miller), dk br g ; star, blaze, snip, white on lower lip, four white legs, brand mark near hind quarter (212).

CAIRO (Mr. Harrison), gr g ; double scar inside arm and thigh (244).

CAP (Mr. Mackey), ch g ; star, snip, blaze, brand C.A.P. on near quarter, saddle mark ; American (42).

CARLOW (Mr. Chinnery), b m ; black points, white marks above off hock (482).

CARLOW (Mr. Church), ch g ; star, white near fore pastern and off hind fetlock (602).

CARME (Capt. Hon. E. Pakenham), b h ; star, blaze, snip, brand near hind quarter, white hind fetlocks (571).

CARTE DE VISITE (Mr. J. E. Bailie), b m ; star, narrow blaze, snip, white near hind pastern ; passed for year only (253).

CASHBOX (Mr. H. C. Higgins), ch g ; star, white mark front of near hind fetlock (332).

CATERINA (Major Rimington), br m, 4 ; star, blaze, snip, white lower lip and off hind leg, scars both shoulders (613).

CATHERINE WHEEL (Mr. W. Buckmaster), ch m , white near hind fetlock and coronet, star, white patch off flank (77).

CAT, THE (Mr. D. H. Gibb), ch m ; star, blaze, snip, white hind legs, collar marks (344).

CATTLE QUEEN (Mr. T. B. Drybrough), b m ; branded 530, near hind quarter, two white hind stockings, large blaze (99).

CAVERSHAM (Mr. J. Belleville), b g ; blaze and snip, white hind fetlock, white near fore coronet (263).

CHARMER (Mr. A. S. Maude), b m ; white near hind fetlock (616).

CHIP (Mr. J. L. Read), br m ; star, black points, scar on both knees (462).

26

CHLOE (Mr. F. J. Siltzer), b m ; small star, black points, collar mark near shoulder, line down spine (245).

CLEHONGA (Mr. P. W. Game), ch g, 4 ; star ; not passed (653).

CLOWN (Earl of Airlie), br g ; tan muzzle, black points, few white hairs near side of face (307).

COCKLE (Mr. J. Duckett), b g ; star, white near fore and both hind fetlocks (544).

COLLEEN (Major Manifold), gr m ; scars off side ribs and brisket (190).

COMBAT (Mr. F. Balfour), br g ; brand near hind quarter, fore and near hind fetlocks white, faint star, saddle mark ; Argentine (9).

CONCEIT (Mr. W. J. Drage), ch m ; white off hind leg and near hind pastern, star, blaze, snip (663).

CONCHA (Mr. T. B. Drybrough), gr g ; branded W, near hind quarter, white blaze, snip and lower lip, two large scars on chest (97).

CONFESSION (Mr. H. Savile), b g ; small star, white marks on fore shins (147).

COQUET (Mr. R. St. G. Robinson), gr m ; star, white mark front off hock, white spot front chest (509).

CORONER (Mr. J. C. Harrison), gr g ; brand on both withers white marks on knees, girth marks (104).

CORRALES (Mr. J. Ravenscroft), blk g ; near fore and near hind pasterns white, brand near hind quarter, saddle marks (59).

COSSACK (14th Hussars' Club), gr g ; white marks front of fore shins (624).

COTTON TAIL (Mr. T. B. Drybrough), b g ; brand J.T. near hind quarter, white hind stockings, white hair on flank, star, snip, saddle mark (102).

COUNTY FASHION (Mr. W. Walton), b m ; white near hind coronet, scar near side ribs, scar off side neck (439).

CREAM CHEESE (Capt. Dundas), dun g ; blaze, snip, white leg, branded W near hind quarter, white hind stockings and fore fetlocks ; Argentine (88).

CRÊME DE LA CRÊME (Mr. C. F. Dixon-Johnson), cr m, 4 ; star, blaze, snip, white mane and tail, white near fore and both hind legs, and off hind fetlock white, for season (322).

CREOLE (Mr. T. B. Drybrough), b m ; white mark near hip, star, branded three lines and 536 on off hind quarter.

CRUSADER (Mr. H. Wilson), br g ; very small star, white marks both hind shins, little white near hind heel (267).

CUDDINGTON (Mr. A. Rawlinson), ch m ; white fore fetlocks, white near hind leg, blaze, snip (149).

CURATE, THE (Mr. F. A. B. Fryer), ch g ; star, blaze, snip, small white spot near hind quarter (326).

DADDY (Mr. R. J. Cunningham), b g; small star, scar off hind quarter, saddle marks; not passed (398).

DAINTY (Capt. Whitla), b m; star, blaze, white near hind fetlock, little white off hind shin (304).

DAISY (Mr. Talbot Rice), b m; blaze, white off hind legs, saddle marks (21).

DAISY (Comte de Madre), b m; star, scar near hind quarter, saddle marks (122).

DAISY (Mr. H. P. Dangan), ch m; star, snip, off hind leg white and inside near hind coronet, black patch near hip (600).

DAISY (Mr. Lloyd), b m; white spot near shoulder, black points (601).

DAME MARJORIE (Mr. J. L. Hunter), br m; star, white near fore and near hind fetlocks (349).

DANDELION (Mr. McCreery), ch g, 4; little white upper lip, white near hind pastern; passed for season (232).

DANDELION (Major Alexander), blk g; star, narrow blaze, snip, white hind fetlocks, grey off fore pastern, white ticks all over (534).

DANDY (Comte de Madre), gr h; flea-bitten on face, white near fore fetlocks, docked rat tail, off ear snipped (16).

DANDY (Mr. R. C. Barton), b g; black points, scar back of off hind and near fore legs (554).

DANIEL (Mr. G. H. Pilkington), br g; star, white hind legs (385).

DAPHNE (Mr. E. B. Sheppard), b m; white hairs, black points, saddle marks off side (85).

DAPHNE (Mr. J. M. Walker), b m; star, black points (415).

DARLINGTON (Mr. E. Makins), b br g; black points, white mark on off fore leg (427).

DARLY (Mr. Flanagan), b m; star, white mark front of hind shin and back of both fore legs (609).

DEAREST (Capt. Whitla), ch m; black spot front of near thigh (305).

DELIA (Mr. A. E. Batchelor), b m; black points (270).

DEVONSHIRE LAD (Mr. W. R. Bindloss), ch g; star, blaze, snip, white near hind leg and off hind pastern, scars on both sides of neck (300).

DEWDROP (Mr. J. G. Fort), blk g; faint star, white spot front off hind shin and both fore legs (484).

DIAMOND (Mr. W. Buckmaster), ch m; star, blaze, snip, white lower lip, brand near shoulder (418).

DIAMOND (Capt. Bruce), blk m; star, black points, saddle marks (357).

DICK (Mr. J. Livingstone), b g, 4; star, very narrow blaze, white near hind pastern and off hind fetlock; this season only (557).

26*

DICK (Mr. H. C. T. Rice), br g ; small scar off hind quarter, scar on both knees (667).

DISPUTE (Mr. F. J. Siltzer), rn m ; black points, two hind pasterns white, star, saddle marks (69).

DOCTOR, THE (Mr. J. C. Harrison), gr g ; brand both withers, white marks both knees, girth marks (104).

DR. JIM (14th Hussars), ch h ; star, narrow blaze, snip, white marks above near knee and hock, white mark hind fetlock (620).

DODO (Mr. S. Savile), b m ; black points, few white hairs on forehead, saddle marks (31).

DOE (Mr. C. Wilson), wh g ; spotted pink muzzle, small snip, blemish above knee (225).

DOE, THE (Mr. J. Watson), b m ; few white hairs on forehead, black points, scar back of near hind leg, over-reach scar both fore coronets, black mark down back (236).

DOLLY (Lord R. Manners), b m ; star, blaze, snip, white off fore fetlock, white marks on withers (470).

DOMINO (Mr. F. Balfour), dun g ; four white legs, white face, brand near hind quarter ; Argentine (7).

DON PEDRO (Mr. W. Buckmaster), b g ; black points, saddle marks, girth marks both sides (79).

DOT (Mr. Ross), b m ; black points, small scar front of chest (546).

DRISSE (Mr. R. P. O'Reilly), b m ; black points, small star, white marks off flank (558).

DROMORE (Mr. Hale), b g ; star, scars on near shoulder, saddle marks ; over height (184).

DRUG (Mr. Spender Clay), b g ; off hind fetlock white, a little white near hind coronet, star, narrow blaze, snip, saddle mark (47).

DUCHESS (Lord Kensington), b m ; star, narrow blaze near fore and both hind fetlocks white (157).

DUCHESS (Dr. Colgan), b m ; very small star, white off hind fetlock, white mark top of hind quarter (530).

DUCHESS OF STRATHBLANE (Mr. R. Hudson), ch m ; star, very narrow blaze, snip, white hind legs (579).

DUN, THE (Mr. Aubrey Price), dun m ; star, black points, collar marks (487).

DUNMORE (Capt. Pedder), gr g ; white spots face and lips, white off hind coronet and heel (353).

EASTERN ART (14th Hussars), b g ; long star, narrow blaze, large snip, white near fore fetlock and near hind coronet and off hind leg (635).

ECSTASY (Mr. J. W. Murray), dk br g; small star, light brown patch on near hip, black points, collar mark near side (562).

EDINBURGH (Major Rimington), b m ; star, white near hind pastern, white ticks, scars both shoulders (612).

EDWARD (Mr. Hale), b g ; large star, white hind fetlocks, saddle marks (183).

ELIZA (Mr. Ashmore), br m ; long narrow star, scar outside near fore leg, white near fore and off hind coronets, white mark front off hind shin ; not passed (651).

EMMA (Capt. Green), b m, 4 ; small star, scar down back tendon off fore leg, black points (381).

EMMELINE (Capt. Wilson), ch m ; scar, white near hind fetlock and off hind leg (246).

ENNISCORTHY (Mr. J. Clerk), dk br m ; few white hairs outside near hind coronet, small star (66).

ERIS (Mr. C. M. Grenfell), b m, 4 ; star, black points ; this year (501).

ESPERANZA (Mr. R. McCreery), ch m ; star, spots of white all over near side, brand mark off shoulder and off hind quarter (231).

EXCHANGE (Mr. F. Hargreave), br m ; star, saddle marks, collar marks (32).

EYELASH (14th Hussars Club), b g ; star, blaze, snip, white lower lip and legs, brand near hind quarter (623).

FAIR MAID (Mr. S. L. Barry), b m ; star, very narrow blaze, white off hind fetlock (449).

FALLUCA (Col. Green-Thompson), b m, 4 ; small star and snip, white near hind fetlock ; passed for season only (319).

FASHION (Mr. G. A. Miller), b m ; star, white near hind fetlock and off hind heel (153).

FASHION (Col. Green-Thompson), dun m ; black points, mane and tail (317).

FAUGH A BALLAGH (Capt J. Hanwell), b g; white near hind leg and off hind fetlock (242).

FAWN, THE (Earl of Huntingdon), ch m ; star, white patch top of off shoulder, scar on near knee (597).

FETTLE (Mr. Lloyd), b m; star, black strip down hind quarter (595).

FIASCO (Mr. T. Conolly), b m ; black points, white spot on near side under saddle, few white hairs front of brisket (109).

FIDGET (Mr. Soper Whitburn), b m ; black points, girth marks, black stripe down back, white marks below both hocks (379).

FIDGET (Mr. Gibbs), br m ; scar front of face and off knee, black points (646).

FITZ (Major Fenwick), ch g ; star, snip, white off hind coronet (283).

FIZZER II. (Mr. C. Adamthwaite), b g ; star, blaze, snip, white fore fetlocks and off hind pastern (673).

FLASH (Messrs. de Escandon), b m ; black points, white mark off hind shin and inside off fore leg (494).

FLASHLIGHT (Lord Kensington), br g ; brand near hind quarter, white off fore heel (158).

FLEA, THE (Mr. Grogan), gr m ; flea-bitten, large scar near side of back (535).

FLIRT (Mr. Fairfax Lucy), br m ; few white hairs, white near hind heel (261).

FLITTER (Mr. Adams), b m ; white hind coronets (642).

FLORIO (Mr. Bailley), b m ; faint star, black points, scar off side ribs (588).

FLUTE (Mr. E. C. Holland), gr m ; black marks on forehead, white spot on lower lip, white fetlocks (325).

FLUTTER (Mr. Miller), br m ; tan muzzle, small white mark outside and above near hock, scar off side quarter (40).

FLYAWAY (Capt. W. H. Persse), ch h ; star, white near hind coronet and off hind pastern (313).

FLYER (Mr. J. B. Drage), blk br m ; star (658).

FOOLISH GIRL (Mr. P. O'Reilly), br m ; star white hind fetlocks (567).

FORMINA (Mr. Hargreaves), b m ; few white hairs under saddle both sides, small scar near ear (44).

FRANK BROWN (Mr. F. J. Balfour), skewbald g ; star, narrow blaze, snip, white under lip, four white legs, white hairs in tail (168).

FREDDY (Mr. Gouldsmith), b g ; star, narrow blaze, snip, white near hind fetlock (38).

FRIDAY (Mr. H. Blyth), ch m ; star, small scar inside off knee, white patch off shoulder ; not passed (421).

GAIETY GIRL (Mr. E. R. A. Shearman), ch m ; star, blaze, snip, white near fore fetlock and off hind leg (481).

GALWAY (Mr. H. Wilson), ch g ; very faint star and snip (268).

GEISHA (Mr. G. Heseltine), br m, 4 ; star, small white mark on upper lip, grey hairs on flank ; season only (162).

GEISHA (Earl of Airlie), br m ; faint star, white near hind coronet (306).

GENESEE (Mr. G. Bland), b m ; star, blaze, snip, white off hind fetlock (671).

GIFT, THE (Mr. J. G. Fort), gr g ; star, blaze, snip, white lower lip, scar point and top of near shoulder (485).

GILL (Mr. Knowles), br m, a ; saddle and girth marks (139).

GIMCRACK (Major Fenwick), ch m ; star, blaze, snip, white near hind pastern and off hind leg (282).

GINGER (Mr. C. Wheeler), ch g ; star, blaze, snip, white off hind pastern, brand marks near fore and hind quarter (218).

GINGER (Mr. E. C. Holland), ch g ; star, blaze, snip, white hind legs, white off fore fetlock (324).

GINGERBREAD (Mr. A. Rawlinson), ch m ; blaze, snip, white near hind coronet (148).

GIPSY (Mr. F. B. Drage), bk g ; white mark on near eye, little white above near knee (279).

GIPSY (Mr. J. Lockett), br m ; tan muzzle, black points, few grey hairs in mane (407).

GIPSY (Mr. Gill), br m ; small scar back of off thigh (648).

GIPSY (Capt. Paynter), br m ; black points, girth marks (607).

GLEN (Mr. Miller), b m ; white snip on nose, star, narrow blaze, white off fore coronet (39).

GOOD BOY (Comte de Madre), dk br g, 4 ; star, black points, saddle marks (249).

GOSSOON (Mr. A. Joyce), br g ; white spots near side of ribs, black points (582).

GRACE (Capt. B. Daly), ch m ; star, blaze, snip, white off hind fetlock (583).

GREEK GIRL (Comte de Madre), b m ; small star, white snip near hind coronet, saddle marks (19).

GREY GHOST (Mr. R. N. Smyth), gr g ; white marks front off knee, girth marks (345).

GREY LARK (Capt. F. Herbert), gr m ; very small snip, two white marks on off fore shin, small white mark off hind quarter (131).

GREY LEGS (Mr. Jameson), rn m ; faint star, white hairs in tail (587).

GREY SISTER (Mr. C. Beatty), gr m ; snip (659).

GREYLING (Mr. J. Ravenscroft), gr g ; flea-bitten, slight snip, white under lip (56).

GREYSTROKE (Mr. F. Hargreaves), gr h ; scar both sides of withers, collar marks (57).

GUN SHOT (Mr. P. W. Connolly), blk br m, ∠ ; star, black points, white mark near side of neck ; passed for the season (511).

GWEN (Mr. E. A. Herbert), br m, 4 : large star, snip, white near fore fetlock and near hind leg (334).

HALMA (Capt. Heygates), b m ; star, narrow blaze, snip, black points, saddle marks (207).

HAPPY BOY (Capt. Loftus), gr g ; star, narrow blaze, white hind legs, scar outside near knee (552).

HARD TO FIND (Comte de Madre), ch m ; blaze, white near hind fetlock, saddle mark (20).

HARMONY (Capt. L. B. Johnson), b m ; very small star, black points, white specks on both hind quarters, saddle marks (87).

HARMONY (Mr. Ross), ch m ; star, narrow blaze, snip, off hind pastern white, girth marks (547).

HAROUN (Mr. E. A. Herbert), b h ; two white spots off hind quarter, white marks fore shin (335).

HARRISTOWN (Mr. J. W. Archdale), br g ; star, white near hind fetlock (542).

HARROW (Mr. P. J. Bailey), br m ; very small star, white near hind pastern, white mark both knees, mark hind shin (473).

HASSAN (Mr. J. L. Lawlor), b g ; star, white near fore pastern and near hind coronet (320).

HECTOR (Capt. W. F. Collins), b g ; star, blaze, snip, brand near hind quarter, saddle marks both sides (111).

HEREFORD (Capt. H. McMicking), b m ; star, black points (347).

HESTER (Mr. J. W. Archdale), ch m ; star, black patch off hip (541).

HONEYMOON (Capt. B. Hartopp), ch m ; scar, blaze, snip, saddle marks (50).

HONEY O (Mr. P. W. Connolly), b m, 4 ; star, near hind coronet white ; this season only (510).

HOUNSLOW (Mr. T. W. Conolly), b g ; star, few white hairs on face, white upper lip, grey hairs in tail, white near hind pastern (211).

IMPULSE (Capt. W. Kirk), ch m ; star and snip, white hind fetlock and near fore coronet, white patch near hind quarter (295).

INDIAN (Mr. C. Wheeler), ro g ; scar near side of neck, brand on off side neck and off fore quarter (219).

INNISKILLING (Major Richardson), b g ; star, blaze, snip, white hind fetlocks, collar marks (640).

IRISH GIRL (Mr. A. C. Hamilton), b m ; black points, scar inside off thigh, white mark front of off hock, white mark above near knee (514).

ISABEL (Mr. G. A. Lockett), ch m ; star on forehead, white off hind coronet with chesnut spots on it, saddle and girth marks (81).

ITALIAN (Mr. Soper Whitburn), br m ; star, white inside near hind coronet (417).

JACK (Mr. Knowles), ch h ; blaze, snip, white near hind pastern and near fore pastern, off fore pastern partly white, saddle marks (123).

JACKO (Mr. Shearman), b g ; star, blaze, snip, black points, girth marks (451).

JACK SHEPPARD (Mr. Neil Haig), ch g ; star, blaze, snip, white lower lip and legs, black patch off cheek, large brand near hind quarter, girth marks (617).

JACKY (14th Hussars Club), b g ; star, narrow blaze, snip, white near hind fetlock, white mark off hind shin (637).

JAMRACK (Mr. J. M. Walker), b g ; star, blaze, snip, white near hind fetlock, brand near hind quarter (416).

JELOOLY (Mr. Archdale), b m ; small star, black points, scar over near eye (540).

JENNY (Mr. N. Curzon), br m ; black points, few grey hairs on croup (370).

JERRY (Hon. T. Brand), ch m (383).

JESS (Capt. C. D. Bruce), ch m ; star, white hind fetlocks, spots all over body (173).

JEWESS (Lord W. Bentinck), b m ; star, snip, white lower lip, off hind leg white, mark on poll (382).

JIM JAM (Mr. C. Wilson), iron gr m ; white spot each side of neck (254).

JINNY (Mr. Stapleton), b m ; saddle and girth marks, small white patch near side of ribs (186).

JOE (Mr. W. R. Bindloss), b g ; black points (299).

JOE (Mr. G. K. Ansell), ch g ; very narrow star, blaze, snip, white near hind leg, brand near hind quarter (343).

JOEY (Mr. T. M. S. Pitt), b h ; star, snip, white near hind fetlocks, large scar top of both shoulders (316).

JOHNNY LONGTAIL (Capt. Miller), blk g ; large star, white hind fetlocks, brand near hind quarter, scar near shoulder (170).

JORROCKS (Mr. D. G. Irvine), b g ; black points, small star, scar off knee and off side of brisket, girth marks (409).

JORROCKS (Mr. E. S. Jackson), gr g ; brand off hind quarter, large scar off shoulder (328).

JORROCKS (Mr. Gill), ch g ; very faint star, white off hind fetlock, white hairs on off fore shin (650).

JOSEPH (Mr. A. M. Knowles), skewbald g ; off eye white, brand near hind quarter, small black spot off hind coronet (215).

JOSEPH (Mr. L. Flanagan), br g ; collar and saddle marks (614).

JOSEPHINE (Mr. J. Lockett), br m ; black points, scar both sides of brisket, collar marks (405).

JUANITA (Mrs. C. Wheeler), b m ; black points, small white spot off side of neck (220).

JUBILEE (Capt. B. Johnson), br m ; star, near hind coronet white, white marks inside front of off fore coronet, saddle marks (86).

JUBILEE (Mr. J. M. Walker), br m ; white near hind pastern and off hind fetlock (413).

JUNO (Mr. L. C. Wynne), b m ; small star, white off hind fetlock (516).

KARDIR (Mr. Maurice), wh g ; snip on lower lip, scars near and off side of neck and back (189).

KATE (Mr. F. A. B. Fryer), br m ; faint star, black points, white spots above both knees (327).

KATE (Dr. Colgan), ch m ; small snip, white hairs off side of neck (533).

KATE (Major Williams), br m ; black points, small white mark off wither, white marks front of near hind shin and back of near heel (585).

KATHLEEN (Colonel Parks), b m ; star, black points, saddle marks, little white on upper lip (196).

KATHLEEN (Capt. C. D. Bruce), br m ; tan muzzle, small star, saddle marks (132).

KATHLEEN (Mr. L. C. Winn), b m ; white hind fetlocks, white patch on wither (515).

KID, THE (Mr. E. A. Wigan), b h ; star, white near hind coronet, white spots over back, scar on near hind quarter (496).

KILALA (Mr. F. C. Pilkington), br m ; long star, white marks over off hock, saddle marks (126).

KILMOON (Mr. T. Conolly), br m ; white hind pasterns, star, saddle marks (108).

KISMET (Capt. J. Hanwell), gr g ; narrow blaze, snip, white lower lip, scar near hind quarter (241).

KITCAT (J. M. Walker), blk br m ; star, black points, grey hairs over body and tail (414).

KITTEN (Mr. F. Balfour), ch m, 4 ; star, blaze, snip, white near hind leg ; passed for season only (432).

KITTY (Mr. H. Bentley), b m ; star, snip, white mark outside near fore arm, white spot near hind quarter (64).

KITTY (Mr. Greenwood), br m, 4 ; little white on off hind heel and inside both fore heels, star, small snip ; passed for season only (65).

KITTY (Mr. H. Spender Clay), b m ; small star, three white fetlocks, near fore coronet white (135).

KITTY (Mr. Aldridge), b m ; small white spot on back rib off side, faint black mark down back (180).

KITTY (Mr. Goff), br m ; star, narrow blaze, white near hind fetlock, large saddle marks off side ; not passed (204).

KITTY (Mr. J. H. Locke), b m ; white off hind pastern, small star, girth marks (570).

KITTY (Mr. Flanagan), br m ; faint star, white near hind coronet and off hind fetlock, white mark front of fore shin (610).

KNIGHT, THE (Mr. J. L. Hunter), gr h ; flea-bitten marks on face and neck, blemish off side of neck (350).

KRECT CARD (Mr. Long), rn g ; large star, black points, girth marks (606).

LADY ALYS (Mr. F. B. Drage), br m ; faint star, white inside off hind pastern (293).

LADY CLARE (Mr. A. Gold), b m ; star, white near ore and near hind fetlock, and grey off hind fetlock ; not passed (420).

LADY DUNKIRK (Mr. A. Rawlinson), b or br m ; black points, black line along back (151).

LADY FLORENCE (Mr. P. P. O'Reilly), b m ; small star, snip, black points, white marks on legs (564).

LADY FREDERICK (Mr. R. P. O'Reilly), ch m, 4 ; star, blaze, snip, white lower lip and hind fetlocks ; this season (577).

LADY GRAY (Mr. F. B. Drage), gr m ; white off hind fetlock, scar on off knee (294).

LADY HAUGHTY (Mr. E. W. Edmondson), b m ; small star, black points, spot near fore leg (404).

LADY PERCY (Mr. J. H. Locke), b m ; star, blaze, snip, white off hind fetlock, and white mark front of near hind shin (565).

LADY VIC (Brig.-Surg. Wooley), b m ; black points, star, narrow blaze, girth marks ; not passed (555).

LANCER (Major Richardson), gr h ; several small scars both hind quarters, white mark off fore leg (639).

LASSIE (Mr. R. L. Mullens), b m ; star, blaze, snip, brand near shoulder, white fetlocks (302).

LAVENDER (Mr. Goff), gr h ; large snip, white chin, white near hind leg and off hind pastern ; over height (206).

LI (Mr. H. R. Fairfax-Lucy), ch or br g ; very small star (260).

LIGHTFOOT (Hon. D. Marjoribanks), rn g ; small star, brand on near shoulder (171).

LILY (Mr. J. Scott-Robson), b m ; star, black points, saddle marks (425).

LITTLE RAKE (Mr. A. T. Neilson), b m ; black points, scar inside off hock, white marks front of near fore and off hind shin (390).

LITTLE WONDER (Mr. H. C. Higgins), b g ; star, white hind legs with black spots, white near fore fetlock (331).

LONDON (Mr. R. H. Collis), gr h ; blemish near side loin, white mark point of near hock (450).

LONG SHOT (Mr. P. W. Conolly), drk br g ; very small star, black points (512).

LOO (Mr. E. C. Judkins), b m, 4 ; star, snip, white mark near hind fetlock, collar mark off side (435).   Passed for this season only.

LOVE TOKEN (Mr. Symons), b m ; long narrow star, snip, white hind and off fore fetlocks (592).

LUCIFER (Mr. Symons), b g ; star, white near hind fetlock and off hind pastern, white fore heels, girth marks (591).

LUCY GLITTERS (Capt. Sykes), b m ; white near hind fetlock ; white mark front near hind shin and below off hock (314).

LULLINGTON (Earl of Harrington), ch m ; scar outside near knee, saddle marks (93).

LU LU (Mr. H. C. Bentley). white h, Arab ; not passed (654).

MADEMOISELLE (Mr. C. A. L'Estrange), gr m ; small snip, white mark inside both knees, girth marks (519).

MADEMOISELLE NITOUCHE (Mr. T. H. Jackson), br m ; white near hind fetlock, collar mark (476).

MADGE (Mr. M. H. Tristram), blk m ; star, white near fore fetlock and near hind coronet (478).

MAGGIE MURPHY (Mr. G. K. Ansell), b m ; small star, white hind fetlocks (342).

MAGIC (Capt. Maxwell), dun m, 4 ; star, narrow blaze, small snips white hind legs, white tail (137).

MAGPIE (Mr. F. C. Muriel), gr m ; white marks front of both hind shins and below both knees ; not passed (355).

MAHARAJAH (Mr. E. H. Wigan), gr h ; small snip, white mark off fore leg (497).

MAID OF KENT (Capt. Schofield), b m ; star, small blaze, black points, blemish outside near shoulder, girth marks (278).

MAJOR (Mr. F. A. Belleville), rn g ; star, snip, white hairs in tail (145).

MAKE HASTE (Capt. Renton), b h ; small star, white marks on wither, small white spot off side neck (94).

MANDARIN (Mr. F. Balfour), b m ; brand near hind quarter, white spot off flank, saddle marks (8).

MANGO (Mr. J. Lockett), br h ; very small star, white mark off side of ribs, scar front of off elbow (406).

MANIFESTO (Capt. R. M. Sanders), b h, 4 ; star, narrow blaze, snip, white near hind coronet and off hind leg, and white fore leg (442)

MANITA (Royal Horse Guards Club), b m ; star white spots, scar point of near shoulder and near side of face, G. L. near side of neck, A. L. P. near shoulder, scar outside near arm, Z. I. R. near quarter, scar in front of near hock (285).

MANOR FLEECE (Mr. Learmouth), ch m ; two small snips, chin white, white hind legs, white marks off fore leg, saddle marks (199).

MARIA (Mr. H. C. T. Rice), blk br m ; small saddle marks (668).

MARTIN (Mr. F. C. Muriel), br g ; near hind coronet and heel white, small star and saddle marks ; not passed (356).

MARVEL (Mr. H. C. Cogswell), br g ; star, black points, white mark inside both knees (433).

MATADOR (Lord Villiers), gr g ; blaze and snip, white under lip, white hind fetlocks (210).

MATCHLESS (Mr. W. H. Lambton), b g ; star, white near fore coronet and hind fetlock, white hairs in tail (221).

MAVOURNEEN (Earl of Huntingdon), gr m ; white muzzle, white marks round eyes, collar marks (594).

MAY BE (14th Hussars), ro m ; star, blaze snip, white near hind leg and off hind fetlock, girth marks (618).

MAY BOY (Mr. F. J. Siltzer), b g ; black stripe on spine, white off hind pastern (72).

MAY FLY (Mr. C. A. D'Estrange), br m ; black points, scar point of off hock, girth marks (520).

MAY FLY (Capt. Loder), b m ; small star, white hind fetlocks, white hairs in tail (375).

MEDDLESOME (Capt. Jenner), b m ; black points, star, off hind white, saddle marks (22).

MEDIA LUNA (Mr. J. Ravenscroft), d g ; black stripe, white socks, off hind pastern white, star, narrow blaze, brand near hind quarter (61).

MELODY (Mr. H. Fielden), b m ; star, narrow blaze, black points, flecked with grey (360).

MERMAID (Capt. F. Herbert), br m ; near hind coronet white, scar inside off hind fetlock, saddle marks (129).

MERMAID (Mr. F. C. Muriel) ; not passed (354)

MERMAID II. (Messrs. E. D. and G. A. Miller), or m ; star, white off hind fetlock (656).

MERMAID III. (Mr. C. Adamthwaite), br m ; white hind fetlocks (672).

MERRY LEGS (Mr. S. M. Dennis), b m ; small star, narrow blaze, snip, white off hind fetlock (394).

MERRY THOUGHT (Mr. F. J. Balfour), b g ; black points, brand near hind quarter (664).

MICHAEL (Mr. T. A. Clarke), gr g ; large star, white near hind fetlock, white marks near flank (384).

MICK (Mr. C. O'Hara), b g ; star, white hind fetlocks, white spot off hind quarter (526).

MICKY FREE (Mr. R. T. Cunningham), dk gr g ; saddle marks (397).

MIDGE (Mr. A. SEYMOUR), dun m ; star, stripe down back, white near fore heel (136).

MIDNIGHT (Capt. W. Kirk), blk m ; white near hind fetlock, scar on near shoulder (297).

MIDNIGHT (Mr. Lloyd), blk m ; scar inside off fore heel, collar mark (596).

MIKE (Mr. Talbot Rice), br g ; off fore and near hind coronets white, white marks on off hind coronet, saddle marks, small star and snip, brand near hind quarter (53).

MILKMAID (Mr. Peel) gr m ; white off hind fetlock, collar scars (202).

MINNIE (Capt. Askwith), br m ; star, narrow blaze, snip, white off hind fetlock, white ticks (475).

MINOR (Mr. Rourke), b m ; black points, very faint saddle marks (550).

MISS BANTAM (Mr. R. Hudson), br m ; white patch lower lip. white marks, both shoulders, white mark off side flank (581).

MISS BARRY (Major Alexander), b m ; scar back of both hocks, white near fore heel, girth marks (529).

MISS FINCH (Mr. A. T. Neilson), b m ; small star, black points, white spots on off fore leg (395).

MISS MAC (Mr. T. M. S. Pitt), ch m ; star, blaze, snip, white fore legs (315).

MISS MACKEY (Mr. C. Beatty), b m ; star, snip, scar off hip, white near fore pastern and near hind fetlock (670).

MIST (Capt. Nolan), gr m ; flea bitten marks on head, scar off side wither, saddle marks (192).

MOMUS (Mr. Russell), gr m ; white snip, little white lower lip, white off hind leg (176).

MONA (Mr. Russell), b m ; white marks front of all four shins, saddle marks (178).

MONK, THE (Mr. Gouldsmith), b m ; white face, two white hind fetlocks, saddle marks (37).

MONTANA BELLE (Mr. T. B. Drybrough), b m ; brand near hind quarter, brand near shoulder, very small star, white spot off shoulder (100).

MOONLIGHT (Capt. A. R. Mosley), gr h ; large blemish both sides of withers (323).

MOONLIGHT (Mr. Anderson), b m ; star, blaze, snip, both flanks ticked white (538).

MOONRAKER (Capt E. W. Clowes), b g ; white hind legs and off fore leg, stockings, brand near hind quarter, star, snip, saddle marks (112).

MOSES (Capt. Kennedy), ch g ; star, blaze, snip, white off fore fetlock, white off fore pastern, white spots near hind quarter, brand top of both shoulders ; not passed.

MOSQUITO (14th Hussars), blk m ; white hind coronets, white marks on fore legs, scars inside both arms (629).

MR. BROWN (Mr. J. D. Gouldsmith) br g ; black points, scar near hind quarter (358).

MUDIR (Major Middleton), br h ; four white legs, white blaze, snip and lower lip, branded both sides of neck (96).

MUSKET (Mr. S. Reynolds), gr g ; snip, white off hind fetlock, white scar near side of neck (388).

MY GIRL (Mr. P. W. Connolly), b m ; star, black points, ticked white (513).

MY LADY (Mr. J. H. Locke), b m ; black points, white near side of ribs (569).

MYSTERY (Mr. A. T. Neilson), b g ; star, blaze, snip, white off hind pastern (389).

MYSTERY (Mr. W. Buckmaster), b m ; star, white spots on back, very short dock (78).

N (Comte de Madre), b m ; white spot off fore heel, black points, star, white saddle marks near side (18).

NAAMAN (Capt. Schofield), b h ; star, narrow blaze, snip, white near hind leg, white mark near fore pastern and off leg (237).

NAMELESS (Capt. C. H. Paynter), dun m ; white hind fetlocks (330).

NAMELESS (Sir W. R. Nugent), gr g ; white mark front of near fore and near hind shins, large white mark near side of back (572).

NANCY (Mr. Russell), b m ; saddle marks, small spot upper lip, docked (177).

NANCY (Capt. Green), b m ; black points, scar front off hind shin (373).

NANCY (Mr. H. J. Smith), b m ; black points, collar mark (467).

NAPPER (Mr. T. Conolly), ch m ; white near hind fetlock, star, saddle marks, inside off hind pastern white, off ear split (107).

NARRAMORE (Mr. Gill), br m ; small star front of off stifle, saddle marks (649).

NELLA II. (Mr. R. Hudson), ch m ; star, blaze, snip, white mark near side of ribs, saddle mark (578).

NELLIE GRAY (Capt. Ellison), gr m ; star, both fore coronets white, saddle mark (455).

NEPENTHE (Capt. R. M. Sanders), dk br h ; very small star, both hind pasterns white, scar inside both fore arms, saddle marks (443).

NEWBRIDGE (Lord W. Bentinck), b g ; star, white near hind fetlock and hind coronets, white scar on both knees ; not passed (480).

NICOTINE (Mr. F. Balfour), blk g ; white near fore brand near hind quarter, brown muzzle ; Argentine (3).

NIGGER (Mr. Mackie), br g ; few white hairs in forehead, both, hind fetlocks and near fore coronet and heel white, brand on off shoulder and both hind quarters (165).

NIGHTLIGHT (Capt. Jenner), blk g ; both hind fetlocks white, brand near hind quarter, large blaze (23).

NIGHTMARE (Hon. R. Ward), rn g ; four white legs, white face, brand near hind quarter (288).

NIMBLE (Mr. Jameson), ch m ; star, faint blaze, black spots over body, girth marks (586).

NINA (Capt. Egerton Green), b m ; star, very narrow blaze, snip, near hind fetlock white, off hind coronet white, saddle marks (374).

NORAH (Mr. Goff), blk m ; small star, white spot front of off shoulder, white marks off flank, white marks front of both stifles (205).

NORAH (Capt. Ferrars), ch m ; star, white off hind fetlock, white mark near shoulder, saddle marks, white spot near eye (208).

NORVAL (Mr. H. C. Cogswell), br g ; star, black points, white near hind leg ; passed for the season (433).

NUGGET (Mr. J. Scott-Robson), ch g ; very small star, blaze, white spot near nostril, white near hind coronet, brand near hind quarter, white near side of face and off hind fetlock (426).

OAK APPLE (Mr. C. M. Grenfell), br m ; star, scar near hind pastern, black points (502).

OLD NICK (Mr. Anderson), b g ; star, scar off side neck (536).

OPAL (Mr. Shearman), blk m ; star, blaze, snip, near hind pastern and off hind fetlock white, saddle mark (452).

OSMAN (Capt. F. Herbert), b h ; small star, near hind fetlock white, saddle mark (172).

OSWALD (Mr. F. H. Wise), b g, 4 ; very faint star, white hind fetlocks ; passed for season (603).

OTTO (Mr. Peel), b g ; star, little white on lower lip, off hind coronet white, little white on near hind and both fore heels, brand off hind quarter, white hairs all over body (203).

PACHA (Mr. F. Hargreaves), light gr h ; branded inside both arms and both thighs (58).

PADDY (Mr. Gill), blk br g ; white near hind fetlock (652).

PADISHA (Dr. A. Findlater), b g ; star, white hind fetlocks, saddle marks (437).

PANCHO (Mr. J. Ravenscroft), dun g ; faint stripe on back, branded near hind quarter, star, very small snip (62).

PASTIME (Mr. C. Wilson), ch g ; white hind legs and stockings and near fore stocking, off fore coronet white, blaze, snip (257).

PEDRO (Mr. W. D. P. Watson), gr h ; fleabitten face and neck, scar off side back, all feet partly white (105).

PERFECT CURE (Mr. Nickalls), skewbald g ; spotted, star, white hind fetlocks (666).

PETACAS (Mr. J. Ravenscroft), b g ; near hind pastern white, brand near hind quarter D, under lip white (60).

PETER PIPER (Marquis of Tullibardine), blk m ; little white on hind heels, saddle marks (286).

PETTICOATS (Mr. F. Balfour), b m ; blaze, narrow white stripe down face, brand near hind quarter, coronet and inside near fore foot white, saddle marks ; Argentine (6).

PHILLIPA (Capt. W. Kirk), dk br or blk m ; near hind coronet white, white mark below off hock, saddle marks (296).

PINTAIL (Mr. J. Drage), br m : near hind pastern and foot white, very faint star, small saddle marks (15).

PLAY BOY (Major H. T. Fenwick), ch g ; near hind stocking white, blaze, star, snip, lower lip white, near hind leg white, saddle marks (280).

PLAY BOY (Mr. J. R. M. Malone), b g ; star, white hind fetlocks (576).

PLAYFUL (Messrs. Miller), blk br m, 4 ; black points, few white hairs on wither, small saddle marks (659).

POKER (Mr. H. H. Wilson), br m ; small white mark on near shoulder, saddle marks, black points (269).

POLLY (Mr. Talbot Rice), ch m ; white hind stockings, star, blaze, snip, saddle marks (52).

POLLY (Mr. Collis), ch m ; star, narrow black snip, brand 8 near hind quarter (465).

POOKA (Earl of Huntingdon), gr m : white marks near fore leg, small scar outside near fore pastern (593).

PORTFIRE (Mr. E. A. Wigan), br g ; faint star, white mark near hind pastern and off hind and fore legs, near fore fetlock grey (498).

POTEEN (Mr. L. Vandeleur), ch m, 4 (247).

PRATTLE (Major H. T. Fenwick), b m ; star, saddle and girth marks (281).

PRIEST (Mr. Sheppard), gr g ; branded near hind quarter (84).

PRIESTESS (Capt. W. Neilson), b m ; black points, collar and saddle marks (445).

PRIMROSE (Sir H. de Trafford), b m ; white off hind pastern, very small star, small white mark on off side neck, saddle marks (128).

PRIMROSE (Mr. R. T. Cunningham), blk g ; star, narrow blaze, near hind leg white, saddle marks, grey forehead (390).

PRINCE (Mr. Carbutt), gr g ; blaze, snip, white lower lip, branded near hind quarter (187).

PRINCE CHARLES (Mr. G. A. Lockett), ch g star, blaze, snip, both fore and near hind legs and off hind fetlock white, saddle and girth marks (422).

PROFESSOR (Queen's Bays Club), b g ; black points, small scar near side of neck and near side of ribs, saddle marks (309).

27

PRU (Capt. Mackenzie), gr g ; blaze, snip, scar near shoulder (48).

PSALM (Capt. Bernard Daly), ch m ; grey hairs on body, faint star (584).

PUBLICAN (14th Hussars), ch g ; star, blaze, snip, white lower lip and near fore coronet, and near hind leg and off hind fetlock (622).

QUICK SHOT (Capt. Bidgood), b m ; black points, star, white hairs in mane (506).

QUICKSILVER (Mr. G. Hardy), gr m ; saddle marks, few white hairs off fore heel (29).

QUICKSTEP (Mr. Bailey), b m ; black points, white marks and scar on both knees, saddle marks (474).

RABBIT (Sir W. R. Nugent), ch rn ; star, blaze, snip, white near hind leg and off fore coronet ; season (573).

RACHAEL (Capt. Neilson), br m ; small star, black points, small saddle mark off side (444).

RAGS (Mr. Neil Haig), ch m ; star, narrow blaze, snip, white near hind leg, black patch both hind quarters ; not passed (372).

RAINBOW (Mr. J. Watson), b g ; star, black points, faint black strip down spine, blemish on near knee (266).

RANEE (Mr. S. M. Dennis), rn m ; star, off fore and off hind fetlocks white (299).

RASPER (Miller Bros.), bright b g ; near hind foot and coronet white, white saddle marks (5).

RATAPLAN (Mr. R. W. Hudson), ch g ; star, blaze, snip, white lower lip and hind legs and off fore coronet, saddle marks (364).

RATTLER (Mr. J. Fitzgerald), br m ; white near hind fetlock, scar outside off hock (522).

REBECCA (Dr. Colgan), b m ; white mark inside off knee (531).

RED HEART (Mr. Aldridge), ch m ; star, blaze, snip, little white hind coronets, saddle marks, black patch off shoulder (179).

RED PRINCE (Mr. S. Savile), ch g, Arab ; white off fore coronet, long star, snip, white marks above near hock (30).

RED START (14th Hussars), ch m ; star, narrow blaze, large white patch off hind quarter (636).

REGAL (Mr. Winterbotham), b m ; star, blaze, snip, white lower lip and inside near hind fetlock, white marks on both fore coronets, saddle marks (371).

REGINA (Mr. L. C. D. Jenner), b m ; blaze, snip, black points, mark on withers (258).

RESTLESS (Mr. G. A. Miller), very dk br m ; star, tan muzzle (4).

REX (Mr. R. W. Hudson), b br h ; star, white spot on lower lip, white hind and off fore fetlocks, collar marks (365).

REX (Major B. G. Lewis), b g ; faint star, white mark back of legs, girth marks (560).

REY (Mr. Aubrey Price), b m ; star, inside near hind coronet white (488).

ROB ROY (Mr. A. Suart), b g ; black points, saddle marks (491).

ROCFIELD (Capt. Wing), ch g ; star, blaze, snip, white hind legs, saddle marks (182).

ROCKET (Mr. J. Harris), b g ; star, blaze, snip, white hind fetlocks (321).

ROEBUCK (Mr. G. Heseltine), rn g ; small star, saddle marks, white hairs in tail (431).

ROEDEER (Earl of Airlie), b m ; faint star, snip, white hind fetlocks, and near fore fetlock (308).

RONALD (Mr. G. A. Lockett), b g ; faint star, snip, white near hind heel, saddle marks (83).

ROSA BONHEUR (Mr. E. F. Dease), b m ; black points, small scar off hip ; not passed (575).

ROSAMOND (14th Hussars), b m ; star, white near hind fetlock (630).

ROULETTE (Dr. A. Findlater), b or ch m ; star, blaze, snip, white hind pasterns and fore legs, girth marks (436).

ROULETTE (14th Hussars), b m ; very faint star, black points (625).

ROULETTE (Mr. E. S. Jackson), ch m ; star, blaze, small white spots lower lip, near hind fetlock white, saddle marks (328A).

RUBICON (14th Hussars), blk g; white fore pasterns, white hind fetlocks, white brand near hind quarter (634).

RUBRICK (14th Hussars), ch g ; star, narrow blaze, snip, white lower lip and near fore fetlock and hind legs, brand off hind quarter (632).

RUBY (Capt. Wing), b m ; star, blaze, snip, white lower lip and fore fetlocks and off hind fetlock, saddle and girth marks (181).

RUBY (Mr. F. Pilkington), ch g ; star, blaze, snip, white lower lip and all four legs white, brand near hind quarter (402).

RUFUS (Mr. H. P. Dangan), ch g ; white near fore coronet, white spots on wither, girth marks (599).

RUFUS (Col. Anderson), br g ; star, black points (605).

RUSTIC (Capt. Richards), b m ; star, black points (251).

SABBATH (Mr. Rourke), br g ; star, blaze, snip, white lower lip and near hind pastern, white marks above both knees (548).

27*

SAGE HEN (Mr. T. B. Drybrough), gr m ; branded, near shoulder, near hind foot white, off hind foot partly white (98).

SAID KHAN (Mr. R. A. D. Fleming), br h ; black points, white spots all over fore legs, scar both flanks, near ear clipped (430).

SAILOR (Mr. E. A. Wigan), gr g ; faint snip, white lower lip, brand off hind quarter (495).

ST. CLAUS (Dr. Watson), gr h ; blaze, snip, near fore and hind legs white (223).

SAMBO (Mr. S. M. Dennis), br g ; star, blaze, snip, scar both sides of neck and near side of back, white spots on all legs, saddle marks (400).

SAMBO (Mr. P. W. Nickalls), b g ; white hind fetlocks double brand near hind quarter, small star, very narrow blaze, white saddle marks ; Argentine (1).

SANDOW (Miller, Bros.), b g ; all four legs white up to fetlocks, brand near hind quarter, star, saddle marks ; Argentine (11).

SAN FELIPE (Mr. W. McCreery), gr g ; very small snip, little white on lower lip, scar under off eye, off side back and front of near fore arm (226).

SANTANA (Mr. W. McCreery), b m ; black points, white spot near side of neck, inside off fore arm, and back of off hind quarter, saddle marks (229).

SANTA ROMONA (Mr. W. McCreery), dun m ; star, hind fetlocks white, black mark down back, saddle marks (227).

SANTIAGO (Mr. F. Swetenham), gr g ; brand on hind quarters, white legs, snip, lower lip white (262).

SAPPERTON (Mr. H. T. Timson), ch m ; star, blaze, snip, hind fetlocks white, saddle and girth marks (367).

SAVAGE (Earl of Harrington) dun g ; star, blaze, snip, brand near hind quarter, saddle marks (274).

SCANDAL (Mr. Grogan), gr m ; white near hind leg, white marks off shoulder and off side neck (528).

SCRUMPTIOUS (14th Hussars), b m ; star, snip, two white spots front off hind coronet (645).

SEABREEZE (Mr. T. B. Drybrough), ch m ; star, blaze, brands 736 on near hind quarter and X on near forequarter, grey hairs in tail and body, scar front of near hock (101).

SEAGULL (Capt. F. H. Milsom), gr g ; off hind feet and off fore heel white, snip near nostril, saddle marks (27).

SEA PEARL (Mr. D. G. Irvine), ch m ; star, blaze, snip, white near fore and both off legs and near hind fetlock, collar and saddle marks (408).

SEA PIE (Mr. P. O'Reilly), b m ; black points, star, scar off hind quarter, saddle marks (565).

SEARCHLIGHT (Messrs. Miller), piebald g ; star, blaze, snip, white lower lip, both hind legs and near fore leg and off hind fetlock (660).

SECOND-HAND (Brig.-Surg. Dooley), b m; black points, few white hairs on shoulders, scar off side of ribs, saddle marks; not passed (556).

SECRET (Mr. F. Siltzer), b m; black points, scar off fore shin (429).

SELIM (Mr. W. Lee-Pilkington), ch g; star, narrow blaze, small snip, white fetlocks, saddle marks (392).

SELINA (Col. Campbell), b m; black points, white mark over off eye (518).

SENTIMENT (Mr. A. Price), b or br m, 4; black points, saddle marks; passed for the season (490).

SERPOLETTE (Mr. Maurice), br m; star, white near hind coronet and heel and off hind fetlock (188).

SHABA (Mr. A. E. Batchelor), flea-bitten gr g; small collar mark near side, saddle mark (271).

SHARZADA (Mr. Soper Whitburn), gr h; white marks above near hock, white near hind fetlock and off fore fetlock, saddle marks (377).

SHEIK (Mr. A. E. Batchelor), b g; star, saddle marks, small blemish off side neck (272).

SHELLBACK (Mr. J. Ravenscroft), dun g; small star and snip, near hind pastern white, brand near hind quarter (63).

SHELL DUCK (Mr. R. O'Reilly), b m, 4; star, snip, white mark on croup, ticked with white hairs; passed for the season (559).

SHERLOCK (14th Hussars), gr g; white hind fetlocks (619).

SHOOTING STAR (Earl of Shrewsbury), br m; white near hind heel, white splash off hind heel, star, saddle marks (2).

SHOP GIRL (Mr. R. L. Mullens), b m; star, white hind fetlocks and near fore heel, saddle marks (301).

SHOT SILK (Capt. Bidgood), br m; star, white hind fetlocks, white hairs in tail, ticked white (505).

SHUCKBORO (Mr. J. Drage), b g; saddle marks, few white hairs top of wither (67).

SILVERTAIL (Mr. Tresham Gilbey), b m; star, blaze, snip, white hind fetlocks, silver tail and hairs, saddle marks (106).

SILVER TALLY (Mr. Rourke), gr m; small scar off side forehead; this season only (551).

SINCERITY (Mr. A. M. Knowles), b h; long snip, off hind fetlock white, saddle marks, scar over off eye (248).

SINGEWICK (Capt. H. McMicking), gr m; star, white near hind pastern (348).

SIRMON (Major Galbraith), ch m; white near fore pastern and near hind fetlock, scar off hip, girth marks (615).

SISTER BESSIE (Col. Campbell), b m; star, black points, scar off hind quarter (517).

SISTER SUE (Mr. Anderson), blk m ; scar over near eye, and collar and girth marks (537).

SKIT (Capt. Hon. E. Baring), b g ; black points, two white spots off hind shin, small saddle marks (457).

SKITTLES (Mr. W. R. Bindloss), b m ; scar near hind quarter, white mark front of off hind shin, saddle mark (298).

SKITTLES (Mr. W. Walton), b g ; very small star, off hind fetlock white, small saddle mark (438).

SKYLIGHT (Mr. Learmouth), b g ; star, black points, little white upper lip, saddle marks, small scar top of withers (200).

SLAPJACK (Mr. T. B. Drybrough), br g ; snip, white hind fetlocks, brand near hind quarter (119).

SLAVE (Mr. F. Balfour),br g ; star, narrow blaze, snip, white lower lip and hind stockings, brand on near quarter, saddle marks (169).

SLAVIN (Miller Bros.), b g ; white off hind pastern and off fore fetlock and pastern, white near fore heel, white stripe on nose, brand near hind quarter (10).

SLIGO (Mr. T. Conolly), br m ; grey hairs in tail and body, star, saddle marks (110).

SLIGO (Earl of Harrington), br m ; small star, saddle marks, tan muzzle (163).

SNIP (Mr. F. B. Drage), br m ; white hind pasterns, few white hairs on near side of face (292).

SOCKS (Mr. Drage), ch m ; three white stars on chest, both hind fetlocks white, white stripe (41).

SODA (Mr. R. W. Hudson), gr h ; long snip, off fore fetlock white, scar above off hock and on near hip (363).

SOUBRETTE (Capt. Hanwell), b m ; star, blemish near knee (273).

SPECULATION (Mr. Smith), b m ; black points, grey hairs off side of back, saddle marks (468).

SPHYNX (Capt. F. Herbert), wh h ; scar on wither, small snip, little white on lower lip (174).

SPITFIRE (Mr. H. C. Higgin), b m ; white near hind coronet and off hind heel, white marks front of fore shins, saddle marks (333).

STAR (Capt. Dundas), dun g ; narrow blaze and snip, black legs, brands on near hind quarter and off hind quarter, white off hind pastern (89).

STRATHCONAN (Capt. Campbell), gr g, 4 ; large blaze and snip, white chin, four white legs (195).

STRATHRUIN (Mr. G. Heseltine), ch m ; star, narrow blaze, snip, white near hind stockings, saddle marks (243).

STRIPES (Mr. F. Bald), dun g ; very small star, brand near hind quarter, blemish down front of shoulder (265).

SULTAN (Mr. W. Lee Pilkington), gr g ; snip, near hind fetlock white, collar marks (391).

SULTAN (Mr. Carbutt), b g ; star, blaze, snip, white lower lip, white off fore coronet and heel and off hind coronet and near hind fetlock, saddle marks (185).

SUNBEAM (Mr. R. Beck), b m ; narrow blaze, snip, white hind fetlocks, saddle marks (144).

SUNBEAM (Mr. Soper Whitburn), ch m ; star, white hind fetlocks, saddle marks (378).

SUNRISE (14th Hussars), ch m ; star, blaze, snip, white lower lip, near hind pastern, off hind and off fore fetlocks, white spot near hind quarter, scar inside off hock (633).

SUNSHADE (Mr. Freakes), ch m ; white hind stockings, star, blaze, snip, saddle marks (46).

SUNSHINE (Mr. J. H. Gouldsmith), ch m ; star, narrow blaze, snip, white lower lip, fore coronets and off hind leg, saddle marks (361).

SURPRISE (Mr. A. Rawlinson), ch g ; star, narrow blaze, snip, white near hind fetlock, off hind and near fore pasterns, saddle marks, blemish near side of neck ; not passed (259).

SURVEYOR (Capt. R. N. Smyth), piebald g ; star, snip, brand on near hind quarter (346).

SUSAN (Major B. G. Lewis), b m ; star, black points, saddle marks, white marks front of near hind shin and back of off fore leg, white hairs in mane (561).

SUSAN (Mr. W. H. Lambton), br m ; black points, few white hairs for star, saddle and girth marks (222).

SUSPENSE (Capt. L. K. Jenner), ch m ; blaze, collar and saddle marks, white hind fetlocks (24)

SWALLOW (Mr. J. Fitzgerald), b m ; star, black points, white hairs down face, girth marks (521).

SWEEP (Mr. C. Adamthwaite), blk g ; star, black points, very small saddle mark (676).

SWEETWATER (Mr. T. B. Drybrough), gr g ; branded W near hind quarter, scar near flank (117).

SYREN (Mr. E. Makins), blk m ; very small star, black points, saddle marks ; not passed (428).

SYREN (Mr. W. J. Jones), blk m ; small star, small saddle marks (662).

TAFFY (Comte de Madre), iron gr g ; white spots outside near fore arm and both sides of neck, saddle marks (54).

TAME CAT (Mr. J. Fitzgerald), b m ; star, white off hind fetlock, scar off shoulder (524).

TARAL (Mr. Clarence Wilson), br g ; big star, streak, snip, both hind pasterns white, white fore heels, brand C.T. on near hind quarter (256).

TEAL (Mr. J. Drage), bl br m ; star, tan marks both sides of muzzle (14).

TEDDY (14th Hussars), br m ; black points (631).

TEETOTUM (Mr. C. O'Hara), b m ; star, very narrow blaze, white near fore fetlock and near hind leg, black patch on back, girth marks (525).

TELEGRAM (Mr. W. Buckmaster), b br m ; star, black points, white marks above knees ; not passed (419).

TEMPLAR (Mr. Miller), ch g ; white near hind coronet, off hind sock white, off fore leg white, brand near hind quarter (35).

TERRY (Mr. T. B. Drybrough), b g ; black points, brand on near hind quarter, saddle marks (73).

TESSY (Comte de Madre), b m ; star, short blaze, snip, near hind fetlock white, saddle marks (55).

THUNDERBOLT (Mr. Hunt), b g ; star, snip, white fore pasterns and near hind fetlock and off hind heel (611).

TIMEKEEPER (Mr. J. Watson), br g ; black points, few white hairs on forehead ; over height (235).

TIPCAT (Messrs. Miller), blk br m ; white near hind coronet, white hairs in tail (661).

TIP TOP (Mr. H. Lawson), br g ; small star, black points, white spot off stifle (213).

TIP TOP (Mr. Gouldsmith), b g ; few white hairs for star, little white on upper lip, black points, slight saddle mark on top (138).

TOMASSINA (Mr. J. Watson), b or br m ; very small star, white hind coronets, scar off shoulder (234).

TOMMY (Lord R. Manners), br g ; white hind coronets (471).

TOM TAYLOR (Capt. Persse), ch g ; white near hind leg and off hind fetlock, white mark near hind quarter (312).

TOP, THE (Mr. McCreery), b m ; small white spot off shoulder, small white marks on wither, black points ; passed for season only (230).

TOPS (Mr. McCreery), dk ch m ; star, white mark inside near hind fetlock, white spot off side of neck and near shoulder (228).

TREATY (Mr. J. L. Reid), br m ; very faint star, black points (461).

TRÈS SEC (Mr. A. Seymour), b g ; star, very narrow blaze, black points (277).

TRILBY (Mr. E. de Escandon), b m ; star, blaze, snip, white hind legs, girth marks (492).

TRIUMPH (Mr. J. Lyons), b g ; star, blaze, snip, white outside near hind pastern, small white spot off hind quarter.

TROUTCATCHER (14th Hussars), b g ; white marks near hind and both fore legs, girth marks (638).

TRUANT (Mr. A. Suart), b m ; star, white hind fetlocks (503).

TULIP (Mr. Chinnery), b g ; white near hind pastern, small saddle mark ; for this season (448).

TURKISH DELIGHT (Marquis of Tullibardine), dk br h ; star, very small snip, white near hind fetlock, scar point of off shoulder (287).

TWITTER (Mr. P. P. O'Reilly), b m ; white marks back of all four legs and front of fore legs (563).

UNKNOWN (Hon. W. Nugent), b g; branded $\frac{R}{R}$ near hind quarter, small snip, saddle marks (121).

UNKNOWN II. (Mr. C. D. Seymour), br m; very small star, off hind fetlock white, saddle marks (146).

VALPARAISO (Mr. Learmouth), b g ; white near hind leg and off hind fetlock, star, narrow blaze, two large brands on near hind quarter (194).

VAMPIRE (Capt. Schofield), b g; star, narrow blaze, snip, near hind fetlock white, near fore fetlock grey, saddle mark, brand near hind quarter (376).

VENTRE A TERRE (Mr. G. K. Ansell), b m ; scars front and near hind fetlocks, white mark front of off fore shin, black points (340).

VENUS (Capt. C. H. Paynter), b br m ; black points, saddle and girth marks (329).

VERVEINE (Mr. W. J. Drybrough), b m, 4 ; black points, black stripe down back, saddle mark (657).

VIXEN (Mr. Gills), b m, 4 ; black points, scar over near eye ; passed for season (647).

WAIF (Lord Kensington), ch m ; white off hind fetlock and near hind coronet, saddle mark (155).

WALLER (Mr. F. J. Mackey), gr g ; white legs, branded R near shoulder (43).

WALNUT (Capt. W. H. Persse), light br g ; black points, saddle marks (310).

WATCHSPRING (14th Hussars), b g ; star, snip, white near fore and near hind coronets, white marks fore legs (621).

WATERFALL (Mr. H. T. Timson), blk m ; star, white marks front of off fore shin, saddle marks (368).

WATSY (Capt. Paynter), b br m ; star, white off hind fetlock, scars point of off shoulder and off hip (608).

WEASEL (Mr. G. A. Miller), b g ; star, blaze, snip, white near fore and both hind fetlocks, brand on hind quarters, white spots all over (154).

WEASEL THE (Mr. W. J. Drybrough), b g ; off fore pastern white, star, saddle and girth marks (655).

WELSH MAID (Mr. R. St. G. Robinson), br m ; black points (508).

WHANGEE (Mr. W. Buckmaster), b m ; white star on forehead, saddle marks (80).

WHIST (Mr. E. C. Judkin), ch m ; star, blaze, snip, white lower lip, near hind fetlock, and off hind leg (434).

WHITE KNIGHT (Major H. T. Fenwick), gr g ; flea-bitten, brand near hind quarter, white fore fetlocks (284).

WHITE THORN (Hon. R. Ward), b m ; saddle marks, few white hairs on forehead, slight scar above off eye (289).

WHY NOT (Major Middleton), ch h ; small snip, white fore pasterns and near hind stocking, saddle marks (95).

WILD CAT (Mr. J. Fitzgerald), b m ; very small star, black points, scar back of near hock, white mark inside near knee (523).

WILD DRAKE (Mr. J. Drage), gr g ; star, near hind leg white to fetlock, white on wither ; season only (12).

WILD DUCK (Mr. J. Drage), gr m ; white near hind fetlock, saddle marks both ribs, two on off, one on near side (13).

WILLIAM (Capt. W. Neilson), br g ; black points, tan muzzle (25).

WINNIE (Mr. R. W. Hudson), ch m ; star, narrow blaze, near hind fetlock white, saddle marks (366).

WOLFCATCHER (Mr. T. B. Drybrough), ch g ; star, grey hairs, branded 6∽ near hind and near fore quarters (75).

WONDER (Comte de Madre), br m ; near white hind fetlock, star and faint blaze, tan muzzle (17).

WONDER (Capt. A. Richards), br m ; very small star, both hind fetlocks white (250).

WOOD QUEST (Mr. A. Joyce), b m ; black points, white mark off side of neck, saddle marks (553).

WOOD QUEST (Mr. R. W. Hall-Dare), b g ; white off hind fetlock (589).

YELLOW BOY (Mr. W. H. Lambton), dun g ; black points, faint black mark down back, saddle marks (224).

ZAMBRA (Hon. J. Dawnay), br h ; star, white hind fetlocks, licked with white over body (369).

ZAZEL (Mr. E. de Escandon), br m ; very faint star, black points, white spots on fore and hind legs, girth marks (493).

ZERO (Mr. J. Drage), br m ; white patches on near hind coronet, grey hairs in tail (68).

ZIGZAG (Mr. S. M. Dennis), b g ; small star, black points, saddle marks (401).

ZOEDONE (Mr. C. M. Grenfell), drk br g ; star, snip, black points, small saddle marks (500).

MEASURED PONIES UNNAMED.

Mr. G. Hardy's ch m ; star, blemish near hind tendon (28).

Capt. Mackenzie's b g ; brand near hind quarter (49).

Mr. Brinton's b g ; both fore pasterns white, brand near hind quarter, faint star, small snip ; not passed (114).

Capt. A. D. Miller's b g ; star, near hind leg white, saddle and girth marks (115).

Capt. A. D. Miller's br m ; small star, saddle marks, scar off knee (116).

Mr. J. Moore's b m ; very small star, black points, collar scars (193).

Col. Park's b m ; off hind heel and coronet white, saddle marks, faint black mark down back (197).

Capt. Harrison's gr h ; large snip, white lower lip, near fore and near hind legs and off hind coronet white ; not passed (198).

Mr. E. B. Sheppard's blk m ; star, saddle marks, blemish part of near shoulder (252).

Mr. Clarence Wilson's ch g ; two white hind stockings and near fore stocking and off fore coronet, blaze, snip (257).

Earl of Harrington's b m, 4 ; star, blaze snip, white lower lip passed for season (275).

Capt. H. Sykes' ch h ; star, large scar front of chest, white mark front of near hind shin (311). ͺ

Capt. Ferrar's gr h ; snip, white lower lip, white off hind and both fore legs (380).

Mr. Henderson's b g ; star, snip, brand near shoulder, saddle and girth marks (460). ͼ

Mr. Chinnery's ch g ; small star, hind fetlocks white (447).

Capt. Meyrick's b m ; star, blaze, white mark near hind coronet, saddle mark (456).

Mr. H. B. Cresswell's b m ; black points, off fore coronet white, white marks on wither, saddle marks (458).

Mr. H. B. Cresswell's ch g ; star, blaze, snip, near hind coronet and off hind fetlock white, brand both shoulders near stifle (459).

Capt. Byng's br m ; star, blaze, small snip, near fore and near hind fetlocks white, off hind pastern white, saddle marks (463).

Capt. Byng's b m ; star, narrow blaze, snip, both hind pasterns white, saddle marks (464).

Capt. Kennedy's b m ; small star, black points, white mark top of near shoulder, saddle and girth marks (477).

Mr. Edge's blk m ; saddle and girth marks (527).

Mr. W. A. Tilney's gr h ; star, blaze, snip, white near fore leg and hind fetlocks, little white on off fore pastern (626).

Mr. W. A. Tilney's gr h ; few white spots near side of face, scar near hip and both sides of back (627).

Mr. Adam's ch g ; faint star, white hind fetlocks, white brand near hind quarter (641).

Mr. Peel's b g, 4 ; star, white hind fetlocks ; passed for season (643).

POLO PONIES MEASURED AND REGISTERED AT HURLINGHAM, 1898.

A 1 (Mr. L. McCreery), red roan m ; star, large spots on both hind quarters. No. 742.

AARON (Capt. Ramsey), gr h ; blaze, snip, white lower lip and hind legs, black mark near off side of neck. No. 1084.

ABDUL (Mr. B. Montgomery), ch h ; star, blaze, snip, near hind leg and off hind fetlock white, ticked with white off flank, white spots on neck. No. 1245.

ABDULLA (Mr. W. F. Robinson), bay h ; off hind coronet white. No. 1085.

ABSENT FRIEND (Major K. MacLaren), dun g ; star, near hind coronet white. No. 1086.

ADELA (Messrs. E. D. & G. A. Miller), gr m ; white face, collar marks. No. 1261.

ADOHR (Capt. H. Steed), gr m ; white face, flea-bitten, collar marks. No. 1018.

AIROSA (Capt. R. Alexander, Rifle Brigade), ch m ; star, white hind fetlocks, 4 years, passed for season. No. 1087.

ALEXANDRA (Mr. W. A. Cooper), drk br m ; white marks near and off side ribs. No. 969.

AMAZON (Mr. J. W. Hornsby), ch m ; star, blaze, snip, off hind fetlock white, scar off shoulder. No. 853.

ANGEL (Messrs. E. D. & G. A. Miller), ch m ; star, snip, white near hind leg, off hind coronet and off fore fetlock. No. 1258.

ANN (Colonel de Robeck), ch m ; star, blaze, snip, near hind fetlock white, scar near fore shin. No. 995.

ARAB STAR (Miss A. Gore-Booth), ch h ; star, blaze, snip, 3 years (passed for season only). No. 1042.

ARGENTINA (Sir Thos. Fowler), b g ; branded 5 near hind quarter, white off hind coronet and heel. No. 801.

ATHOS (Mr. A. E. Batchelor), b g ; star, blaze, snip, white hind fetlocks, brand near shoulder, scar off side of neck. No. 1088.

ATTACK (Capt. Heygate), b m; star, blaze, white hind fetlocks, collar marks. No. 1089.

AVOCA (Mr. B. Montgomery), b g; star, near hind fetlock white. No. 1243.

BABBIE (Mr. Bernard Kidd), ch m; star, scar front of near hind shin. No. 862.

BACCHANTE (Mr. E. Lloyd), blk m; small star and snip, grey hairs in flank, collar marks. No. 869.

BAGNAL (Mr. F. J. Balfour), b g; off hind fetlock white, brand near hind quarter. No. 928.

BANJO (Mr. F. J. Balfour), b g; star, blaze, snip, lower lip, off hind coronet, near fore leg white, brand off hind quarter. No. 927.

BANJO (Mr. W. B. Longsdon), ch g; blaze, snip, white lower lip, near hind leg, and off fore fetlock, white spots on both fore legs. No. 1212.

BANSHEE (Mr. A. Withers), ch m; stars, black spots on hind quarters ticked with white. No. 1076.

BARMAID (Mr. R. L. Geanes), b m; star, snip, white hind and near fore fetlocks, 4 years. Passed for season. No. 1091.

BARNABY (Messrs. Withers), b g; near hind coronets, and off hind fetlock white. No. 752.

BARNIE (Mr. A. C. Master), b g; white face, lower lip, near and off hind legs and off fore fetlock, collar marks. No. 1090.

BARON, THE (Mr. O. T. Slocock), ch g; star. No. 979.

BARONESS (Mr. H. Scott-Robson), b m; faint star, near hind fetlock white, brand near hind quarter, saddle and girth marks. No. 743.

BARONESS (Mr. J. W. Hornsby), gr m; white spots near hip and off shoulder, saddle and girth marks. No. 852.

BARONET (Colonel de Robeck), br g; star, saddle marks. No. 1005.

BEAN (Mr. Balfour), ch g; star, brand near hind quarter, saddle marks. No. 893.

BECKY SHARP (Messrs. Withers), b m; star, blaze, snip, off hind leg white, scar back of off shoulder. No. 753.

BELINDA (Mr. H. C. McNeile), gr m; scar off hip, collar marks. No. 793.

BENDER (Mr. James Farmer), 5 yrs., b m; star, snip, near hind fetlock white. No. 802.

BENDIGO (Mr. W. Buckmaster), b g; brand near shoulder, scar outside near hock. No. 840.

BERYL (Capt. Loftus), br m; star, near hind fetlock white. No. 954.

BETTY MARTIN (Messrs. Withers), ch m ; star, white spot near shoulder. No. 758.

BIDDY (Major G. Bouverie), blk m ; star, white spots on both hind shins. No. 783.

BIOGRAPH (Mr. A. Rawlinson), ch g ; star, blaze, white spot upper lip and near jaw, brand off hind quarter. No. 1201.

BIRDSEYE (Mr. Balfour), skewbald g ; white face, lower lip and legs, brand near hind quarter. No. 907.

BISHMULLA (Major O'Hara), b h ; star, blaze, snip, white fetlocks, white marks above hocks and knees. No. 1235.

BLACK BASS (Capt. Bidgood, R.A.), blk g ; off hind coronet white. No. 1032.

BLACKBERRY (Messrs. E. D. and G. A. Miller), blk m ; small star. No. 1265.

BLACK BESS (Dr. Dooley), drk br m ; tan muzzle. Two years (passed for season only). No. 1044.

BLACKBIRD (Mr. R. P. O'Reilly), br m ; star, near hind fetlock white. No. 1047.

BLACKBIRD (Mr. T. G. Gibson, Jr.), blk m ; star, snip. No. 1092.

BLACK DIAMOND (Mr. W. H. Jay), blk g ; off hind coronet white. No. 781.

BLACKIE (Mr. W. F. Robinson), blk g ; white spots near fore leg. No. 1196.

BLACK JANE (Dr. T. O'Mearn), blk m ; star, blaze, snip, lower lip, near hind coronet, and off fore fetlock white. No. 947.

BLACK LEG (Messrs. E. D. and G. A. Miller), blk g ; star, blaze, both hind fetlocks and fore coronets white. No. 1266.

BLACKMAN (Capt. Egerton Green), blk g ; faint star. No. 860.

BLACKWATER (Mr. T. Cradock), b m ; star, scar near hind quarter. No. 1250.

BLACK WILLIAM (Capt. Egerton Green), blk g ; saddle and girth marks. No. 1273.

BLACK WITCH (Mr. J. Watson), blk b m ; scar off fore coronet. No. 1248.

BOOMERANG (Mr. A. Hugh Bainbridge), br m ; star, white spot off shoulder. No. 1080.

BO-PEEP (Sir Thos. Fowler), 5 yrs., drk b m ; near hind coronet white, scar near fore shin. No. 803.

BOSSEYE (Mr. J. Ravenscroft), b g ; white face, lower lip and legs, brand off hind quarter, ticked with white. No. 899.

BOULAK (Mr. T. D. Pilkington), b g ; star, blaze, snip, white spots over body. No. 866.

BRANDON (Mr. W. A. Cooper), gr g ; star, girth marks, 4 yrs.
(passed for season only). No. 970.

BRIDEGROOM (Mr. F. H. Wise, 13th Hussars), gr g ; star, near
hind fetlock white. No. 1020.

BROWN MOUSE (Mr. W. H. Jay), br m ; star, near hind fetlock
and off hind coronet white. No. 776.

BUCKLE (Messrs. E. D. & G. A. Miller), blk m ; star, snip, both
hind fetlocks white. No. 1260.

BUCKSHOT (Mr. O. Sullivan), ch g ; star, blaze, near hind fetlock
white. No. 1064.

BUEN CRIOLLO (Mr. F. E. Kinchant), ch g ; star, blaze, snip,
lower lip and near hind fetlock white, scar outside near hind pastern,
brand off hind quarter. No. 917.

BUMBLE BEE, late Vie Roack (Mr. S. I. Roack), br m ; star,
white hind fetlocks. No 952.

BUNGAY (Mr. Jules Wuidart), b m ; star, white hind fetlocks.
No. 1093.

CAHIRMEE, late Catarina (Major Rimington), br m ; star, blaze,
snip, white lower lip, off hind fetlock and near fore coronet. No. 1012.

CAPRICE (Mr. E. Lloyd), b m ; star, scar off fore fetlock, collar
marks. No. 868.

CAPT. JINKS (Mr. H. Scott-Robson), b g ; small star, hind fetlocks
and fore coronets white, brand on both quarters, saddle marks. No. 686.

CARMEN (Mr. H. Scott-Robson), b g ; star, lower lip and hind
leg white, white hairs in tail, brand near hind quarters. No. 685.

CARTE DE VISITE (Mr. G. A. Miller), drk b m ; star, blaze,
snip, white near hind fetlock. No. 1094.

CARTON (Colonel de Robeck), br m ; white spot near ribs. No.
1003.

CASE SHOT (Mr. W. S. Heather), b m ; star, near hind coronet
white. No. 1040.

CASSANDRA (Viscount Belgrave), b m ; star, white near hind leg,
scar near flank. No. 1095.

CASTANCE (Mr. Glen Williams), ch g ; star, blaze, snip, white hind
coronets, white marks on jaws, brand near hind quarter. No. 1096.

CASTOR (Mr. J. Ravenscroft), b roan g ; white face, lower lip, off
hind and both fore legs, and near hind coronet, white patches both sides,
brand near hind quarter. No. 929.

CATCH'EM (Hon. O. Hastings), ch g ; star, blaze, snip, white off
hind leg, scar off shoulder. No. 959.

CATTERICK (Mr. A. G. Dalgety), 6 yrs., gr g ; dark spot near side
of ribs, white mark near fore leg. No. 804.

CHACARERO (Mr. A. J. Stourton), gr g ; snip, lower lip white,
brand near hind quarter, scars both shoulders. No. 741.

CHANCE (Mr. H. Scott-Robson), ch g ; star, small snip, off hind coronet and near fore fetlock white, brand off quarter. No. 744.

CHAPPIE (Mr. C. Innes Taylor), dun g ; white face, lower lip, both hind and near fore legs, and off fore fetlock, brand near hind quarter. No. 786A.

CHEEPER (Mr. Balfour), blk g ; star, brand near hind quarter, saddle marks. No. 895.

CHELMSFORD (Mr. W. Braikenridge), ch g ; star, blaze, snip, white lower lip, off fore coronet and hind legs, 4 yrs. Passed for season. No. 1206.

CHINAMAN (Capt. Egerton Green), br g ; girth marks, small scar inside off thigh. No. 767.

CHOPETTE (Capt. Ramsey), ch m ; white marks both sides of ribs, white spot off hind shin. No. 1097.

CINDERELLA (Hon. F. White), b m ; star, near hind and off fore fetlock white, brand near fore quarter. No. 910.

CIRCE (Mr. A. Rawlinson), ch m ; star, white hind fetlocks, white mark near forearm. Passed on appeal. No. 1202.

CIRCUS GIRL (Mr. R. S. Clayton), br m ; star, snip, white lower lip, near fore and near hind fetlocks. No. 1098.

CLEMENTINE (Capt. Loftus Bryan), b m ; scar about point of near hock. No. 1226.

COBNUT (Major Rimington), b m ; small white spot near hind quarter, white hind coronets. No. 990.

COBWEB (Mr. W. Buckmaster), b m ; star, near fore coronet and both hind and fore fetlocks white. No. 842.

COCOA (Mr. A. Pyke), ch g ; star, blaze, off hind fetlock white. No. 1099.

COFFEE (Mr. C. Adamthwaite), dun m ; star, blaze, snip, lower lip and near hind fetlock white. No. 740.

COME-ON (Mr. L. McCreery), br m ; small star, snip, collar, girth and saddle marks. No. 739.

COMPETITOR (Messrs. E. D. & G. A. Miller), br m ; star, white spot off ribs. No. 676A.

COQUETTE (Mr. H. Scott-Robson), blk m ; white hind fetlocks, brand near quarter. No. 738.

COQUETTE (Mr. Leighton), blk m ; near hind fetlock white. No. 865.

CORDOVA (Mr. Balfour), br g ; star, brand near hind quarter, white patch off side of back. No. 894.

CORLICAN (Capt. Loftus Bryan), b m ; star, off hind fetlock white, white mark below near elbow. No. 1227.

COUNTESS (Mr. W. H. Jay), b m ; scar on face, girth and saddle marks. No. 782.

28

COUNTESS (Mr. John Nettleton), ch m ; star, blaze, snip, collar marks. No. 798.

CRESCENT (Capt. H. de B. de Lisle), br m ; star, snip. No. 1254.

CRY HELP (Mr. P. W. Connolly), ch m ; star, white mark off hind quarter, 4 years (passed for season only). No. 1031.

CRYHELP (Mr. Peel, R.H.A.), b g ; star, snip, white hind fetlocks. No. 1008.

CRYSTAL (Capt. A. Butler), blk br g ; white spots off ribs. No. 1100.

CROSS-PATCH (Mr. L. McCreery), roan m ; star, spotted muzzle, off hind fetlock and off fore coronet white, scar off fore shin, large spots both hind quarters. No. 737.

CUCKOO (Messrs. Withers), b m ; star, blaze, snip, white hind fetlocks. No. 754.

CURRAGH (Mr. C. de Robeck), b g ; star, near fore coronet white. No. 1221.

DAIRIUS (Mr. A. Suart), b g ; star, blaze, snip, near hind coronet white. No. 1068.

DAISY BELL, by Zither (Mr. W. H. Jay), b m ; scar off fore coronet, white spots off shoulder, collar marks. No. 768.

DAISY BELLE (Dr. Colgan), drk br m ; star, white marks both forelegs. No. 961.

DANCE (Mr. F. J. Mackey), red roan g ; white face and legs, brand off hind quarter and near side neck. No. 736.

DANDY (Mr. F. A. Gill), br g ; girth and saddle marks. No. 684.

DANDY (Mr. G. Heseltine), br g ; star, snip, off hind coronet white, brand near shoulder, and near hind quarter. No. 1211.

DAPSTER (Mr. James Farmer), 5 yrs., br g ; star, snip, off hind fetlock white, collar marks. No. 805.

DARKIE (Mr. A. C. Master), blk g ; star, white hind fetlocks ; 4 yrs. ; passed for the season. No. 1101.

DARRY (Mr. G. Doman), b m ; star, scars off side rib, and off shoulder. No. 1102.

DAY BOY (Capt. Brooksbank, 14th Hussars), b g ; star, off hind fetlock white. No. 1016.

DAWN (Capt. H. de B. de Lisle), ch m ; star. No. 1255.

DEAR BOY (Mr. Balfour), b g ; star, near hind leg white, brand near hind quarter, saddle marks. No. 888.

DEAREST (Capt. T. T. Macan), br m ; scars on neck, faint star, white mark off knee. No. 871.

DEAREST (Mr. P. W. Connolly), b m ; star, blaze, snip, off fore fetlock white. No. 1037.

DELIGHT (Mr. G. Doman), br m ; star, ticked with white hairs. No. 1103.

DEUCE ACE (Mr. O'Sullivan), dun m ; star, blaze, both hind and near fore fetlocks white. No. 1052.

DIAMOND (Mr. A. Rawlinson), drk br m ; tan muzzle, white mark both knees, saddle marks. No. 735.

DIANA (Mr. John Nettleton), gr m ; black spots off shoulder and ribs, white marks back of hind legs. No. 795.

DIANA (Mr. J. W. Hornsby), b m ; scar, white mark on neck. No. 858.

DICE BOX (Colonel de Robeck), b g ; star, blaze, snip, white mark inside both knees. No. 996.

DINAH (Mr. H. D. McNeile), dun m ; black stripe down back, scar near shoulder. No. 792.

DODO (Mr. Charles T. Craig), gr m ; near hind fetlock white, white mark front off hind shin. No. 806.

DOLLY VARDEN (Mr. L. McCreery), b br m ; star, faint blaze, scars outside off hind leg, near fore shin and near shoulder, saddle and girth marks. No. 734.

DON, THE (Mr. H. C. Higgin), gr h ; white spots on muzzle, black and brown spots over body. No. 1104.

DONISHALL (Messrs. E. D. & G. A. Miller), b g ; near hind coronet white. No. 1270.

DORMILON (Mr. Balfour), br g ; star, snip, off fore and hind fetlocks white, brand near hind quarter. No. 896.

DOROTHY (Mr. T. L. Moore), ch m ; star, blaze, snip, white hind fetlocks. No. 1220.

DUCHESS (Capt. Brooksbank, 14th Hussars), ch m ; star, white hind fetlocks, scar near hind shin. No. 1017.

DUN, THE (Colonel W. A. Cardwell), dun m ; scar front off hind shin, and tack off fore leg, saddle and collar marks. No. 807.

DUNDALK (Mr. Alfred Withers), gr m ; blaze, snip. No. 1105.

DUSTER (Mr. H. Scott-Robson), ch g ; face, lower lip, hind legs, and near fore coronet white, brand off quarter. No. 733.

EASTBOURNE (Mr. H. Lawson), b g ; star, white near hind coronet. No. 1106.

EILEEN (Colonel W. A. Cardwell), br or b m ; scar off fore coronet, white mark back of near fore leg, saddle marks. No. 808.

EMILY (Dr. T. O'Mearn), br m ; star, blaze, snip, both hind and near fore fetlocks white. No. 946.

EMMA (Capt. Egerton Green), b m ; star, white mark off fore leg and off side of neck. No. 764.

EMPRESS (Mr. John Nettleton), b m ; star, white marks on near hind shin, off hind leg and off flank, saddle marks. No. 797.

28*

ERIN (Mr. J. W. Hornsby), roan m ; star, near hind fetlock white, white marks outside off hocks. No. 1107.

EVA (Mr. Bernard Kidd) ; star, white mark left quarter and both shoulders. No. 861.

EVERGREEN (Mr. W. E. Grogan), gr m ; star, blaze. No. 966.

EXCHANGE (Mr. W. S. Heather), ch m ; star, blaze. No. 1041.

EXPRESS (Mr. A. Withers), b g ; white spots near hind quarter, scar both sides hock, collar marks. No. 1075.

FAIRY (Mr. F. A. Gill), b m ; star, white spot on withers. No. 683.

FAIRY BLAST (Hon. O. Hastings), ch m ; star, white spot near flank. No. 974.

FANCY (Major K. MacLaren), b m ; star, blaze, snip, off hind coronet white. No. 1108.

FARM VIXEN (Capt. E. Makins, 1st Dragoons), dun m ; star, blaze, snip, white hind fetlocks. No. 788.

FATMA (Mr. T. Cradock), gr m ; snip, white spot lower lip, near hind fetlock white. No. 1251.

FAUGH-A-BALLAGH (Mr. Rupert S. Gwynne), br or b g ; off hind fetlock, saddle marks. No. 809.

FAWN, THE (F. A. Gill), ch m ; star, blaze, snip, both hind fetlocks white. No. 1272.

FEO (Mr. C. Innes Taylor), blk g ; star, white hind fetlocks and fore legs, brand near hind quarter. No. 785.

FIDGET (Colonel W. A. Cardwell), b g ; faint blaze, snip, fore coronets white, saddle marks. No. 810.

FIDGET (Mr. Charles T. Craig), light b or dun m ; small white star, black lines down back. No. 811.

FIDGET (Capt. Carey), ch m ; star, blaze, snip, white spot on lower lip, near hind fetlock and off hind coronet white. No. 1109.

FIGET (Dr. T. O'Mearn), b m ; star, snip, white lower lip, brand off ear. No. 963.

FILE, THE (Mr. Balfour), b g ; star, snip, off hind fetlock white, brand off hind quarter. No. 890.

FIREFLY (Capt. A. Butler), ch m ; white face, lower lip and both hind and near fore legs, black patch off hock. No. 1110.

FIRST POP (Mr. F. J. Townsend), 4 yrs., b g ; near hind coronet white. Passed for the season only. No. 812.

FIZZER (Mr. W. H. Jay), blk g; off hind fetlock white. No. 775.

FLASH (Mr. W. H. Jay), b m ; near hind fetlock and off hind coronet white, scar on near flank. No. 771.

FLICKAMAROO (Marchioness of Downshire), br m ; scar off side of neck. No. 1111.

FLIRT, THE (Mr. E. Targett), b m ; star, 4 yrs. Passed on appeal for season. No. 1112.

FLIRT (Mr. H. Scott-Robson), blk m ; white hind fetlocks, scar and brand near quarter. No. 732.

FOLLOW ME (Mr. L. McCreery), 4 yrs., br m ; small star, small white spot off hind quarter. Passed for the season only. No. 731.

FOLLY (Capt. R. Peel, 2nd Life Guards), b m ; black stripe. No. 730.

FOLLY (Colonel de Robeck), b m ; white spot below off hock, off hind coronet white. No. 993.

FOX (Mr. T. F. Cooke), br g ; near hind coronet white. No. 1233.

FRECKLES (Mr. H. Way), b g ; star. No. 1208.

FREDDY (Mr. A. Robinson), b g ; white marks on both hind and near fore tendons, brand near hind quarter. No. 1200.

FRIDAY (Mr. Herbert Blyth), ch m ; star, white mark off shoulder. No. 769.

FRITZ (Mr. R. R. Baker), 5 yrs., b g ; scar both knees, small saddle marks. No. 813.

FRIVOLITY (Mr. A. Hugh Bainbridge), b m ; dark spot off ribs. No. 1081.

FUSEE (Messrs. Withers), b m ; star, blaze, snip, near hind and off fore fetlock white. No. 756.

GADFLY, late Rourke's Drift (Messrs. Millers), ch m ; star, blaze, snip, lower lip, near hind and off fore leg white. 4 years. Passed for season only. No. 944.

GAUCHO (Mr. A. J. Stourton), blk g ; star, blaze, snip, lower lip and legs white, brand near hind quarter. No. 729.

GAY BOY (Mr. F. J. Balfour), ch g ; star, blaze, snip, lower lip, both hind and off fore legs white, brand near hind quarter, white spot near ribs. No. 925.

GEISHA (Mr. Godfrey Heseltine), br m ; star, scar point of chest. No. 875.

GENERAL, THE (Mr. H. C. Talbot Rice), b g ; near hind coronet white, scar outside near fore leg. No. 1113.

GEORGIA (Mr. W. Braikenbidge), b g ; white spots on hind quarters, white spots off knee. No. 1205.

GIGOLETTE (Mr. Godfrey Heseltine), b br m ; star, upper lip, near hind fetlock and off hind coronet white. No. 874.

GINGER (Messrs. Withers), ch m ; star, blaze, snip, scar near fore arm. No. 755.

GINGER (Mr. J. Fulton), ch g ; white face, both hind legs and off fore fetlock. No. 1114.

GIPSY (Mr. T. B. Godman), br m ; near hind fetlock white, saddle marks. No. 850.

GITANA (Mr. C. Innes Taylor), ch m ; face, lower lip, both hind legs and fore fetlock white, 4 years. Passed for season only (on appeal). No. 787.

GO BANG (Mr. H. Wilson), b m ; star, near hind fetlock grey and white, white marks both fore legs. No. 1115.

GO BANG (Mr. L. McCreery), b g ; star, blaze, snip, near hind fetlock white, scar off side of back. No. 728.

GOLD LEAF (Colonel de Robeck), ch m ; white spots both fore legs. No. 1002.

GOOD COMPANY (Capt. Paynter), b m ; white hind fetlocks. No. 1116.

GOOD GIRL (Mr. James Farmer), 6 yrs., b m ; star, narrow blaze, small snip, off hind coronet white. No. 814.

GOOSE, THE (Mr. W. E. Grogan), gr m ; white hind coronets, saddle and girth marks. No. 967.

GRANNY (Mr. W. C. Symon), gr m ; blaze, white marks on fore legs. No. 1210.

GRASSHOPPER (Mr. H. Scott-Robson), b g ; blaze, snip, lower lip and legs white, brand near hind quarter. No. 727.

GREY BROTHER (Mr. J. Clarke), gr g ; white hind legs, saddle marks. No. 726.

GREY LEG (Mr. R. Robinson), gr g ; white eyelids, white spots on muzzle, off hind fetlock white, brand near hind quarter. No. 1117.

GREY LEG (Mr. A. C. Kenyon Fuller), gr g ; white marks above both hocks and fore legs, scar both sides of ribs. No. 1118.

GREYLING (Capt. Loveband), gr m ; scar near hind fetlock, white spot near ribs. No. 1001.

GUNSHOT (Mr. P. W. Connolly), blk m ; star, scar near nostril. No. 1030.

GROUSE (Mr. E. Booth), br g ; star. No. 1247.

HAIDÉE (Capt. A. Butler), drk b m ; star, blaze, snip, white hind fetlocks, white spots front of chest, near shoulder and neck. No. 1119.

HARLEQUIN (Mr. F. J. Townsend), 4 yrs., ch m ; star, blaze, snip, collar marks, white legs, black spot near hind quarter. Passed for season only. No. 815.

HARP STRING (Capt. Loftus), b g ; off hind coronet white. No. 957.

HEATHER BELLE (Mr. H. C. Cavendish Fitzroy), ch m ; star, white spot near and off ribs. No. 843.

HEIRESS (Messrs. E. D. & G. A. Miller), bay roan m ; star, blaze, snip, near hind leg white, white marks both hind quarters. No. 1268.

HIGH LIFE (Mr. L. McCreery), 4 yrs., ch m ; star, blaze, snip, off hind fetlock and off fore coronet white, scar off quarter. Passed for the season only. No. 725.

HONESTY (Messrs. E. D. & G. A. Miller), blk m ; star, blaze, snip, off hind fetlock white, saddle marks. No. 724.

HONEY (Mr. Stanley Mortimer), cr g ; off hind leg and off fore fetlock white, brand near hind quarter. No. 876.

ICICLE (Mr. F. J. Balfour), wh g ; black spots over body, brand near hind quarter. No. 924.

IDA (Mr. A. Suart), ch m ; star, blaze, snip, white lower lip, hind legs ticked with white hairs. No. 1072.

INDIO (Mr. C. Innes Taylor), br g ; scar outside of hock, saddle marks. No. 786.

INNISBEG (Mr. E. Booth), ch m ; star, blaze, off hind fetlock white. No. 1246.

INQUISITIVE (Messrs. E. C. & G. A. Miller), b m ; off hind coronet white. No. 1267.

IRISH GIRL (Messrs. E. D. & G. A. Miller), b m ; white spot near side of ribs. No. 1269.

IT (Earl of Harrington), ch m ; star, blaze, snip, off hind coronet, near hind and off fore fetlocks white, 4 yrs. Passed for season. No. 848.

IVY (Capt. Egerton Green), ch m ; star, blaze, snip, near hind fetlock white. No. 859.

JACK (Mr. Blois), dun g ; white face, lower lip, jaw, both hind and near fore legs and flanks, brand near hind quarter. No. 1121.

JACK (Mr. L. A. Howard), blk g ; white hairs on face, and collar marks. No. 1120.

JACK (Mr. J. Richards), b g ; near fore coronet white. No. 1059.

JACK-IN-THE-BOX (Mr. W. H. Jay), b g ; saddle and girth marks. No. 778.

JACQUETTE (Sir Thos. Fowler), b m ; faint star, few white hairs on forehead, near hind coronet white, collar marks. No. 816.

JANE (Mr. W. E. Grogan), b m ; star, off hind fetlock and coronet white, grey hairs in tail. No. 965.

JEANNETTE (Mr. H. Scott-Robson), blk m ; near hind coronet white, brand near quarter. No. 723.

JENNY (Major K. MacLaren), dun m ; star, blaze, snip, white lower lip, near hind and off fore fetlocks. No. 1122.

JERPOINT (Mr. W. A. Cooper), b m ; faint black line down hind quarters, saddle and girth marks. No. 941.

JESSIE (Mr. A. W. B. Spencer, 13th Hussars), ch m ; star, blaze, snip, lower lip white, black spot near ribs, scar near fore coronet. No. 1014.

JEST (Mr. A. Rawlinson), ch m ; star, blaze, near hind fetlock white. No. 722.

JESTER (the Duchess of Newcastle), b g ; star, white near hind fetlock and near fore coronet, white spots off fore coronet, 4 yrs. Passed for season. No. 1207.

JILL (Mr. Herbert H. Wilson), ch m ; scar near loin, saddle marks. No. 749.

JIMIMA (Capt E. W. Pedder), b m ; white spots on fore legs. No. 1123.

JINNIE (Mr. E. C. Sandars), gr m ; white spots on upper lip, scars off ribs, flea-bitten face. No. 1124.

JINNY (Mr. Gerald W. Hobson), ch m ; star, blaze, scar both hind quarters, white spots off hind quarter. No. 1083.

JOE COTTON (Mr. Stanley Mortimer), ch h ; face, lip and legs white, white spots over body. No. 880.

JUANITA (Mr. S. Yearsley), blk m ; brand near hind quarter, white marks above both knees. No. 1078.

JUDITH (Capt. Heygate), roan m ; white face, lower lip and legs, white spots over body. No. 1125.

JUDY (Mr. J. Alexander), gr m ; white marks near ribs. No. 949.

JUDY (Mr. H. Goodman), b m ; star, blaze, snip, near hind fetlock white. No. 1009.

JUDY (Mr. P. P. O'Reilly), b m ; star, white hind fetlocks. No. 1055.

JUMPS (Mr. A. J. Stourton), b g ; star, blaze, snip, lower lip and legs white, brand near hind quarter. No. 949A.

KATHLEEN (Mr. C. Adamthwaite), br m ; star, blaze, snip, off hind coronet white. No. 720.

KICKAMAROO (Mr. T. L. Moore), br m ; star, white hind coronets. No. 1217.

KILDARE (Mr. J. Reid Walker), br m ; star, saddle and girth marks. No. 719.

KINGFISHER (Mr. J. W. Lamont), gr g ; white spot on lower lip, scar and brown spots on face. No. 1126.

KITTIE (Mr. J. E. Cairnes), b m ; star, near hind fetlock white. No. 1127.

KITTY O'BRIEN (Mr. Neil Haig), b m ; star, near hind fetlock white, collar marks. No. 1128.

KLONDIKE (Mr. F. Freke), drk b g ; white off hind fetlock, scar near hind quarter. No. 1074.

KLONDYKE (Mr. Balfour), blk g ; star, blaze, snip, lower lip, off hind fetlock, near hind and both fore legs white, brand near hind quarter. No. 905.

LADY BIRD (Capt. A. M. Balfour, R.A.), br m ; star, large scar off fore coronet, saddle marks. No. 817.

LADY BIRD (Mr. James Farmer), b m ; star, snip. No. 818.

LADYBIRD (Mr. C. P. Stedall), b m ; star, white marks both flanks. No. 1129.

LADY CICELY (Colonel W. H. Walker), gr m ; star, white spot point of off shoulder, 4 years. Passed for season. No. 1130.

LADY FREDERICK (Mr. R. P. O'Reilly), ch m ; (re-measured, see No. 577). No. 1046.

LADY GEORGINA (Dr. Dooley), br m ; star, blaze, snip, white lower lip and both hind fetlocks, 4 years. Passed for season only. No. 1051.

LADY GOLIGHTLY (Earl of Harrington), b m ; star, saddle and girth marks. No. 847.

LADY GOUGH (Mr. A. C. Kenyon Fuller), b m ; star, off hind coronet, near fore and near hind fetlocks white, white marks off fore legs. No. 1131.

LADY GOUGH (Mr. R. Hudson), b m ; star, blaze, snip, white lower lip and near hind leg, white hairs in tail. No. 1053.

LADY KITTY II. (Mr. S. Yearsley), b m ; white spots near hind quarter, black line down back, white mark above off hock. No. 1077.

LADY PAT (Major K. MacLaren), skewbald m ; star, blaze, snip, white legs, brand near side of back, collar marks. No. 1132.

LADY-IN-WAITING (Mr. J. W. Lamont), b m : star, blaze, snip, near fore and near hind fetlocks, and off fore coronet white. No. 1133.

LARKY PRINCESS (Mr. L. C. Wynne), gr m ; near hind fetlock white. No. 1036.

LATCH KEY (Hon. G. Ward), blk m ; star, near hind fetlock white, white marks both fore legs. No. 1134.

LEIVISTA (Mr. F. E. Kinchant), br g ; star, snip, near hind and off fore fetlocks white and grey, brand near hind quarter. No. 918.

LIMPIAS (Mr. H. Scott-Robson), ch g ; star, blaze, snip, lower lip and near hind leg white, black mark down back, brand near shoulder. No. 718.

LISRYAN (Mr. P. P. O'Reilly), br m ; white spots both hind quarters. No. 1054.

LOBSTER (Hon. F. White), b g ; near hind coronet and off hind leg grey, brand near hind quarter. No. 913.

LOCUST (Mr. Follet Holt), dun g ; star, blaze, near hind and both fore fetlocks white, brand near hind quarter. No. 886.

LOOK-OUT (Mr. L. McCreery), gr roan g ; star, snip, white hind fetlocks. No. 717.

LUCINDA (Capt. Egerton Green), ch m ; star, white hind legs and near fore fetlock. No. 1066.

LUCY LOCKET (Capt. E. Makins, 1st Dragoons), b roan m ; star, collar marks. No. 870.

LUIDA (Mr. John Nettleton), br m ; star, saddle and girth marks. No. 799.

LUNA (Mr. Balfour), piebald g ; face, lower lip, hind legs and near fore leg white, brand near hind quarter. No. 897.

LUNATIC (Mr. A. Rawlinson), b g ; star white marks front of off fore and off hind shin, scars on off knee, near fore shin and off fore arm, saddle marks. No. 690.

McCLAY (Mr. Peel, R.H.A.), b m ; star, blaze, grey hairs in flank and tail, off hind fetlock white. No. 1007.

MACK (Mr. F. J. Balfour), blk g ; star, saddle and girth marks, brand near hind quarter. No. 926.

MADELINE (Sir Thos. Fowler), 5 yrs., br m ; small star, off hind coronet white. No. 819.

MAGIC (Mr. O. T. Slocock), b m ; star, near hind coronet white. No. 976.

MAGNET (Mr. D. Hudson), br m ; star, near hind legs and off hind fetlock white. No. 1135.

MAHOMET (Mr. R. S. Clayton), blk g ; star, snip, white marks above both hocks and off knee, scar near side of neck. No. 1136.

MAKEHASTE (Mr. Balfour), b g ; face, lower lip and legs white, brand off hind quarter, white patch near hip. No. 891.

MAMELUKE (Mr. H. Scott Robson), ch g ; star, blaze, snip, off hind coronet white, brand near quarter, saddle marks. No. 716.

MANNERS (Mr. Balfour), b g ; star, both hind and off fore fetlocks white, brand near hind quarter. No. 908.

MAORI KING (Mr. Follet Holt), drk br g ; brand near hind quarters, saddle marks. No. 885.

MARCH HARE (Capt. Hare), b g ; star, near hind fetlock white. No. 1045.

MARIA (Mr. Innes), b m ; star, snip, off hind coronet white. No. 998.

MARIA (Mr. F. Belleville), iron gr m ; star, scar off ribs, grey hairs in tail, saddle marks. No. 715.

MARIOSA (Capt. R. Alexander), b roan m ; star, snip, white hairs in tail. No. 1137.

MARITANA (Mr. J. Fitzgerald), b m ; star, 4 years (passed for season only). No. 1029.

MARJORY (Mr. A. Suart), b m; star, white hind fetlocks. No. 1070.

MARLEY (Mr. Collins), b m; white hind coronets, white spots off fore fetlock. No. 1230.

MARRON GLACÉ (Capt. Campbell Johnson), ch m; star, blaze, snip, white hind legs and near fore fetlock, white spots in tail. No. 1138.

MARTINGALE (Hon. H. Scott Robson), b br g; star, blaze, snip, lower lip and near fore and both hind fetlocks white, brand off quarter. No. 713.

MASTER THOMAS (Mr. John Henry Elliott), b g; star, white hind fetlock, saddle marks. No. 820.

MATCH BOX (Messrs. Withers), ch m; face, lower lip, near hind leg white, off hind leg partly white, 4 yrs. (season only). No. 763.

MATILDA (Mr. B. C. Kidd), b m; star, scar near forearm. No. 1139.

MAY (Mr. T. S. Greenway), drk ch m; star, blaze, brand near shoulder, white spot near hind quarter. No. 1141.

MELBORNE (Mr. W. A. Cooper), ch g; star, snip, white hind fetlocks. No. 940.

MENELIK (Mr. A. J. Stourton), roan g; face, lower lip, lower jaws and all legs white, large white marks both flanks. No. 714.

MENZIES (Mr. C. Sheather), ch m; star, near hind fetlock white. No. 1142.

MERCEDES (Mr. R. Hudson), br m; collar marks, near hind coronet white. No. 1229.

MERCURY (Mr. J. W. Hornsby), gr g; hind fetlocks, near fore fetlocks and off hind coronet white, saddle marks. No. 854.

MERMAID, by Sea Horse (Mr. W. H. Jay), dun m; star, blaze, off hind fetlock, near hind and both fore coronets white. No. 773.

MERMAID (Capt. J. Hanwell), b m; star, off hind fetlock white. No. 1140.

MERMAID (Mr. R. L. Geanes), b m; off hind fetlock white, 4 yrs. (passed for season). No. 1143.

MERMAID (Mr. W. E. Grogan), br m; star, snip, wart scar near side of neck. No. 968.

MERRY HORN (Mr. Alfred Withers), ch g; star, blaze, near hind coronet white, white spot near side of neck and off shoulder. No. 1199.

MERRY MAID (Mr. A. J. Pilkington), b m; few white hairs both sides of ribs, 4 yrs. (passed for season). No. 1058.

MERRY THORNE (Capt. Bidgood, R.A.), ch g; star, blaze, snip, near hind leg white, 4 years (passed for season only). No. 1034.

MICKEY FREE (Hon. O. Hastings), b g. No. 977.

MIDNIGHT (Capt. Campbell Johnston), drk br m; star, off hind fetlock white, white off stifle. No. 1144.

MILKMAID (Capt. T. Macan), br m ; scar outside near hock, saddle marks. No. 846.

MINX (Mr. T. F. Cooke), br m ; star, near hind coronet white, white mark near fetlock. No. 1232.

MISS CICELY (Colonel W. H. Walker), gr m ; white spots off hind quarter. No. 1145.

MISS FORTUNE (Colonel de Robeck), drk br g ; star. No. 1004.

MISS LAX (Mr. R. R. Barker), 5 yrs., b m ; star, large snip, narrow blaze, saddle and girth marks. No. 821.

MISS MEATH (Mr. A. G. Dalgety), 5 yrs., b m ; saddle marks near side. No. 822.

MISS MEGG (Mr. James Farmer), br m ; star, small white spot in mane, scar near fore leg, saddle marks. No. 823.

MISS POLLY (Mr. J. W. Hornsby), b m ; star, blaze, snip, saddle and girth marks. No. 855.

MISS REILLY (Dr. Dooley), b m ; star. No. 1050.

MISS SHARP (Mr. A. Dalgety), 5 yrs., b m ; star, narrow blaze, snip, few grey hairs in mane. No. 824.

MISS SULLIVAN (Mr. O'Sullivan), ch m ; star, blaze, snip, near hind fetlock and off hind coronet white. No. 1062.

MISTER ORD (Mr. Neil Haig), blk g ; star, blaze, snip, white lower lip and legs, brand near hind quarter. No. 1146.

MISTLETOE (Mr. H. Lawson), b m ; star, blaze. No. 1147.

MOLLY (Mr. R. Lonsdale), b m ; star, snip, white lower lip, both hind and off fore fetlocks. No. 1033.

MOLLY BAWN (Mr. A. Topham), blk m ; star, snip, white hind fetlock. No. 1022.

MONA (Mr. James Farmer), 5 yrs., b m ; star, blaze, lower lip white, white legs. No. 825.

MOONLIGHTER (Mr. J. R. Aspinall), gr ; blaze, snip, white lower lip and near fore and off hind fetlocks. No. 1148.

MOONSTONE (Mr. R. St. G. Robinson), br g ; tan muzzle. No. 1026.

MORGIANA (Mr. C. C. Wilson), ch ; star, blaze, snip, white near fore and near hind fetlocks, white mark near hind shin, 4 yrs. (passed for season). No. 1204.

MOSES (Capt. Ramsey), gr g ; snip, white lower lip and near hind fetlock. No. 1149.

MOSQUITO (Mr. Balfour), br g ; snip, near hind fetlock white, brand near hindquarter. No. 892.

MOUSE (Mr. Hamilton Russell), drk br m ; near hind fetlock, off hind coronet white. No. 1150.

MUFTI (Mr. H. C. Higgin), gr g ; off ear snip. No. 1151.

POLO PONIES, 1898.

445

MULLINGAR (Mr. O'Sullivan),b m ; star, near hind fetlock and off hind coronet white. No. 1063.

MUSCIPSULUS (Mr. H. F. Ford), ch m ; star, blaze, snip, both hind and near fore fetlocks white. No. 864.

MY GIRL (Mr. J. Gouldsmith), b m ; star, blaze, snip, white hind fetlocks. No. 992.

NANCY (Capt. T. Macan), b m ; star, blaze, snip, both hind and near fore fetlocks white, scar point of near shoulder. No. 845.

NAWAB (Mr. A. E. Gostling), br h ; star, blaze, snip, both hind and near fore fetlocks white. No. 1152.

NELLIE (Mr. J. T. Wigan, 13th Hussars), b m ; star 4 years (passed for season only). No. 1013.

NETTLE (Mr. E. B. Sheppard), b m ; star, off hind coronet white. No. 1153.

NIGHT STAR (Mr. J. Adamthwaite), br m ; star, white hind fetlocks, collar marks. No. 826.

NOBBY (Mr. A. E. Gostling), drk b h ; star, near hind fetlock and off hind coronet white, scars off ribs. No. 1155.

NOISETTE (Mr. R. St. G. Robinson), ch m ; star, blaze, snip, near fore and near hind fetlocks and off hind coronet white, 4 years (passed for season only). No. 1025.

NORA (Mr. T. S. Greenway), dapple gr m ; near hind fetlock white. No. 1156.

NUN, THE (Mr. W. S. Heather), blk m. No. 1039.

NUTCRACKER (Major Rimington), drk b m ; star, white marks both sides of ribs, scar front of hind fetlock. No. 989.

OLIVE (Mr. Godfrey Heseltine), b m ; near hind coronet white, scars on both hocks. No. 873.

ON THE HOP (Mr. L. McCreery), ch g ; near hind fetlock white, black spot off quarter. No. 712.

OOFBIRD (Mr. A. Watts), b m ; tipped with white both flanks. No. 1238.

OVERO (Mr. Follett Holt), piebald g ; face, lower lip, and legs white, brand on both hindquarters. No. 916.

PATCHWORK (Mr. W. H. Jay), skewbald m ; star, blaze, snip, lower lip and legs white, 4 years (passed for season only). No. 777.

PEARL, late Miss Roark (Messrs. Millers), gr m ; white marks both sides of ribs. No. 943.

PEBBLE (Mr. W. Buckmaster), br m ; saddle and girth marks. No 841.

PEGGY (Mr. H. Tudor), b m ; star, off hind fetlock white, mark down back. No. 1157.

PEGGY (Capt. L. Bryan), b m ; scars near hind quarter, off ribs and near fore pastern. No. 1214.

PET (Mr. F. A. Gill), br m ; star, saddle and girth marks. No. 682.

PETACAS (Mr. F. E. Kinchant), gr g ; black spots over body, scar on off ribs, brand near hind quarter. No. 919.

PETER (Mr. J. Fulton), b g ; star, collar marks, white spot off forearm. No. 1158.

PET FOX (Mr. C. de Robeck), blk g ; star, snip, white fore coronet and hind fetlocks. No. 1219.

PHŒBE (Mr. John Henry Elliott), b m ; star, small snip, grey hairs on face, off hind fetlock white, saddle marks. No. 827.

PHŒNIX (Capt. T. Macan), b m ; star, white near hind fetlock, scar and white mark off fore leg. No. 872.

PHYLLIS (Mr. Alfred Withers), drk br m ; star, fired both hocks. No. 1198.

PHYSICIAN (Mr. H. Scott Robson), b piebald g ; face, lower lip and all legs white, brand near quarter. No. 711

PICASO (Colonel W. A. Cardwell), blk g ; star, blaze, snip, white hind fetlocks, brand near hind quarter. No. 828.

PICQUET (Mr. Wilson), blk br m ; white hairs on poll, white spot inside both knees. No. 1159.

PINTO BILL (Mr. T. B. Drybrough), piebald g ; face, near fore and hind legs and off knee white. No. 745.

PINWIRE (Major Rimington), b m ; star, blaze, snip. No. 991.

PLAYFUL (Mr. F. Belleville), br m. No. 710. (Measured last year as a 4 year-old. See No. 659).

PLEDGE (Capt. L. Bryan), b m ; star, blaze, snip, white lower lip and off fore coronet, white hairs in tail. No. 1215.

PLOUGHBOY (Sir F. Burdett), drk br g ; near hind coronet white, scar off shoulder and near flank. No. 1160.

PLUNGER, THE (Mr. A. Blyth), b g ; star, blaze, snip, scar on forehead, near hind and both fore fetlocks white, black spot on back ; passed on appeal. No. 1163.

POLICY (Sir H. F. de Trafford), ch m ; star, blaze, off hind coronet white. No. 681.

POLLUX (Mr. J. Ravenscroft), br g ; star, blaze, snip, lower lip, off hind and both fore legs and flanks white, brand near hind quarter. No. 887.

POLLY (Mr. H. Goodman), drk br m ; star, white hind fetlocks. No. 1011.

POM-POM (Mr. W. Blumson), gr g ; white legs, brand on both fore legs. No. 935.

POPCORN (Mr. Stanley Mortimer), ch g; white face and lower lip, white spots over body, branded near cheek, near, fore, and hind quarters. No. 878.

PORTENO (Mr. F. E. Kinchant), b g; star, blaze, snip, white lower lip and legs, branded both hind quarters. No. 920.

PORTO RICO (Major Porteous), blk g; star, snip, white hind fetlocks, brand near hind quarter, white hairs in tail. No. 1161.

POTEEN (Capt. H. Clifton Brown), ch m; scar off fore pastern. No. 1162.

PRAIRIE FLOWER (Mr. T. Anderson), b m; star, near hind leg and off hind fetlock white. No. 958.

PRECILLA (Capt. H. de B. de Lisle), b m; star, near hind fetlock white. No. 1257.

PRINCESS (Mr. H. Scott Robson), b m; off hind fetlock white, brand near quarter. No. 709.

PRINCESS (Mr. J. Alexander), ch m; star, blaze, snip, white lower lip, off fore and off hind fetlock white. No. 980.

PUCK (Capt. H. de B. de Lisle, bay g; star, blaze, snip, white lower lip, both hind fetlocks white, both fore coronets white. No. 1252.

QUEEN BEE (Mr. H. N. Magill), b m; star, blaze, snip, white lower lip and hind fetlocks. No. 1236.

QUEEN BEE (Mr. J. W. Hornsby), ch m; star, blaze, snip, white hind legs, white hairs over near ribs. No. 856.

QUEENIE (Mr. W. Walton), b m; near hind coronet white, white marks above both knees. No. 1164.

QUICKSILVER (Mr. Balfour), b m; brand near hind quarter. No. 884.

QUIEN SABE (Mr. H. C. Higgin), ch g; star, blaze, white lower lip, both hind and off fore legs, brand near fore quarter, ticked with white hairs. No. 1193.

RAJAH (Mr. A. Watts), gr g; star, blaze, snip, white spots on muzzle. No. 1241.

RAKE, THE (Mr. E. Coovel), gr g; white mark near ribs. No. 746.

RANGER (Mr. Stanley Mortimer), br g; white hind heels, star, brand near fore and hind quarters. No. 881.

RAPID RHONE (Mr. A. Rawlinson), roan m; grey hairs in tail, saddle and girth marks. No. 881A.

RAT, THE (Capt. N. Curzon), drk br g; near hind coronet white. No. 1165.

RATTLER (Messrs. Withers), br g; star, snip, near fore and near hind fetlocks white. No. 761.

RECKLESS (Capt. H. de Lisle), gr m ; star, off hind fetlock white. No. 1256.

RED RAG (Mr. D. Hudson), b m ; star, snip, near hind fetlock white, white marks inside both ears. No. 1166.

RED ROBIN (Mr. W. S. Heather), ch m ; star, blaze, snip, white hind fetlocks. No. 1038.

REDSKIN (Mr. Follet Holt), b g ; star, white hind fetlocks, brand near hind quarter, saddle marks. No. 915.

REDSTART (Mr. Lister), ch m ; star, blaze, snip, white lower lip, near hind fetlock and off fore coronet. No. 1203.

REGALIA (Capt. H. de B. de Lisle), ch m ; star, blaze, near fore and hind fetlocks white. No. 1253.

RELIEF (Major K. MacLaren), ch m ; star, blaze, snip, white lower lip and fetlocks. No. 1167.

RIBBON (Mr. E. C. Judkins), blk m ; star, near hind coronet white. No. 1168.

RISKY (Mr. C. P. Stedall), b g ; star, blaze, snip, white fetlocks. No. 1169.

ROARK VIXEN (Mr. S. I. Roark), br m ; white spot off ribs, saddle marks. No. 953.

ROBIN (Mr. Scott Robson), ch g ; star, blaze, snip, near hind leg and off fore fetlock white, brand near side chest. No. 708.

ROBIN GREY (Mr. T. L. Moore), gr g ; white spots on head and neck. No. 1218.

ROCKET (Mr. P. E. Hardwicke, 1st Dragoons), ch g ; star, blaze, snip, white lower lip and hind legs, white hairs in flank. No. 791.

ROGER (Mr. T. F. Cooke), ch g ; white face, lower lip and legs. No. 1234.

RONDO (Mr. Stanley Mortimer), ch g ; star, blaze, white hind fetlocks, brand near shoulder. No. 879.

ROSA (Mr. H. Scott Robson), roan m ; face, lower lip, flanks and all legs white, brand near hind quarter. No. 707.

ROSAS (Hon. F. White), ch g ; star, blaze, snip, white hind legs and fore fetlocks, brand near hind quarter. No. 911.

ROSEMARY (Messrs. E. D. & G. A. Miller), b m. No. 1264.

ROSETTE (Mr. J. W. Hornsby), ch m ; star, blaze, snip, white hind fetlocks, 4 years, passed for the season. No. 1170.

ROSIE (Mr. A. Boyd-Rochfort), b m ; star, near hind fetlock white, white marks off hock. No. 1043.

ROYAL BOY (Mr. A. Boyd-Rochfort), b g ; star, blaze, snip, white lower lip and all legs. 4 years, passed for season only. No. 1061.

RUBY (Mr. F. J. Mackey), b g ; white hind fetlocks, faint black mark down back, white mark off shoulder, saddle and girth marks. No. 706.

RUBY (Colonel W. A. Cardwell), ch g ; star, blaze, snip, lower lip white, near hind fetlock and off hind coronet white, brand near hind quarter, white spots on body. No. 830.

SAILOR (Mr. W. A. Cooper), ch g ; star, white mark off side neck. No. 972.

SALLY (Mr. R. C. Barton), b m ; star, near fore fetlock white. No. 1056.

SANDOW (Capt. Loftus), b g ; white hairs off coronet, girth marks. 4 years, passed for season only. No. 956.

SANDOW (Mr. W. H. Jay), b g ; white near hind coronet. No. 774.

SARDINE (Mr. Ernest Denly), 6 yrs., b m ; near hind fetlock white. No. 831.

SATIRE (Mr. J. W. Hornsby), ch g ; star, off hind fetlock and near hind coronet white. No. 857.

SAUCY (Mr. F. A. Gill), gr m ; forehead and hind coronets white, scar near fore shin. No. 680.

SEABREEZE (Mr. A. Suart), br m ; star, blaze. No. 1071.

SEAGULL (Mr. A. Watts), g m ; flea-bitten, blaze, snip, collar marks. No. 1237.

SEALIA (Capt. Egerton Green), ch m ; off hind fetlock white. No. 765.

SECOND HAND (Dr. Dooley), b m ; scars near hind fetlock and off fore shin. No. 1048.

SECRET (Hon. O. Hastings), ch m ; star, blaze, black spots off ribs, black spot near knee. No. 960.

SECRET (Messrs. E. D. & G. A. Miller), ch m ; star, blaze, snip. No. 1259.

SECRETARY (Mr. Balfour), ch g ; star, blaze, snip, near hind fetlock and off hind leg white, brand near hind quarter. No. 889.

SEE-SAW (Sir Thos. Fowler), 5 yrs., ch g ; white star on forehead, white hind fetlocks. No. 832.

SELIM (Messrs. Withers), ch m ; star, saddle and girth marks. No. 757.

SERF BELLE (Mr. Max Angus), b m ; star, blaze, snip, saddle marks. No. 705.

SERPENT (Mr. Herbert H. Wilson), b m ; off hind fetlock white, star. No. 748.

SHEIK (Mr. A. Watts), bh ; near fore fetlock and off fore coronet white. No. 1240.

SHOP GIRL (Mr. H. C. C. Fitzroy), gr m ; star, white hind fetlocks. No. 844.

SILK (Capt. Egerton Green), b m ; scar on near loin, collar marks. No. 766.

29

SILVER BELL (Mr. James Farmer), 6 yrs., b m ; small star, white hind fetlocks and near fore coronet. No. 833.

SILVERDALE (Mr. A. Topham), drk br g; snip, white hind fetlocks. No. 1021.

SILVERLOCK (Mr. James Farmer), 5 yrs., gr m; star, narrow blaze, snip, white hind fetlocks, white spot near fore leg. No. 834.

SILVERLOCK (Capt. A. Carstairs), gr m ; blaze, snip, white hind fetlocks, white mark near fore leg. No. 1171.

SILVERLORN (Mr. John Nettleton), b m ; star, ticked with white, collar marks, white marks off flank. No. 800.

SILVERTAIL (Mr. F. H. Wise, 13th Hussars), br m ; star, blaze, snip, white lower lip and near hind coronet, white hairs in tail, ticked with white. No. 1019.

SINKAH (Mr. A. Watts), ch h ; star, blaze, snip, white spot on lower lip, white legs. No. 1242.

SLIPPERS (Mr. J. Wormald), b m ; off hind fetlock white. No. 1209.

SMITH O'BRIEN (Mr. Balfour), ch g ; star, blaze, brand near hind quarter, black spots near hind quarter, saddle marks. No. 904.

SMUTT (Capt Loftus), br g ; star, blaze, near hind coronet white. No. 995.

SNOWBALL (Messrs. Withers), gr g ; snip. No. 759.

SNOWFLAKE (Mr. B. Montgomery), g h ; flea-bitten, snip. No. 1244.

SOAP-SUDS (Mr. A. Rawlinson), gr g ; off hind leg and fore coronets white, saddle marks. No. 703.

SO EASY (Mr. L. McCreery), br m ; star, near hind and fore fetlocks white, saddle marks. No. 704.

SOPHIA (Mr. J. Alexander), ch m ; star, blaze, snip, both hind fetlocks white. No. 962.

SORCERER (Mr. A. J. Curnick), br g ; star, snip, white hind fetlocks. No. 1172.

SOUVENIR (Mr. Ernest Denly), 5 yrs., iron gr m ; star, white spots off ribs. No. 835.

SPEC (Capt. J. Hanwell), b m ; star, blaze, snip, white lower lip, hind legs and off fore fetlock. No. 1173.

SPINSTER (Mr. O. T. Slocock), b m ; scar off fore shin, 4 yrs. (passed for season only). No. 975.

SPIRTLE (Sir Thos. Fowler), 5 yrs., b m ; faint star, near hind fetlock white, saddle and girth marks. No. 836.

SPOT WHITE (Capt. A. M. Balfour, R. A.), blk g ; white star and snip lower lip, off fore and near hind fetlocks white, white spot off side of neck, saddle marks. No. 837.

SPRIGHTLY (Colonel de Robeck), b m ; star, blaze, white hind fetlocks, scar over near eye. No. 1225.

SPRIGHTLY (Mr. Balfour), blk g ; white hind fetlocks, brand near hind quarter, saddle marks. No. 906.

SPRINGJACK (Mr. Balfour), drk br g ; star, near hind fetlock white, brand near hind quarter, scar off fore leg. No. 900.

SPRING ROSE (Mr. A. Hill), b m ; star, near hind fetlocks and fore coronets white. No. 1174.

SQUIB (Colonel W. A. Cardwell), ch g ; white hairs in mane, scar on both hocks, saddle marks. No. 838.

SQUIRREL, THE (Mr. J. Wormald), ch m ; black spot near cheek, white hairs top of withers, near fore coronet white. No. 1067.

STANDARD (Mr. A. Rawlinson), b m ; star, blaze, snip, off fore and off hind fetlocks white, collar marks. No. 1175.

STAR III. (Colonel de Robeck),) drk br m ; star, blaze, white spot lower lip, both hind fetlocks and near fore coronet white. No. 1000.

STEIN (Dr. T. O. Mearn), b m ; star, snip. No. 964

STELLA (Mr. C. de Robeck), drk br m ; star, blaze, snip, off hind coronet white. No. 1222.

STELLA (Messrs. Withers), br m ; star, near hind fetlock and off hind coronet white. No. 750.

STELLA (Mr. John Nettleton), ch m ; star, blaze, snip, white spots near and off hind quarters, flanks ticked with white, saddle and girth marks, 4 yrs. Passed for season only. No. 796.

STITCH IN TIME (Mr. A. C. Kenyon Fuller), b g ; scar near hind quarter. No. 1176.

STRAWBERRY (Hon. F. White), roan g ; star, blaze, snip, white lower lip and legs, white patches on body, brand near hind quarter, scars on neck. No. 912.

SUDDEN THOUGHT (Mr. Follet Holt), wh m ; black spots on fore quarters and ears, brand near hind quarter. No. 914.

SULTAN (Mr. Ernest Denly), 4 yrs., blk g ; small blemish off side of neck. Passed for the season only. No. 839.

SUNRISE (Mr. J. Adamthwaite), b m ; star, small snip, saddle and girth marks. No. 931.

SUNSET (Mr. J. Adamthwaite), br m ; star, narrow blaze, snip, saddle and girth marks. No. 932.

SUNSHINE (Mr. F. J. Townsend), 5 yrs., ch m ; star, blaze, snip. No. 933.

SWALLOW (Capt. Vernon, Rifle Brigade), blk g ; star, blaze, snip, brand near hind quarter, both hind and off fore fetlocks white. No. 1015.

SWEEP (Mr. T. B. Godman), blk g ; star, snip, white hind fetlocks, off fore fetlock and near fore coronet. No. 849.

SYMPATHY (Messrs. E. D. & G. A. Miller), b m ; star, both hind fetlocks white. No. 1263.

29*

SHE (Earl of Harrington), br m ; small star, scar on wither.   No.
  1263A.

TAFFY (Mr. F. J. Balfour), br g ; star, blaze, snip, white lower lip,
  both hind and off fore legs, and near fore fetlock, brand near hind quarter.
  No. 922.

TARA (Mr. J. E. Cairnes), gr g ; snip, white lower lip and hind
  legs. No. 1177.

TARPAULIN (Capt. E. Makins, 1st Dragoons), b m ; star.   No.
  790.

'TELEGRAPH (Mr. W. H. Jay), ch g ; star, snip, near hind fetlock
  white, collar mark, 4 yrs.   Passed for season only.   No. 780.

TELEPHONE (Messrs. Withers), br m ; star, off hind fetlock white,
  scar near fore fetlock. No. 751.

TEMPÉ (Mr. H. M. Hardy), br m ; white mark about point of near
  hock. No. 1228.

TERRE-TERRE (Mr. Glen Williams), skewbald g ; brand near
  hind quarter. No. 1178.

TERROR (Mr. W. Graham McIvor), ch m ; star, blaze, snip, off
  hind leg and near fore coronet white, 4 yrs.   Passed for season only.   No.
  883.

TESSIE (Mr. J. E. Cairnes), b m ; star, scar off hip.   No. 1179.

THREE CHEERS (Mr. L. McCreery), ch m ; blaze, snip, lower lip
  and off fore leg white. No. 700.

TINKER (Mr. F. J. Balfour), b g ; star, snip, white lower lip and
  hind fetlocks, brand near hind quarters.   No. 921.

TIPPLES (Mr. W. H. Jay), b m ; white hind fetlocks.   No. 779.

TIP-TOP (Sir Thos. Fowler), 5 yrs., blk g ; near hind coronet white,
  scar near hind leg. No. 934.

TIT BITS (Mr. A. Pyke), drk ch m ; star, white marks on face and
  legs, off hind fetlock white. No. 1197.

TOM (Mr. F. J. Mackey), blk g ; white hind fetlocks, saddle marks.
  No. 702.

TOMBOY (Mr. F. J. Balfour), br g ; star, blaze, white lower lip and
  fetlocks, brand near hind quarters.   No. 923.

TOM CAT (Mr. W. C. Symon), b g ; star, white hind legs and near
  fore coronet. No. 1180.

TOM TIDDLER (Messrs. E. D. & G. A. Miller), b g ; star, white
  spot near side of ribs. No. 1262.

TOM TIT (Mr. J. Watson), br g ; scar with white hair near side of
  neck. No. 1249.

TOM TIT (Mr. A. E. Gostling), b g ; star, white hind and off fore
  leg. No. 1181.

TOM TIT (Mr. J. W. Murray), b g ; star, blaze, snip, near hind leg
  white. No. 1057.

TONY (Mr. Balfour), skewbald g ; white face, lower lip and legs, branded both hind quarters. No. 898.

TOPPER (Mr. Balfour), b g ; star, blaze, snip, white lower lip, near hind fetlock and off hind leg, brand near hind quarter. No. 909.

TOPSY (Messrs. Withers), blk m ; faint star. No. 752.

TORRITO (Mr. A. J. Stourton), b g ; star, brand near hind quarter. No. 701.

TREASURE (Capt. R. Peel, 2nd Life Guards), b g ; star, white hind fetlocks, saddle and girth marks. No. 679.

TRILBY (Capt. A. M. Balfour, R.A.), b or br m ; small star, white hind fetlocks, saddle marks. No. 936.

TRIUMPH (Mr. R. Hudson), b g ; star, blaze, snip, near hind coronet white, scars on neck. No. 1060.

TRIXIE (Mr. F. Hargreaves), ch m ; star, blaze, snip, lower lip and hind legs white. No. 699.

TROOPER (Mr. H. Scott Robson), b g ; star, brand near quarter, white hairs in tail. No. 698.

TURCO (Mr. T. F. Cooke), ch h ; star, near hind fetlock white, scar off ribs. No. 1231.

TWILIGHT (Mr. A. Suart), b m ; star, blaze, snip both hind and near fore fetlocks white. No. 1069.

VACUNA (Mr. H. Scott Robson), b g ; face, near fore and both hind legs and off coronet white, brand near quarter, white mark near side of neck. No. 697.

VALENTINE (Mr. Balfour), ch g ; white face, lower lip, hind legs, off fore leg and near fore coronet, brand near hind quarters, ticked with white. No. 903.

VANITY (Mr. Balfour), ch m ; star, blaze, snip, white lower lip, hind legs, off fore leg, and near fore fetlock, brand near hind quarter. No. 902.

VENDETTA (Colonel de Robeck), b m ; star, near hind fetlock and off fore coronet white. No. 999.

VENTURE (Mr. Balfour), blue roan g ; near hind coronet and off hind fetlock white, black spots over body, brand near hind quarter. No. 901.

VERVANE (Mr. J. Drybrough), br m ; saddle marks. No. 678.

VICTOR (Mr. L. O. P. Learmont, R.H.A.), b g ; star, white spot near hind shin and off fore shin. No. 1006.

VICTORY (Mr. G. A. Miller), br m ; star, scar on off hock. No. 1182.

VIOLET (Capt. A. E. Webb), br m ; star. No. 1223.

VIVANDIÈRE (Mr. Innes), ch m ; star, blaze, white hind legs, black spot near hind quarter. No. 997.

VIVANDIÈRE (Mr. E. Burne), dun m ; star, blaze, snip, white spot on lower lip, near hind leg white. No. 1183.

VIXEN (F. A. Gill), b m ; white spots near ribs. No. 1271.

VIXEN (Mr. Herbert H. Wilson), b m ; white spots both sides of neck. No. 747.

VIXEN (Viscount Belgrave), ch m ; white hind fetlocks. No. 1184.

WALL EYE (Mr. W. Edge), gr g ; off eye white, snip, lower lip and both hind legs white. No. 971.

WALNUT (Mr. Glen Williams), ch g ; star, blaze, snip, white hind and off fore leg, brand near hind quarter. No. 1185.

WARRIOR (Mr. J. Fitzgerald), ch g ; star, blaze, snip, black spots both hind quarters. No. 1028.

WASP (Mr. Glen Williams), b g ; white face, lower lip, hind coronets, near fore fetlock and off fore leg, brand near hind quarter. No. 1186.

WATCHFUL (Mr. James Farmer), 5 yrs., b m ; faint star. No. 937.

WATCHMAN (Messrs. Withers), b g ; star, brown spot off hind quarter, white spot on poll. No. 760.

WAVELET (Mr. Glen Williams), b g ; star, blaze, snip, near hind fetlock white, brand near hind quarter, ticked with white. No. 1187.

WEASEL (Mr. A. Watts), b m ; star, with bay spot, blaze, snip. No. 1239.

WELSH HARP (Mr. James Farmer), 5 yrs., ch m ; faint star, white hind coronets. No. 938.

WESTBURY (Mr. Stanley Mortimer), b g ; branded near fore and hind quarters and cheek. No. 877.

WHISKEY (Mr. D. Hudson), blk m ; white hairs in flank, near hind and both fore fetlocks white. No. 1188.

WHITESOCKS (Mr. J. Drage), br g ; star, blaze, snip, white fetlocks, saddle and girth marks. No. 696.

WHITE STOCKINGS (Mr. C. Sheather), b m ; white face, lower lip and hind legs. No. 1189.

WHITE WINGS (Mr. W. H. Jay), gr m ; flea-bitten marks on the head. No. 772.

WILD BOY (Mr. H. Tudor), br g ; star, blaze, snip, white lower lip, hind fetlocks and near fore coronet. No. 1190.

WILD BOY (Mr. L. F. Archdale), br g ; near fore coronet white. No. 951.

WILDFLOWER (Capt. L. Bryan), b m ; scar point of near shoulder. No. 1213.

WILD GIRL (Mr. L. F. Archdale), b m ; white spots near ribs, white marks off ribs. No. 950.

WILLIE D (Mr. F. J. Mackey), ch g; star, near hind leg white, black line down back, white spot off hind quarter. No. 594.

WINK (Mr. Glen Williams), dun g; star, scar on face, white hind fetlocks, brands near hind quarter. No. 1191.

WINNIE (Mr. H. C. Talbot Rice), b m; scar near knee. No. 1192.

WISDOM (Mr. E. Lloyd), b br m; star, white hind fetlock. No. 867.

WISDOM (Colonel de Robeck), b m; star, blaze. No. 994.

WISE GIRL (Mr. James Farmer), 5 yrs., drk br m; saddle marks. No. 939.

WITCH, THE (Mr. S. Yearsley), ch m; star. No. 1079.

WOODY (Major George Bouverie), b m; star, white marks, both hind and off fore shins and near knee. No. 784.

XX (Major M. F. Rimington), b m; star, white marks on fore fetlocks. No. 1224.

YELLOW FELLOW (Mr. J. Drage), dun g; star, blaze, snip, off hind fetlock white, saddle marks. No. 695.

YELLOW JACK (Dr. T. O'Mearn), ch g; star, snip, off hind fetlock white, collar marks. No. 945.

ZARA (Mr. H. Goodman), b m; faint black line down hind quarters. No. 1010.

ZELIE (Mr. Leonard), ch m; star, blaze, snip, white spots near side of neck and near hind quarter. No. 1216.

UNNAMED PONIES.

Mr. J. Bartlett's ch g; star, snip, white legs, white spots over body. No. 1154.

Capt. Loftus' gr m; blaze, white spot back of near fore leg, 4 yrs. Passed for season only. No. 973.

Dr. W. O'Mearn's br m; star, near fore coronet and both hind fetlocks white, scar near fore leg. No. 942.

Mr. J. Drage's gr g. No. 689.

THE FOLLOWING PONIES WERE NOT PASSED.

CHANCE (Mr. B. C. Kidd), ch m ; star, blaze, near hind fetlock white. No. 1195.

CRESS (Mr. G. Turner), ch m ; star, snip, near hind leg and off fore fetlock white. No. 948.

DOUBTFUL (Mr. F. Hargreaves), ch m ; star, blaze, near hind fetlock and off hind heel white, saddle marks.

DULCIE (Mr. O. T. Slocock), b m ; wart mark near stiffle. No. 978.

GOOD BOY (Count J. de Madre). No. 930.

GREY BIRD (Mr. F. A. Gill), gr g ; snip, lower lip and all fetlocks white. No. 677.

JOEY (Mr. Gerald W. Hobson), ch g ; star, blaze, snip, white hind legs and near fore fetlock. No. 1082.

MISS SHOT (Dr. Dooley), drk br m ; star. No. 1049.

OLIVETTE (Mr. A. Suart), ch m ; star, blaze, snip, near hind fetlock white, black patch near hind quarter, light and black patch off hind quarter. No. 1073.

POLLY (Mr. E. Folley), b m ; wart marks in flank, 4 yrs. No. 1027.

PRINCE THORNE (Capt. Bidgood, R.A.), ch g ; star, blaze, snip, near hind fetlock and near fore coronet white. No. 1035.

SARAH (Mr. T. S. Greenway), drk b m ; white marks above near hock, off hind coronet white. No. 3094.

SYLVIA (Mr. John Nettleton), br m ; star, snip, both fore and hind heels white, white mark near side of neck, saddle marks off side. No. 794.

TURNER (Mr. J. Watson), b m ; star, snip, both hind fetlocks white, white spots off shoulder. No. 882.

VARDYA (Mr. E. E. Mason), b m ; star, blaze, snip. No. 1065.

POLO PONIES MEASURED AND REGISTERED
AT HURLINGHAM, 1899.

———◆———

ABBOTT, THE (Capt. Belfield), gr g; near hind fetlock white scar in front of near hind fetlock. No. 0299.

ABDOOLAH (Capt. C. E. G. Morton), gr g; collar mark. No. 0105.

ACORN (Major G. M. Eccles), br m; star, narrow blaze, snip. Passed for season. No. 0430.

ACORN (Earl of Harrington), ch g; star, near fore and near hind fetlocks white. No. 0624.

ACTRESS (Major G. M. Eccles), br m; few grey hairs in forehead, near hind leg grey, black patch off side of ribs. Passed for season. No. 0431.

ACTRESS (Mr. J. C. Harrison), b m; near hind fetlock white. No. 0609.

ADA (Mr. C. Adamthwaite), br m; star, few white hairs on face both flanks ticked with white, collar marks. No. 0217.

ADELA (Messrs. E. D. & G. A. Miller), gr m; white face, collar marks. No. 010.

AFTER ME (Mr. Ashgill Colville), blk m; star, narrow blaze, snip, both hind fetlocks white, off coronet white. No. 052.

AFTER THE BALL (Mr. Leonard Bucknall), b g; star, scar on forehead. No. 0157.

ALI BABA (Capt. Lionel Lindsay), ch h; star, blaze, lower lip white, both hind fetlocks white, scars both sides of neck. No. 0676.

ALLAZAN (Mr. J. Lawson), ch g; star, scars on all four legs, brand near hind quarter. No. 0218.

ALICE (Miss B. Stafford), ch m; white hairs over head and fore quarters. Passed for season. No. 0377.

ALL FOURS (Mr. A. Withers), blk m; all four fetlocks white with black spots. No. 0329.

ALMA (12th Lancers' Pony Club), b g; small star, near hind fetlock, off hind coronet white. No. 0145.

AMBERITE (Miss Rawson), ch m ; star, small snip, near hind
coronet white, collar marks. No. 0450.

AMELIA (Mr. J. B Southey), br m ; star. No. 0488.

ANCIENT, THE (Mr. T. Anderson), br m ; star, narrow blaze,
snip, both hind fetlocks white. No. 0451.

ANGEL (Messrs. E. D. & G. A. Miller), ch m ; star, snip, near hind
leg white, off hind coronet white, off fore fetlock white. No. 07.

ANGELA (Capt. F. Egerton Green), blk br m ; faint star, both
hind fetlocks white. No. 0172.

ANGELINA (Mr. J. Adamthwaite), ch m ; star, blaze, snip, near
hind coronet white. No. 094.

ANTELOPE (Mr. H. Fielden), br g ; both hind fetlocks white. No.
0112.

ARAB STAR (Miss A. Gore-Booth), ch g ; star, narrow blaze, small
snip. Passed for season. No. 0378.

AREA BELLE (Colonel de Roebeck), b m ; star, near hind fetlock
white, white marks above off hock, small scar off shoulder. No. 0677.

ARGENTINE (Messrs. H. C. Richards & Leigh), roan g ; small star,
small snip, black spots over ribs and hind quarters, faint brand near fore
quarter. No. 187.

ATOM (Mr. R. Hudson), b g ; star, blaze, snip, grey hairs near side
face, scar off hind quarter. No. 0361.

ATTORNEY, THE (Mr. Grogan), br g ; near hind and off fore
coronets white, collar marks. No. 0452.

"BABETTE" (Mr. A. Withers), b m ; star, snip, near hind and·
both fore fetlocks white. Passed for season. No. 0330.

BADMINTON (Mr. H. Percy Woodcott), b g ; white face, both
hind legs white, near fore fetlock white, collar marks. No. 035.

BALLET (Mr. H. J. D. Clerk), b m ; near hind coronet, off hind
fetlock white. Passed for season. No. 0219.

BALLS (Mr. D. M. Gray), gr h ; snip, scar outside forearm, white
mark near hock. No. 0537.

BANK HOLIDAY (Mr. W. S. Buckmaster), b m ; star, collar
marks. No. 0124.

BANKER (Mr. Edge), b g ; star, white mark on front of off fore
and off hind shin. No. 0453.

BANTAM (The Earl of Harrington), b g ; "H" branded on near
flank, faint star, (broad), both hind and off fetlocks white, black spots, scar
off quarter. No. 0625.

BAROMETER (Mr. R. H. H. Eden), br g ; star, snip, near hind
fetlock white, scars near fore leg. No. 049.

BARONESS (Major Carew), blk br m ; faint star. No. 0101.

BATTLE (Capt. de Lisle), b m ; few white hairs on forehead, faint
grey patch off hind quarter, black points. No. 0627.

BAYLEAF (Messrs. Richards & Leigh), br g; star near hind coronet white, few white hairs front of off fore shin. No. 0188.

BAYLEAF (Mr. A. C. C. Keyon Fuller), b m ; white spot lower lip, near hind fetlock and both fore legs white, white marks above both knees. No. 0258.

BEGGAR'S MAID (Major Alexander), br m ; white face, lower lip white, both hind and off fore legs white. No. 0454.

BELINDA (Major Kennedy), br m ; star, few white hairs on face, snip, both hind fetlocks white, black spots, near fore coronet white. No. 0259.

BELLA (Mr. H. Fielden), b m ; star, white hairs in tail. No. 0114.

BEN AZREK (Mr. Cecil, 8th Hussars), gr h ; white face, lower lip white, near hind and near fore legs white, off hird fetlocks white, white patch on thighs. No. 0489.

BENJAMIN BINNS (Mr. C. McNeill), b g ; star, off hind fetlock black and white, ticked with white hairs. No. 0675.

BERTHA (Mr. J. W. Hornsby), b m ; both hind coronets white. No. 0626.

BESS (Mr. Nettleton). br dun m ; star, collar mark. No. 0297.

BESSIE (Mr. A. E. Fair), blk m ; star, blaze, snip, lower lip white, near hind coronet white, off fore fetlock white with black spots. No. 0300.

BESSIE (Capt. Paynter, 6th Dragoons), blk m ; white hairs both sides of neck. No. 0490.

BESSY (Mr. J. O. Jameson), b m ; star, near hind coronet white. No. 0538.

BETSY (Major Kennedy), br m ; star, near hind fetlock and off hind coronet white with black spots. No. 0260.

BETTY (Mr. R. C. Barton), ch m ; star, narrow blaze, lower lip white. No. 0362.

BIDDY (Mr. R. Hudson), br m ; star, scar front of near hind fetlock. No. 0539.

BILBERRY (Mr. M. E. M. Ballera), br m ; small star, near hind fetlock white, white marks both fore and both hind legs, collar marks. No. 0540.

BILLY (Mr. N. H. Scott), b h ; few white hairs on face, snip, near hind fetlock white, flanks ticked with white hairs. No. 0646.

BILLY BELLEW (Mr. W. S. Buckmaster), b g star, blaze, snip, near hind fetlock white, brand near fore quarter. No. 0291.

BILLY BOY (Lieut.-Colonel D. T. Hammond), b g ; small star, snip, both hind fetlocks white. No. 0379.

BLACKBERRY (Messrs. E. D. & G. A. Miller), blk m ; small star. No. 014.

BLACK LEG (Messrs. E. D. & G. A. Miller), blk g ; star, faint blaze, both hind fetlocks and fore coronet white. No. 015.

BLACKBERRY TART (Mr. Tresham Gilbey), drk br m ; star, black points, small collar marks. No. 0293.

BLANFORD (Mr. H. Percy Woolcott), b m ; star, white spots over face, snip, off hind coronet white, collar marks. No. 033.

BLAZES (Mr. Goodman), ch m , star, blaze, near hind leg white ·with chesnut spots. No. 0678.

BLUEBAGS (Mr. C. C. Goldsmith), gr m ; large snip, lower lip white, near hind leg white, black patch near flank. No. 0220.

BLUEBEARD (Mr. G. K. Ansell), blk g ; star, few white hairs on face, near fore fetlock grey. No. 0541.

BLUESKIN (Polo Club, 8th Hussars), roan g ; star, both hind fetlocks white, brand near hind quarter. No. 0491.

BOBBY (Mr. Hugh Rainey), br g ; near hind fetlock white, off fore fetlock grey. No. 0380.

BONES (Capt. B. Daly), b m ; faint star, small snip, near hind coronet white. No. 0679.

BOOKMAKER (Capt. Vernon), b g ; black points, no distinctive marks. No. 0542.

BOOTS (Mr. G. H. A. White), b g ; star, blaze, snip, white spot upper lip, both hind and near fore fetlocks white, collar marks. No. 0301.

BOUGHTON (Capt. McMicking), b g ; star, bay black legs. No. 0261.

BOY, THE (Mr. T. C. Higgins), b g ; star, blaze, snip, black line down croup, off hind fetlock white. No. 0381.

BRANDON (Mr. W. A. Cooper), gr g , white marks on both fore heels. No. 0382.

BRAT, THE (Mr. Grogan), br m ; small star, small snip. No. 0455.

BRAY (Mr. J. Roark), br m ; star, narrow blaze, snip. No. 0456.

BRILLIANTINE (Messrs. Richards & Leigh), b m ; star, off hind fetlock white, scar off fore arm, collar marks, black patches near ribs. No. 0189.

BRODERICK (Mr. Todds), b g ; small star. Passed for season. No. 0543.

BROWN PRINCE (Mr. H. F. Wickham), blk br g ; ticked with white hairs, collar mark. No. 0680.

BRUNETTE (Capt. C. Grey), blk m ; small white mark outside near fore leg. No. 0262.

BUBBLE (Capt. J. Murray, 14th Hussars), b m ; small scar off hip· No. 0383.

BUCK, THE (Mr. T. R. Denny),blk dun g ; star, small snip, white spot lower lip, all four legs white, brand near hind quarter. No. 0544.

BUCKLE (Messrs. E. D. & G. A. Miller), blk m ; star, small snip, both hind fetlocks white. No. 09.

BUDMARSH (Capt. Langworthy), b g ; star, narrow blaze, lower lip white. No. 0131.

BULLET (Capt. Makins), b m ; star, collar marks. No. 0127.

BUSYBODY (Mr. H. J. D. Clerk), ch m ; star, few white hairs on face, near hind fetlock white, white spot near ribs, ticked white hairs both flanks. Passed for season. No. 0221.

BUTT, THE (Hon. A. Hastings), ch m ; star, blaze, snip, lower lip white, near hind leg white. No. 071.

CALIPH III. (Mr. W. F. Taylor), ch g ; star, blaze, snip, both hind fetlocks and off fore coronet white. No. 0222.

CALM (Mr. J. C. de Las Casas), ch m ; white face, lower lip white, both hind legs white, ticked with white hairs on body. No. 0628.

CARMEW (Mr. C. H. Reade), gr m ; grey legs, white spot near side of neck. No. 0457.

CAROLINE (Mr. A. Withers), b m ; star, near hind coronet white with black spots, off hind coronet white. Passed for season. No. 0331.

CARPENTER, THE (Capt. Wormald), br g ; star, faint snip, near hind fetlock white. No. 0135.

CASTLE RANGER (Mr. H. J. Townsend), b m ; star, off fore and near hind fetlocks white, narrow blaze. No. 030.

CATCH-A-PENNY (Mr. J. Roark), b m ; star. No. 0459.

CERBERUS (Mr. Goodman), b g ; white face, near hind and off fore fetlocks white with black spots, off hind leg white. No. 0681.

CHANCE (Mr. H. C. Talbot Rice), b g ; star, blaze, snip, lower lip white, near fore fetlock and hind coronet white. No. 0223.

CHELMSFORD (Mr. W. Brackenridge), ch g ; star, blaze, snip lower lip white, off fore coronet white, both hind legs white. No. 0667.

CHERRY (Mr. M. E. M. Butler), b m ; star, near fore coronet white, few white hairs front of near shoulder. No. 0545.

CHERRY WHISKEY (Polo Club, 8th Hussars), b g ; star, narrow blaze, snip, off hind fetlock white, brand near hind quarter. No. 0492.

CHIRGWIN (Mr. Meredith), b m ; star, blaze, snip, both hind fetlocks white, white hairs both flanks. No. 0546.

CHRISTOPHER (Capt. F. Egerton Green), b g ; star, near fore and off hind fetlocks white. Passed for season. No. 0668.

CHROME YELLOW (Polo Club, 8th Hussars), ch g ; white face, lower lip white, both hind legs white, near knee white, brand near hind quarter. No. 0493.

CIGARETTE (Sir J. H. P. Hume Campbell), b m ; faint star, collar mark. No. 0166.

CIVILY (R.A. Polo Club), b m ; star, blaze, snip, white mark lower lip, both hind fetlocks white, collar marks. No. 0303.

CLEMENTINE (Mr. J. Adamthwaite), b m ; star, blaze, snip, off hind fetlock white. No. 023.

CLEMENTINE (Mr. Symon), b m ; star, blaze, snip, lower lip white, both hind legs white with black spots, near fore fetlock white with black spots. No. 0302.

CLONDA (Mr. R. H. H. Eden), gr m ; scar off hind quarter, faint marks above knees. No. 043.

CLOVER (Mr. J. H. E. Holford), roan m ; both hind fetlocks white. No. 0116.

COCK OYSTER (Hon. O. Hastings), gr g ; star, snip. No. 069.

COLLEEN (Messrs. Richards & Leigh), b m ; star, blaze, off hind fetlock white, same leg grey, collar marks. No. 0190.

COLWORTH (Capt. Loftus), gr m ; snip, near hind fetlock white, off hind and off fore coronets white. No. 0458.

COMET (Mr. R. H. H. Eden), roan g ; star, blaze, snip, brand both quarters, off hind fetlock and off fore coronet white. No. 047.

COMMODORE (Mr. W. Graham McIvor), flea-bitten grey g ; large white marks, star, blaze, snip, lower lip, white, all four legs white, brand near hind quarter. No. 0610.

CONNOLLY, MISS (Mr. P. W. Connolly), ch m ; star, white patch on off quarter. No. 0536.

CONSTANCE (Mr. J. Richards), br m ; star, ticked with white hairs. Passed for season. No. 0363.

COOMBATTI (Major Longfield), br g ; star, both fore and near hind fetlocks white, brand near hind quarter. No. 0163.

COQUETTE (Mr. P. Leighton), blk m ; near hind fetlock white, scar in front off hind shin. No. 0182.

COQUETTE (Mr. G. Hewson), b m ; star, black spot on face, small collar marks. No. 0432.

CORBHEY (Mr. O'Reilly), b m ; faint star. Passed for season. No. 0682.

CORDITE (Mr. S. M. Russell), gr g ; snip, lower lip white, both hind and near fore fetlocks white. Passed for season. No. 0384.

CREOLE (Mr. R. St. G. Robinson), b m ; white spots on face, near hind coronet grey. No. 0433.

CRESCENT (Capt. de Lisle), br m ; star, snip. No. 03.

DAFFODIL (Capt. F. J. Dalgety), dun m ; star, blaze, snip, off hind fetlock white. No. 0285.

DAIMAN (Major Longfield), piebald g ; brand near hind quarter, Argentine. No. 0162.

DAN (Mr. A. Withers), b g ; off hind fetlock white. No. 0332.

DAUNTLESS (Mr. Malcolm Moncrieffe), ch g ; star, narrow blaze, near hind leg white, off hind and both fore fetlocks white ticked grey hairs, faint brand, white mark near fore quarter. No. 0191

DAWN (Capt. de Lisle), ch m ; star. No. 04.

DAWN (Mr. Malcolm Moncrieffe), gr m ; snip, both lips white, both hind fetlocks white, near fore leg and off fore fetlock white, scar off fore fetlock. No. 0192.

DAWN (Capt. E. Haygate), b m ; star, faint blaze, snip, white spot upper lip. Passed for season. No. 0224.

DAYLIGHT (Mr. James Farmer), ch g ; narrow blaze, lower lip white, off hind leg up to hock white, black spot on off hind quarter. No. 080.

DEERHOUND (Mr. Malcolm Moncrieffe), gr g ; small snip, brand near hind quarter, collar marks. No. 0193.

DELEICE (Capt. Williams), ch m ; star, white spots over muzzle and face, near hind fetlock white with chesnut spots. No. 0583.

DELIGHT (Mr. R. P. O'Reilly), br m ; few white hairs on forehead few white hairs in mane. Passed for season. No. 0364.

DEMON (Mr. J. D. Gouldsmith), blk br m ; star, No. 028.

DESERT KING (Capt. Parsons), br h ; star, scar inside both thighs, off hind fetlock white. No. 0304.

DEXTER (Mr. Malcolm Moncrieffe), b g ; star, few white hairs on face, snip, off hind coronet white, slight brand near fore quarter. No. 0194.

DIADEM (Sir Thomas Fowler), b m ; faint star, near fore coronet white, collar marks. No. 057.

DIAMOND (Mr. W. Hardcastle), blk br h ; snip. No. 0647.

DIAMOND (Mr. A. Withers), b g ; off hind fetlock white. No. 0333.

DIANA (Mr. R. H. H. Eden), b m ; star, narrow blaze, near hind fetlock white. No. 050.

DIANA (Prince Alexander of Teck), blk m ; white spot off flank. No. 0118.

DICK (Mr. Robert Allen), b g ; faint star, white mark above both knees. No. 0263.

DIDO (R.A. Polo Club), b m ; star, blaze, snip, white spot lower lip, near hind fetlock white. No. 0305.

DILKHUSH (Colonel Henrieques), gr m ; star, blaze, both hind legs white, white marks on hind and fore legs. Passed for season. No. 0306.

DIOMED (Mr. W. Campbell), ch g ; star, blaze, snip, both hind legs white, off fore fetlock white. No. 0434.

DIVES (Mr. Malcolm Moncrieffe), b g ; star, both hind legs white, scar front of off fore shin, collar mark, brand rear hind quarter. No. 0225.

DOATIE (Mr. J. E. Dykes), b m ; star, lower lip white, both hind fetlocks and near fore fetlocks white with black spots. No. 0385.

DOCTOR (Mr. O. T. Slocock), br g ; star, off fore and off hind coronet white. No. 0460.

DOLL (Mr. Meredith), br m ; faint star. No. 0547.

DOLLAR, Miss (Mr. Dixon Johnson), b m ; star, off hind fetlock white, ticked with black hairs. No. 0548.

DOLLY (Mr. W. Prevost, 14th Hussars), br m ; star, snip, near fore fetlock white. No. 0494.

DOLPHIN (Mr. Malcolm Moncrieffe), ch g ; star, blaze, snip, white, spot upper lip, off hind leg white, ticked white hairs, brand near fore quarter. No. 0195.

DOMINO (Mr. R. H. H. Eden), skewbald m ; star, tan muzzle. No. 045.

DOMINO (Mr. Malcolm Moncrieffe), gr g ; snip, both lips white, both hind legs and near fore leg white, brand both fore quarters, large scar off fore coronet. No. 0196.

DON, THE (Capt. J. W. Yardley), ch g ; star, near hind coronet and off fore fetlock white. No. 0386.

DONISHALL (Mr. C. H. Reade), b g ; very faint star. No. 0461.

DONISHULL (Messrs. E. D. & G. A. Miller), b g ; near hind coronet white. No. 019.

DONZEA (Mr. J. Lawson), b m ; near hind fetlock white with black spots, white marks off fore leg. No. 0226.

DORCAS (Mr. Malcolm Moncrieffe), gr m ; brand near shoulder. No. 0227.

DOREEN (Mr. T. Anderson), ch m ; star, narrow blaze, snip, both hind legs white. No. 0462.

DOROTHY (Mr. H. Lindemere), b roan m ; star, narrow blaze, snip, lower lip white, both hind fetlocks and off fore fetlock white. No. 0334.

DORRIS (Mr. J. Roarke), br m ; long narrow blaze, small snip, both hind fetlocks white. No. 0463.

DOUBTFUL SPEC. (Mr. A. Kenyon Fuller), b m ; star, near hind and near fore fetlock white, with black spots. No. 0264.

DOVE, THE (Mr. W. Gillman), gr m ; faint snip, near hind coronet and off hind fetlock white. No. 0307.

DOWN (Capt. Hall), ch m ; star, blaze, snip, near hind and both fore legs white, off hind fetlock white, scar off side of neck. No. 0495.

DRAGOON (Mr. Malcolm Moncrieffe), b g ; star, faint snip, white spot lower lip, white mark off fore coronet, brand near fore and near hind quarter, large scar front of chest. No. 0197.

DRIVEN BACK (Mr. James Farmer), br m ; star, narrow blaze, snip, near hind fetlock white. No. 073.

DROGHEDA (Capt. Langworthy), ch m ; star, very faint blaze, white spot near hind quarter, black spots both hind quarters. No. 0133.

DROMORE (Capt. Hall), br m ; star, snip, white hairs on face, both hind fetlocks white, off fore coronet white. No. 0496.

DRUSILLA (Mr. J. Adamthwaite), b m ; black points, no marks. No. 088.

DUMPTY (Capt. J. A. Bell Smyth), blk g ; star, both hind fetlocks white, near fore coronet white, all with black spots. No. 0549.

DUNWATER (Mr. C. H. Rankin), dun m ; star, both hind fetlocks white. No. 0119.

DURANZA (Mr. J. Lawson), br g ; scars on face, brand near hind quarter, white marks both fore legs. No. 0228.

EDITH (Capt. F. Egerton Green), br m ; white marks both fore shins. No. 0141.

EILEEN (Mr. Mort, 8th Hussars), b m ; star, narrow blaze, collar mark. No. 0497.

ELASTIC (Mr. Kenneth Allison), b g ; faint star, near hind and both fore coronets white. No. 0365.

ELECTRIC (Sir Thomas Fowler), ch g ; white tail, white marks on neck. No. 054.

EMERALD (Mr. J. B. Dale), ch m ; star, blaze, snip, near hind fetlock and off hind coronet white. No. 0629.

ENID (Mr. Todds), b m ; small saddle mark, girth mark off side. No. 0550.

ENNISCORTHY (Mr. L. C. Swifte), b g ; star, small snip, scars off stifle and fetlock. No. 0597. Re-named from " Rusty Buckle."

ENNISKILLEN (Mr. A. Withers), b br g ; both fore coronets white, near hind fetlock white. No. 0335.

ERIN (Major Carew), ch m ; star, blaze, snip, both hind fetlocks white, white patch off ribs. No. 0171.

ERRIS (Mr. Erskine Booth), b m ; star, blaze, near hind fetlock and off hind leg white. No. 0387.

ETHEL (Mr. A. Withers), br m ; few white hairs on forehead and face, white spot off forearm. No. 0336.

EVA (Mr. Hugh Rainey), ch m ; star, blaze, snip, near hind and near fore fetlock white. Passed for season. No. 0388.

EXCELSIOR (Mr. J. L. Sandall), br g ; star, narrow blaze and small snip, white spot upper lip, ticked with grey hairs, near hind fetlock white. No. 0389.

FALSE PRIDE (Mr. A. J. Cunnick), b m ; black spot below off stifle, scar front of off fore pastern. Passed for season. No. 0338.

FANATIC (Capt. C. E. G. Morton) b g ; star, narrow, blaze, snip, all four fetlocks white. No. 0106.

FANCY (Mr. Arthur Wrench), ch m ; star, blaze, snip, both hind legs white, off fore fetlock tipped with white hairs. Passed for season, No. 0390.

30

FANCY (Mr. J. W. Nolan), b m ; star, both hind fetlocks white with black spots, collar marks. No. 0684.

FAREWELL (Mr. H. Rich), br m ; white spot near side of ribs. Passed for season. No. 0337.

FARRELL, MISS (Mr. Warden), b m ; star, blaze, snip, both hind and off fore fetlocks white with black spots. No. 0551.

FATIMA (Mr. T. Craddock), gr m ; near hind fetlock white. No. 0391.

FAVOURITE (Mr. Threlfall, 8th Hussars), b g ; white face, lower lip white, black spots upper lip, near hind fetlock and off hind leg white, brand near hind quarter, collar mark. No. 0498.

FAWN, THE (Mr. F. A. Gill), ch m ; star, blaze, snip, both hind fetlocks white. No. 021.

FAWN, THE (Mr. T. Craddock), b m ; white face with bay spots, lower lip white, near hind leg white, white hairs in tail. No. 0392.

FELIX (Mr. J. Adamthwaite), ch m ; star, blaze, near hind coronet white. No. 091.

FERUS (Mr. R. Hague Cook), br g ; star, both hind fetlocks white. No. 0648.

FETLOCK II. (Mr. Rasbotham), ch g ; star, blaze, snip, lower lip and lower jaw white, both hind and near fore legs white, collar marks. No. 0552.

FIGGET (Mr. E. Lloyd), b m ; star, narrow blaze, snip, near fore and near hind fetlocks white with black spots. No. 0292.

FIZZER II. (Mr. Wickham), b h ; star, snip, both hind fetlock and near fore fetlock white with black spots. No. 0553.

FLIRT (Mr. W. B. Hayes), ch m ; star, white hairs down face, near hind fetlock white. Passed for season. No. 0393.

FLIRT (Capt. C. Wilson), ch m ; star, near hind fetlock white. No. 0394.

FLORA (Mr. H. Rainey), blk or drk ch m ; star, blaze, snip, off hind fetlock white. No. 0395.

FLY (Mr. E. Sullivan), br m ; a few white hairs in mane. No. 0397.

FOLLY (Mr. T. O'Meara), b m ; star, narrow blaze, snip, white spot lower lip. No. 0396.

FORBIDDEN FRUIT (Major Rimington), b g ; star, small collar mark. Passed for season. No. 0554.

FRANK (Capt. J. A. Bell Smyth), br m ; star, narrow blaze, off hind fetlock white with black spots, small white spot near shoulder. No. 0555.

FREEDOM (R.A. Polo Club), ch g ; white face, both hind legs white, ticked with white hairs. No. 0308.

FRIAR TUCK (Capt. J. W. Bidgood, R.A.), blk br g ; faint star, near fore fetlock grey. Passed for season. No. 0435.

FROLIC (Mr. J. C. de Las Casas), ch m ; star, small snip, near hind fetlock white, collar marks. No. 0630.

FROLIC (Mr. J. F. Church), ch m ; white face, both hind legs and off fore fetlock white. No. 0611.

FULL STOP (Capt. F. Egerton Green), b m ; white face, lower lip white, both hind legs white.

GAIETY (Mr. W. K. Carew), br m ; star, blaze, snip, lower lip white. Passed for season. No. 0436.

GALLOP ON (Major R. T. Lawley), b g ; star. No. 097.

GAME BOY (Mr. W. K. Carew), b g ; star, narrow blaze, snip, ticked with white hairs, near hind fetlock white. Passed for season. No. 0437.

GAME CHICKEN (The Keyasham Stud Company), ch g ; star, white hairs down face, white spot off hind quarter, and off fore quarter, and near hind quarter. No. 0398.

GAMMON (Mr. A. G. Dalgety), b g ; bay, black points, no distinguishing marks. No. 0649.

GAY LADY (Mr. T. O'Brien), b m ; star, narrow blaze, snip, both hind fetlocks white. Passed for season. No. 0399.

GAY MAN (Messrs. Richards and Leigh), b g ; star, faint white mark off hind coronet, black patch off shoulder, scar near ribs. No. 10198.

GEM (Mr. C. Adamthwaite), b m ; star, faint black mark down croup. No. 0229.

GENTLE IDA (Mr. Ballactus), b m ; scar near side of neck. No. 0556.

GIPSEY (Mr. F. T. Colgan), gr m ; small snip, white spots lower lip. No. 0465.

GIPSY LEE (The Polo Club, 14th Hussars), b m ; star, narrow blaze, both hind fetlocks white. No. 0500.

GIPSY MAIDEN (Elmsall Ludwich Stud, Hatfield), blk m ; white mark near hip, both flanks ticked white, white marks both fore legs. No. 0199.

GIRTON GIRL (Capt. Oldnall), b m ; star, narrow blaze, both hind coronets white, scar off side of neck. No. 0309.

GLADYS (Sir Henry Rawlinson),b m ; star,near hind fetlock white, white spots off hind and near fore leg. No. 0176

GLORY QUALE (Mr. N. F. Archdale), b m ; star, near hind fetlock and off hind coronet white. Passed for season. No. 0464.

GOAT, THE (Mr. A. Bellville), b g ; star, blaze, snip, lower lip white, both hind and off fore legs white. No. 0296.

GOBANG (Mr. J. Windart), b m ; small star, near hind coronet white, collar marks, white marks both fore legs. No. 0339.

GO BETWEEN (Mr. R. P. O'Reilly), br g ; faint star. No. 0366.

30*

GOLDEN GATE (Lord Villiers), b m ; white mark front of near hind shin, scar above off knee. No.0230.

GOLDING, MRS. (Mr. W. R. Wyndham), gr m ; star, lower lip white. No. 0265.

GOODSPECK (Mr. James Farmer), b m ; white coronet near hind, collar marks. No. 079.

GRAPE SHOT (Capt. J. W. Bidgood), br m ; star, off hind coronet white. No. 0437.

GREEDY BOY (Mr. G. K. Ansell), gr g ; white mark inside both knees and in front of off hind shin, scar off nostril. No. 0557.

GREEN SLEEVES (Mr. J. Lawson), br m ; star, faint snip, near hind fetlock white, with small black spots, scars on all four legs. No. 0231.

GREY FRIAR (Mr. James Farmer), gr g ; snip, near fore coronet white. No. 085.

GREY FRIAR (Mr. T. Hudson), gr g ; star, blaze, snip, both hind fetlocks white, off fore coronet white. No. 0466.

GREY GOWN (Mr. J. Lawson), gr g ; star, blaze, snip, lower lip white, off ear split, scar above near knee, brand near hind quarter. No. 0232.

GREY LEG (Major D. E. Wood, 8th Hussars), gr g ; both hind coronets white, collar marks, brand near hind quarter. No. 0499.

GREY LEG (Capt. Campbell Johnstone), gr g ; blaze, snip, white spot lower lip, collar marks. No. 0310.

GREYLING III. (Mr. M. E. M. Butler), iron gr m ; black points, no distinctive marks. No. 0558.

GREY PRINCE (Mr. James Farmer), gr g ; near hind fetlock white. No. 084.

GUINEVERE (Mr. G. Heseltine), drk b m ; faint star, small scar off stifle. No. 0287.

HALLELUJAH (Mr. P. R. Denny), gr g ; near hind fetlock white. No. 0559.

HEIRESS (Messrs. E. D. & G. A. Miller), b roan m ; star, blaze, snip, near hind leg white, white marks both hind quarters. No. 017.

HEMIS (Mr James Adamthwaite), b m ; off hind fetlock white. No. 093.

HERMIT (Sir Thomas Fowler), gr g ; white face, off hind and near fore coronets white. No. 059.

HERON (Mr. James Adamthwaite), b g ; star off cheek. No. 090.

HIS NIBS (Mr. W. S. Buckmaster), br g ; star, both hind fetlocks white with black spots, brand near fore quarter. No. 0290.

HIRUNDO (Capt. Vernon), drk br g ; star, blaze, snip, lower lip white, both hind and near fore legs white, brand near hind quarter. No. 0560.

HOMECIA (Mr. James Farmer), b m ; both hind fetlocks white, white marks inside both hind quarters. No. 078.

HOUSEMAID (Mr. J. D. Gouldsmith), b m ; star near hind leg. No. 026.

HOVE (Capt. Grey), b m ; star, blaze, scar inside near fore coronet. No. 0266.

HOVIS (Major E. D. Kennedy), br g ;large collar mark on off side. No. 0621.

HUNTING HORN (Mr. Brennan), ch g ; star, narrow blaze, snip, all four legs white. Passed for season. No. 0467.

HUNT THE SLIPPER (Mr. Percy Bullivant), b m ; star, off hind fetlock white, off fore fetlock grey. No. 0173.

HURRIED SHEET (Major Douglas Haig), gr g ; star, brand near hind quarter. No. 0103.

HUSHEEN (Mr. Charles B. Toms), ch m; star, blaze, snip, lower lip white, off hind leg white. No. 0130.

IN AND OUT (Capt. L. Bryan), b m ; star, lower lip white, all four fetlocks white. Passed for season. No. 0561.

INQUISITIVE (Messrs. E. D. & G. A. Miller), b m ; off hind coronet white. No. 016.

IRISH GIRL (Messrs. E. D. & G. A. Miller), b m ; white spot near side of ribs. No. 018.

IT (Earl of Harrington), ch m ; star, narrow blaze, small snip, off hind fetlock white, near fore coronet white with spots. No. 0631.

IZAVE (Mr. E. Ballesty), ch g ; star, narrow blaze. No. 0367.

JACK (Capt. B. Daley), b g ; star, white hairs top of wither. No. 0562.

JACK, MRS. (Capt. C. G. Mackenzie), ch m ; star, narrow blaze, snip, near hind fetlock white, off fore fetlock white, faint brand off fore quarter. No. 0311.

JACKO (Mr. Hugh Rainey), gr g ; snip, lower lip white, both hind legs white, collar marks. No. 0400.

JACK TAR (Mr. Wylam, 8th Hussars), br g ; snip, near hind fetlock white, brand near hind quarter. No. 0501.

JAMES (Mr. H. J. D. Clerk), drk br g ; star, snip, near hind fetlock white, small scar near hind quarter. No. 0233.

JANE (Mr. A. Withers), b m ; small star, collar mark. No. 0340.

JEDDAH (Capt. Mussenden), b g ; star, small snip, off hind and near fore fetlocks white, brand near hind quarter. No. 0502.

JILL (R.A. Polo Club), gr m ; scar in front of hind shin. No. 0312.

JIM (Major L. Haywood, R.A.M.C.), b g ; star, narrow blaze, snip, off hind fetlock white. No. 0368.

JIMMY (Mr. C. C. Goldsmith), b h ; star, snip, upper lip white, near fore and both hind fetlocks white, off fore coronet white, and collar marks. No. 0234.

JINNET (Mr. John Carpenter), ch m ; star, narrow blaze, snip, off hind fetlock white, white patch near hip. No. 0401.

JOAN OF ARC (Mr. Robinson), b m ; star, blaze, snip, off hind fetlock white, white mark front of near hock. Passed for season. No. 0563.

JOHN BROWN (Mr. James Farmer), b g ; small scar on front of near hind fetlock. No. 075.

" J.P." (Capt. C. G. Mackenzie), skewbald g ; white face and chin, all four legs white. No. 0313.

JUGGINS (Mr. Wainwright), ch g ; star, blaze, snip, lower lip white, scar outside near knee. No. 0314.

KATHLEEN (Mr. C. E. Hunter), b br m ; star, collar marks. No. 0632.

KEEPSAKE (Major Longfield), b m ; faint star. No. 0165.

" K. H." (Hon. C. G. Gore Langton), gr g ; brand near fore shoulder. No. 0564.

KHALID (London Polo Club), gr h ; scar near knee, flea-bitten all over body. No. 0122.

KHALIFA (Mr. Cecil, 8th Hussars), gr m ; white mark above off hock. No. 0503.

KHEDIVE, THE (Mr. J. Roark), ch g ; star, blaze, snip, lower lip white, near fore coronet and off hind fetlock white. No. 0468.

KILGIBBON (Capt. L. Bryan), b g ; star, white hairs off side of wither. No. 0565.

KILLACOOLEY (Capt. L. Bryan), b g ; star, off hind fetlock white, white spots on coronet. No. 0566.

KITTEN, THE (Mr. J. Adamthwaite), b m ; white mark on front of near fore fetlock, white mark on neck. No. 092.

KITTY (Mr. John Nettleton), b m ; large snip, narrow blaze, star, black points, no marks. No. 0148.

KITTY (Mr. O'Brien, 8th Hussars), br m ; star, near hind fetlock white, white mark on croup. Passed for season. No. 0504.

KITTYWYNK (Mr. Charles B. Toms), b m ; star, scar off hip. No. 0139.

KLONDIKE (Mr. Eyre Lloyd), b m ; star, black points, no distinctive marks. No. 0633.

KODAK (Capt. Hall), br m ; black points, no distinctive marks. No. 0505.

LADY (Mr. A. E. Fair), b m ; star, blaze, snip, lower lip white, both hind and near fore legs white, off fore fetlock white. No. 0315.

LADY (Mr. G. F. Richardson), ch m ; star, narrow blaze, both hind legs white. No. 0402.

LADY, THE (Mr. James Farmer), blk m ; small white spot point of near shoulder. No. 097.

LADY BIRD (Mr. James Farmer), b m ; snip, near hind coronet white. No. 081.

LADYE (Mr. W. Graham McIvor), ch m ; star, blaze, white spot lower lip, off hind leg and near fore coronet white, white-and-black patch near hind quarter. No. 0612.

LADY GEORGINA (Colonel Dooley), br m ; star, blaze, snip, lower lip white, both hind fetlocks white, ticked with grey hairs. Passed for season. No. 0568.

LADY GIRTON (Capt. Mackenzie), b m ; small star. No. 0328.

LADY GODIVA (Mr. Pando Kirk), dun ch m ; star, blaze, snip. No. 0403.

LADY KISSER (Major Duff, 8th Hussars), br m ; collar mark. No. 0506.

LADY LOVE (Mr. F. E. Sanford Pakenham), b m ; collar marks. No. 0439.

LADY OF QUALITY (Mr. Percy Bullivant), br m ; faint star. Passed for season. No. 0174.

LADY PAT (Mr. T. Moore), b m ; star, both hind fetlocks white, white hairs mane and tail. No. 0569.

LADY PERRY (Capt. L. Bryan), b m ; small scar off side of jaw. No. 0570.

LADY SOPHIA (Mr. T. D. Pilkington), br m ; lightly ticked with white hairs over body, collar marks. No. 0184.

LADY UXBRIDGE (Major Carew), drk br m ; star, few white hairs on forehead, off hind fetlock white. No. 0169.

LADY VIC II. (Lieut.-Colonel G. F. Dooley), b m ; star, snip. No. 0369.

LAMBKIN (Mr. A. Withers), b g ; star, blaze, snip, lower lip white, all four fetlocks white with black spots. No. 0360.

LANDLADY (Mr. James Farmer), b m ; star, narrow blaze, snip, both hind fetlocks white. No. 083.

LANGRISHE (Major Rimington), blk br g ; white spots off ribs. No. 0567.

LAURA (Mr. John Nettleton), drk br m ; faint star, faint snip, both fore fetlocks white. No. 0155.

LEAH (Mr. W. Neilson), br m ; white spot near shoulder. No. 0235.

LEAVE IT TO ME (Mr. H. S. A. Sandford), ch m ; star, blaze, snip, white marks on both fore shins. No. 068.

LEN (Mr. J. J. Stafford), b m ; star, both hind coronets white, ticked with grey hairs, collar marks. No. 0404.

LILAC (Mr. C. E. Amphlett, 6th Dragoons), dun m ; black stripe down back and tail. No. 0507.

LILLIE (Mr. John Nettleton), br m ; large star, near fore coronet white. No. 0153.

LILLOUTH (Mr. A. Suart), ch m ; star, narrow blaze, near hind fetlock white. No. 0634.

LIMA (Mr. A. F. Houlder), b g ; star, white mark lower part of face, near hind fetlock white with black spots, brand near hind quarter. No. 0341.

LIMELIGHT (Mr. Hargreaves), br g ; star. No. 0236.

LIMERICK (Mr. A. Withers), ch g ; star, white hairs on face, both hind fetlocks white. No. 0342.

LIMITED MAIL (Major Rimington), b g ; star, narrow blaze, both hind fetlocks white, collar marks. No. 0571.

LITTLE TOM (Miss Langrishe), b g ; both hind coronets white. Passed for season. No. 0405.

LIVELY(Mr. T. W. Connolly), b m ; faint black mark down croup, black points. No. 0440.

LONDONDERRY (Mr. G. K. Ansell), b m ; black spots on face, few white hairs on tail. No. 0572.

LUCKY (Mr. H. W. Turner), b m ; large scar on face. No. 0343.

LUDLOW LAD (Messrs. Richards & Leigh), b g ; star, near hind fetlock white, white mark back of both fore legs. No. 0200.

MACKBRIGS (Capt. R. Ellison), ch g ; white face, lower lip white, near fore and both hind legs white, off fore fetlock white, white marks over body. No. 0161.

MACKINSTRY (Mr. J. Lawson), br m ; near hind fetlock grey, scar front off hock, white collar marks, off ear split. No. 0237.

MADCAP (Capt. H. Greathed), b m ; star, black points, black line down croup, small collar mark. No. 0650.

MADGE (Mr. John Nettleton), b m ; white face, lower lip white, all four legs white. No. 0149.

MADGE (Mr. H. T. C. Parker), b m ; star, both hind fetlocks white. No. 0573.

MAGGIE (Mr. W. M. Cobbett), mottled br m ; star, white spot near hind leg. No. 0651.

MAGIC (Mr. John Nettleton), br g ; near fore and both hind legs white, brand near hind quarter, off hind fetlock white. No. 0151.

MAGIC (Capt. H. Greathed), b m : star, few white hairs on face, off hind fetlock white, off fore fetlock grey and white, white spots off hind quarter. No. 0652.

MAGPIE (Mr. J. Roark), br m; star, snip, lower lip white, off fore coronet white. No. 0469.

MAHDI (Capt. Sir Keith Fraser), white h; scar off hind quarter. No. 0111.

MAIA (Capt. Bell Smyth), ch m; near fore coronet white with chestnut spots, black patches off hind quarter. No. 0685.

MAIDEN OVER (Mr. W. P. Monkhouse, R.H.A.), b m; star, blaze, snip, near hind fetlock white, scar off shoulder. No. 0508.

MALTESE CAT (Mr. F. H. Wise), b m; star, near hind fetlock white with black spots. No. 0574.

MAINSPRING (Mr. C. McNeill), br m; star, white spots near shoulder. No. 0238.

MANIFESTO (Mr. Leonard Bucknall), b g; star, narrow blaze, large snip, lower lip white, near hind coronet, near fore and off hind legs white. No. 0156.

MAPLE SUGAR (Mr. J. Lawson), ch m; star, off hind fetlock white, off fore coronet white, collar marks. No. 0239.

MARCHIONESS (Capt. Brooke), b m; faint star, off hind fetlock white, collar marks. No. 0575.

MARGUERITE (Mr. Lomer, 8th Hussars), dun m; star, narrow blaze, snip, both hind coronets white, white hairs in mane. No. 0509.

MARION (Lieut.-Col. Sir H. Johnson), drk br m; faint star, faint snip. No. 0576.

MARQUIS (Mr. A. Withers), br g; near hind fetlock white. No. 0344.

MARY (Mr. Denny), ch m; star, blaze, snip, scar off side of neck. No. 0577.

MARY (7th Hussars' Polo Club), br m; near hind fetlock white. No. 0121.

MARY, MISS (Mr. R. G. Tarbett), br m; star, snip, both hind fetlocks white. No. 0408.

MARY MEATH (Major Honner), b m; star, near hind coronet white, black spot off fore quarter. No. 0406.

MASTERPIECE (Mr. H. S. A. Sanford), b g; star, blaze, snip, all four fetlocks white. No. 067.

MATCHLESS (Mr. W. B. Hayes), br m; star, off hind fetlock and near coronet white with black spots. No. 0407.

MAY (Capt. Brooke), drk br m; scar both sides of brisket. No. 0578.

MAY MORN (Major Rimington), drk br m; star, near hind fetlock white with black spots, near fore coronet white. No. 0579.

MAY QUEEN (Capt. Bonham), b m; near hind leg grey on outside, small white marks both fore legs. No. 0267.

MEDDLAR (Mr. Digby C. Martin), b g; black, bay points, saddle marks. No. 062.

MEDIUM (Mr. A. Withers), b br m ; faint star, off hind fetlock white with black spots. No. 0345.

MELLON (Mr. Digby C. Martin), b m ; star, narrow blaze, snip, black points, saddle marks. No. 065.

MERMAID (Mr. A. Withers), b m ; star, near hind coronet white, brand near hind quarter. No. 0346.

MERRIMAC (Capt. de Lisle),br g ; star,scar inside off fore coronet. No. 0268.

MERRY ANDREW (Mr. J. Adamthwaite), blk g ; star, both hind fetlocks white. No. 089.

MERRY GIRL (Capt. Bell Smyth), b m ; star, narrow blaze, both hind fetlocks white with black spots, off fore coronet white with black spots. No. 0686.

MERRY MAID (Mr. A. J. Pilkington), b m ; black points, few grey hairs in mane. No. 0370.

MERRY THORN (Capt. J. W. Bidgood, R. A.), ch g ; star, blaze, snip, upper lip white, near hind fetlock white. No. 0441.

MICKIE FREE (Hon. O. Hastings), b g ; small scar on front of shin off hind leg. No. 070.

MICKIE FREE (Mr. A. Withers), b m ; star, short blaze, near hind coronet white. No. 0347.

MIKE (Mr. H. Straker), ch g ; star, blaze, snip, lower lip white, both hind legs and near fore fetlock white, collar mark, brand near fore and near hind quarter. No. 0654.

MIKE (Mr. R. Bourke), ch g ; star, blaze, small snip, black patches near hind quarter. No. 0655.

MILKYWAY (Capt. Makins), gr m ; white face, lower lip white, both fore fetlocks white. No. 0126.

MILLIE SIMPSON (Mr. A. Kenyon Fuller), ch m ; star, white marks front of near hind leg and front of off fore fetlock. No. 0269.

MILLY (Capt. B. Daley), ch m ; star, blaze, snip, white hairs outside of off hock, scar off side neck. No. 0580.

MINNOW (Mr. H. Percy Woolcott), b g ; star, narrow blaze, near hind fetlock white, off fore fetlock grey. No. 034.

MINX (Mr. R. F. Courage), br m ; small white spots back of both fore legs. No. 0669.

MISCHIEF (Capt. H. Greathed), gr m ; star, white spots upper lip. No. 0653.

MISFIT (Mr. John Hetherington), b br m ; few white hairs on forehead, both hind fetlocks white with black spots. No. 0348.

MISS LUSK (Mr. W. Lindsay), ch m ; star, blaze, snip, lower lip white, near fore leg white, ticked with white hairs. No. 0606.

MISS ROSE (Mr. Burke), b m ; both hind fetlocks and near fore coronet white. No. 0581.

MYSTERY (Mr. Turbetts), b m ; white spot near side of ribs, collar marks. No. 0582.

MODESTY (Mr. Swift), b m ; white spots front of off fore shin. No. 0583.

MOLLY (Polo Club, 8th Hussars), blk m ; star, both hind fetlocks white, ticked with white hairs. No. 0510.

MONA (Mr. J. Adamthwaite), b m ; black points, saddle marks. No. 095.

MONA (Earl of Leitrim), br m ; white muzzle, white eye-lids, scar front of chest. No. 0409.

MONK, THE (Mr. W. M. Cobbett), b g ; faint star, brown patch off hind quarter, scar off shoulder. No. 0656.

MONKEY (Capt. C. Grey), roan g ; star, faint black mark down croup. No. 0270.

MOONSTONE (Mr. R. St. G. Robinson), br g ; black points, no distinctive marks. No. 0442.

MOSES (Mr. A. A. Montgomery), b br g ; scar front of off hind shin. No. 0316.

MOSQUITO (Mr. A. Findlater), b m ; star, brand near side of neck, black line down croup. No. 0349.

MOSS ROSE (Mr. Digby C. Martin), b m ; star, near hind coronet white. No. 064.

MOUNTEBANK (Mr. H. R. Fairfax Lucy), blk m ; faint star, both hind coronets white. No. 0134.

MOUSE, THE (Capt. H. B. Dalgety), br m ; star, near hind coronet white. No. 0108.

MUFFIN (Mr. W. Graham McIvor), piebald g ; black spots on muzzle, brand near hind quarter. No. 0613.

MULATTO (Mr. W. S. Buckmaster), b m ; faint star. No. 0670.

MULBERRY (Mr. Digby C. Martin), b m ; small star, scar on forehead, white collar mark. No. 066.

MUSCAT (Mr. W. George Mawer), b g ; star, blaze, snip, lower lip white, off hind fetlock white with black spots, collar marks. No. 0185.

MUSKET (Mr. T. D. Pilkington), gr g ; snip, off hind fetlock and near fore fetlock white, scar near side of neck. No. 0183.

MYRTLE (Mr. Digby C. Martin), b m ; star, near hind and off fore fetlocks white. No. 063.

MYSTERY (Mr. D. T. Slocock), b m ; black points, no distinctive marks. No. 0470.

NAAS (Mr. C. de Robeck), b br m : star, few white hairs on face. No. 0584.

NANCY (Major R. T. Lawley), br m ; small scar on face. No. 098.

NARCISSA (Mr. W. Lindsay), b m ; small white spot off shoulder. No. 0585.

NEBULA (Earl of Shrewsbury and Talbot),ch m ; star, off hind fetlock and off fore coronet white. No. 0240.

NEGOTIATOR (Mr. J. Murphy), b g; star, snip, white hairs on face, both hind fetlocks white. No. 0586.

NELLIE (Mr. John Nettleton), ch m ; star, scar on both knees. No. 0147.

NELLY (Mr. J. T. Wigan), b m ; faint star, small scar near stifle, small white spot near side of neck. No. 0614.

NEWBRIDGE (Mr. Tilney, 14th Hussars), gr g ; both hind fetlocks white, brand near fore and near hind quarter. No. 0511.

NIGHT EXPRESS (Mr. G. K. Ansell), drk br m ; faint star, near hind fetlock white with black spots, off hind coronet white. No. 0587.

NILE (Major Bainbridge), b m ; large star, narrow blaze, snip, both hind fetlocks white, black spots near hind fetlock, collar marks, white spot off side jaw. No. 0180.

NIPON (Mr. H. Percy Woolcot), b g; star, off hind coronet white. No. 036.

NIPPER (Capt. R. Ellison), b g ; star, snip, near hind fetlock white, both sides of wither branded. No. 0167.

NITA (Mr. F. St. Lawrence Tyrrell), blk br m ; star. No. 0443.

NOISETTE (Mr. W. F. Taylor), b m ; faint star, large scar near side of chest. No. 0241.

NOISETTE (Mr. R. St. G. Robinson), ch m ; star, blaze, snip near fore fetlock white, off hind coronet white, all with chestnut spots. No. 0444.

NORA (Mr. Stewart Dackett), b m ; faint star, faint snip, near hind fetlock white. Passed for season. No. 0471.

NORAH (Mr. A. Withers), ch m ; white hair on forehead, scars on face, black spots both hind quarters, collar marks. No. 0350.

NOVELTY (Mr. Swift), drk br m ; star, off hind fetlocks white with black spots, collar mark. No. 0588.

NUGGET (Capt. the Hon. J.Beresford), ch g ; star, blaze, snip, star behind near shoulder, collar mark. No. 0105.

NUN, THE (Mr. J. L. Lamont), b m ; star, faint blaze, small white marks near hind leg. No. 0317.

ORDERLY (Mr. J. Lawson), br m ; star, blaze, snip, white chin, both hind legs and near fore fetlock white, collar marks. No. 0242.

OZONE (Mr. Nettleton), b m ; star, near hind fetlock white with black spots. No. 0298.

PAINT BRUSH (Capt. J. Hanwell), grey g ; narrow blaze, small snip, both fore fetlocks white with black spots, off hind fetlock white. No. 0186.

PALEFACE (Capt. Langworthy), roan g ; white face, lower jaw white, both hind legs white, white marks both knees. No. 0132.

PALEFACE (Polo Club, 8th Hussars), b g ; white face, lower lip white, all four fetlocks white, brand near fore and near hind quarter. No. 0512.

PANCHITTA (Mr. A. Bellville), b m ; star, narrow blaze, small snip, near hind fetlock white. No. 0289.

PANTS (Mr. W. Lindsay), ch g ; star, blaze, near hind and near fore fetlock white, off fore coronet white. No. 0589.

PARMA VIOLET (Capt. F. Egerton Green), br m ; star, snip. No. 0143.

PARMA VIOLET (Capt. Williams), b g ; faint black mark down croup, white hairs top of wither. No. 0590.

PATCH (Lord W. Bentinck), b g ; star, both hind fetlocks white, white patch near flank. No. 0615.

PATCH WORK (Mr. R. H. H. Eden), skewbald m ; star, blaze, snip, lower lip white, small scar outside near hock. No. 046.

PATIENCE (Polo Club, 8th Hussars), drk br m ; star, narrow blaze, both hind fetlocks and off fore coronet white. Nc. 0513.

PATRICIA (Mr. F. H. Wise), ch m ; star, blaze, snip, both hind legs white, scar near hind shin, ticked with white hairs. No. 0591.

PAVYMAID (Messrs. Richards & Leigh), ch m ; few white hairs on forehead, near fore and off hind legs white with chestnut spots. Passed for season. No. 0201.

PEARL (Capt. F. D. Hickman), gr m ; small white spot lower lip, both hind fetlocks white. Passed for season. No. 0446.

PEARL (Mr. W. Hardcastle), br m ; star, narrow blaze, snip, near fore coronet white, near hind coronet white with black spots. No. 0657.

PEARL, THE (Mr. Guy Gilbey), b m ; both hind fetlocks white with black spots. No. 0635.

PEARLEY (Lord Villiers), ch m ; star, large snip. No. 0243.

PEGGY BAKER (Major Rimington), b m ; star, white spot off ribs. No. 0592.

PEPITA (Capt. Clifton Brown), b m ; few white hairs on forehead, near hind fetlock white, white spots both fore and near hind legs. No. 0616.

PET, THE (Capt. The Hon. J. Beresford), ch m ; star, blaze, snip, both hind fetlocks white, white spots all over body. No. 0104.

PETER (Mr. J. S. Bakewell), gr g ; snip, white spot on muzzle, black spots on face, collar marks. No. 0244.

PHEASANT, THE (Major E. D. Kennedy), b m ; near hind coronet white. No. 0622.

PHIL (Mr. C. E. Hunter), ch g ; star, silver mane, few white hairs in tail. No. 0636.

PHILLIPINE (Mr. J. Hetherington), b m ; off hind coronet white, faint black line down croup. No. 0351.

PHOSPHORUS (Sir Thomas Fowler), b m ; black marks, white mark near hind shin. No. 056.

PICKAXE (Polo Club, 8th Hussars), b g ; white face, lower lip white, both hind legs white, off fore fetlock and near fore coronet white, brand near quarter. No. 0514.

PIG, THE (Capt. Sir K. Fraser), b m ; faint star, near hind coronet white. No. 0110.

PINKIE (Mr. T. R. Denny), white g ; black spots on body, pink muzzle, brand near hind quarter. No. 0593.

PINTO (Mr. J. Lawson), br m ; white face and lower lip, large white patch both flanks, scar front of both hind legs, white marks both fore legs. No. 0245.

PIRATE (Mr. T. Anderson), gr g ; narrow blaze, snip, both hind and near fore fetlocks white. No. 0472.

PLUM DUFF (Mr. W. B. Hayes), b g ; black points, no distinctive marks. No. 0410.

POLLY (Mr. J. C. Nolan). dk b m ; star, white mark upper lip, few white hairs in tail. No. 0411.

POLLY IV. (Mr. Wate), br m ; star, collar mark. No. 0594.

POLLUX (Polo Club, 8th Hussars), roan g ; white face, lower lip white, both fore and off hind legs white, white patches both flanks, brand near hind quarter. No. 0515.

POST GIRL (Messrs. Richards & Leigh), b m ; star, few white hairs on face, snip, white spot upper lip, near hind fetlock white. No. 0202.

POTEEN (Mr. Erskine Booth), b m ; star, near hind fetlock and off hind coronet white, both hind legs grey. No. 0412.

PRECILLA (Capt. de Lisle), br m ; star, near hind fetlock white. No. 06.

PRETENDER (Mr. de Las Casas), ch g ; white face, near hind legs white, white spot near hip. No. 0637.

PRINCE (Mr. R. Brown), ch g ; star, near hind fetlock white, off fore coronet white, ticked with white hairs both flanks, white spots off hind quarter, and black spot on croup. No. 0445.

PROFESSOR (Mr. B. A. Wilson), b g ; faint star, ticked with white over hind quarter, small black spot near side of back. No. 0286.

PRUSILLA (Messrs. Richards & Leigh), b m ; scar near flank. No. 0203.

PTARMIGAN (Capt. Makins), gr m ; scar off side of face. No. 0125.

PUCK (Capt. de Lisle), b g ; star, blaze, snip, lower lip white, both hind fetlocks white, both fore coronets white. No. 01.

QUEEN (Mr. Robert N. Allen), b m ; star, both hind fetlocks white with black spots. Passed for season. No. 0271.

QUEENIE (Mr. John Nettleton), b m ; star, narrow blaze, snip, near hind fetlock white. No. 0152.

QUEEN OF THE CASTLE (Mr. Farmer), ch m ; star, narrow blaze, small white mark near hind coronet. No. 096.

QUHARRIE (Mr. N. F. Archdale), br g ; near fore coronet white with black spots. No. 0473.

QUICKSILVER (Mr. G. P. Sechiary), b m ; black points, no distinguishing marks. No. 0352.

QUIEN SABE (Capt. B Daley), ch m ; star, small scar near hind quarter. No. 0687.

RACHAEL (Mr. R. H. H. Eden), blk m ; black points, small saddle marks. No. 044.

RAINBOW (Capt. C. E. G. Martin), b g ; star, both hind coronets white, brand near shoulder. No. 0107.

RAINBOW (Capt. de Lisle), b g ; star, snip. No. 0272.

RAJAH (Sir Thomas Fowler), blk g ; star, both hind fetlocks white. No. 058.

RANDINO (The Hon. A. Hastings), ch h ; star, white mark on off fore shin. No. 072.

RATCATCHER (Capt. G. Wynne), br m ; star, white line on face, snip, ticked with white hairs, off hind leg and off fore fetlock white. No. 0447.

READE, MISS (Mr. C. H. Reade), b m ; black points, no distinctive marks. Passed for season. No. 0623.

RECKLESS (Capt. de Lisle), gr m ; star, off hind fetlock white. No. 05.

REDFIELD (Major Honner Brannontoun), b g ; star. No. 0516.

RED LANCER (Mr. Montgomery), ch g ; star, blaze, snip, lower lip white, off fore and both hind legs white. Passed for season. No. 0318.

REDSKIN (Polo Club, 8th Hussars), roan g ; star, both hind and near fore fetlocks white, brand near hind quarter. No. 0517.

REDWING (Mr. H. Fielden), ch m ; narrow blaze, white marks both fore legs. No. 0113.

REGULICI (Capt. de Lisle), ch m ; star, blaze, near fore and near hind fetlocks white. No. 02.

REJECTED (Mr. J. D. Gouldsmith), b m ; star, snip, both hind fetlocks white, collar marks. No. 027.

REVELATION (Sir Thomas Fowler), gr m ; star, off hind coronet white. No. 061.

REVOLUTION (Mr. W. E. Grogan), ch g ; star, blaze, snip, both hind fetlocks white. No. 0688.

RINGLET (Capt. Vernon), ch m ; star, small snip, lower lip white, near hind fetlock white, scar front of off hind shin. No. 0595.

RODELIA (Mr. G. M. Harris), roan m ; bay face. Passed for season. No. 0413.

ROSE (Mr. John Nettleton), b m ; star, off fore fetlock white. No. 0154.

ROSEIAS (Mr. H. Fielden), b g ; star, narrow blaze, near hind fetlock white. No. 0115.

ROSEMARY (Messrs. E. D. & G. A. Miller), br m. No. 013.

ROSETTE (Mr. G. B. Game), b m ; hind quarter ticked white hairs, scar off side of ribs. No. 0353.

ROSETTE (Capt. C. S. Coghill), roan m ; star, near hind fetlock white. No. 0319.

ROSS-DROIT (Mr. J. H. Locke), b g ; near fore fetlock grey and white. No. 0414.

ROULETTE (Mr. F. W. Perry), b m ; near and off eyelids white, off nostril white, near hind fetlock white with black spots, small collar mark. No. 0689.

ROUSE (Capt. H. McMicking), dun m ; star, blaze, lower lip white, dark brown line from wither to tail. No. 0273.

RUBY (Mr. R. H. H. Eden), ch m ; star, blaze, snip, lower lip white, off hind and near fore fetlock and coronet white, scar on neck. No. 048.

RUBY (Mr. E. H. Pease), br m ; faint star, black points, white mark near hind quarter. No. 0658.

RUBY (Mr. E. C. Holland, 6th Dragoons), b m ; star, near fore coronet white. No. 0518.

RUBY (Major Milton), b m ; small star, small snip, off hind fetlock grey, collar mark. No. 0596.

RUFUS (Mr. H. A. Bellville), ch g ; star, narrow blaze, faint snip, near hind fetlock white. No. 0246.

RUPHIS (Mr. J. O. Jameson), ch g; star, near hind coronet white. No. 0690.

SABANITA (Messrs. Richards & Leigh), drk b m ; star, white spots off coronet. No. 0204.

SAINT (Mr. W. Hardcastle), blk br h ; faint star, near fore and hind coronet white. No. 0659.

SALOPIA (Mr. P. Leighton), ch m ; few white hairs on lower jaw. No. 0146.

SAMMY (Capt. F. Egerton Green), ch g ; star, blaze, snip, lower lip white, near hind fetlock white, white mark off ribs. No. 0140.

SAMMY (Mr. A. H. McClintock), gr g ; large white patch off ribs. No. 0415.

SAMSON (Mr. J. Adamthwaite), b g ; star. No. 025.

SANDY (Major R. T. Lawley), b h ; white spots all over body. No. 0100.

SANDY (Mr. de Las Casas), ch g ; star, blaze, snip, upper lip white, white spots on muzzle, both hind legs and both fore fetlocks white, collar marks. No. 0638.

SAPHIRE (Mr. Hardcastle), b m ; star. No. 0671.

SATAN (Mr. Vander Byl), gr g ; both hind legs white, white marks both fore legs, scar off side neck. No. 0519.

SATELLITE (Mr. A. Withers), ch m ; star, narrow blaze, small snip, near hind fetlock white, ticked with white hairs. No. 0672.

SAUCE BOX (Mr. J. V. Southey), gr g ; snip, lower lip white, both hind fetlocks white. Passed for season. No. 0520.

SAVERNAKE (Mr. A. E. Gostling), b g ; star, snip, scar on forehead, both hind fetlocks white, white marks on all four legs. No. 0354.

SCOTTY (Capt. F. J. Dalgety), br m ; small star, both hind fetlocks white with black spots. No. 0284.

SCRIBE (Capt. Loftus Brien), gr g ; snip, near fore and near hind fetlocks white. No. 0691.

SEABIRD (Mr. J. B. Dale), ch m ; star, narrow blaze, snip, all four fetlocks white. No. 0639.

SEAL (Major Kennedy), b m ; black points, small collar marks. No. 0274.

SEALE (Mr. H. B. Harrison), br m ; white face, and near off hind fetlocks white. No. 052.

SECRET (Messrs. E. D. & G. A. Miller), ch m ; star, narrow blaze, small snip. No. 08.

SELOUS (Major Lawley), br g ; white spots all over body. No. 0170.

SENTIMENT (Capt. E. Heygate), b m ; off ear split. No. 0247.

SHAKER, THE (Capt. F. Egerton Green), b g ; faint star, faint snip. No. 0142.

SHAMROCK (Lord Radnor), b g ; star, few white hairs on face and on pole, white hairs front of chest. No. 0205.

SHANNON (Capt. Belfield), gr g ; star, blaze, snip, both hind legs white. No. 0320.

SHANNON (Mr. A. Withers), blk g ; star, near hind coronet white, scar above off knee. No. 0355.

SHEBEEN (Lord Radnor), b m ; white hairs back of near hind leg ; and back and front off fore leg. No. 0206.

SHEEN (Lord Radnor), ch g ; star, blaze, snip, both hind legs white, near fore fetlock white, collar marks, white hairs mane and tail. No. 0207.

SHEILAH (Colonel Clowes, 8th Hussars), b m ; star, snip, lower lip white, near hind leg and off hind coronet white, near fore fetlock white, collar marks. No. 0521.

31

SHELLFISH (Lord Radnor), b m ; faint star, black line down croup, ticked white hairs both flanks. No. 0208.

SHILELAGH (Mr. G. Bent Ollivant), blk g ; few white hairs inside both knees. No. 0159.

SHORT ODDS (Mr. J. Craddock), b g ; near hind fetlock white. No. 0416.

SHOT (Lord Radnor), blk m ; white mark front of off fore and off hind shin, collar mark. No. 0209.

SHROLE (Mr. O. T. Slocock), b g ; star, collar mark. No. 0474.

SHY LASS (Mr. G. N. Midwood), b m ; small star, faint snip. No. 0417.

SHYLOCK (Mr. R. H H. Eden), ch h ; scar above each hock, and above each knee, and on near shin, white mark off hip. No. 041.

SIGNET (Mr. J. Adamthwaite), b m ; collar marks. No. 022.

SILKWORM (R.A. Polo Club), b g ; star, snip, white hairs on face, both fore and off hind legs white, brand off hind quarter. No. 0321.

SILVERLORN (Mr. C. Elliot), b m ; star, black points, scar near fore fetlock, collar marks. No. 0660.

SILVERSTAR (Mr. J. D. Gouldsmith), b m ; star, snip, near hind and near fore fetlocks white. No. 029.

SILVERTAIL (Mr. James Hobbs), b g ; star, blaze, snip, near hind and off fore fetlocks white, grey hairs in tail. No. 038.

SILVERTAIL (Prince Alexander of Teck), b m ; star, blaze, snip, near hind coronet white, off fetlocks white, white marks both flanks. No. 0117.

SILVERTAIL (Mr. T. P. Godman), b m ; star, near hind fetlock and off hind coronet white, ticked with white hairs. No. 0129.

SILVERTAIL (Mr. J. D. Gouldsmith), b m ; star, off hind fetlock white with black spots. No. 0248.

SIMON (Capt. Henderson), br g ; star, small snip. No. 0522.

SIMPLICITY (Capt. Deare, 8th Hussars), br m ; star, narrow blaze, snip. Passed for season. No. 0523.

SISS (Mr. C. B. Houston), br m ; star, narrow blaze, small snip, white spots off hind quarter, collar marks. No. 0418.

SISTER ADA (Mr. W. R. Wyndham), gr m ; white marks, upper and lower lips, white mark outside near hind hoof, white spots near flank. No. 0275.

SISTER MARY (Capt. E. Makins), br m ; white face, lower lip white, near fore fetlock white. No. 0128.

SISTER SUE (Mr. James Farmer), ch m ; star. No. 086.

SISTER SUE (Mr. O. C. Francis), ch m ; star, blaze, snip, small white spot lower lip, near hind fetlock white, small black spot off hind quarter. No. 0276.

SISTER SUE (Mr. T. J. Stafford), b m ; small star, both hind coronets white. Passed for season. No. 0419.

SISSY (Lord Radnor), b m ; faint star, both hind fetlocks white. No. 0210.

SKYLARK (Capt. Fordyce Buchan), br m ; star, with black spot, near hind fetlock white and grey with black spots, white spots over fore and hind quarters. No. 0322.

SLAP JACK (Mr. P. R. Denny), ch g ; white face, lower lip white, near hind and both fore legs white, brand both hind quarters, white and black spots over body. No. 0599.

SLIGHT MARE (Mr. Leonard), blk br m ; grey patch outside off quarter. No. 0600.

SNAP (Lord Radnor), b g ; star, near hind coronet white, spot, few white hairs in tail. No. 0211.

SOCIETY (Mr. Morris), b m ; white hairs on face, star, all four coronets white, white spot off hind coronet. Passed for season. No. 0601.

SODA (Capt. Williams), br m ; faint long star, small snip, both hind fetlocks white with a black spot, scar point of off shoulder. No. 0692.

SOLITUDE (Mr. Alex. J. Hutchinson), ch m ; star, faint black line down croup, black patch off hind quarter. No. 0277.

SOLOMON (Mr. J. S. S. Mowbray), ch g ; star, snip, both hind and off fore legs white, near fore fetlock white. No. 0420.

SOUTHEY (Capt. Deare, 8th Hussars), b g ; star, white hairs on face, faint snip, near hind fetlock and off hind coronet white. No. 0524.

SPENT (Mr. E. C. Sandars), b m ; off hind fetlock white. No. 0323.

SPIDER, THE (Mr. P. Bullivant), ch m ; star, both hind legs white, scar inside off hind leg. No. 0177.

SPINACH (Mr. A. G. Dalgety), b m ; faint star, few white hairs off fore quarter. No. 0661.

SPINK (Mr. Edge), gr m ; near hind fetlock and off hind coronet white. No. 0475.

SPINNING WHEEL (Capt. Henderson, 8th Hussars), b m ; white hairs on face, white marks near fore leg. No. 0525.

SPLASH (Mr. Denny), b m ; white face, white mark off fore leg, scar off shoulder. No. 0602.

SPOT (Polo Club, 8th Hussars), ch g ; white face, lower lip white, both hind and off fore fetlocks white, brand near hind quarter. No. 0526.

SPOT WHITE (Mr. H. Straker), ch g ; star, blaze, snip, white spot lower lip, near hind leg and off hind coronet white, scars both sides of neck. No. 0662.

SPRIG (Mr. B. Daly), ch m ; star, both hind legs white, off fore fetlock white, collar marks. No. 0421.

SPRING TIME (Mr. H. A. Robinson), b g ; few white hairs in forehead, off hind fetlock white with black spots, near hind coronet grey. No. 0422.

31*

SPRING JACK (Mr. H. Chippendall Higgin), b g ; star, blaze, snip, off hind coronet white, near fore fetlock white, white mark near fore and off hind leg, brand off fore quarter. No. 0617.

SQUAW (Mr. O. T. Slocock), ch m ; star No. 0476.

STAFFORD (Mr. H. A. Bellville), gr m ; very small scar in front of chest. No. 0249.

STAR (Mr. J. Vaughan), b m ; star, off hind fetlock white. No. 0120.

STAR (Lord Radnor), b m ; faint black mark down croup, collar marks. No. 0212.

STARLIGHT (Mr. G. D. Armstrong), ch m ; white face, near hind white, white spot near shoulder and off side of neck. No. 0158.

ST. CLOUD (Capt. C. Grey), b m ; star, very faint blaze, snip, near hind fetlock white. No. 0278.

STELLA (Capt. Holmes), b m ; near fore and near hind fetlocks white. No. 0663.

STILL TRUE (Mr. H. Mogill), br m ; faint star, off hind and off fore fetlocks white. Passed for season. No. 0371.

STONEYBROKE (Mr. Jones, 8th Hussars), blk g ; scar near ribs, white spot off fore shin. No. 0527.

STORM (Messrs. Richards & Leigh), b br m ; star, off hind fetlock white, scar near fore coronet. No. 0213.

ST. OSYTH (Capt. F. Egerton Green), b m ; large star, narrow blaze, near fore fetlock grey, near hind fetlock white, black patch off hind quarter. Passed for season. No. 0673.

STURDY (Capt. L. Bryan), b g ; small snip, both hind fetlocks white. Passed for season. No. 0603.

SULTAN (Mr. Percy J. Trouncer), blk g ; small blemish off side of neck. No. 037.

SULTAN (Mr. R. H. H. Eden), br g ; star, both hind fetlocks white. No. 039.

SUNBEAM (Mr. J. O. Jameson), b m ; star, near hind coronet white with black spots, faint black mark down croup. No. 0179.

SUNBEAM (Mr. H. H. Smiley), b m ; star, narrow blaze, off hind coronet white, ticked with grey hairs. No. 0423.

SUN FLOWER (Mr. T. J. Stafford), ch m ; snip. Passed for season. No. 0424.

SUNRISE (Lord Radnor), br m ; star, white spot inside near fore coronet. No. 0214.

SUNRISE (Mr. F. M. Freake), b m ; large snip. No. 0252.

SUNSHINE (Mr. Talbot Rice), b m ; faint star, off hind fetlock white, near hind coronet white. No. 0250.

SUNSHINE (Mr. F. A. Bellville), br m ; star, blaze, snip, off hind fetlock white with black spot, white spot near fore coronet, ticked with white hairs. No. 0251.

SURPRISE (Polo Club, 8th Hussars), b g ; star, blaze, snip, all four legs white, white mark on neck, brand near hind quarter. No. 0528.

SUSAN (Mr. J. Adamthwaite), blk m ; very faint star. No. 024.

SWALLOW (Mr. T. Anderson), iron gr m ; black points, no distinctive marks. No. 0477.

SWEEP (Mr. H. F. Hardy), drk br g ; white hairs top of wither. No. 0529.

SWIFT (Mr. Stewart Duckett), b m ; scar above near knee, scars near cheek. No. 0478.

SYLPH (Mr. J. Lamont), b br m ; black points, no marks of identity. No. 0324.

SYMPATHY (Messrs. E. D. & G. A. Miller), b m ; star, both hind fetlocks white. No. 012.

SYNTAX (Mr. A. Withers), b g ; star, short blaze, near hind and near fore fetlocks white with black spots. No. 0356.

TAR BOX (Mr. Meredith), b g ; small star. Passed for season. No. 0604.

TELEPHONE (Mr. Fairfax), br m ; star, off hind fetlock white with black spots. No. 0288.

TELEPHONE (The Earl of Harrington), ch m ; star, blaze, snip, near hind and fore fetlocks white, off hind coronet white, collar marks. No. 0640.

THAMES (Mr. H. Rich), b br m ; few white hairs on forehead, off hind fetlock and off fore coronet white. Passed for season. No. 0357.

THURSDAY (Major Kennedy), b m ; faint star, near hind fetlock white with black spots, near fore coronet white with black spots. No. 0279.

TICK-TICK (Sir Thomas Fowler), ch m ; star, both hind and off fore fetlocks white, near fore coronet white. No. 060.

TILA (Mr. R. H. H. Eden), br m ; star, snip, both hind fetlocks white. No. 042.

TILLY (Mr. Ballesty), br m ; star. Passed for season. No. 0372.

TINKER (Mr. J. L. Moore), b g ; star, narrow blaze, both hind fetlocks and near fore coronet white. No. 0605.

TIP (Colonel Clowes, 8th Hussars), ch g ; white face, scar outside both hocks and inside near knee, collar marks. No. 0530.

TOFF, THE (Mr. James Farmer), ch g ; star, narrow blaze, snip, lower lip white, near hind leg and off hind coronet white. No. 074.

TOKAR (Major Bainbridge), dun m ; star, blaze, snip, white patches both ribs, collar marks. No. 0181.

TOMMY (Lt.-Colonel A. D. Neeld), b g ; star, near hind coronet white. No. 0160.

TOM TIDDLER (Messrs. E. D. & G. A. Miller), blk g ; star, white spot near side of ribs. No. 011.

TONY (Captain Brooke), b g; star, blaze, snip, near hind fetlock white with black spots. No. 0253.

TOPSY (Mr. J. Hetherington), gr m ; faint black spot top of near hind quarter, scar over near eye. No. 0358.

TRAVERTY (Mr. J. Craddock), br m ; star, near hind coronet white with black spot, ticked with grey hairs, collar marks. No. 0693.

TRICKY (Mr. J. Fitzgerald), ch m ; star, blaze, snip, near hind leg white. No. 0448.

TRILBY (Miss Norah Kavanagh), gr m ; snip, both hind fetlocks white. No. 0425.

TRILBY (Sir A. Vere Foster) b m ; star. No. 0426.

TRILBY II. (Mr. James Farmer), b m ; star, off hind fetlock white. No. 082.

TULIP (Mr. Eyre Lloyd), b m ; few white hairs on forehead and face, faint black mark down croup. No. 0641.

TULLOW (Mr. A. M. Swift), b m ; star, near hind fetlock white. No. 0427.

TULLOW (Mr. J. Murphy), b m ; star, faint snip, white hairs in tail. Passed for season. No. 0479.

TWINKLE (Mr. Erskine Booth), b m ; star, blaze, snip, scar point of off shoulder. No. 0428.

UMBRELLA (R.A. Polo Club), ch m ; star, brand near fore and near hind quarters, black patch off ribs. No. 0325.

UNCLE SAM (Capt. Fitzgerald), ch g ; few white hairs on forehead, both hind fetlocks white, brand near hind quarter. No. 0618.

UNCLE SAM (Mr. H. Straker), b g ; star, scar near nostril, near hind fetlock white, brand off hind quarter. No. 0664.

UNKNOWN, THE (Mr. A. F. Maude), br m ; star, near fore and both hind fetlocks white, off fore coronet white. No. 0429.

VANITHE (Miss A. Gore Booth), ch m ; star, narrow blaze, white hairs off hind quarter and near shoulder, ticked white hairs both flanks. Passed for season. No. 0449.

VENGEANCE (Mr. T. Anderson), b g ; black mark down back, black points. No. 0486.

VERA (Mr. O. J. Wilson), ch m ; star, blaze, snip, lower lip white, near hind coronet white, scar off flank. No. 0373.

VICTORINE (London Polo Club), b m ; star, white spot near hind quarter. No. 0123.

VIOLET (Mr. John Nettleton), ch m ; star, faint snip, white patch off shoulder. No. 0150.

VIXEN (Mr. F. A. Gill), b m ; white spots near ribs   No. 020.

VIXEN (Mr. J. Roark), br m ; faint star, faint snip, both hind legs white. No. 0480.

VIXEN (Major D. E. Wood, 8th Hussars), gr m ; all four coronets white. No. 0531.

VIXEN (Mr. R. Hague Cook), ch m ; faint star, large scar off side of neck. No. 0665.

VOUVRAY (Mr. C. C. Goldsmith), dun m ; star, narrow short blaze, snip. No. 0254.

WAIF, THE (Mr. J. P. Godman), br m ; star, scar off side of neck. No. 0130.

WALES (Mr. James Farmer), b m ; small white spot near hind quarter. No. 076.

WATER PROOF (Mr. Robert N. Allen), br g ; no marks of identity. No. 0280.

WATER RAT (Mr. R. H. H. Eden), gr g ; lower lip white, near hind leg and off fore fetlock white. No. 040.

WEARY (Major Longfield), br m ; small star. No. c164.

"W." " H." (Mr. F. J. Mackey), b g ; brand near shoulder and near hind quarter. No. 0255.

WHALEBONE (Mr. F. J. Barwicke), b m ; white mark front of off hind and off fore legs, small scar front of near shoulder   No. 0295.

WHEAT EAR (Mr. A. Withers), ch m ; star, blaze, black spot on forehead, near hind fetlock and off hind leg white. No. 0359.

WHITE FACE (Major Carew), br g ; star, narrow blaze, lower lip white, near hind fetlock white. No. 0102.

WHITE HEATHER (Mr. P. Bullivant), gr g ; narrow blaze, large snip. No. 0175.

WHISPER (Mr. Glynne Williams), dun g ; near hind and near fore fetlocks white, brand near hind quarter. No. 0619.

WIDOW, THE (Mr. O. T. Slocock), b m ; faint star.   No. 0481.

WIDOW, THE (Mr. O. C. Francis), b m ; star, blaze, snip, lower lip white, all four fetlocks white. No. 0281.

WIGRAM (Major R. T. Lawley), b g ; no marks of identity.   No. 099.

WILDFIRE (Mr. T. B. Drybrough), b m : both hind fetlocks and near fore fetlock white, scar above off knee. No. 0178.

WILD FLOWER (Major Kennedy), b m ; a few white hairs on forehead, snip, off hind fetlocks white. No. 0282.

WISDOM (Mr. J. J. Roark), br m ; star, narrow blaze, lower lip white, near hind coronet white, white spot off hind coronet, ticked white hairs over body. No. 0482.

WOEFUL (Mr. Glynne Williams), roan g; both hind fetlocks white, brand near hind quarter. No. 0256.

WRETCHED (Mr. H. Rich), blk m ; star, blaze, snip, ticked white hairs over body. No. 0137.

ZENITH (R.A. Polo Club), blue roan g; star, black spots, both hind and off fore fetlocks white, near fore coronet white, brand near hindquarter. No. 0326.

ZERO (Capt. Vernon), b g ; star, narrow blaze, small snip, near fore and off hind fetlocks white, brand near hind quarter. No. 0598.

ZITHER (Capt. J. W. Hare), b m ; star, very narrow blaze, near hind fetlock white. No 0374.

ZODIAC (R.A. Polo Club), blue roan g ; star, blaze, snip, white lower lip, both hind fetlocks white, brand near hind quarter. No. 0327.

THE FOLLOWING PONIES WERE NOT PASSED.

BIDDY (Mr. R. Hudson), br m ; small star, scar near hind fetlock. No. 0375.

BOWINE STAR (Capt. Loftus Brien), br m ; star, near hind fetlock white, off hind fetlock white with black spots. No. 0695.

CHARTREUSE (Mr. W. E. Grogan), b m ; star. No. 0694.

DAISY (Mr. F. P. Colgan), gr m ; no marks of identity. No. 0487.

DANDY (Mr. Ernest A. Dormer), b g ; star, blaze, and with little white near fore coronet. No. 053.

DEMON (Capt. Loftus), blk g ; scar near side of face. No. 0484.

DUBLIN (Mr. C. de Robeck), br g ; scar, back and sides near knee, white mark top of wither, saddle and girth marks. No. 0696.

GAOLSTON (Earl of Longford), br m ; star, narrow blaze, snip, both hind legs white. No. 0168.

GINGER (Capt. C. Levita), b g ; small star, collar marks. No. 0620.

GIPSY (Capt. Adams), b m ; star, small snip, near fore fetlock white, collar marks. No. 0283.

HARE, THE (Mr. F. Eassie), b g ; star, blaze, snip, both hind and near fore fetlocks white. No. 0532.

HORROR (Mr. H. Rich), b m ; star, near hind fetlock white. No. 0131.

JEALOUSY (Mr. R. Hudson), br m ; scar off hind quarter, collar marks. No. 0376.

KATHLEEN II. (Capt. Deare, 8th Hussars), ch m ; white face, both hind fetlocks white, scar outside near fore fetlock. No. 0533.

KENSINGTON (The Earl of Harrington), b g; faint black line down back, small star, black points. No. 0645.

LIMIT (Mr. Las Casas), br m ; faint star, white marks on all four legs. No. 0644.

MACK (Mr. W. G. Deare), b g; star, near hind fetlock white, collar mark. No. 0697.

MIDGE (Mr. C. de Robeck), br m ; star, white hairs on face, white hairs off side of withers. No. 0533.

NORMANDY GIRL (Mr. H. Percy Woolcott), b m white marks near hind quarter. No. 031.

PHLEON (Mr. Nettleton), br m ; scar outside off fore fetlock, body ticked with white hairs. No. 0643.

RABBIT (Mr. G. B. Ollivant), blk g ; few white hairs on forehead, brand near hind quarter. No. 0674.

RAINCLOUD (Col. de Robeck), blk br m ; faint star, both hind fetlocks white, black spots both hind coronets. No. 053c.

ROCKET (Mr. H. Percy Woolcott), br g ; star, blaze, snip, both hind fetlocks white. No. 032.

SEAL (Lord Radnor), b m ; star, blaze, snip, near fore leg grey down front of shin, faint black mark down back. No. 0216.

SHYLOCK (Lord Radnor), b g ; star, blaze, snip, white spot upper lip, both hind coronets white, scar front of off hock. No. 0215.

SILVER (Capt. Loftus), gr m ; snip. No. 0483.

SIR PATRICK (Mr. C. de Robeck), br g ; dun muzzle. No. 0608.

STELLA (Mr. F. B. Savill), ch m ; star, narrow blaze, near hind
    fetlock white.   No. 0294.

STRABOE (Mr. J. Murphy), b m ; faint star, faint snip.   No.
    0485.

TEMPÉ (Mr. H. F. Hardy, 14th Hussars), br m ; black points no
    marks of identity.   No. 0535.

TOMMY (Mr. G. Heseltine), b g ; few white hairs on off shoulder
    and off hind quarter.   No. 0642.

WARRIOR (Mr. C. Butler), b g ; near fore coronet white.   No.
    0698.

WATERHEN (Mr. W. Hardcastle), b m ; white spots on all four
    legs, fired both fore legs, scars on wither.   No. 0666.

WILD FOX (Mr. Meredith), b br g ; star, near hind fetlock white.
    No. 0607.

491

POLO PONIES MEASURED AND REGISTERED
AT HURLINGHAM, 1900.

————◆————

AMETHYST (Capt. Loftus), br g ; faint star, scars both hocks.　No. 0786.

ARABSTAR (Miss A. Gore Booth), ch g ; star, blaze, small snip. No. 0831.

ARDAGHOWEN (Mr. W. R. Fenton), gr m ; scar on face, scar on near ribs and hip.　No. 0832.

ARGENTINE (Mr. A. J. Palmer), gr g ; white face, lower lip white, brand near hind quarter. No. 0700.

ASTHORE (Mr. F. W. O'Hara), ch m ; few white hairs on face, near hind fetlock white, white mark off hind quarter. No. 0833.

ASTON (Mr. J. W. Hornsby), b g ; faint star, brand near hind quarter, white spots on body. No. 0935.

AU REVOIR (Mr. T. J. Roach), gr m ; off hind coronet white, white spots off ribs. No. 0787.

AZIZ (London Polo Club), g h ; star, blaze, snip, lower lip white, scar near shoulder, off hind quarter and all four legs white. No. 0897.

BALLET (Mr. H. J. D. Clerk), b m ; near hind coronet and off hind fetlock white. No. 0737.

BAYLEAF (Messrs. E. D. & G. A. Miller), b m ; star, blaze, snip, off fore fetlock white, lower lip white. No. 0738.

BEAUTY (Capt. C. Trower), gr m ; flea-bitten, small black patch on off shoulder. No. 0739.

BEAUTY BOY (Mr. S. W. Russell), gr g ; white face, lower lip white, both hind and near fore legs white. Passed for season. No. 0865.

BELINDA (Mr. W. G. Dease), b m ; star, faint snip, white hind fetlocks. No. 0788.

BISCUIT (Mr. L. Darell), ch m ; star.　No. 0936.

BLACKBIRD (Mr. W. Hardcastle), blk m ; star.　No. 0731.

BLACKMARIA (Hon. Charles Cavendish), blk m ; black mane, on white marks. No. 0740.

BLACKTHORN (Mr. W. Hardcastle), blk br g ; star, white spot on off hind coronet. No. 0732.

BLOATER (Major Honner), b br m ; star, scar near hind shin. No. 0866.

BLUE STOCKING (Mr. W. B. C. Burdan), br m ; star, faint snip, lower lip white, all four fetlocks white. No. 0701.

BOBS (Mr. F. W. O'Hara), br g ; faint star, scar each side near fore fetlock. Passed for season. No. 0834.

BOXIANA (Mr. Foxhall Keene), b m ; white hairs on face, snip, brand near hind quarter, scar off hind quarter. No. 0937.

BRAKESPERE (Capt. Loftus Bryan), gr g ; near fore and near hind coronet white. No. 0789.

CABMAN (Mr. W. J. Edge), b g ; star, snip, off hind fetlock white, collar marks. No. 0790.

CÆSAR (Mr. James Farmer), gr g ; small white patch off shoulder. No. 0741.

CALIPH (Mr. C. K. O'Hara), br g ; white hairs on forehead, snip, near fore coronet white. No. 0836.

CAMERON (London Polo Club), br or dun g ; star, blaze, snip, lower lip white, both hind and near fore fetlocks white, off fore coronet white, brand near hind quarter. No. 0898.

CANTLE (London Polo Club), ch g ; star, snip, near fore fetlock and off hind coronet white, brand off hind quarter, white mark off fore coronet. No. 0899.

CASSIA (Mr. C. K. O'Hara), ch m ; star, blaze, snip, lower lip white, off hind leg white, black line down back. No. 0835.

C. D. B. (Mr. J. A. F. Cochrane), b g ; near hind fetlock white, white mark off hip. No. 0867.

CHAIRMAN (Mr. C. Dillon), ch g ; star, blaze, snip, both hind and off fore legs white, white spots off side of neck. No. 0868.

CHAMOIS (Mr. J. Fitzgerald), br m ; star, blaze, snip, lower lip white, near hind leg white. No. 0837.

CHARLIE (Mr. A. Gold), b g ; small white spot near side of neck, small scar near hind quarter. No. 0927.

CHÉ (Mr. F. Daniell), br g ; star, near hind and off fore fetlocks, white, near fore coronet white, brand near hind quarter. No. 0928.

CHUB (Mr. P. Kelly), br m ; star, snip, near hind and near fore fetlocks white. No. 0791.

COFFEE COOLER (Mr. Foxhall Keene), ch m ; star, blaze, snip, lower lip white, near hind fetlock white. No. 0938.

COLUMBINE (Mr. C. K. O'Hara), br m ; small scar off side of face. Passed for season. No. 0838.

COQUETTE (Mrs. Prosper Liston), drk ch m ; star, white hairs in mane, collar marks. No. 0869.

CORKY (Mr. T. J. Longworth), b g ; white hairs on face, collar mark, faint black line on croup. No. 0702.

CRONJE (Mr. W. G. Deane), br g ; near hind fetlock white. No. 0792.

CRUSOE (Mr. C. C. Gouldsmith), br g ; scar off hind heel. No. 0703.

CRYSTAL (Mr. C. Webb), gr m ; star, collar marks. Passed for season. No. 0839.

CURDS AND WHEY (Mr. T. J. Longworth), dun m ; star, blaze, small scar off shoulder. No. 0704.

CURRAGH (Mr. W. Hardcastle), b g ; ticked with white, star, narrow blaze, snip. No. 0733.

CZARINA (Mr. Frank Newman), drk ch m ; star, white hairs off hind coronet, scar off hind leg. No. 0913.

DAISY (Mr. H. B. Harrison), b m ; star, white mark on near ribs. No. 0705.

DAPHNE (Mr. H. W. Montgomery), b br m ; star, near hind coronet white. No. 0742.

DENNIE (Mr. Bernard Daly), drk br m ; near hind coronet and off hind fetlock white, scar off fore pastern. No. 0870.

DIANA (Mr. Ernest Deney), br m ; grey hairs over face, near hind fetlock and near fore coronet white. No. 0706.

DICE BOX (Mr. Francis F. Daniell), b g ; faint white mark off fore fetlocks, scars all four heels. No. 0707.

DINAH (Mr. Nettleton), br m ; star, near hind coronet white, white spot off hind coronet. No. 0906.

DIVARSION (Messrs. Slocock), br m ; blemish inside near fore fetlock. No. 0793.

DO-DO (Capt. Loftus), b m ; both hind fetlocks white. No. 0794.

DON JOHN (Mr. J. W. Hornsby), b g ; star, faint blaze, brand near fore quarter. No. 0939.

DUM-DUM (Mr. J. Adamthwaite), b m ; white face, near fore and near hind fetlocks white. No. 0708.

DUM-DUM (Mr. T. J. Roach), ch m ; star, blaze, snip, white spots on hind quarters, white mark near forearm and shoulder. No. 0795.

ECARTÉ (Mr. M. Moncrieffe), ch g ; star, blaze, snip, wall eye off side. No. 0743.

ECLIPSE (Mr. M. Moncrieffe), b g ; faint star, brand near hind quarter. No. 0744.

EGRET (Mr. M. Moncrieffe), cream g ; white face, lower lip white, brand near hind quarter and near side neck. No. 0745.

EMPIRE (Mr. M. Moncrieffe), ch g ; star, narrow blaze. No. 0746.

EMPRESS (Mr. P. W. Connolly), b m ; both hind fetlocks white, black line down back. Passed for season. No. 0840.

EMU (Mr. M. Moncrieffe), b g ; both hind fetlocks white, brand near hind quarter. No. 0747.

ENTERPRISE (Mr. M. Moncrieffe), b g ; star, blaze, snip, both hind fetlocks white, brand near hind quarter. No. 0748.

ERIN (Mr. W. Hardcastle), dun m ; small star. No. 0734.

EXILE (Mr. M. Moncrieffe), drk ch g ; white face, lower lip white, both hind and off fore legs white, near fore coronet white, brands off hind quarter. No. 0750.

EXPRESS (Mr. Foxhall Keene), b g ; faint star, all four fetlocks white, scar point of near shoulder. No. 0941.

EXPRESS (Mr. M. Moncrieffe), b g ; off hind fetlock white. No. 0751.

EUCHRE (Mr. M. Moncrieffe), ch g ; star, small blaze, brand near hind quarter. No. 0749.

EVELYN (Mr. W. Brackenbridge), ch m ; star, scar off forearm. No. 0940.

FAIRY QUEEN (Messrs. E. D. & G. A. Miller), ch m ; star, blaze, snip. No. 0752.

FILTER (Mr. J. Adamthwaite), br g ; star. No. 0709.

FIRE FLY (Mr. F. D. Hickman), ch m ; star, near fore fetlock white. No. 0796.

FLANAGAN (Mr. J. M. Teid), b g ; star, narrow blaze, snip, near fore fetlock white. No. 0841.

FLORA (Mr. John N. Cahill), roan m ; large blaze, near hind leg white, white hairs in tail. No. 0871.

FORBIDDEN FRUIT (Major A. E. Jenkins), b g ; star. No. 0872.

FRANCISCO (Mr. Auberon Stourton), b g ; star, small snip, near hind fetlock white, brand near hind quarter. No. 0900.

FRANKIE (Mr. Francis F. Daniell), blk g ; star, narrow blaze, snip, lower lip white, all four legs white, brand near hind quarter. No. 0710.

FRIENDSHIP (Earl of Shrewsbury and Talbot), b m ; white marks below off hock. No. 0922.

FUZZY (Mr. Thomas Anderson), b g ; white hairs on forehead, snip. No. 0797.

GAIETY (Mr. W. K. Carew), br m ; star, blaze, snip, white spot lower lip. No. 0842.

GAMEBOY (Mr. W. K. Carew), br g ; star, white hairs on face, snip, near hind fetlock white. No. 0843.

GIPSY MAID (Mr. John Rich), b m ; faint star, near hind fetlock white. Passed for season. No. 0711.

GIPSY QUEEN (Colonel Campbell), gr m ; star, white spots over body. No. 0844.

GLORY (Mr. N. F. Archdale), b m ; star, both hind fetlocks white. No. 0798.

GOODENOUGH (Mr. Foxhall Keene), br g ; few white hairs on face, both hind fetlocks white, brand near hind quarter, scar off hind quarter. No. 0942.

GOWNBOY (John Jones & Son), ch h ; star, blaze, snip, ticked with white hairs. Passed for season. No. 0754.

GREYWING (Messrs. E. D. & G. A. Miller), gr m ; both hind fetlocks white, near fore fetlock white. No. 0753.

HAILSTORM (Mr Aubrey Price), ch g ; white face, near fore and near hind legs white, off fore coronet white, white mark off fore fetlock. No. 0755.

HAILSTORM (Mr. J. W. Hornsby), ch m ; star, blaze, snip. No. 0943.

HANDY ANDY (Dr. Furlong), b g ; small scar near side of neck. No. 0799.

HANDYMAN (Mr. James Farmer), dun g ; white hairs in mane and tail, white spot both sides of neck, collar marks. No. 0712.

HARDBAKE (Mr. L. Darrell), dun m ; star, blaze, snip, lower lip white, off hind fetlock and both fore fetlocks white. No. 0944.

HELIDON (Mr. Guy Bethel), ch h ; star, blaze, snip, lower lip white, both hind legs and near fore leg white, off fore fetlock white. Passed for season. No. 0901.

HOLDUP (Mr. Foxhall Keene), b g ; star, both hind fetlocks white, brand near fore quarter. No. 0945.

HYACINTH (Mr. J. D. Gouldsmith), b m ; star, narrow blaze, near fore and both hind fetlocks white. No. 0713.

JACK (Mr. Auberon Stourton), blk g ; white and black head, all four legs white, black spot off hind fetlock. No. 0929.

JAMAICA (Mr. J. Henry Stock), b br m. Passed for season. No. 0756.

JEFFRIES (Mr. Foxhall Keene), gr g ; white spots on muzzle, brand near fore quarter, scar off hind quarter. No. 0946.

JET (Capt. Loftus), blk m ; small scar near fore shin. No. 0800.

JOKER (Mr. C. K. O'Hara), ch g ; faint star, blaze, snip, white spot lower lip, both hind fetlocks white. No. 0845.

JORROCKS (Mr. James Farmer), dun g ; faint star, near hind coronet white. No. 0757.

JUDGE (Mr. J. W. Hornsby), br g ; star, blaze, snip, small spot lower lip, white near fore fetlock, brand near hind quarter. No. 0947.

JUST IN TIME (Mr. C. Buckmaster), ch g ; star, narrow blaze, faint snip, both hind legs white, scar near shoulder. No. 0930.

KAKI (Mr. T. Wilson Lynch), gr m ; off hind fetlock white. No. 0873.

KATHLEEN (late MISS TORMENTOR) (Mr. R. Yerburgh), b m ; faint star, near hind coronet white. No. 0758.

KIERNAN (Mr. E. A. Shaw), br g ; star, off hind coronet white, collar marks. No. 0874.

LADY ABBESS (Mr. A. F. Maude), ch m ; star, white mark off hind quarter. Passed for season. No. 0846.

LADY BIRD (Mr. E. E. Cockett), b m ; star, blaze, snip, both hind and off fore legs white. No. 0759.

LADY BOBS (Mr. James Farmer), br m ; star, near hind coronet white. No. 0714.

LADY BROWNFIELD (Mr. Foxhall Keene), ch m ; star, blaze, snip, near hind fetlock white, off fore fetlock white, near fore coronet white. No. 0948.

LADY EDIE (Mr. Evan T. Prichard), ch m ; white star on forehead, near fore fetlock white. No. 0715.

LADY OF QUALITY (Mr. Percy Bullivant), br m ; faint star. No. 0907.

LADYSMITH (Mr. W. B. Hayes), b m ; faint black mark down back, scar front of off hind fetlock. No. 0875.

LENA (Mr. J. W. Hornsby), ch m ; star, blaze, both hind fetlocks white, white spots hind quarter. No. 0949.

LITTLE FLO (Mr. F. G. Trollope), b m ; scar outside near hind fetlock. No. 0760.

LITTLE PLAYMATE (Mr. A. F. Maude), br m ; few white hairs. No. 0847.

LITTLE SHOT (Major G. M. Eccles), br m ; small scar near fore shin. No. 0848.

LOCKATT (Mr. John Watson), ch g ; star, near hind coronet and off fore fetlock white. No. 0950.

LOTTY (Hon. Aubrey Hastings), b m ; few white hairs in mane. No. 0716.

LOVE LOST (Mr. P. W. Connolly), br m ; collar marks. No. 0849.

LUCILLA (Mr. Nickalls), b m ; no white marks.   No. 0761.

LUCY (Mr. A. Dugdale), b m ; small star, both hind fetlocks white.
No. 0951.

LYDDITE (Mr. F. Daniell), dun g ; star, near hind fetlock white,
brand both hind quarters.   No. 0931.

MAGIC (Mr. John McDonald), drk b g ; star, white hairs on face,
near fore fetlock and off fore coronet white.   No. 0801.

MAHOMED (Miss A. Gore Booth), b br g ; black points, no marks.
Passed for season.   No. 0850.

MAMIE (Mr. Foxhall Keene), ch m ; star, blaze, snip, near hind
fetlock and both fore legs white, brand near hind quarter.   No. 0952.

MANGUS (Capt. Fitzgerald), br m ; star, blaze, snip, lower lip
white, all four legs white.   No. 0908.

MARGARET (Mr. Nettleton), ch m ; star, blaze, snip, white spot
lower lip.   No. 0909.

MARIGOLD (Messrs. E. D. & G. A. Miller), b m ; star, white
mark off hind shin.   No. 0762.

MAVOURNEEN (Mr. W. Hardcastle), cream m ; small star, off
hind leg white.   No. 0735.

MELODY (Mr. Norris Midwood), b m ; black points, no marks.
Passed for season.   No. 0802.

MERRY MAID (Mr. Nettleton), b m ; star, both hind fetlocks
white.   Passed for season.   No. 0910.

MERRY RATTLE (Mr. P. W. Connolly), ch m ; star, blaze, snip,
near hind and off fore fetlocks white, off hind leg white.   No. 0851.

MISS CRAFTY (Mr. H. B. Harrison), ch m ; white face,
lower lip white, both hind legs white, black spot near fore coronet.   No.
0717.

MISS HEALY (Mr. W. C. Meredith), br m ; small star, faint white
marks off shoulder and neck, white mark off hock.   No. 0803.

MISS MURPHY (Mr. P. O'Reilly), b m ; star, collar marks, scar
near side of face.   No. 0876.

MISS SHEPPARD (London Polo Club), b m ; faint star, white
marks lower jaw.   No. 0902.

MISS TAFFY (Mr. W. Redlington), br m ; star, narrow blaze, snip,
off hind fetlock white.   No. 0763.

MOLLIE (Mr. J. Cradock), b m ; large blaze, near hind leg and off
fore fetlock white, white spot front of chest.   No. 0877.

MONEYGOULD (Mr. A. F. Maude), br m ; near hind fetlock
grey.   No. 0852.

MOTHER'S FAVORITE (Mr. James Farmer), b br m ; near hind
fetlock black and white.   No. 0718.

MOUNTAIN MAID (Mr. Foxhall Keene), b m ; star, both hind
fetlocks white, scars front of both hocks.   No. 0954.

MRS. JACK (London Polo Club), ch m ; star, white hairs on face, snip, near hind fetlock and off fore coronet white, brand off fore quarter. No. 0903.

MRS. O'SHEA (Mr. James Farmer), b m ; both hind fetlocks white. No. 0719.

MY LADY (Mr. Walter Lindsay), ch m ; star, narrow blaze, snip, both hind fetlocks white. No. 0804.

MY QUEEN (Mr. W. B. Hayes), br m ; white face, white spot lower lip, both hind legs white. No. 0878.

NAMELESS (Mr. Aubrey Price), b m ; star, white marks on back and front of off hind leg. No. 0764.

NELL (Mr. T. J. Longworth), br m ; white marks both hind quarters. No. 0720.

NO (Mr. A. Boyd Rochford), dun m ; both hind fetlocks white, black line down back. Passed for season. No. 0879.

NORA (Mr. Stewart Duckett), b m ; faint star, faint snip, near hind fetlock white. No. 0805.

NOTELESS (Hon. O. Hastings) ch m ; star, blaze, snip, white spot lower lip, near hind fetlock white, white mark front of off hind fetlock, off fore fetlock white. No. 0911.

OAK APPLE (Mr. J. Cradock), ch m ; star, blaze, snip, both hind fetlocks white. No. 0880.

ODDS ON (Mr. J. W. Nolans), b m ; near hind fetlock white, white spots off shoulder and off side of neck, white mark near ribs. No. 0881.

ONYX (Capt. Loftus), br m ; faint star, near fore coronet white. Passed for season. No. 0806.

PA (Earl of Harrington), ch g ; white face, lower lip white, near hind and both fore legs white, off hind coronet white, white marks over body, scar off forearm, brand near hind quarter. No. 0914.

PADDY (Messrs. Slocock), b g ; white face, lower lip white, wall eye. No. 0807.

PAT (Mr. Herbert A. Gaildene), b br g ; off hind coronet white, slight collar marks. No. 0882.

PATIENCE (Mr. C. Adamthwaite), b m ; faint star, faint snip, near fore coronet white. No. 0765.

PEANUT (Mr. H. B. Harrison), b m ; star, off   fetlock black and white, near fore fetlock grey. No. 0721.

PEARL (Mr. F. D. Hickman), gr m ; scar off hind   , flea-bitten marks on head. No. 0808.

PEELER (Mr. F. Daniell), b br g ; star, white spot lower lip, near hind fetlock white, brand near hind quarter. No. 0932.

PEGGY (Mrs. Thompson), ch m ; star, near hind fetlock white, white patch near ribs, collar marks. No. 0883.

PETER (Mr. H. B. Harrison), br g ; faint star. No. 0722.

PETTICOAT (Mr. Eastwood Bigger), b m ; both hind coronets white. No. 0884.

PILGRIM (Mr. J. Adamthwaite), br g ; faint star and blaze, snip, faint collar mark off side. No. 0723.

PINKEEN (Mr. H. P. Wilson), ch m ; few white hairs on forehead, near hind coronet white, off hind and off fore fetlocks white, white spot off hind quarter. No. 0885.

PIPINS (Mr. W. E. Grogan), b m ; star, near hind coronet white with black spots, off hind coronet white. No. 0809.

PIRATE (Mr. W. F. A. B. Richardson), b g ; star, blaze, snip, lower lip white, white spot off hind coronet, white marks off fore coronet. No. 0886.

PLAGUE (Mr. W. E. Grogan), blk m ; star, blemish on face. No. 0810.

POST BOY (Mr. W. E. Grogan), ch g ; star, blaze, snip, white marks near hind fetlock, white hairs in tail. No. 0811.

PRESIDENT (Mr. Aubrey Price), b g ; star, snip, near fore and near hind coronets white, off hind fetlock white, brand near hind quarter. No. 0766.

PRIMROSE (Mr. E. Hodgson), ch m ; star, small snip, off hind fetlock white with chestnut spots. No. 0767.

PRIMROSE (Mr. J. Watson), ch m ; star, white hairs on face, near hind fetlock white, collar marks, white marks on hind quarters. No. 0933.

PRINCE (Mr. John Carpenter), b g ; star, collar marks, off fore coronet white. No. 0887.

PRUDENCE (Mr. C. C. D'Arcy Irvine), b m ; star, blaze, snip, near hind leg white. No. 0853.

QUEEN (Mr. T. L. Moore), b m ; star, blaze, snip, near hind leg white. No. 0812.

QUEENIE (Mr. F. G. Trollope), br m ; white marks front of near fore and near hind legs. No. 0768.

QUICKSILVER (Mr. Frank Newman), grey m ; small snip, white mark lower lip, collar marks. No. 0915.

RAGS (Earl of Harrington), b g ; star, small snip, near hind fetlock white. Passed for season. No. 0916.

READCOMBE LASS (Hon. O. Hastings), ch m ; white face. No. 0725.

RED LETTER (Mr. H. Barker), ch m ; star, both hind legs white. No. 0724.

32*

REDSKIN (Mr. Aubrey Price), ch m ; star, white marks off ribs, collar marks. No. 0769.

REPULSE (Mr. G. A. Miller), ch m ; star, narrow line down face, snip, white mark front of off hock. No. 0923.

REWARD (Mr. Tresham Gilbey), b m ; star, blaze, scar near hind quarter. No. 0770.

ROLI-POLI (Mr. S. R. Selman), b m ; faint star. No. 0771.

ROSA (Mr. J. W. Hornsby), roan m ; both hind fetlocks white. No. 0955.

ROSARY (Mr. Menzies), ch m ; scar near forearm. Passed for season. No. 0953.

ROSEGLASS (Mr. George F. Richardson), b br m ; star, collar marks. No. 0888.

ROUGE (Mr. C. Creed), b m ; black points, small white mark on back. No. 0854.

ROYAL SALUTE (Mr. J. Henry Stock), br g ; black streak down back. No. 0772.

ROYALTY (Mr. James Farmer), gr m ; near hind coronet white, white marks off hind and both fore coronets. No. 0773.

ROYALTY (Messrs. Slocock), br m ; star, blaze, snip, lower lip white, off hind fetlock white. No. 0813.

SADIE R. (Mr. E. Hudson), gr m ; near fore fetlock white and black. Passed for season. No. 0774.

ST. MORITZ (The Keynsham Stud Company), ch g ; star, black patches over hind quarters. Passed for season. No. 0778.

SAMPLE (Mr. A. Rawlinson), b m ; small scar outside near hock, white hairs off hind quarter. No. 0917.

SANCHO (London Polo Club), br g ; white face, lower lip white, both hind and off fore legs white, white marks all over body, brand both hind quarters. No. 0904.

SAPHIRE (Capt. S. J. Loftus), ch m ; white hairs on face and off hind coronet. Passed for season. No. 0814.

SARAH (Mr. W. A. Rawlinson), b m ; star, both hind legs white. No. 0775.

SCENE SHIFTER (Mr. C. W. Meredith), ch g ; off hind coronet white. Passed for season. No. 0815.

SCHOOL BOY (Dr. Colgan), b g ; white hairs on forehead. No. 0816.

SEAGULL (Dr. Colgan), gr m ; no marks of identity. No. 0817.

SEAGULL (Mr. H. Straker), gr g ; brand off fore quarter, scar on forehead. No. 0956.

SHOPGIRL (Colonel T. Cuthell), ch m : star, blaze, snip, near hind leg white, off hind coronet white. Passed for season. No. 0905.

SHRAPNEL (Mr. James Farmer), br m ; slight blemish back of near hock. No. 0727.

SILVER (Capt. Loftus), gr m ; snip, white and black spots lower lip. No. 0818.

SILVER SAND (Mr. T. J. Longworth), ch g ; star, near hind leg and off hind fetlock white. No. 0726.

SNOWDROP (Mr. G. A. Miller), gr m ; black spots both shoulders and off ribs. No. 0924.

SOCIETY (Mr. A. Rawlinson), br g ; star, blaze, snip, both hind fetlocks white. No. 0919.

SPARKLETT (Mr. H. Thursby), b m ; star, near fore leg grey, near hind leg white. No. 0776.

SPION KOP (Mr. Haskins), ch g ; star, collar marks. No. 0819.

SPOOF (Mr. Francis F. Daniell), b g ; star, blaze, snip, lower lip white, both hind legs and near fore fetlock white, white marks both ribs, brand near hind quarter. No. 0728.

SPRING (Messrs. E. D. & G. A. Miller), br m ; white spots off ribs. No. 0777.

SPRITE (Mr. John Leonard), roan m ; faint star. No. 0820.

STELLA (Mr. W. Hardcastle), b m ; star, narrow blaze, large snip, both hind legs white, both fore coronets white. No. 0736.

STRAYSHOT (Mr. P. W. Connolly), br m ; small white mark inside left knee. No. 0855.

STRONGBOW (Major Alexander), ch g ; white face, lower lip white, all four legs white. No. 0821.

SUGAR STICK (Miss Alice Kennedy), br m ; star, small collar marks ticked with hairs. No. 0889.

SUNBEAM (Mr. R. St. G. Robinson), b m ; off hind fetlock white, white spot off hind quarter, ticked with white. No. 0856.

SUNFLOWER (Mr. T. H. O. Pease), ch m ; star, blaze, snip, off hind coronet white. No. 0779.

SWEEP (Mr. W. A. Rawlinson), br g ; star, small snip, both hind and near fore fetlocks white. No. 0780.

SYLVAN LADY (Mr. J. Fitzgerald), ch m ; near hind fetlock white. No. 0857.

TAILER (Mr. C. K. O'Hara), ch g ; star, narrow blaze, dark line down back. No. 0858.

TAXIANA (Mr. Foxhall Keene), b m ; star, small snip, near hind fetlock white, brand near fore quarter, scar near hind quarter. No. 0957.

TELEPHONE GIRL (Mr. M. Quinn), ch m ; star, blaze, snip, lower lip white, black spots on body, collar marks. No. 0822.

TETSY (Mr. N. F. Archdale), br m ; off hind fetlock white. No. 0823.

THE JUDGE (Miss Helen Tyrrell), br g ; both hind fetlocks white. Passed for season. No. 0781.

THE SPY (Mr. Aubrey Price), ch g ; star, blaze, snip, near fore coronet white, white mark on croup, collar marks. No. 0782.

TILLY (Mr. Eugene Ballesty), br m ; star. No. 0890.

TOAST RACK (Mr. A. R. Fairfax Lucy), gr g ; scar front of neck, white spot near ribs. No. 0912.

TO PAY (Mr. Ernest Brown), ch g ; star, blaze, snip, near hind leg, near fore fetlock, and off fore coronet white, collar marks. No. 0891.

TOSS UP (Mr. P. W. Connolly), dun m ; white hairs on forehead, near hind fetlock white. No. 0859.

TOTTY (Hon. Aubrey Hastings), br m ; star, white hairs on face, near hind fetlock white, white marks off ribs. No. 0729.

TRICKS (Mr. J. W. Hornsby), b m ; star, narrow blaze, snip, near hind coronet and off hind fetlock white. No. 0918.

TWINKLE (Mr. L. C. Wynne), br m ; star, both hind fetlocks white, white mark off shoulder. No. 0860.

UTILITY (Messrs. E. D. & G. A. Miller), b br g ; star. No. 0783.

VANITY (Mr. H. Stanley), b br m ; star, white spot near ribs. No. 0892.

VELVET (Mrs. E. H. Pack Beresford), b m ; star, blaze, snip, both hind and near fore fetlocks white, white spots near fore leg. No. 0824.

VICTORIA (Messrs. Slocock), b m ; star, blaze, snip. No. 0825.

VIXEN (Mr. H. P. Wilson), ch m ; star, blaze, snip, white spot upper lip, near hind fetlock, off hind coronet, and near fore leg white. No. 0893.

WANCHEE (Mr. F. G. Trollope), b m : star, faint snip, white marks front of near fore and near hind legs. No. 0784.

WATERFORD (Mr. H. Barker), b g ; off hind fetlock and near fore coronet white, collar marks. No. 0730.

WINK (Mr. P. W. Connolly), br h ; star, white hairs on face, both hind legs white. No, 0861.

WISDOM (Mr. Aubrey Price), b br m ; near hind fetlock white. No. 0785.

YES (Mr. A. Boyd Rochfort), br m ; off hind coronet white. No. 0894.

ZULUKA (Dr. Furlong), br m ; faint star, near hind fetlock white. No. 0826.

THE FOLLOWING PONIES WERE NOT PASSED.

BLACK WATCH (Mr. John Leonard), blk br m ; near hind fetlock white, with black spots. No. 0827.

BOBBINS (Mr. A. Gold), light ch m ; white hairs on face, faint snip, near fore fetlock and off hind coronet white, white mark off hip. No. 0934.

CERES (Capt. Walker Leigh), b m ; star, blaze, snip, near hind fetlock and off hind leg white. No. 0920.

CHARLIE'S AUNT (Capt. F. Egerton Green), b m ; star, blaze, snip, near hind coronet white. No. 0925.

CHRISTOPHER (Capt. F. Egerton Green), b g ; star, near fore and off hind fetlocks white. No. 0926.

DICKEY (Mr. W. Murphy), b or br g ; star, narrow blaze, snip, scar near hind fetlock. No. 0828.

EL SOVEY (Capt. Loftus Bryan), b m ; star, narrow blaze, snip, both hind fetlocks white. No. 0829.

LADY MAY (Mr. A. Suart), b m ; scar off side ribs and outside near knee. No. 0958.

LOTTERY (Mr. W. Buckmaster), b m ; faint star, both hind coronets white. No. 0921.

MULDOON (Colonel Campbell), gr g ; scar near hind fetlock and off hind quarter. No. 0864.

NO GO (Mr. C. W. Meredith), b m ; star, blaze, snip, scar near hind coronet, ticked with white hairs on flanks. No. 0830.

OLIVE (Mr. G. P. Russell), b m ; small white spots near hind quarter and inside off hind coronet. No. 0959.

PATBOY (Mr. J. H. Locke), b g ; star, white hairs both ribs. No. 0895.

PHŒBE (Mr. Gerald Hardy), b m ; few white hairs on face. No. 0960.

RASSENDYN (Mr. W. K. Carew), ch g ; star, white hairs on face, all four fetlocks white. No. 0863.

RIGOLETTO (Mr. A. Boyd-Rochfort), b g ; black points, no marks. No. 0896.

VIVANDIÈRE (Mr. J. Fitzgerald), br m ; small star, white marks off hind quarter. No. 0862.

POLO PONIES MEASURED AND REGISTERED AT HURLINGHAM, 1901.

———◆———

ABBESS, THE (Mr. W. E. Crogan), b m ; few grey hairs o h Coronet. No. 173.

ABRAHAM (Mr. Bernard Wilson), b g ; few grey hairs in forehead. No. 366.

ADAM HILL (Captain W. Neilson), gr g ; flea-bitten head, behind elbows and in flanks. No. 439.

ADVANCE (Mr. T. L. Walker), br m ; scar N H heel No. 572

ALERT (Messrs. Miller), ch g ; star, race, snip, both fore pasterns and backs of fetlocks, both hind stockings. No. 367.

ALEXANDRA (Mr. R. H. H. Eden), bl m. No. 541.

ALICE (12th Lancers Club), ch m ; star, snip, scar N H tendon. No. 263.

ALLFOURS (Messrs. Slocock), ch g ; star, race, snip, white legs, stripe running up to hock of N/H. No. 490.

ALLY SLOPER (Mr. A. Hastings), b g ; o h ½ fetlock. No. 379.

AMELIA (12th Loncers Club), ch m ; blaze, race, snip, o f fetlock, N/H stocking, o/H pastern. No. 264.

AMPELOPSIS (Captain Phipps Hornby), b g ; small spot as star, small white mark inside N/F cannon bone. No. 542.

ANEMONE (Mr. E. Blakiston Houston), br m ; few grey hairs as star, double transverse stripe above N/ shoulder point. No. 315.

ARROW, THE (Captain W. H. B. Long), b m ; faint star N side, scar N/ shin, o/H coronet black marks. No. 258.

ARTHUR'S LOVE (Mr. J. J. Stafford), ch m blaze face o f stocking, N/H pastern and up back of fetlock. No. 225.

ASH TRAY (Mr. E. M. Stewart), b m; star, race, B H ½ fetlock. No. 328.

ATHANSIA (Mr. W. G Dease), b m ; few grey hairs forehead. No. 491.

BABY NIGGER (Mr. O. Hastings), bl g ; permanent irregular, scar both sides of wither. No. 380.

BALD FACE (Mr. E. Rotheram), dk b g ; blaze, broad race, whole snip and underlip, B/N fetlocks and B/O pastern. No. 302.

BALSORROCK (Captain W. Neilson), b m ; star N H pastern, O H heel. No. 440.

BARBED WIRE (Mr. James Fitzgerald), gr g ; light forehead, O F coronet, B/H fetlocks upwards to point in front. No. 290.

BARMAID (Mr. C. Adamthwaite), ch m ; long star, snip, small white patch N/F heel. No. 5.

BARMAID (Mr. L. M. Ryan), br m ; star, race, few grey hairs o hip and small grey spot O/ quarter. No. 492.

BAR NONE (Mr. J. W. Hornsby), dark b g ; N H fetlock. No. 462.

BAY LEAF (Mr. Allen Gott), b m ; star, B H fetlocks, 2 marked knees. No. 530.

BAZAAR (Mr. N. Haig), dark grey m ; light forehead and both cheeks, spot O/ quarter (season only). No. 340.

BEATLE (Mr. T. J Roark), bl m ; star, B H pasterns and back of fetlocks. No. 493.

BEAUTY (Captain Hickman), blk m ; star, race, broad snip O F coronet. No. 283.

BEAUTY BAY (Mr. Mortimer Russell), gr g ; white face, lower lip light, N/F leg and B/H legs light coloured. No. 226.

BELL (Mr. C. B. Houston), br m ; spot B H shins and inside of knee. No. 332.

BELLA (12th Lancers Club), gr m ; dark patch near side of forehead, N/F fetlock and O/H pastern and back of fetlock. No. 265.

BENEFIT (Mr. A. Byrne), black m ; N H heel and patch in front of same coronet. No. 184.

BENEFIT (Mr. H. B. Harrison), ch m ; few grey hairs on forehead, N/H heel and inside coronet white. No. 52.

BERNEY (Mr. John Sandall), b g ; small star inside N H coronet. No. 110.

BERNICIA GIRL (Mr. Sandilands), ch m ; star and race B H stockings. No. 381.

BERYL (Mr. Neil Haig), gr m ; N H coronet. No. 341.

BESS (Mr. Evan T. Pritchard), b m ; white spot, O H shin. No. 531.

BETTY (Mr. Glover), ch m ; small star, faint race, snip B H socks. No. 463.

BIDDY (Mr. R. Maxwell), b m ; star (season only) No. 281.

BIJOU (Mr. W. C. Eustis), dun b m ; bald under both eyes. No. 400.

BIRDIE (Mr. M. Quinn), br m ; star race, linear scar inside o f heel. No. 471.

BIRD OF FREEDOM (Messrs. Slocock), ch m ; blaze face, N F leg white. No. 124.

BITHNER MARE (Mr. W. McCreery), b m ; N H coronet and heel. No. 368.

BLACKIE (Colonel H. de Roebeck), bl m ; star only. No. 112.

BLACK JACK (Captain W. Hall), bl g ; star, N'F coronet. No. 111.

BLACK PEARL (Mr. J. Hornsby), bl m ; white marks top wither, spots o/ side. No. 574.

BLIND MAN'S BUFF (Mr. Percy Bullivant), b g ; small star, N H coronet. No. 399.

BLUEY (Mr. N. Haig), gr m, "M" N shoulder. No. 424.

BOUTCHIE (Mr. J N. Malone), gr m ; flea bitten head and both shoulders. No. 306

BRAMBLE (Mr. W. McCreery), dark b g blaze, N H fetlock. No. 369.

BRAMPTON (Mr. J. Drage), ch m ; star snip. No. 6.

BRITANNIA (Mr. E. Hughes), br m ; spot for race o H half fetlock with black markings. No. 339.

BROTHER JOHN (Mr. James Farmer), dk br g. No. 53.

BROWN BETTY (Mr. H. Morris), black m. No. 185.

BROWN VARNISH (Mr. G. K. Ansell), b g ; star, N H coronet and heel with black marks in coronet, No. 186.

BRUNO (R.A. Polo Club), b m ; star, bald round eyes. No. 441.

B & S (Mr. J. M. Richardson), b g ; star, snip N H coronet. No. 96.

BUCK SHOT (Mr. Dawson), br g ; star, race, snip B H fetlocks, N F pastern, and back of.fetlock, brand M. No. 464.

BUSTER (Mr. L. Morough Ryan), b g ; heel and small patch in front of same coronet (season only). No. 187.

BUSTLE (Mr. A. M. Caldecott-Smith), br m ; scar N'H heel. No. 494.

BUTTERCUP (Mr. A. Stourton), ch m ; star, race, snip. No. 425.

BUTTERFLY (Messrs. Miller), br m ; few grey hairs as star, permanent scar in front of o/F fetlock and o/H coronet. No. 7.

BUTTERSCOTCH (Mr. R. G. O. Chesin), ch m ; o knee marked, grizzled patch top of N/ quarter. No. 279.

CAMERON (Mr. J. Hargreaves), b g ; star, race, snip B H pasterns. No. 543.

CAPRICE (Mr. J. Hargreaves), b m ; star. No. 544.

CARLOW (Captain L. Bryan), b g ; star, few grey hairs outside N/F heel. No. 472.

CAROLINA (Captain Egerton Green), b m ; star, snip and N/ nostril. No. 342.

CANTERBURY (12th Lancers Club), br g ; small line as star, few white spots about F/ fetlocks. No. 266.

CAT (Messrs. Slocock), b m ; no white. No. 125.

CHAIN SHOT (Mr. W. K. Carew), b m ; little white O H heel. No. 227.

CHALMINGTON (Captain H. L. Lithgow, R.H A.), br g ; grizzled star. No. 442.

CHANCE (Messrs. Slocock), b m ; permanent scar in front of N H joint. No. 126.

CHARITY (Mr. James Farmer), b m ; star, slight race O H coronet. No. 54.

CHARITY (Mr. J. Bellville), gr m ; large scar under N side of body. No. 401

CHARITY (Mr. M. Quinn), br m ; few grey hairs for star, patch of grey in front of O/ hock. No. 473.

CHARLIE (Mr. R. Lonsdale), ch g ; star N/H pastern, and ½ fetlock. No. 272.

CHARLIE (Mr. A. F. Houlder), br g ; star, snip B H pasterns. No. 481.

CHARLIE'S AUNT (Captain F. Egerton Green), b m ; star, race, snip. No. 1.

CHARLTON (Captain Lithgow, R.H.A.), dk br g ; grey mar k,N/ shoulder, all fetlock joints. No. 443.

CHELTENHAM (Captain F. Egerton Green), dk b g ; star, with grizzled edge, small snip, N/F, small marking in front of coronet and heel, O/F coronet, N/H ½ fetlock (season only). No. 457.

CHESHIRE (Mr. R. H H. Eden), b m , long star, snip N H coronet, O/H fetlock (season only). No. 545.

· CHICKANE (Mr. C. Brownlow), br m ; star, race, snip to O side, N/F fetlock, N/H ½ stocking, O/H pastern. No. 319.

CHICKEN (Mr. F. Barbour), dun m ; star O H coronet. No. 313.

CHIEFTAN (Mr. A. Stourton), b or br g ; grey hairs on nose, N F ½ fetlock, B/H fetlocks. No. 455.

CHIFF CHAFF (Captain Osmaston), br m ; collar marks, O H heel and inside coronet. No. 278.

CHIPS (Mr. J. W. Hornsby), bl g ; O H heel and spot in front of same coronet. (Season only.) No. 465.

CHRISTOPHER (Captain F. Egerton Green), b g ; star, N F pastern, and O/H pastern and fetlock. No. 269.

CLARA (Mr. W. B. Hayes), bl br m ; star, spot centre back. No. 228.

CLEMENTINA (Mr. S. A. Watt), bl br m ; star. No 496.

CLIMBER (Mr. James Farmer), ch m ; star, race, snip, N H coronet and heel. No. 55.

CLIP (Mr. James FitzGerald), ch m ; star. No. 289

CLOISTER (Mr. J. Hargreaves), b g ; small white mark N, shin, few grey hairs front of O/H leg, just above hock. No. 546.

CLONMEL (Messrs. Slocock), br m ; star, race, faint snip inside both hind coronets. No. 127.

COCKSHOT (Mr. F. P. Colgan, M.D), ch g ; blaze, O'H fetlock, O/H pastern.

COLLENSO (Mr. J. Eaton Dykes), ch g ; blaze, race, snip O H pastern, No. 229.

COMO. NO. (Mr. R. P. Wilson), b g ; star, race, sn p, four pasterns N/H, one lightest. No. 547.

CONFIDENCE (Mr. T. L. Moore), br m ; star, race, snip, to N nostril. No. 188.

COOLIE GIRL (Mr. R. A. Fleming), bl br m ; small grizzled star. No. 402.

COUNT, THE (Mr. A. Dugdale), br g ; inside $\frac{1}{2}$ of N/H coronet and heel. No. 532.

COUNTESS (Mr. T. Linton), b m ; lot of saddle marks and fired inside hocks. No. 230.

COUNTESS (Mr. W. E. Drury), ch m ; broad race N H fetlock, O H pastern, ches. markings on coronets, white markings under body. No. 583.

COWBOY (Mr. J. Hargreaves), gr g ; almost white. No. 548.

COWSLIP (Messrs. Miller), bl m ; B F pasterns and N F fetlock, with black coronet markings. No. 8.

COWSLIP (Mr. W. B. Hayes), dun m ; faint crescentic star. No. 497.

CRAFTY (Mr. James Farmer), b g ; small star, grizzled ring round it, snip B/H stockings. No. 56.

CRONEY (Mr. A. Findlatt), b g ; grizzled patch for star. (Season only.) No. 482.

CRYSTAL (Mr. C. Webb), gr m ; star, B F hee's light, legs dark. No. 274.

CRYSTAL (Mr. J. Hargreaves), gr m ; dark with light head, O H fetlock, and N/H coronet lighter. No. 549.

CURRAGH (Mr. A. Price), bl br m ; saddle marks. No. 44.

CURRANTS (Mr. Owen Wynne), br m ; small star, slightly to N side of forehead. No. 276.

CUSHLA (Mr. Percival), blk m. No. 275.

CUTTY SARK (Mr. N. Haig), gr m ; white, with large scar near side of body. No. 343.

CYMBAL (Captain E. D. Miller), br m; N H fetlock with bl ring round coronet. No. 426.

DAINTY (Mr. R H. H. Eden), br m; few grey hairs forehead snip. No. 550.

DAIRYMAID (Mr. F. P. Colgan, M.D.), ch m; O H pastern. No. 129.

DAISY (Mr. R. W. Hall Dare), br m; star, race, snip, underlip, O H fetlock, N/H ½ fetlock. No. 231.

DAPPLE (Mr. C. W. Meredith), gr m; dark legs, star, N F coronet, O/F pastern. No. 189.

DAY (Mr. B. Daly), ch g; blaze, snip, underlip, O F pastern, O H pastern, and N/H stocking. No. 113.

DEATH OR GLORY (Messrs. Slocock), b m; star. No. 130.

DELIGHT (Messrs. Slocock), b roan m; star, slight race, N H fetlock. (Season only.) No. 151.

DICK'S DAUGHTER (Mr. E. G. Hope Johnstone), ch m; blaze. No. 232.

DISCORD (Mr. J. Bellville), b g; star inside O shin. No. 403.

DOCTOR, THE (Dr. Ridd), b g; star long race, B F coronets. No. 174.

DOCTOR, THE (Mr. J. Farmer), blk g; star, N H coronet. No. 86.

DOLLAR (Mr. P. W. Perry), b m; clot for star, small race snip, scar back O/ heel. No. 474.

DON, THE (Mr. R. H. H. Eden), b g; few grey hairs forehead, broad snip N/ nostril. No. 551.

DON CARLOS (Mr. H. Learmonth), bl g; blaze, underlip O F and N/H fetlocks, angular mark N/F coronet. No. 552.

DORCHAT (Mr. J. E. Brandt), dk b g; star, N F coronet and heel, and O/H coronet. (Season only.) No. 97.

DOROTHY (Mr. A. W. Perkins), ch m; star, race, N H fetlock. No. 427.

DOROTHY (Mr. L. M. Ryan), whole coloured rich dark ch m. No. 498.

DOUBLE X (Mr. G. Heseltine), ch g; star, race, snip, O F pastern, N/ fetlocks, large scar inside O/ hock. No. 456.

DRAGON (Mr. R. H. H. Eden), b g; grizzled mane and tail. No. 553.

DREAM, THE (Mr. C. Death), b m; star. No. 175.

DRUMFIN (Mr. J. W. Connolly), gr g; star, N F coronet, N H fetlock light. (Season only.) No. 285.

DUCHESS (Mr. G. S. Reade), b roan m; saddle-marks, girth-marks under centre of body. No. 336.

DUCHESS, THE (Mr. J. Adamthwaite), dun m ; blaze, o h stockings. No. 87.

DUMPS (Captain H. D. O. Ward), gr g ; chestnut, flea-bitten neck and shoulders. No. 444.

DYNAMITE (Mr. W. E. Drury), ch g ; few grey hairs forehead, spot as snip, b/h stockings No. 584.

EILEEN (Mr. C. Brownlow), dk b m ; star, snip, b f pasterns, n h fetlock, o/h outside coronet. No. 318.

ELDORADO (Mr. N. Learmonth), br g ; star, n f both hind fetlocks, No. 554.

ELLA (Captain F. Egerton Green), b m ; n h heel. No. 267.

EL LUCERO (Mr. N. Learmonth), br g ; star, n f pastern. No. 555.

EMERALD (Captain Loftus), br m ; blaze, race, snip n h fetlock, o/h heel. No. 500.

EMIGRANT (Mr. M. Moncrieffe), b g ; blaze, race, snip n h fetlock, o/h coronet, small white mark. No. 25.

EMMA (Mr. C. H. T. Reade), b m ; large star, grizzled, snip n h $\frac{1}{2}$ fetlock, white o/f coronet. (Season only). No. 132.

EMPRESS (Captain G. B. Gosling), gr m ; o f and n h light legs. No. 190.

EMPRESS (Mr. J. Carpenter), br m ; blaze face, n h fetlock. No. 233

EMPRESS (Mr. W. B. Hayes), br m ; grizzled race and snip, scar outside n/h fetlock. (Season only.) No. 501.

ENCORE (Mr. M. Moncrieffe), br g ; blaze, faint race, snip. No. 26.

ENID (Captain Egerton Green), b m ; snip n nostril. No. 370.

ENSLIN (Captain Egerton Green), bl m ; star. No. 344.

ERIC (Mr. M. Moncrieffe), b g ; star, snip both pasterns. No. 27.

ESTHER (Mr. W. G. Dease), br m ; large star, n f coronet, b h pasterns. No. 191.

EVEN MONEY (Mr. O. Hastings), b m ; crescent star, n h coronet, o/h pastern. No. 382.

EXCESS (M. C. Brownlow), b m ; star, race, broad snip. No. 325.

EXCHANGE (Messrs. Slocock), b g ; a few grey hairs on forehead. No. 133.

EXILE (Mr. A. Buchanan Baird), b g ; star race, snip to o nostril. (Season only.) No. 483.

FAIRY (Mr. B. H. Nicholson), b m , small star, n f heel grizzled. No. 404.

FAIRY, THE (Mr. L. K, Woods), iron gr m ; spot on N′ side hind heels white. No.176.

FAITH (Mr. J. Bellville),ch m ; star, race, snip. No. 405.

FANATIC (Captain C. L. Graham), dk b g ; star, o f ½ fetlock, o/H fetlock. (Season only). No. 327.

FANCIFUL (Mr. T. J. Burrows), gr m ; flea-bitten cheeks and forehead. No. 192.

FANNY (Mr. H. Deering), br m ; B′H fetlocks, B F pasterns, white (black coronet markings in all fours). No. 134.

FANNY (Mr. J. L Walsh), bl m ; star, race, snip, o/H coronet, little white N/H coronet and heel. No. 234.

FAR FAR (Miss Clare Woolmer), ch m ; star, race, snip o/H stocking and N/H pastern. No. 3.

FAVORITE (Sir Vere Foster), b m ; N/H pastern, o/F heel, and little in front of coronet. No. 235.

FESTIVAL (Mr. A. Price), br m ; N/F heel, little white outside same, coronet grizzled. No. 45.

FIDGET (Mr. J. T. Burrows), br m ; small star, B/H pasterns. No. 193.

FILBERT (Mr. M. Moncrieffe), b g. No. 28.

FIREFLY (Mr R. H. H. Eden), b m ; o/H pastern, white patch N/ shoulder. No.556.

FIREFLY (Mr. M. Moncrieffe), b g; blaze, race, broad snip. No. 30.

FIRST SHOT (Mr. S. H. Wallace), b m. No. 502.

FLASH (Mr. E. F. Dease), b m ; star, spot on N/ side wither. No. 311.

FLASH LIGHT (Mr. M. Moncrieffe), ch g ; star, N/H fetlock. No. 30.

FLASH LIGHT (Mr. A. Dugdale), b m ; scar inside N/H coronet, No. 533.

FLICK-A-MAROO (Messrs. Miller), ch m ; blaze, face, underlip, N/F fetlock, o/H fetlock, N/H stocking. No. 9.

FLIP (Captain E. D. Miller), b g ; grizzled, star, N/F pastern, o F and N/H ½ fetlock, o/H coronet. No. 406.

FLIRT (Captain Hickman), b m ; star, N/H pastern, faint ring, small patch N/ quarter. No. 282.

FLIRT (Mr. R. H. H. Eden), rn m ch roan ; faint star. (Season only.) No. 557.

FLORADORA (Mr. J. Farmer), ch m ; star, N/H pastern, small grizzled spot, o/H water line. No. 57.

FORGER (Mr. M. Moncrieffe), b g ; large star, snip N/F and B/H fetlocks. No. 31.

FORGET-ME-NOT (Mr. M. Quinn), dun m ; star, N/H pastern, o/F and B/H socks. No. 475.

FORTRESS (Mr. M. Moncrieffe), dk b g ; no white, branded bar across back of thigh, and cross on outer side, N/ second thigh. No. 32.

FORTUNE (Mr. M. Moncrieffe), dk b g ; snip on N, nostril. No. 33.

FOXHALL (Mr. E. H. Baker), b g ; few grey hairs o forehead. No. 489.

FRAGMENT (Mr. M Moncrieffe), br g ; few hairs for race, snip over N/ nostril. No. 34.

FRAMPTON (Captain Lithgow, R.A.), blk m ; small spot on forehead, O/H coronet. No. 445.

FRIAR (R.A. Polo Club), b g ; N F coronet, O F pastern, B H fetlocks. No. 446.

FRIAR (Mr. M. Moncrieffe), dk b g ; O'F pastern, B H pasterns, and ½ fetlock, N/F coronet. No. 36.

FRIAR, THE (Mr. B. Blunsome), gr horse ; scar above o knee. No. 88.

FRIDAY (Mr. M. Moncrieffe), bl br g ; B H coronets, black markings above hoof. No. 35.

FROLIC (Mr. M. Moncrieffe), dk b g ; blaze, race, snip, N F and N/H coronet. O/H fetlock. No. 37.

FROSTY (Mr. M. Moncrieffe), ch roan m , curved race N H ½ stocking. No. 38.

FUGITIVE (Mr. M. Moncrieffe), ch g ; star, race, disconnected snip N/F, O/F, and O/H fetlocks, and N/H coronet. No. 39.

FULLGATE (Mr. R. R. Barker), b m ; B H pasterns, blk spots on coronets. (Season only.) No. 58.

FURY (Mr. M. Moncrieffe), b g. No. 40.

FUSEE (Mr. M. Moncrieffe), ch g ; star, race, disconnected snip. No. 41.

FUSIC (Captain L. Bryan), ch m ; star, race, snip O H stocking. No. 135.

FUZZ (Mr. M. Moncrieffe), dk b g ; star. No. 42.

GALLIA (Mr. L. de Las Casas), ch m ; blaze face, O F pastern, B H ½ stockings. No. 407.

GAMBLER (Mr. J. Leonard), bl g ; few grey hairs on forehead. No. 194.

GAME HEN (Mr O. Hastings), ch m. No. 59.

GARNETT (Captain Loftus), ch m ; star, race, O F pastern, O H inside coronet. No. 136.

GAY DECEIVER (Captain Long), b m ; star. No. 195.

GAUCHO (Mr. N. Learmonth), br g ; blaze underlip. No. 558.

GERALD (Mr. N. Haig), b m ; white marks inside o knee and shin, small mark inside N/H heel. No. 345.

G. G. (Mr. J. W. Nolan), br m ; star, N F and N H coronet, O H fetlock. No. 236.

GINGER (Mr. St. L. G. Stephen), ch horse ; many saddle marks, grey patch below o/ hip. No. 484.

GIPSEY (Mr. E. Bellamy), br m ; star, snip over N nostril. No. 196.

GIPSEY (Major J. Fowle), br m ; star, N H pastern white with black markings. No. 197.

GIPSEY QUEEN III. (Colonel Napier McGill), br m ; star, O H pastern and scar o/ heel. No. 303.

GIRAFFE (Mr. T. J. Roarke), b m ; little faint white mark in front of N/H coronet. No. 137.

GLASS O' GROG (Mr. Stephenson Grigg), gr g ; flea-bitten, light bay spots, N/H leg light coloured. No. 338.

GLENTASK (Mr. R. M. Douglas), br g ; few grey hairs as star, N H coronet (season only). No. 317.

GOAT, THE (Mr. H. A. Gairdine), b m ; scar front o' fetlock, grey tick in coat. No. 504.

GO BANG (Messrs. Miller), br m ; small grizzled patch for star. No. 10.

GOLLYWOG, THE (Miss Wilson), dun g ; star, snip, white mane and tail. No. 218.

GOOD LUCK (Messrs. Slocock), b g ; star, B H fetlocks, white. No. 138.

GOUCHO (Messrs. Dennis), b g. No. 114.

GRACE (Mr. W. Brackenridge), br m ; star. No. 356.

GRANITE (Captain Loftus), gr g ; 4 white pasterns, light face. No. 503.

GREEN LAWN (Mr. J. Stafford), ch m ; star, race, snip, No. 237

GREGORY'S POWDER (Mr. Maurice F. Dennis), ch g ; race, four white legs, N/ quarter K. No. 115.

GREY BIRD (Mr. W. E. Drury), gr g ; N shoulder. No. 586.

GREY WINGS (Mr. St. L. G. Stephen), gr m ; flea-bitten forehead, neck and flanks. No. 485.

GRIZEL (Mr. N. F. Archdale), gr m ; N/F and B H fetlocks. No. 139.

HANDY ANDY (Mr. A. Hastings), ch g ; star, O H ½ stocking. No. 383.

HAPPY THOUGHT (Major G. M. Eccles), ch m ; star, race, O H fetlock. (Season only.) No. 280.

HARD LUCK (Messrs. Slocock), br m ; star, snip O H fetlock, N H coronet and heel. No. 140.

HARLEQUIN (Mr. H. F. Hardy), b g; star, N F and O H heel. No. 116.

HASSAN (Mr. W. Lindsay), ch g; star, small spot O/ shin   No. 505.

HAWTHORN (Dr. Kelly Patterson), b m.   No. 305.

HAZEL (Mr. G. Morris Midwood), ch m; linear star O H pastern, ½ fetlock. (Season only.) No. 98.

HENRY (Mr. James Farmer), br g; B H coronets.   No. 60.

HEYDAY (Mr. H. F. Hardy), blk g; star, race, N F coronet and inside O/H coronet. No. 117.

HILL DUCK (G. W. S. Willins), b m; faint spinal stripe.   No 99.

HOB NOB (Captain Egerton Green), ch g; blaze face, B F coronets and heels, B/H stockings. No. 371.

IDA (Mr. Jasper Grant), b m; star, snip N H fetlock and up back of leg. (Season only.) No. 334.

IN AND OUT (Major Paynter), b m; small star-fetlocks.   No. 238.

ISAAC (Mr. B. Wilson), red roan g.   No. 372.

JACK-AN-APES (Messrs. Miller), b g; O H coronet and heel.   No. 11.

JACKO (Mr. H. E. Lambe), gr g; slight bay marks over eyes.   No. 559.

JANE (Mr. E. Bellamy), bl br m; N H coronet.   No. 198.

JASPER (Captain Loftus), br g; star, race, snip to N, side, N H pastern. No. 141.

JEMIMA (Mr. W. H. Moreshead), br m; (season only).   No. 199.

JEN HO (Mr. J. Farmer), br g; few grey hairs in forehead.   No. 62.

JESSIE (Mr. H. Barker), b m.   No. 61.

JIM'S PALL (Mr. James Farmer), elevated ridge bone O/ forehead. No. 384.

JOAN (Mr. B. Worthington), bl g; O F coronet, N H fetlock.   No. 239.

JOEY (Mr. A. K. Huntington), br g; star, spot as snip, pasterns, and back of fetlocks. No. 408.

JOHN O'GAUNT (Mr. J. Drage), gr g.   No. 12.

JOHNNY (Mr. Stuart Duckett), b g; star, snip, white mark on N/ side. No. 506.

JUDGE, THE (Miss Tyrrel), dk b g; B H pasterns and up to ½ fetlock joint. No. 108.

JUDGE, THE (Mr. J. Adamthwaite), br g; snip, pasterns, and fetlocks. No. 89.

33*

JULIA (Messrs. Slocock), b m ; B H coronet rings. No. 142.

JUMBO (Mr. W. E. Drury), bay g ; blaze, race, snip N F fetlock, B H fetlocks. No. 587.

JUST IN TIME (Mr. W. Blunsome), ch g ; grizzled blaze, narrow race and snip. No. 64.

JUST IN TIME (Mr. P. W. Connolly), br g ; few warts in front of sheath. No. 286.

KATE (Mr. T. Corrigan), b m. (Season only.) No. 143.

KATE (Mr. E. T. Pritchard), dk ch m ; blaze top of mane, grey inside N/H coronet, O/H fetlock, spot inside of O/ knee. No. 534.

KATHLEEN (Mr. N. Haig), b m ; N H fetlock, O H coronet. No. 346.

KEYSTONE (Mr. M. Moncrieffe), ch g ; small crescent on forehead, scar O/H shin. No. 43.

KHEDIVE (Mr. O. Milling), b g ; star. No. 240.

KIMBERLEY (Mr. R. Blakiston Houston), ch m ; star, O F pastern, N/H outside coronet, O/H fetlock, ches. mark O/H coronet. No. 327.

KING ARTHUR (Mr. Noel Price), b g ; narrow race, N F pastern and back of fetlock, B/H fetlocks. No. 46.

KING JOHN (Mr. A. Price), b g ; blaze, race, broad snip B H fetlocks. No. 47.

KISS IN THE RING (Mr. P. Bullivant), ch g ; blaze face. No. 409.

KITTEN (Mr. L. J. Droffats), b m. No. 241.

KLONDYKE (Mr. J. Farquhar), bl g ; blaze, race, snip underlip, B/F and N/H fetlocks, O/H ½ fetlock. No. 447.

KOORT NONG (Mr. N. Haig), b m ; inside O H heel, branded 829, N/ side hock, enlarged O/ knee. No. 347.

LADY BETTY (Mr. C. C. Gouldsmith), ch m ; blaze, underlip, O F and B/H legs, N/F leg, ches. and white. No. 385.

LADY BIRD (Mr. H. Barker), br m. No. 65.

LADY BIRD (Mr. H. Boden), dk br m ; few grey hairs forehead, and tail and coat. No. 560.

LADY BIRD (Lady Kilmorey), b m ; star, race, snip underlip, O F coronet. No. 242.

LADY BIRD (Mr. J. N. Hone), br m ; (Season only.) No. 296.

LADY CLARE (W. K. Carew), b m ; O F heel, and spot on coronet, O/H spot on outer heel. No. 243,

LADY DEWET (Mr. C. B. Houston), br m ; few spots above F/ knees. No. 331.

LADY FLORENCE (Messrs. Slocock), b m ; few grey hairs on forehead, N/H pastern and ½ fetlock. No. 145.

LADY GOLIGHTLY (Mr. F. Barton), ch roan mare. No. 100,

LADY GEORGE (Mr. O. Milling), ches. m ; star, race, O'H fetlock, N/ heel. No. 244.

LADY GRACE (Mr. J. Farmer), grey coat ticked, bay m ; wart on chest. No. 66.

LADY GREY (Mr. M. Quinn), grey mare, mottled dark grey legs, mottling mixed brown hairs. No. 476.

LADY JANE GREY (Mr. Fosyth Forrest), gr m scar above o/ knee. No. 386.

LADY MASSA (Captain L. Bryan), br m. No. 144.

LADY NELL (Messrs. Slocock), b m ; scar outside O H fetlock. No. 507,

LADY PAT (Captain Jenner), b m ; small dot as star. No. 357.

LADYSMITH (Mr. M. de Las Casas), gr m ; O/F dark, N F light. No. 410.

LADY TOM (Mr. H. B. Harrison), br m ; faint star and race N'H pastern and heel. No. 68.

LADY WHITE (Mr. R. Blakiston Houston), b m ; star, race, snip O/F coronet. No. 320.

LADY WINK (Messrs. Slocock), bl m ; few grey hairs on forehead. No. 146.

LASSIE (Mr. R. Young), ch m ; star, race, snip to N' side, N H coronet and back of heel, N/H fetlock. No. 428.

LATCH KEY (Mr. G. A. Miller), ch g ; star, spot O, shoulder. No. No. 575.

LATCH KEY (Mr. W. Lax), ch g ; star and short race. No. 387.

LEDBURY (Mr. Bell), b g ; two small white marks N' side. No. 576.

LEECH, THE (Mr. G. Barter), b m ; star, scar front N'H fetlock. No. 396,

LETTY LIND (Mr. A. M. Caldecott-Smith), b m; star, N H coronet, and B/H heels. No. 508.

LIMIT, THE ((Mr. W. McCreery), ch m (3 years) ; blaze, N F fetlock, O/F pasterns and stocking, N/H pastern. (Season only.) No. 436.

LINDSEY (Messrs. Slocock), b m ; blaze, race, snip B H fetlocks. No. 147.

LINKMAN (Messrs. Miller), br roan g ; dot race, snip, B H stockings, patch under N/ side body, grey hairs in tail. No. 373.

LIQUEUR (Mr. H. P. Wilson), br g. No. 307.

LITTLE FELLOW (Mr. Harcourt Gold), b g ; star, N'H ½ fetlock. No. 429.

LITTLE HERCULES (Mr. F. C. Nash), ch roan g. No. 388.

LITTLE LADY (Mr. J. Farmer), gr m ; light coloured head, B'H stockings. No. 67.

LOAN (Messrs. Slocock), bl or br m ; brushed o,H fetlock. No. 148.

LOCKET (Captain E. D. Cameron), b m. No. 448.

LOCKSLEY (Mr. W. B. Hayes), b g ; small star, scar inside, o F leg. No. 509.

LOPEAR (Mr. W. E. Drury), b g. No. 589.

LORD BOBBY (Mr. Casson), b g ; star, N'H $\frac{1}{2}$ fetlock o'H fetlock. (Season only.) No. 430.

LORD BOBS (Mr. J. St. P. McArdle), ch g ; star only. No. 245.

LOVELY CASH (Mr. J. Devaney), b m ; bl legs. (Season only.) No. 273.

LUCIANA (Mr. J. Adamthwaite), ch m ; blaze face underlip, N H stocking. No. 69.

LUCILLE (Captain Egerton Green), ch m ; star, faint race, and snip, small white spot outside o/ knee. No. 374.

LUCY GLITTERS (Mr. J. Wormald), b m ; white spot back N' knee. No. 411.

LULU (Mr. William Lax), ch m ; star race, N'F coronet, white mark on o/H coronet, back of tendon. No. 389.

LURLINE (Mr. F. O. Ellison), b m ; star, small white mark front · of o/ shin. No. 431.

MABEL (Mr. N. F. Archdale), br m ; o'H coronet ring. No. 149.

MACAROON (Mr. D. C. Master), dun g ; square star. No. 70.

MADGE (Mr. T. J. Roark), b m ; star, B,H pasterns, o,F coronet. No. 150.

MAD EYE (Mr. R. W. Hali-Dare), dk b g ; star. No. 246.

MAGIC (Mr. F. B. Phillips), br m ; star, snip. No. 201.

MAGIC (Mr. C. W. Meredith), ch m ; N'H $\frac{1}{2}$ stocking, black spot outside o/H coronet. No. 202.

MAHOMET (Captian Paske), b g ; grizzled patch on each side of spine, under saddle. No. 271.

MAINSTAY (Mr. F. Ellison), b br m ; N H pastern. No. 412.

MANDARIN (Mr. F. Newman), gr g ; dark legs, coronet rings. No. 466.

MANIFOLD (Mr. N. Haig), ch g ; blaze N'H $\frac{1}{2}$ stocking, white mark above both eyes on cheek. No. 348.

MANSFIELD (Mr. W. McCreery), bg ; star o,' coronet and heel, B/H fetlocks. No. 375.

MARANGO (Mr. W. McCreery), ch m ; short blaze, scar outside o/H fetlock. No. 376.

MARIE THE RAKE (Mr. N. Haig), br m ; saddle marks, spot N side. No. 349.

MARJORIE (Mr. F. Wise), b m ; very small star, small spot N H heel. No. 413.

MARMALADE (Mr. Digby Master), b or br g. No. 71.

MARMOZETTI (Mr. G. A. Miller), ch m ; star race N H pastern front o/H coronet. No. 577.

MARSH MARIGOLD (Captain Phipps G. Hornby), ch m ; star. o/H coronet. No.561.

MARY ANN (Mr. J. Drage), br m ; star o F and N H fetlocks. No. 13.

MASTER OWEN (Keynsham Stud Company), b g ; star, race B H $\frac{1}{2}$ stockings. (Season only.) No. 101.

MASTER WILLIE (Mr. J. G. Murphy), b g ; star, slight snip inside o/H heel. No. 151.

MATINEE (Mr. F. Ellison), b m ; N H heel o H heel and part of coronet. No. 414.

MAUD (Mr. C. W. Moncrieffe), br m ; clot for star, slight snip N H pastern and back of fetlock, o H fetlock. No. 203.

MAY DAY (Mr. W. Roylance Court), b m ; star snip. No. 578.

MAXIM (Mr. J. T. Roark), ch g ; star, snip, B H coronets. No. 152.

MAY FLOWER (Dr. Kelly Paterson), b m ; small white mark, N H heel. No. 304.

MAY FLY (Mr. J. T. Roark), ch m ; grizzled race. No. 153.

MAY MORN (M. Percy Walcot), ch m ; star, race, snip, to N side, few grey hairs centre N/ quarter. No. 72.

MEADSTONE (Mr. R. Blakiston Houston), br m ; star, race, snip N F coronet, o/F outside coronet festoons in white B/F fetlocks, blk markings in coronet. (Season only.) No. 329.

MEG MERRILIES (Mr. S. Anderson), b m ; star, N H pastern, o H coronet. (Season only.) No. 510.

MELBA (Mr. N. Haig), ch m ; star, race, snip. No. 350.

MELODY (Mr. Digby Master), iron gr m ; bay hairs on face. No. 73.

MERCURY (Mr. F. Wise), b g ; few grey hairs in forehead, B H pasterns and back of fetlocks. No. 415.

MERCURY (Lord C. C. Bentinck), ch g ; star, grizzled race, white spot o/ side behind girth. No. 459.

MERRY LASS (Captain O'Hara), b m ; many saddle marks. No. 295.

MERRY TOM (Mr. J. Drage), b g ; star, mealy legs. No. 579.

MERRY THOUGHT (Mr. A. Dugdale), br m ; spot N′ side. No. 535.

MICROBE (Captain F. Egerton Green), b m ; few grey hairs on forehead. No. 458.

MIDGE (Captain B. Daly), br m ; saddle marks B′ sides and on centre of back. No. 247.

MIKE (Mr. Evan T. Pritchard), ch g ; grey hairs forehead, N′H coronet, ring, o/H pastern, No. 536.

MI LADY (Mr. R. Blackiston Houston), b m ; little grizzled patch inside o/F pastern. No. 314.

MINUET (Messrs. Miller), b m ; both hind coronets, patchy grey marks largest in heels. No. 14.

MIRIAM (Mr. J. Adamthwaite), ch m ; few grey hairs forehead, N/F coronet and heel, No. 580.

MIRIAN (Mr. C. W. Meredith), b m ; few grey hairs forehead. No. 204.

MISS COLONIAL (Mr. J. Farmer), br m ; wart front of neck. No. 74.

MISS GINGER (Mr. W. Lindsay), star, race, disconnected spot as snip, N/F fetlock, o/H stocking. No. 205.

MISS MURPHY (Mr. M. Murphy), ch m; N F coronet, star, B′H pasterns and part of fetlock. (Season only.) No. 299.

MISS OAKLEY (Mr. Digby Master), br m ; large star, race, slight mark N/F heel. No. 390.

MISS POPPET (Mr. A. A. Suffert), bl m ; star, grizzled, race. No. 572.

MISS SANDLEY (Mr. R. H. H. Eden), b m ; o′H pastern, N′H coronet ring. No. 567.

MISS WAREN (Mr. N. Haig), br m ; small white spot above front o/H fetlock. No. 351.

MISTRESS, THE (Mr. M. Quinn), b m ; star, race, snip, N/H sock. (Season only.) No. 478.

MOLLY (Mr. W. Ashmore), dk gr m ; star, N′H pastern. (Season only.) No. 156.

MOLLY BAWN (Mr. W. B. Hayes), liver coloured m ; star, N/H pastern and ½ fetlock. No. 511.

MONA (Mr. W. G. Dease), br m ; star, o F coronet, B H fetlocks. No. 118.

MONA (Lord Harrington), b br m ; star, both H′ pasterns and back of fetlocks. No. 358.

MOONSTONE (Mr. Digby Master), ch m ; star, race inside N/F coronet inside o/H coronet. No. 391.

MOORHEN (Mr. R. W. Fearnley), ch m ; star, short connected race, grey hairs on top of wither. No. 102.

MORGLAY (Mr. A. Price), br m ; X-shaped star, N H coronet. No. 48.

MOVEMENT (Mr. N. E. Price), b m ; blaze race, sn p, spot over N/ nostril, B/H ½ stockings. No. 49.

MOYRA (Mr. F. Wise), bl m ; star, N H heel. No. 416.

MUSCIC (Mr. Digby Master), gr m ; light mottled. No. 75.

MUSTAPHA (Mr. B. Worthington), b g ; star, race, snip, N F white over knee, B/H stockings. No. 248.

MY FANCY (Mr. N. F. Whelan), br m ; scar on inner and back part O/H tendon. No. 154.

MY LADY (Messrs. Slocock), b m ; few grey hairs forehead, snip. No. 155.

MY LADY (Mr. Stewart Murray), gr m ; brown tick, especially about body. (Season only.) No. 310.

NALBUND (Mr. P. H. Sandilands), ch g ; star, race, snip to O/ side. No. 392.

NAN (Mr. R. R. Barker), br m ; star. No. 76.

NANCY (Mr. E. M. Stewart), ch m ; star and race, (to O/ side), snip B/H stocking. No. 330.

NANCY (Mr. W. B. C. Burden), b m ; star, race snip, N H fetlock. No. 393.

NATTY (Mr. B. H. Nicholson), ch m ; star, race, white spots B/ sides of neck, O/H pastern. No. 417.

NAUGHTY BOY (Mr. W. E. Drury), br g ; few grey hairs forehead, small mark O/H. No. 590.

NEELGANOST (Mr. B. Daly), ch g ; star, race, warts on chest. No. 119.

NELLY (Mr. R. Blackiston Houston), b m ; star, few spots N/ shin. No. 321.

NELLY BLY (Messrs. Slocock), b m ; N H coronet and heel. No. 157.

NETTLE (Mr. J. Farmer), b m ; star, N H coronet. No. 394.

NEVER SAY DIE (Mr. W. G. Edge), b or br m ; star. No. 158.

NEWPORT (Mr. W. C. Eustis), b g ; star, white spots over body and quarters. No. 418.

NIGRETI (Mr. N. Learmonth), bl g ; star, race, snip O H coronet. No. 562.

NIMBLE (Mr. C. H. Richardson), b m ; star, race, snip, N F and B H fetlocks. No. 326.

No. 1 (Messrs. Slocock), b or br g ; few grey hairs forehead, N H pastern, O/H ½ fetlock. No. 159.

NO HUMBUG (Mr. Noel E. Price), ch m ; very small spot forehead, small grey marks front B/F fetlocks. No. 50.

ODDINGTON (Mr. J. R. Ormrod), steel gr m ; white hairs behind girth o/ side. No. 77.

ŒDIPUS (Captain Steeds), dark ch g ; star, race, snip, o'H pastern, fetlock and back leg, spotted all over. No. 15.

ONYX (Captain Loftus), br m ; little semilinear mark forehead, few grey hairs, N/F coronet. No. 160.

OPHIA (Captain E. D. Miller), ch g ; star, race, bald snip, o̤H coronet inside. No. 419.

ORCHID (Captain W. E. H. Steeds), gr m ; b tick side of neck, small blk spot N/ side of neck. No. 512.

ORPHAN, THE (Mr. T. D. Wallis), br g ; o H coronet, ring and back of heel. No. 479.

ORPHAN, THE (Mr. S. Anderson), br m ; star, B H pasterns. No. 513.

OYEZ (Mr. A. Dugdale), b g ; o'H heel and coronet. No. 537.

PADDY (Mr. C. H. Reade), br g ; saddle marks centre of back, permanent scar o/H heel. No. 250.

PALMYRA (Mr. Thomas Anderson), br m ; wide race, snip, N F coronet, B/H ½ stockings. No. 161.

PALNITA (Mr. J. D. Wallis), br m ; faint star. No. 249.

PANIC (Messrs. Miller), blk br m ; angular mark o side under saddle. No. 16.

PANSY (Mr. J. Farmer), liver ch m ; star, race, snip, N̤H coronet. No. 395.

PANTALOON (Mr. Dawson), b g ; large blaze all four stockings to above knees and hocks. No. 467.

PAT (Messrs. Slocock), ch dun g ; dark ch, lighter legs. No. 162.

PATCH (Mr. F. W. O'Hara), b m ; spot o̦' side top neck and o̦' shoulder, various saddle marks. No. 288.

PATIENCE (Mr. J. H. Welch), b m ; star, race, snip, N̦F inside coronet, N̤/H fetlock, o/H leg grizzled. No. 324.

PATIENCE (Mr. Ulric O. Thynne), b m ; small star N' side. No. 359.

PAXTON (Mr. G. A. Miller), dk b g ; 3 white marks N̦ side, one on back. No. 581.

PEARL (Captain Loftus), br m ; blaze, snip, N H pastern, grey tick in coat. No. 514.

PEDLAR (Mr. Evan T. Pritchard), br g ; 2 grey marks on back, scar o/ knee. No. 538.

PILOT (Mr. W. E. Drury), b g ; star N F heel, N̦/H fetlock, o̦H pastern, and patch outside o/F heel. No. 591.

PLAY TOY (Mr. T. J. Roark), ch g ; o̦H coronet. No. 164.

POLEMIC MARE (Mr. Arthur Natus), ch m ; large star, narrow continuous race. No. 103.

POM-POM (Mr. W. E. Grogan), ch g ; star, race, snip to N side, N/H stocking, spot front O/H coronet. (Season only.) No. 515.

POM-POM (Captain Phipps Hornby), br g ; small lineal scar inside front O/ coronet. No. 563.

POP (Mr. E. Bellamy), br g ; star, saddle and girth spots. No. 251.

PRETTY JANIE (Mr. A. Rodgers), br m ; star O H pastern and up inside fetlock. (Season only.) No. 316.

PRICELESS (Mr. R. Whurr), b m ; few grey hairs N side fore top, single spot N/ side. No. 486.

PRIMROSE (Messrs. Miller), b m ; single spot near stifle, two linear marks front N/H shin. No. 17.

PRIMROSE (Mr. T. J. Roark), ch m ; blaze B'H stockings. No. 165.

PRIMROSE DAME (Mr. W. Stourbridge), ch m ; star, grizzled extension over left brow. (Season only.) No. 104.

PRINCE (Mr. Engledon) ; star, disconnected race and snip, few grey hairs in tail. No. 166.

PRINCE (Mr. E. N. McCormick), b g ; blaze, race, snip, with grizzled edge to race, B/H fetlocks. (Season only.) No. 252.

PRINCE, THE (Mr. J. D. Wallis), ch g ; star, race, snip, O H pastern. (Season only.) No. 259.

PRINCESS (Rev. C. Prodgers), br m ; N F coronet and heel, B H coronets. No. 432.

PRINCESS (Mr. E. Rotherham), dk b m ; star, narrow race to snip, over nostril, underlip, N/F coronet, O/F coronet inside, N/H ½ stockings. No. 301.

PRODIGAL (Mr. J. W. Hornsby), gr g ; O H leg light. No. 468.

PUNCH (Hon. O. Hastings), b horse ; star, small hollow over O shoulder point. No. 78.

PUNCH (R.A. Polo Club), gr g ; white mottled quarters. No. 449.

QUALITY (Mr. E. Rotherham), br g ; few grey hairs forehead, B H pasterns. No. 300.

QUEEN (Major Beech), dk b m ; few grey hairs under saddle. No. 18.

QUEENIE (Mr. R. A. Warren), b m ; blaze, scar front O'F fetlock N/H fetlock. No. 516.

QUEENIE (Mr. T. Leonard), br m ; light grizzled saddle mark. (Season only.) No. 200.

QUERY (Messrs. Miller), br m ; large saddle marks O side, small ones N/ side, O/H pastern, few grey hairs front O/F coronet. No. 19.

RABOATH (Mr. W. McCreery), dk b g ; race, snip. No. 433.

RATTLE (Captain E. G. Hardy), ch m ; blaze, race, snip N H coronet, o/H inside fetlock. No 564.

REDBIRD (Mr. W. E. Drury), ch g ; star, faint grizzled race B/H fetlocks. No. 592.

RED HEART (Mr. E. F. Dease), ch m ; star, with grizzled border, narrow race, snip. No. 312.

RED PICKLES (Mr. J. S. Bakewell), ch roan g ; rudimentary corn inside o/ hock. No. 565.

RED ROSE (Lieut.-Colonel Henriques), ch m ; few grey hairs N/ side centre of forehead, o/H pastern and heel, white, with permanent scar on inner and front side of same. (Season only.) No. 105.

REQUISITION (Captain Fielden), gr g. No. 573.

R.H.A. (Mr. A. L. Farrant), gr g ; blaze o/F fetlock B/H stockings. No. 450.

RINGLET (Mr. J. Adamthwaite), ch m ; small star. No. 79.

RISK (Mr. C. W. Meredith), b m ; star race, broad snip to N nostril, N/F, o/H pastern, N/H fetlock. No. 206.

ROCK (Mr. W. E. Drury), b g ; star, snip, B F and O H fetlocks white, white marks N/ side. No. 593.

ROLLO (Mr. C. H. Sheather), b g ; star o H pastern, and tuft o/F fetlock. No. 434.

ROMAN LASS (Messrs. Slocock), gr m ; B/F and o H legs. No. 167.

ROULETTE (Mr. J. Adamthwaite), ch m ; blaze N/H stocking. No. 80.

ROYAL OAK (Mr. R. Good), br g ; blaze, race, small snip O H ½ fetlock. (Season only.) No. 253.

RUBY (Captain Loftus), ch m ; star, broad race N/H fetlock. (Season only.) No. 168.

RUBY (Mr. F. Ellison), ch m ; blaze, underlip N F coronet, N/H stocking o/F fetlock, with band to hock. No. 420.

RUFUS (Mr. A. Dugdale), ch g ; star race, snip. No. 539.

ST. BLAIZE (Captain Phipps Hornby), br g ; blaze, N F stocking, B/H stockings. No. 566.

ST. KILDA (Mr. N. Haig), ch m ; star, narrow race, white spot N/ flank. No. 355.

ST. OSYTH (Captain Egerton Green), b m ; star, snip, N H pastern and ½ of fetlocks white. No. 2.

ST. PAT (Mr. P. J. C. Linnott), ch g ; star, race curving to o/ side, broad snip, N/H fetlock, o/H coronet. (Season only.) No. 216.

ST. PATRICK (Keynsham Stud Co.), bl g ; few grey hairs on forehead, snip, N/F pastern both hind fetlocks. No. 107.

ST. SIEVA (Mr. W. C. Fagan), b m. (Season only.) No. 309.

SAMMY (Colonel Campbell), gr g ; lightly flea-bitten, white mark N F shin, also below and in front of N/ hock. No. 270.

SANTA JÈ (Mr. Glover), b g ; faint star. No. 469.

SANTOI (Mr. A. Rawlinson), br m ; star to N/ side, B/H pasterns and back of fetlocks. No. 360.

SANTOI (Mr. C. Dillon), ch m ; faint race, grey tick in coat over both hip joints. No. 207.

SANTOY (Mr. J Adamthwaite), br m ; star O H heel and back of fetlock. No. 81.

SAPHIRE (Captain Loftus), ch m ; star N H coronet. No. 169.

SARAH (Mr. C. H. T. Reade), br m ; few small spots O S behind saddle flap, few grey hairs under flap N/ side. No. 254.

SAUCY MARY (Mr. N. Haig), b m star. No. 352.

SAVOY, THE (Captain L. Bryan), b m ; star, race, N H pastern and inside fetlock, O/H fetlock. No. 480.

SCHOEMAN (Captain Egerton Green), ch g ; star, race B N stockings. No. 353.

SCHOLAR (Mr. W. E. Grogan), b g ; spot forehead, O H coronet ring. No. 517.

SCOTTY (Mr. M. F. Dennis), b g ; blaze, snip B H legs. No. 120.

SCOUT (Messrs. Miller), ch g ; star race to N side, large snip ascending race from O/ nostril, O/F and O/H coronet, N/H stocking. No. 20.

SEABREEZE (Major Harley), b m ; white mark near bottom end of mane. No. 470.

SEASIDE (Mr. A. Rawlinson), ch m ; large star, Larrow race scar outside N/H shin. No. 92.

SECRET (Mr. P. J. Sinnott), dk b m ; star, short race N F coronet, N/H fetlock, O/H pastern, and ½ fetlock. No. 208.

SENSIBLE (Mr. J. Farmer), b m ; small star B H heels. No. 82.

SEQUEL (Mr. A. Rawlinson), ch m ; star, narrow race B/H coronets, irregular markings. No. 461.

SHAIBOOB (Major J. Fowle), gr horse ; permanent scar on B F coronets. No. 209.

SHAMROCK (Mr. J. Mitchell), br g ; dot on forehead, N/H coronet and heel. No. 435.

SHAMROCK (Mr. A. Rawlinson), b g ; ring for star grizzled race, broad snip underlip, N/F coronet and inside O/F fetlock. No. 93.

SHEILA (Mr. J. B. Charters), br m. No. 308.

SHERIDAN (Mr. W. Lyon Clark), b g blaze, N F fetlock, N/H stocking. No. 377.

SHYLOCK (Mr. P. J. Sinnott), ch g ; star, race, underlip, B/H stockings. No. 210.

SILENCE (Mr. P. J. Sinnott), b m ; small star, B H pasterns, small
black spots on coronets. No. 211.

SILVER (Mr. J. Adamthwaite), b m ; star O H pastern. No. 83.

SILVER (Mr. H. A. Gairdine), ch m star race, mealy tail. No. 518.

SIRDAR (Mr. G. J. Reade), br g saddle marks o side *only*. No.
335.

SKITTLES (Mr. R. H. H. Eden), br m ; few grey hairs, spot o/
knee, mark o/ shin. No. 568.

SLIDEAWAY (Mr. W. E. Drury), ch roan g. No distinctive marks,
more ches than roan. No. 594.

SLIGO (Mr. P. J. Sinnott), bl m ; star, N H pastern O H coronet,
grey patch o/ shoulder. No. 212.

SLIMBOY (Mr. N. Haig), br g ; o H coronet, scar inside O H leg and
N/H leg. No. 354.

SLIPPERY SALL (Mr. T. B. Montgomery), b m ; knob front O F
pastern, prominent forehead. No. 519.

SLYBOOTS (Mr. T. L. Moore), b m ; small vertical linear star.
No. 213.

SLYONE (Mr. P. J. Sinnott), b m ; small star, snip N, nostril. No.
214.

SLY PAT (Mr. T. R. Roark), gr g ; light grey. No. 170.

SNOB (Mr. R. Blakiston Houston), gr m ; dark, mottled with light
coloured head. No. 323.

SNOWBALL (Mr. R. Blakiston Houston), gr m ; light coloured
head, four dark legs. No. 322.

SON JOHN (Mr. J. Bigley), ch gr g ; N F and B/H pasterns. (Season
only.) No. 171.

SONNY (Mr. J. N. Hare), gr g ; star N H pastern, O H small coronet
mark, bay tick in coat. No. 298.

SOPHIA (Mr. W. G. Dease), b m ; small spot o' side saddle. No.
121.

SPANIARD (Major Paynter), b g ; N F coronet and heel. No. 122.

SPARKLET (Mr. J. Pyke Nott), liver ches m ; star, N F coronet.
No. 106.

SPARROW (Mr. W. E. Drury), b g ; star. No. 595.

SPARROW (Mr. R. Sullivan), b g ; star, few grey hairs as snip, grey
ticks in coat. (Season only.) No. 255.

SPIDGER (Mr. Stuart Duckett), b m ; star, B H pasterns. No.
520.

SPRITE (Captain E. D. Miller), bl m ; grizzled star, white marks on
B/F and N/H shins. No. 421.

STARLIGHT (Mr. Jasper Grant), ch m ; star, race, snip, O H fetlock.
No. 333.

STARS AND STRIPES (Mr. A. L. Farrant, R.H.A.), red roan g ; blaze, four white legs over knees and hocks. No. 451.

STEPHANOTIS (Major A. Stoke), br m ; spot, N H heel, O H coronet and heel. No. 452.

STOUT (Messrs. Slocock), b g ; few grey hairs on forehead. (Season only.) No. 172.

STRANGER (Major Paynter), br g ; star, interrupted race and snip, N/H pastern. No. 477.

STRELMA (Mr. P. J. Sinnott), b m ; faint patch under N saddle pannel. No. 215.

STRIPES (Mr. St. L. G. Stephen), br m ; small star, O H $\frac{1}{2}$ fetlock, narrow white ring round body. No. 487.

SUGAR PLUM (Mr. A. Rawlinson), ch m ; long star, both hind stockings. No. 94.

SUMMER LIGHTNING (Mr. G. A. Miller), b m ; few grey hairs on forehead, scar inside O/ forearm, outside O/H shin. No. 361.

SUMMER SHOWER (Mr. G. A. Miller), br m ; grizzled star. No. 362.

SUNDAY (Mr. A. Rawlinson), gr m ; right $\frac{1}{2}$ face light, left face dark, scar both shoulders, N/H heel light. No. 95.

SUNFLOWER (Mr. P. J. Sinnott), b m ; star, O H coronet, spot N/ loin. No. 217.

SUNSHINE (Mr. J. J. Stafford), gr g ; O F heel, light patch below N/H outside. No. 256.

SURPRISE (Mr. E. B. Sheppard), ch g ; star, race, snip, B H fetlocks, N/F coronet. No. 378.

SUSAN (Mr. H. Barker), ch m ; blaze, N F pastern and up back of leg O/H fetlock. No. 84.

SWEETMEAT (Captain Hickman), b m ; faint grizzled star. No. 284.

SWEETS (Mr. J. T. Roark), b m ; star, short race. No. 522.

SWEET WILLIAM (Mr. J. Adamthwaite), b g ; star. No. 85.

SYLPH, THE (Captain H. D. O. Ward), br m ; small linear mark, N/H shin. No. 453.

SYLVIA (Mr. P. J. Sinnott), b m ; star, race, snip, O nostril, N F coronet, B/H fetlocks. No. 257.

TARBOX (Messrs. Miller), br g ; few grey hairs for star. No. 21.

TAMBORINE (Mr. J. N. Hare), b g ; few grey hairs in forehead. No. 297.

TANTRUM (Major G. M. Eccles), b m ; small star, B S under saddle, grizzled patch. No. 277.

THEODORE (Col. H. M. Ridley), bl g ; snip, B H pasterns inside fetlocks and heel. No. 569.

THUNDERSTORM (Messrs. Miller), ches g ; star, race, snip, spot o/ side neck. No. 22.

TINMAN (Mr. N. Learmonth), dun g ; star, N H and B F fetlocks. No. 570.

TIP (Mr. F. Freake), b m ; star. No. 363.

TITANIA (Mr. Ulric O. Thynne), br m ; small star, few grey hairs in tail. No. 364.

TOKER, THE (Mr. Henry Terral), b g ; star, O'F and N H coronet. No. 460.

TOM (Mr. H. A. Gairdine), b g ; blaze, N H fetlock, O H pastern. No. 524.

TOMMY (Mr. J. H. Anketell-Jones), bl g ; saddlemarks, few white dots front of O/F fetlock. No. 260.

TOMMY DOD (Mr. E. T. Pritchard), b or br g ; B F and N/H coronets and heels, blk marks. No. 540.

TOM THUMB (Mr. W. E. Drury), ch g ; blaze face, N F fetlock, B/H high stockings. No. 596.

TOPSEY (Captain Loftus), br g ; snip, N/ nostril, B H stockings, N H fetlocks. No. 177.

TORDILLO (Mr. M. F. Dennis), gr g ; white face, 4 white legs. No. 123.

TORTOISE (Mr. T. J. Roark), br m ; star, O'H coronet ring. No. 178.

TOUCH AND GO (Captain Long), b m ; grizzled right ½ face, few grey hairs right cheek. No. 219.

TOY SHOP (Mr. T. Lewis Moore), mottled gr g ; No. 525.

TRUMPS (Mr. H. A. Gairdine), b g ; few grey hairs on forehead, slight linear snip, N/H pasterns, blk markings inside. No. 526.

TUMBLER (Mr. W. E. Drury), b g ; no white. No. 597.

TURQUOISE (Captain Loftus), ch m ; few grey hairs forehead, N H fetlock, O/H coronet. No. 527.

VESTA (Mr. H. A. Gairdine), b m ; N H pastern, O H coronet, blk marks. No. 528.

VIC (Mr. W. McCreery), ch m ; star, race, snip, N H coronet. No. 437.

VICTOR (Mr. J. J. Stafford), b g ; star, B H pasterns. No. 261.

VICTORIA (Mr. John Barker), b m ; star, N H coronet, O H fetlock. No. 109.

VIXEN (Miss Webber), gr m ; bay tinge in coat. No. 163.

WATCHMAN (Mr. F. W. Perry), br g ; N/F pastern and ½ fetlock, N/H pastern. No. 220.

WELL MOUNT (Mr. R. St. G. Robinson), br g; N/H heel, spot front of same coronet. No. 287.

WEXFORD (Messrs. Slocock), br g. No. 179.

WILLIAM (12th Lancers Club), ch g; star, disconnected race and snip, B/H pasterns and ½ fetlock. No. 268.

WINCANTON (Mr. R. H. H. Eden), b m; inside N F coronet and heel. No. 571.

WINNIE (Mr. J. Adamthwaite), dk ch m; star. No. 91.

WITCHCRAFT (Mr. A. Price), b m; O/H inside coronet and heel, small white mark N/ quarter. No. 51.

WOLVERINE (Messrs. Miller), b m; star, linear saddle marks. No. 23.

WONDER BIRD (Mr. J. Cheshire), ch m; star, race, few white grizzled marks over N/ hip joint. No. 262.

WREN, THE (Hon. O. Hastings), br m; star. No. 90.

YELLOW GIRL (Mr. W. C. Eustis), dun m; small star, blk stripe down back, zebra markings B/F. No. 422.

YORK (Mr. J. Drage), b m; star and scar outside N shin. No. 582.

YOURS TRULY (Mr. H. A. Gairdine), gr m; N F and B/H legs, spot N/ side neck at wither. No. 529.

ZOO (Mr. F. C. Nash), ch m; star, race, snip O F pastern and back of fetlock, O/H inside coronet. No. 397.

1901.—THE FOLLOWING PONIES WERE NOT PASSED.

BEECHNUT (Mr. F. Hargreaves), ch g; star, N'H coronet. No. 438.

BOBS (Mr. F. W. O'Hara), br g; few grey hairs for star, odd markings at upper part N/ knee. No. 293.

BONNIE STAR (Captain L. Bryan), br m; star O H pastern and ½ fetlock, N/H pastern. No. 180.

CHANGE (Captain Leo Wynne), b m; star, race, spot for snip, O H coronet and heel. No. 291.

CLAREEN (Mr. C. W. Creede), br m; star, snip, N H inside coronet, O/H whole coronet white. No. 223.

CORNELIAN (Sir H. de Trafford), ch m; star, race, disconnected and small snip. No. 4.

CORNER BOY (S. Anderson), bl br g; star B,H pasterns. No. 495.

DELIGHT (Messrs. Slocock), br; with white hairs m, star, race, silver topped tail, N/H fetlock. No. 499. (See also under D, in passed for season).

DE WET (Messrs. Slocock), b g; star slightly to N/ side. No. 181.

DRACHMA (Mr. A. L. Farrant), b m; star, race, snip O F and O,H pasterns. No. 454.

FETTERLESS (Earl of Harrington), blk ch m; star, N H coronet, O/H pastern and half fetlock. No. 365.

GAMBLER (Mr. Ashton Clegg), b g; B,H pasterns and heels, grizzled inside N/H leg, dent in muscle of N/ quarter just below tail, few grey spots N/ side body. No. 585.

KATE (Mr. W. E. Drury), b m; small vertical star, O,H fetlock, N/H coronet, permanent scar O/ shoulder. No. 588.

LADY BIRD (Colonel Napier McGill), ch m; blaze face, N,F outside coronet, white marks front of hock. No. 294.

MAGIC II. (Mr. C. W. Meredith), ch m; star, race, dot for snip, B/H, odd shaped coronet markings. No. 224.

MAISIE (Mr. Osmond Hastings), b m; star O,H fetlock, numerous saddle marks, 2 spots on O/ side. No. 398.

NORAH CREINA (Mr. John Leonard), b m; star, race, broad snip O/F coronet. No. 222.

PAUL (Major Carew), ch g; star, N F coronet, B/H fetlocks, grizzled about both quarters. No. 423.

SHEELAH (Mr. B. J. O. Flaherty), blk m; O H pastern and back of fetlock. No. 182.

SILVERSKIN (Messrs. Miller), ches g. No. 24.

SUGAR CANDY (E. Kennedy), br m; point of O ear missing. No. 521.

TWINKLE (Miss Wilson), br m; star only. No. 221.

VICTORIA (Captain Takenham), ches m; rich red ches, star, snip. No. 292.

E. D. MILLER. WALTER JONES. G. A. MILLER. C. D. MILLER.

Rugby Team, 1901. Winners of Hurlingham Champion Cup.

INDEX.

RIDING AND HUNTING. Fully Illustrated with

upwards of 250 Reproductions of Photographs and Drawings. In 1 vol., demy 8vo, cloth. Price 16s. net.

"Capt. Hayes has produced a book which cannot fail to interest, if not to instruct the experienced horseman, and the beginner may learn from its pages practically all that it is necessary for him to know."—*The World.*

" We can imagine no more suitable present for one who is learning to ride than this book."—*Pall Mall Gazette.*

VETERINARY NOTES for HORSE OWNERS.

An Illustrated Manual of Horse Medicine and Surgery, written in simple language, with over 200 Illustrations. New Edition. Revised throughout, considerably enlarged, and incorporates the substance of the Author's " Soundness and Age of Horses." Large crown 8vo, buckram, 15s. net.

" It is superfluous to commend a book that is an established success, and that has gone on from edition to edition extending its usefulness."—*Army and Navy Gazette.*

INFECTIVE DISEASES OF ANIMALS. Being

Part I. of the Translation of Friedberger and Froehner's Pathology of the Domestic Animals. Translated and Edited by the Author. With a Chapter on Bacteriology by Dr. G. NEWMAN, D.P.H. Demy 8vo, 10s. 6d. net.

"The plan of the work is excellent, and the arrangement all that could be desired ; while the translation has been aptly done, and the awkwardness of rendering the original German into English, so common in translations, has been avoided. Dr. Newman's notes on bacteriology form an acceptable addition to the volume. This is a work which no veterinary practitioner who is anxious to be thoroughly up-to-date in his professional knowledge can afford to be without."—*Glasgow Herald.*

THE HORSEWOMAN. A Practical Guide to Side-

Saddle Riding. By MRS. HAYES. Edited by CAPT. M. H. HAYES. With 4 Collotypes from Instantaneous Photographs, and 48 Drawings after Photographs, by J. H. OSWALD BROWN. With numerous Illustrations.

" This is the first occasion on which a practical horseman and a practical horsewoman have collaborated in bringing out a book on riding for ladies. The result is in every way satisfactory, and, no matter how well a lady may ride, she will gain much valuable information from a perusal of ' The Horsewoman.' "—*Field.*

ILLUSTRATED HORSEBREAKING. New and

Cheaper Edition. Large crown 8vo. Price 12s. net.

This Edition has been entirely rewritten, the amount of the letterpress more than doubled, and 75 reproductions of Photographs have been added.

"A valuable addition to the literature of a subject which this author may really be said to have made his own. We do not know another who so happily combines absolute practical knowledge with an attractive literary style."—*Referee.*

LONDON : HURST AND BLACKETT, LIMITED.

THREE NEW WORKS

By CAPT. M. HORACE HAYES, F.R.C.V.S.

HORSES ON BOARD SHIP. A Guide to their Management. By M. H. HAYES. In 1 vol., crown 8vo, with numerous Illustrations from Photographs taken by the Author during a voyage to South Africa with horses. Price 3s. 6d. net.

"We are sure that the book will be found useful and instructive to those who are new to the work of conveying either large or small numbers of horses across the seas."— *County Gentleman.*

"So well-studied and so well-appointed a book cannot but prove of high value to any-one interested in its subject."—*Scotsman.*

"The publication of this book could not have been more opportune. The serious charges which Capt. Hayes—an experienced veterinary surgeon and one of our leading authorities on horse management—makes, from personal experience, will tell their own tale."—*Referee.*

MODERN POLO. By E. D. MILLER. Edited by M. H. HAYES. In 1 vol., demy 8vo, with numerous Illustrations from Photographs and Drawings. Price 16s. net.

BREAKING AND RIDING. Military Commentaries. By JAMES FILLIS, Riding Master-in-Chief to the Cavalry School at St. Petersburg. Edited by M. H. HAYES. In 1 vol., medium 8vo. Fully Illustrated by Photographs and Sketches taken on the spot. Price 16s. net.

LONDON: HURST AND BLACKETT, LIMITED.

Printed in Great Britain
by Amazon